CONTENTS

to Valerie, Deirdre and Allen

PREFACE

I wish to thank the staffs of the following institutions for their assistance: the Public Record Office of Northern Ireland, Belfast – in particular, Bryan Follis and Trevor Parkhill; the Public Record Office, London; the Imperial War Museum, London; the British Library (Reference Division), Newspaper Library, London; the Tom Harrisson Mass Observation Archive, University of Sussex, especially Dorothy Sheridan; the State Paper Office, Dublin; the Northern Ireland Fire Authority, Lisburn; the Ulster Folk and Transport Museum, Cultra; the Royal Ulster Constabulary Museum, Belfast; the British Broadcasting Corporation Written Archives Centre, Reading; the Main Library, Queen's University Belfast; the Central Library, Belfast; the Linen Hall Library, Belfast, especially John Gray and John Killen; and the Bundesarchiv-Militärarchiv, Freiburg, Federal Republic of Germany.

I must also express my gratitude to the Deputy Keeper of the Records, Public Record Office of Northern Ireland, for granting me permission to quote from material deposited there; and I am deeply indebted to the following depositors: Brian Dingwall for giving me access to Lady Spender's diary; the Spender family for Sir Wilfrid Spender's Financial Diary; Michael Duffin for Emma Duffin's diary; W. Topping for the Topping Papers; and Mrs W. Ward for William Ward's notes on the Belfast air raids. Mass Observation material is reproduced by permission of the Trustees of the Tom Harrisson Mass Observation Archive, University of Sussex, and I am particularly grateful to Moya Woodside for granting permission to use her name throughout the text.

Most sincere thanks are also due to those who provided photographs and other material, with which to illustrate the text: Artillery Unemployment Group; Belfast Central Mission; Belfast City Council; *Belfast Telegraph*; Nellie Bell; British Library; Bundesarchiv-Militärarchiv; Arthur Campbell; Ernie Cromie of the Ulster Aviation Society; Drogheda Fire Brigade; Charlie Gallagher; Gallaher Limited; Harland and Wolff; Imperial War Museum; *Londonderry Sentinel*; Bill McCourt; James Mackie and Sons; Ian McQuiston; J. Mercer; National Archives of Canada; Newtownabbey Methodist Mission; Brian Potter; Major H. John F. Potter; Public Record Office of Northern Ireland; Short Brothers; Ulster Folk and Transport Museum; Ulster Museum; United States Army; Kenneth Wakefield; and Wilton Funeral Service.

I extend my thanks to those individuals and institutions whose help and advice were crucial to the completion of this book. Robert Fisk provided me with detailed information regarding possible oral and written sources, and instilled in me some of the enthusiasm which informs his own work. Kenneth Wakefield, an acknowledged authority on the blitz, was constantly willing to offer guidance on numerous points relating to the raids on Belfast and the Luftwaffe records concerning them. I wish to express my gratitude to my publishers, Blackstaff Press, whose expertise and encouragement were vital in shaping the present volume. I also owe a particularly heavy debt of gratitude to the University of Ulster for granting me a Teacher Fellowship, without which this book could not have been written, and especially to Tom Fraser (at Coleraine) and Keith Jeffery (at Jordanstown), who helped guide this text during its formative phase. And I would like to thank Anne Cunningham, who typed the manuscript, for her promptitude and efficiency.

Above all, I must thank the very many citizens of Belfast and elsewhere, whom I interviewed in the course of my research, for their unstinting kindness and patience, their irrepressible humour and their unfailing honesty.

BRIAN BARTON
BELFAST, 1989

I

POVERTY AND PROGRESS

THE PRE-WAR YEARS

The hungry thirties: Trafalgar Court in Belfast's dock area. (Belfast Central Mission)

In Northern Ireland, as in much of Britain, the inter-war years still evoke bitter memories. They are vividly depicted in 'Down the Shankill' by an ex-resident, Winifred Campbell. She recalls:

> Short time unemployment was common enough. It simply meant a tightening of the belt for a while. . . [But] as months stretched into years people began to despair. Every possible economy became the way of life. . . The only thing that people had left was their self-respect and they tried very hard to hold on to this.

The 1920s and 1930s are forever identified in the public mind with economic recession, slum housing, malnutrition, poor health, and, for many, poverty eased inadequately by heavily means-tested benefits. In 1932 violence, rooted in widespread distress, erupted in Belfast, followed three years later by the worst sectarian riots in the city since the troubles when Ireland was partitioned in 1921.

Yet Belfast began the twentieth century as a confident and energetic provincial city in the full flush of its industrial and commercial power. In 1911 its population was 387,000 and had multiplied more than fourteen times since 1800. At the time of World War I it could boast two of the largest shipyards in the world, Harland and Wolff, and Workman Clark. It was the world's most important linen centre, with reputedly its most expansive single textile firm, York Street Flax Spinning Company; it had both the biggest independent tobacco factory, Gallaher Limited, and the most sizeable ropeworks of its kind. In addition, the city contained roughly forty engineering premises and was an important centre for food processing, whiskey distilling and aerated water manufacture. In total, it accounted for one-third of Ireland's entire industrial production. Its banks remained solvent – they had known no failures since the early 1820s.

Along with the rest of Ireland, Belfast's most affluent years were those immediately before partition in 1921; its economic prospects then seemed bright. Physically it remained undistinguished – never able to compete or compare with the grandeur of Dublin. Rather, it had developed as a typical British industrial town, built sturdily and inelegantly. Its saving grace was its setting, a green river valley. Local Unionists attributed the transformation and prosperity of the region to the frugality and enterprise of its Protestant people, and the security and protection of the Union. As a consequence, Belfast Unionists orchestrated the political resistance to Home Rule throughout the north-east, prompting Arthur Griffith, the founder of Sinn Féin, to describe the 'Ulster question' as a 'Belfast city question'.

From 1920, however, both the city and Northern Ireland as a whole entered a prolonged period of persistent and unyielding depression. In the North, on average, 19 per cent of the insured work force was unemployed between 1923 and 1930 and 27 per cent for the years 1931–9; only Wales had a worse record. In Belfast up to one-quarter of the labour force was without work in 1931 and again in 1938 – approximately 50,000 people. One of the most memorable features of its working-class districts during the 1930s were the clusters of gaunt and undernourished men standing idly on street corners. In Ronnie Munck and Bill Rolston's oral history, *Belfast in the Thirties*, Florrie Addley recalls: 'You would have been identified as what corner you stood at. They would say, "Oh, sure you know him, he stands at the corner of Henry Street. . ." They'd nothing else to do, nowhere else to go.' Bryce Millar, then a young shipyard worker, remembers the local convention that 'You could not stand with them until you were over fourteen and had left school.'

The recession was not due to the impact of partition, which had marginal economic consequences. In essence it was caused by the stagnation and decline of Belfast's major traditional industries, in particular, shipbuilding and linen. These giants of the nineteenth century progressively became the dinosaurs of the twentieth. With justification, Sir Crawford McCullagh, the city's longest-serving Lord Mayor, observed that their contraction had been 'brought about by problems over which neither the [Stormont] government nor the municipality has any control'.

During the inter-war years, the shipbuilding industry suffered both from falling world demand and intense new foreign competition, especially from the United States, Scandinavia and Japan. In their response, the two local yards benefited little from the policies adopted by successive Westminster governments; these were, in any case, only marginally effective even in Britain. Between the end of December 1931 and May 1934, during the aftermath of the Wall Street Crash, no ships were launched from Harland and Wolff; 'the grass grew on the slips'. In 1935 the inappropriately nicknamed 'wee yard', Workman Clark, was forced to close, its operations being absorbed by its larger neighbour, Harland and Wolff. Meanwhile, Harland and Wolff itself had built up a massive overdraft – £2.3 million by 1931 – and there was much talk of liquidation. In 1932, the trough of the Depression, employment at the firm plummeted to between two and three thousand; it had been thirty thousand in 1920, a figure never surpassed before or since.

Nevertheless, over the course of the 1930s, the company performed creditably. By May 1934 its work force had recovered to reach ten thousand. In 1935 its tonnage launched was a world record for the year, and in 1938 its total output was the largest for any shipyard in the United Kingdom. A key to its survival was the diversification of production: it built the first diesel-electric trains in the British Isles for the Bangor and County Down Railway Company; more conventional locomotives for North and

Industrial Belfast: the city hall around 1930, backed by extensive warehouses, mills and factories. (Ulster Folk and Transport Museum)

South America and Australia; engines for oil pipelines; and steel structures for shops and cinemas, including the Ritz, which opened in Belfast in 1936. By late 1939 the yard was employing approximately twelve thousand – as many workers as in 1929.

During the 1930s, the linen industry had experienced a substantial and permanent decline in output and exports. This was caused less by increased foreign competition than by a dramatic decline in the level of world demand. As a consequence, less than 40 per cent as much flax was then being processed world-wide as pre-1914. Unforeseeable changes in female fashion were a major reason for this contraction of the market. After World War I, skirts became shorter and required less voluminous layers of the material for underwear. With the modern demand for novelty, the durability of linen clothing became less of an asset. Also, progressively fewer people could afford the retinue of domestic servants needed to launder the cloth properly. Although the Northern Ireland linen industry responded admirably compared to firms in Britain, its work force, none the less, dropped from a wartime peak of ninety thousand to fifty-seven thousand by 1935.

Belfast's unemployment problem was aggravated by a drop in the levels of emigration in the inter-war years, which contributed to an increase in the numbers looking for work. The population of the city rose by almost 50,000 between 1911 and 1937 to 437,000, by which time over one-third of the people of Northern Ireland lived within its boundaries. A proportion of this growing labour force was absorbed into the engineering sector, which revived in the 1930s, or into the expanding building industry. A minority found employment in the small number of new firms which were attracted to the North. The most important of these was the aircraft factory of Short and Harland. The company was formed in June 1936 against the background of deepening international tension in Europe and beyond. As a consequence, earlier that year, the Royal Air Force placed so large an order for Sunderland flying boats from Short Brothers of Rochester that it could not accommodate the increased demand and was forced to expand its productive capacity. Belfast offered a unique and irresistible range of inducements; a skilled labour force, much of it made redundant from the shipyard; a deep-water dock; a hugh stretch of sheltered water in Belfast Lough, ideal for flying boats; and an airport, with fifteen-hundred-yard runways, built on some of the four hundred acres of slobland recently reclaimed by the local Harbour Commission. By August 1937 construction at Sydenham had been completed and the production of land and marine aircraft had begun. Within two years, the firm was employing two thousand workers; in wartime this rose to a peak of over twenty thousand.

However, like most regions in the United Kingdom, Northern Ireland found it difficult to attract new industry. It lacked raw materials, it was remote from GB markets, and its transport costs were higher than in Britain. In addition, Northern Ireland ministers were unable, and those at Westminster were unwilling, to provide adequate financial attractions to

Belmont Street, off the Woodstock Road, in February 1939: cobbled streets, gas lights and cramped unhealthy housing. Large families were raised in these grim conditions. (Ulster Folk and Transport Museum)

potential investors. Stormont legislation, introduced for this purpose in 1932 and 1937, succeeded in creating only 279 new jobs. This abysmal record prompted Tommy Henderson, an Independent Unionist MP, to enquire whether 'if the Government set up a few fish shops they would not give more employment'. Overall, the North's economy slipped further behind the performance of the United Kingdom as a whole. Additional jobs were not being created quickly enough to absorb its growing work force or to compensate for the decline of its basic industries. As a result, by 1938 no region in Great Britain had a higher percentage of unemployed workers.

None the less, during the inter-war years, conditions for the vast majority of the population improved substantially. Between 70 and 80 per cent of Northern Ireland's insured work force remained in employment throughout, and between 1932 and 1937 the number of those in work rose by 15 per cent; some were absorbed by expanding sectors of industry, while others found jobs in education, commerce and government. This growth was almost identical to the level of increased employment in Scotland, the north of England, and Wales. Average real income per head in Northern Ireland rose 10–15 per cent between the wars, a figure once again very similar to regions in Great Britain outside the South-east and the Midlands.

Throughout Northern Ireland a measurable improvement took place in health, housing, life expectation and the overall quality of life. Electricity generation proceeded rapidly, particularly after the creation of the electricity board in 1932, and consumption trebled over the next six years – a faster growth rate than in the United Kingdom as a whole. Leisure activities became more varied. In September 1924 a BBC transmitter was established locally, and by 1939, roughly half of Northern Ireland households had a wireless set. Among the upper and middle classes, the number of private motor cars on the North's roads increased ten fold between 1919 and 1937; for the population as a whole, car ownership rose from one for every sixty families to one for every seven. Golf, yachting and cricket became more popular, mirroring social developments in Britain. Up to thirty thousand spectators watched rugby internationals at Ravenhill and five hundred thousand gathered to see the first Ards TT race in 1928.

However, beneath this surface of middle-class affluence there lurked deep chasms of social deprivation throughout Northern Ireland. For many of those living in working-class areas of Belfast, unemployment, low wages, high rents, overcrowding, poverty and ill health were part of the inescapable reality of urban life. Their existence and true extent only began to be realised when they were brutally exposed by the German air raids on the city during the spring of 1941. The social inequality that permeated Belfast society was graphically illustrated when one of the directors at Gallaher's tobacco firm had the misfortune to catch pneumonia. He lived above the company's offices in York Street. In *Belfast in the Thirties* Florrie Addley recalls

> sitting while they laid turf because he was coming up to a crisis. . . they tied up the knocker in case there would be a noise, and we would have noticed this and be told as children: 'Oh, be very quiet and keep away; there's a crisis coming.' Well, this had happened to him and they laid turf, carts and carts of turf, laid from Earl Street to Brougham Street to deaden the noise of the trams; so they must have been – to us they were very, very wealthy.

Bryce Millar can vividly recall some of the features of his childhood home in Michael Street in north Belfast during the 1930s – the cramped rooms with their bare boards, the water tap behind the front door (there were no bathroom facilities), and the flickering light from naked gas flames. No comprehensive survey of such conditions was undertaken until 1944. However, in 1941, several months after the blitz and at a time when twenty-six thousand people had been officially evacuated from Belfast, Dr Thomas Carnwath undertook an inquiry into all matters relating to health in the city. His generally unfavourable report was an indictment of his employers, the Belfast Corporation. He observed that there were 'undoubtedly bad areas' of housing. He listed some of them: 'Edward Street, courts and passages off the Newtownards Road, the Ravenhill Road, between North

A Sunday breakfast at the North Belfast Mission. Men received meals if they wore suits and attended the church service. (Newtownabbey Methodist Mission)

Queen Street and York Street, Cromac Street'. The most common defects were 'damp, mouldering walls, many of them bulging, rickety stairs, broken floors [and] crumbling ceilings'. Some of the houses were 'mere hovels, with people living in indescribable filth and squalor'. Large families had been raised in these 'unsavoury conditions'; some of the tenants had been in occupation for twenty years. Nevertheless, rents were high, 'considering the nature of the accommodation'; 1s.9d. (9p) per week for a 'small attic which it was an adventure to approach', and up to 3s.8d. (18½p) for rooms on other floors. The report concluded that 'overcrowding was confined to very poor people [living in] worn out houses, without back passages and of obsolete design, situated in narrow streets and cul-de-sacs'. The worst excesses were discovered in large tenement houses 'in decayed neighbourhoods, sublet with one or two rooms each, with half a dozen families in a house originally built for one and rents up to 9/0 [45p] per room'.

Other contemporary surveys confirmed these gloomy findings. One indicated that in parts of the city such as Smithfield, up to 10 per cent of houses were each occupied by two or more families. Also in 1941 an independent study of Lonsdale Street, off the Crumlin Road, found that a total of 190 people were living in twelve houses. Adrian Robinson, a senior civil servant at the Ministry of Home Affairs, described the finding as 'typical of the bad areas of the city'. During 1942 and 1943, ministry officials conducted further inquiries into both city-centre and more suburban districts, including North Queen Street, Dock Street, Henry Street and Whiterock Gardens. They concluded that houses with seven to eight rooms, occupied by seventeen to thirty people, was the norm, a 'typical return of the number of persons in each house in a working class street'. In their view, 'housing conditions in Belfast are as bad as they can possibly be; gross overcrowding prevails. . . The position has become so acute that, even under war conditions, some remedial action is considered essential.' In fact they suggested that it was 'politically necessary to do something' for the 'good of morale'. The 1944 Stormont government inquiry did nothing to lessen the officials' sense of urgency.

Housing conditions in the city during the late 1930s were of course less bleak than these statistics would suggest. They had, after all, deteriorated significantly from September 1939. Owing to the conflict, virtually no houses were built and maintenance work was neglected at a time when, ironically, Northern Ireland's population reached its fastest growth rate since the Famine of 1845–9. Also, the blitz caused very extensive damage to residential property, particularly in Belfast; some of the very densely populated districts suffered most. None the less, a major housing problem already existed even before the outbreak of war. From 1936, Medical Officers of Health repeatedly advised the Belfast Corporation that ten thousand houses for which it was responsible were 'unfit for human habitation' and 'inimical to health'. Accordingly, they condemned them for demolition but no action was taken. In 1939 a Stormont government spokesperson stated that there were two thousand 'insanitary houses' inside the city boundaries.

Looking back in 1942 and 1943, Ministry of Home Affairs officials themselves considered that during the inter-war years housing had been 'allowed to lag behind England very materially'. Adrian Robinson, secretary to the ministry, pointed out that the Northern Ireland government had made available 'no grants whatsoever of the same kind' as in Britain and had not attempted a slum-clearance scheme of 'any sort, kind or description'. Thus in Great Britain £200 million was paid in housing subsidy; in Northern Ireland just £3 million, 'half of what it should be'. In England and Scotland over three hundred thousand slum houses had been demolished and the people rehoused, while 'nothing was done here'. During the inter-war period, four million new houses were built in Britain compared to only fifty thousand in Northern Ireland.

In successive housing acts, Stormont ministers were consistently less generous than their counterparts at Westminster. However, they did labour under crippling financial difficulties. Their lack of capital is reflected in the

Needy children with mugs of milk provided by the Belfast Central Mission. (Belfast Central Mission)

poor quality of all public services in the North during these years. Both from preference and necessity, they relied on private enterprise to provide the much-needed houses, with encouragement from the local authorities. Dr Carnwath reached the conclusion in his report that 'private effort can not be relied upon', that the 'main responsibility' therefore rested with the Belfast Corporation and 'the fact that little or nothing has been done is a grave reflection on its housing administration'.

The city's Unionist-dominated council perpetuated its habitual and malignant record of municipal corruption, favouritism rather than ability determined the pattern of appointments. Its political composition and its practice of discrimination against the city's Catholic population in the allocation of jobs and contracts served to deepen sectarian division and further alienate the minority community (23.8 per cent of the total in 1937). Councillors were conservative in outlook and lacking in energy, and constantly provided minimal services whether in housing, health, education or support for mothers and children. They sought to justify their inactivity in the face of the city's pressing social problems by casting responsibility on to the Government. From the early 1920s, there were recurrent hints that they would be suspended and replaced by commissioners, as had happened in Dublin for similar reasons. For too long Stormont ministers proved reluctant to take this decisive step, as they feared the political consequences. (In fact the Belfast Corporation was not suspended until 1942.)

Although the corporation was given every encouragement by the Stormont government to provide housing for the underprivileged, it was responsible for the construction of a mere twenty-five hundred dwellings between the wars. During these years, a total of almost thirty thousand houses were built in Belfast, mostly by private contractors and with the help of a government subsidy. However, government officials themselves were aware that these did 'practically nothing to meet the needs of the poor working class', as only the higher-incomed artisan and the lower middle class could afford their rent. None the less, George B. Hanna, Junior Minister of Home Affairs, was well pleased with them, suggesting that they would be perfect for three or four children,

> a clean and tidy wife [and a father] who does not want to go out either to a public house or to a Local Option meeting, he wants his *Evening Telegraph* – and after having patted the children on the head and said good night to them he sits down in that house which is his own or becoming so more and more every day.

This view was not shared by one Northern Ireland senator, James McMahon of the Nationalist Party, who commented:

> If you saw these houses you would wonder how anyone could live in them and certainly if anyone died upstairs, he would have to be taken out through the window because you could not get a coffin downstairs.

He concluded that no family could possibly remain in one for 'any considerable length of time'.

Clearly, appalling housing conditions persisted in some areas throughout the inter-war period. Taking a broader perspective, however, when compared with regions of Britain, neither Belfast nor Northern Ireland appears to have been uniquely disadvantaged. Between 1926 and 1937, one-sixth of the population of the North moved into new houses. Although proportionately fewer dwellings were constructed locally than in other parts of the United Kingdom, the relative demand for them was smaller than in Britain. Northern Ireland had a slower rate of population growth, its marriage rate was lower and it experienced comparatively little internal migration. In Belfast itself, the housing stock in 1919 was much newer than in most British cities, reflecting its more recent growth. It probably avoided some of the worst excesses of overcrowding and hardship associated with industrialisation elsewhere. In 1937 it had an average of 0.88 persons living per room. In 1931 the equivalent figure for Glasgow was 1.57, for Edinburgh 1.15 and for Scotland as a whole 1.27.

Dr Carnwath considered that Belfast's housing did not compare unfavourably with other towns of similar size in England. Even so, he felt convinced that it was a cause of the city's 'poor health record'. This poor record was itself evident in the faces and demeanour of many working-class people. In *Belfast in the Thirties*, Paddy Scott recalls:

> I remember going over to Queen's as a student, walking over the Antrim Road, and one of the incidents which struck me then, which left an indelible

At the North Belfast Mission, undernourished children were given ultra-violet treatment for rickets, caused by vitamin D deficiency. The dark glasses protected their eyes from the glare. (Newtownabbey Methodist Mission)

> mark in my memory, was seeing young children with deformed legs, gaunt looking; I subsequently discovered it was rickets due to malnutrition. I also noticed the women were gaunt, lifeless and particularly the young men. . . their eyes were lifeless, expressionless, which gave me the impression that they were people who had lost all hope.

The experience had a 'tremendous effect' upon Scott: it made him a socialist. It was knowledge of these conditions that prompted Dr William Lyle, Unionist MP for Queen's University Belfast, to plead for the formation of a Ministry of Health, during his maiden speech in October 1942. The House listened in 'tense silence' to his allegation that in the 'slaughter of innocents', the Stormont government had 'out-Heroded Herod'.

In 1931 life expectancy at birth in Northern Ireland was 57.1 years, a figure similar to the rest of Europe and to other parts of the United Kingdom. However, although public health showed a measurable improvement in the North during the inter-war period, it remained poor by modern standards and there was much preventable illness and death. Maternal and infant mortality rates in the North were 50–60 per cent higher than in Britain and childbirth carried increasing rather than diminishing risks for Northern Ireland women. Maternal mortality actually rose substantially (by one-fifth) between 1922 and 1938, while the infant death rate remained alarmingly high. Belfast had a lamentably poor record for both. In the late 1930s, roughly eight hundred babies died in the city each year during the first twelve months of life (one out of every ten live births). In 1940 the proportion lurched even further upwards to one in eight. This was the highest level since 1920, and about twice the comparative figure for Liverpool or Manchester. In a modern continental city such as Amsterdam, the proportion had dropped to one in thirty on the eve of World War II.

In 'Down the Shankill', Winifred Campbell observes:

> Child mortality was a sadly accepted part of life and it was rarely that a whole family would reach adulthood. It was reasonable to assume that a family would lose at least one child. When asked how many in the family, the answer might be 'four living and two dead'.

In *Belfast in the Thirties*, Anne Boyle recalls how these sad statistics affected her own family:

> There was so much infant mortality that it seemed as if every week blue-baby coffins were coming out of every street. I had three brothers and a sister dead before they were two years old, out of eleven of us.

Dr Carnwath believed that the cause of this appalling death rate was not 'primarily' the poor quality of Belfast's housing, or indeed its water supply, its means of sewage disposal or system of refuse collection. Rather, it was its personal medical services which he held to be mainly responsible. He considered that they fell 'far short of what might reasonably be expected in a city of its size and importance'. Midwifery was poor; no provision of special foods was made for expectant mothers; nor was any attempt made to detect anaemia, to monitor difficult pregnancies or to educate women in cleanliness; few health visitors were employed to check on infants' progress. In 1938 the Report of the Maternity Services Committee estimated that maternal mortality could be halved merely by providing better facilities such as these. For many working-class women, bad health was endemic. They were underfed and overworked, and maternity itself was a dangerous occupation. Bryce Millar remembers that when his mother reached her confinement, she refused to take more than three days off work; the family could not afford to go without her wages for longer. She would come home from the mill and ask him to go and fetch the nurse. At first as a young child, he felt perplexed; he had no idea why she should feel in need of medical attention.

Among infants, the major causes of death were diarrhoea and pneumonia, the latter frequently developing out of whooping cough and measles. These illnesses were mainly due to defective knowledge of child-care and of course the lack of hygiene – unclean milk, hands, teats, bottles, floors, clothes, yards and houses. Such conditions must also have contributed to the fact that in the late 1930s, 51 per cent of all deaths in Belfast under fifteen years of age were caused by infectious diseases; this was 25 per cent higher than English county boroughs. Meanwhile school medical inspectors reported a marked increase in the incidence of vermin and nits, and of skin diseases, which could disrupt sleep and spread from the pupils to other members of their families. Bad teeth were inevitable when the education authority appointed just one dentist for every twenty-three thousand children; the average throughout England and Wales was one for every six thousand.

Much death and disease could have been avoided by a modest increase in expenditure on rudimentary health education and on medical care. Overall, Belfast's health services were poor by British standards. Ultimately the blame lay with the Belfast Corporation and the Board of Guardians. The precise division of responsibility between them was unclear but, in any case, both were inactive, niggardly and conservative in approach, tending to regard the provision of medical care as a parental duty. The Northern Ireland government was unable to increase its level of grant support towards the development of existing health services: once again the 'whole difficulty was finance'. Owing to the acute shortage of capital, departmental inquiries made recommendations that were never implemented.

For the adult population, working conditions in the city's major industry were a traditional source of ill health and even of premature death. At the shipyard the conditions were primitive: employees were exposed to high noise levels; filth; the lack of proper sanitary provision; and inadequate protection, either from the weather or from their machinery. In the linen mills the inhalation of flax dust caused restricted breathing, bronchitis and lung disease. It was said that 'You would always know a doffer': before World War I, a doctor described how, at the age of thirty, their appearance 'begins to alter, the face gets an anxious look, shoulders begin to get rounded – in fact, they become prematurely aged, and the greatest number die before the age of forty-five years'.

However, tuberculosis was the most virulent killer of young adults in Belfast; it was commonly referred to euphemistically as going 'into a decline'. During the late 1930s, it accounted for 49 per cent of all deaths in the age group fifteen to twenty-five and for 38 per cent of those between twenty-five and thirty-five. There were roughly four hundred fatalities from the disease in the city each year, the highest total relative to its size of any county borough in the United Kingdom. Although the mortality rate from tuberculosis fell sharply throughout Northern Ireland (by 40 per cent between 1922 and 1938), it constantly remained 20 per cent higher than in Great Britain. It was caused partly by inferior medical services but was mainly due to poor-quality housing and low standards of nutrition. It receded as living standards rose, and social and sanitary conditions improved. In the North, average incomes were substantially lower than in Britain (by at least one-third), and there was almost certainly more malnutrition as a result. During the late 1930s, school medical inspectors in Belfast reported increased numbers of physical 'subnormals' and of those definitely undernourished. They considered their findings to be significant,

A used-clothes shop at Smithfield market, 1937. Cast-off clothes and shoes were all many poor people could afford. (Ulster Folk and Transport Museum)

a clear indication of the lack of nutrition widespread among the city's pupils. As Winifred Campbell observed in 'Down the Shankill':

> The first priority was the rent. That must be paid, otherwise a family could be evicted and their belongings seized in lieu of rent. Next came food, a necessity of life. A long way behind came fuel, clothes, utensils, bedding.

Meat consumption in Northern Ireland was 30–40 per cent below British levels – it was a luxury for some even over the Christmas period. In *Belfast in the Thirties* Leo Boyle recalls seeing 'people going down to Sawer's on Christmas Eve and waiting on the remnants of the turkeys, buying gizzards and turkeys' necks. They couldn't afford a turkey or a chicken, and made soup out of that.'

Two independent church studies, both conducted in the late 1930s, provide some insight into the very considerable levels of poverty in working-class areas of Belfast. The first was an inquiry carried out by the Methodist Church Temperance and Social Welfare Committee on behalf of the Belfast District Synod into a new housing estate, a two-penny tram ride from the city centre. Over seven hundred households were researched just before

Christmas 1937. Over half of the sample, 376 households, were at least partially dependent on some form of state benefit. A poverty line or minimum income was devised which was regarded as barely enough to meet the most basic human needs of the occupants, such as rent, food, fuel, gas, electricity and clothing. None the less, the committee found that the incomes of 58 per cent of the households surveyed fell below the minimum laid down, and that for those entirely dependent on public financial support, the proportion rose to 80 per cent.

The second inquiry was held by the social services committee of the Irish Presbyterian Church. It examined a 'representative working-class area' of 436 households during the period November 1938 to February 1939. In part its purpose was to 'bring home to the conscience of the church the very serious state of affairs in Belfast and every industrial city in the United Kingdom'. Their poverty line was 'very harshly drawn' by a professional economist and was based both on the British Medical Association's 1933 assessment of minimum food requirements and the criterion adopted by the pioneering social investigator Seebohm Rowntree. A family income was calculated that would provide the least considered necessary for its health and strength to be maintained. No allowance was made for spending on 'luxury' items such as tobacco or amusements. The study concluded that at least 33 per cent of the families were in 'considerable economic distress', and that a further 29 per cent were living under conditions which were 'barely sufficient and probably intolerable for any length of time'.

If the scale of the deprivation, highlighted by both surveys, shocked those who read them, its causes were more predictable. A key factor was unemployment; it had begun to move upwards once more in 1937. A very high proportion of those relying on state benefits did not have enough on which to survive. Most pensioners were also living in poverty, and it was regarded as 'inevitable' in households with two or more young children. A further crucial element was the low level of wages, especially as prices rose sharply after 1936. In the Methodist Church survey it was found that one-third of those families fully dependent on wages were below the poverty line. In some cases, distress was caused by poor financial management, but this was not easy to avoid where householders had insufficient earnings to provide for contingencies. As a consequence, food and clothes were acquired on credit and any major item of expenditure, such as furniture, was often bought on hire purchase. Clearly, a burden of debt at high interest rates proved difficult to avoid and could very quickly accumulate.

During his boyhood in Ballymacarrett before World War II, Jimmy Penton experienced the reality of the poverty that lay behind these depressing statistics. He was 'born and bred under the gantries', and recalls the well-beaten track to Cupples's pawnshop on the Newtownards Road or, as an alternative source of ready cash, the 'two wee Jew men', Appleman and Fink, money lenders well-known throughout the neighbourhood. Driven by hunger, he regularly stood with friends at the gates of the shipyard, waiting for the workers to come off their shift and offer them 'crusts left over from their piece'. As he said: 'It filled a hole.' At 10 p.m. on Saturdays his mother would walk to Davey Esther's butchers shop on Dee Street, hoping that he would 'give her something for one or two pence'. When Jimmy's brother was dying, the doctor was sent for; it was widely assumed that when he failed to arrive, it was because he was uncertain of receiving his fee of 2s.6d. (12½p).

Collective poverty helped generate a strong sense of community spirit. In 'Down the Shankill', Winifred Campbell recalls: 'Any event, happy or sad, became the business of the street and was openly discussed. Advice was freely given, invited or not. Doors were left open.' Children were brought up in an 'extended family' made up of neighbours as well as relatives; 'the street reared you'. In order to survive, families shared the necessities of life. In her experience, 'help, such as it was, was given and received with simple dignity'. Every possible economy became instinctive and routine:

> Soup was made from bones instead of meat. Scraps of bread were made into boiled plum duff. Small pieces of soap were rendered down into a sort of cleaning jelly. Teeth were cleaned with salt and water and men gave each other a haircut. Only powdered ash from the fire was thrown away; every cinder was carefully picked out to back the fire. The floors had to be scrubbed with water only in order to save the precious soap. Little boots went from child to child until they were past wearing. Even then, they were filled with dampened coal dust and used for fuel. Men and women had only the clothes they stood up in – all the others had long since gone to the pawn shop or been made over for the children. . . They were remarkably courageous. . . they were all in the same boat.

Tightly drawn communal bonds also held open the prospect of finding work, whether through friendship with a factory foreman or contacts within the Church or the Orange Order. At the shipyard, Masonic membership or family links with the firm were vital in determining the allocation of jobs available. Jimmy Penton later recalled: 'It was a tradition; my father put my name down.' It was only later, as a trade-union official, that he began to realise fully the extent of Masonic influence.

Means of escape from this dismal environment were few. The educational system provided little such opportunity during the inter-war years. Although substantial improvement took place in the provision of elementary schools and in teacher training, in 1937 just 7 per cent of Northern Ireland school children received a secondary education. Only one in twenty of these had their fees paid. The number of assisted places at university level was derisory – a mere twenty-one each year between 1924 and 1938.

With such a pervasive and sustained experience of poverty in working-class areas, the growth of support for socialist candidates in central and local government might reasonably have been expected. However, this did not take place; Unionist control of the Belfast Corporation remained unshaken, indeed almost unchallenged, from the early 1920s. The party consistently held over fifty of the sixty seats in the council chamber, the remainder being virtually monopolised by Nationalist representatives. During the trough of the Depression in 1932, just three of the city's fifteen wards were contested, and this fell to two in 1934. Although the Northern Ireland Labour Party won thirteen seats in 1920, it never again approached this level of success. Instead, it struggled to remain a significant force even in its heartland – the central areas of Belfast and the docks. Its performance in the city's parliamentary elections was similarly unimpressive.

Many factors contributed to the Northern Ireland Labour Party's record of impotence and ineffectiveness. Its ambitions were constantly thwarted by the divisiveness of sectarianism and the ambiguity of its position on the partition issue. Despite the prevalence of distress and need, its commitment to socialism was not necessarily a vote-winner. The Catholic Church condemned it as incompatible with Catholicism; the appeal of its candidates in strongly nationalist constituencies was, in any case, lessened by their almost exclusively Protestant, trade-unionist background. Moreover, its demands

Pre-war Belfast: Royal Avenue on a wintry day. (Arthur Campbell)

were frequently pre-empted by the Unionist government, which operated a step-by-step policy with Great Britain, resulting in the fruits of British Labour Party victories being implemented in Northern Ireland. Ministers succeeded in buying off potential opposition with major cash social services rather than stunting it with nakedly sectarian appeals. In addition, the electoral system benefited the Unionist Party. It gained most from the abolition of proportional representation which significantly reduced the level of electoral competition. It also developed a highly effective and well-disciplined party machine which could and did apply very powerful and emotive pressures to the electorate to vote for the preservation of the Union. Working-class voters in Protestant areas, Jimmy Penton remembers, almost felt 'intimidated to vote' Unionist, while known Labour supporters were likely to 'get their windows in'.

None the less, there was a strong tradition of Independent Unionism. Tommy Henderson, one of its best-known figures and certainly its most voluble, is recalled by Winifred Campbell in 'Down the Shankill':

> Patriotism and loyalty had become so much a part of politics that to vote against the Unionist Party was regarded almost as an act of treason. . . It was different in Shankill ward: we had an opposition candidate, Unionist of course but independent. He was a local man who had painted a picture of William of Orange, complete with a white horse, on the gable of his street, Weir Street. These paintings were treated with great respect and unveiled as ceremoniously as a priceless work of art. As well as a successful painter, Tommy Henderson was a sensible, clear-thinking man and he soon became the idol of the district. When he addressed the people, it was obvious that he had a power to hold their interest. His fame, his ideas and plans for the working class became known all over the Shankill.

When he was nominated as a candidate, she adds, 'People were strongly behind him and it was certain that the Unionist Party had a fight on its hands.'

That poverty should have contributed to outbreaks of violence was always likely. Belfast had an unenviable tradition both of disorder and of 'holy war'. Bryce Millar lived near the community divide at Isabella Street in the York Street area. Watching his father move quietly to the fireplace, pick up a poker and crouch behind the downstairs front window, is among his earliest recollections. Outside there would be an ominous silence before bricks and stones began cascading through the shattered panes.

In *Voices and the Sound of Drums* Patrick Shea noted the emergence of both the Falls and the Shankill, the Catholic and Protestant heartlands, as 'great nurseries of religious intolerance'. Yet from the moment of his arrival in the city, he had been struck by the fact that these

> closely packed, neighbouring streets had so much in common. . . equally touched by economic depression, bad housing, by the dictates of autocratic employers, by participation in foreign wars, by emigrating sons and daughters, by social change, by the emergence of organized labour.

On occasion, as he observed, 'they looked like making common cause and turning their combined anger on the people and the institutions they saw as their oppressors'. The Outdoor Relief riots of 1932 are among the few instances when they did so and, for some, they are among the most cherished episodes in the history of the city's labour movement.

The context was one of deepening economic depression and mounting distress; both were global in their impact. In due course agitation and violence erupted not just inside Northern Ireland, but in Dublin, numerous British cities and indeed throughout much of the western world. By September 1932, seventy-eight thousand people were unemployed in Belfast: 28 per cent of the insured work force. As the recession in the city continued, the number of those who had exhausted their claim to state benefits rose and, with no other options open, they looked to the Belfast Board of Guardians for assistance. Its thirty-four members, middle class and almost exclusively Unionist, were profoundly unsympathetic in their response. This was partly because they did not regard it as their function to provide the help requested. They considered that their proper role was the relief of 'chronic distress' – the old, the ill, the orphans – and that it was the moral and financial responsibility of the state to assist the 'ordinary' able-bodied unemployed.

Moreover, board members were convinced that to offer too generous a level of support would discourage those in need from looking for jobs, and so, in their view, 'subsidize idleness' and inhibit self-sufficiency. They were particularly critical of the numbers of young applicants in their twenties, many of them married and with families, who 'had not worked and are apparently not anxious to work'. The insensitive jibe by board chairwoman, Lily Colman, that there was 'no poverty under the blanket', caused widespread resentment. It did not escape the attention of the guardians that 60 per cent of their claimants were Catholics, mainly from west Belfast and, it was suspected, eager to 'get as much as they can from the rates'.

Some of the board's fears were not entirely misplaced. Even though earnings were substantially lower in Northern Ireland than in Great Britain, the Stormont government paid the same level of British social benefits. As a result, the local unemployed could claim financial assistance which came close in value to the average local wage, particularly in the case of married men with children. (During World War II evidence would suggest that a minority of the work force, perhaps 4–5 per cent, chose to remain without jobs 'even when there was a large excess demand for labour in the United Kingdom as a whole and probably also in the province'.)

In essence, the guardians were more concerned with protecting the rates than with protecting the poor. The grants they gave were very heavily means-tested and much lower than in comparable cities in the United Kingdom. They were described by the Presbyterian Church in Belfast as 'inadequate to provide the barest necessities of life'. Even the unionist *Belfast News-Letter* reported that recipients of Outdoor Relief were on the

Cobblestone defences in Baker Street on the Lower Falls during riots in 1932; St Peter's Pro-Cathedral looms in the background. (Public Record Office of Northern Ireland)

'verge of starvation'. When a torchlit protest meeting was held at the Custom House on Monday, 3 October 1932, sixty thousand people attended. Outdoor Relief workers then organised a hunger march on Stormont to coincide with the opening of the autumn session of the Northern Ireland parliament. It had been planned for 11 October, but twenty-four hours earlier, it was banned by the Ministry of Home Affairs under the Special Powers Act. However, on the appointed day crowds began to assemble as arranged and soon non-sectarian rioting erupted. It was rooted in widespread distress and in emotions which had been inflamed by demonstrations and oratory. It spread rapidly from the Catholic Lower

Falls into the Protestant districts of west Belfast and across the River Lagan into Ballymacarrett. Eventually, under pressure from both the Government and the Belfast Corporation, the Board of Guardians was forced to increase relief payments.

The co-operation between the two communities proved to be brief and, in the longer term, unproductive: Patrick Shea observed that 'inherited religious prejudice and fostered fears were too strong for the bonds created by immediate and real grievances'. Continuing unemployment and competition for work also gave a sharper edge to ancient hatreds. Even in 1932, Catholic pilgrims on their way to the Eucharistic Congress in Dublin had been stoned at Great Victoria Street Railway Station. During the period which followed, sectarian tensions gradually mounted. They were stirred by the jubilee celebrations for George V in 1935, which nationalists boycotted, and they were stimulated still further by the activities of the Ulster Protestant League. This was a small but extreme body, which exerted an influence beyond its numbers.

Throughout the late spring and early summer of 1935, persistent, violent, though relatively minor, incidents occurred, mainly in the York Street–docks area of the city. These escalated into full-scale rioting on 12 July. Dawson Bates, the Minister of Home Affairs, had at first banned all processions, but then capitulated to the Orange Order's demands for exemption. It is probably impossible now to reconstruct with accuracy the precise source of the sectarian confrontation that resulted. As the Orangemen returned from the Field at Belmont in east Belfast, a small riot broke out at Stewart Street, near the city centre. When the parade reached the Lancaster Street area, a heated dispute outside a public house may have provided the flash point for the later, large-scale outbreak. Rioting, sniping and arson lasted for three weeks in the Falls–Shankill area, during which the Royal Ulster Constabulary was supported by the army and the B Specials. Eleven people were killed, most of them Protestant, and 574 injured; there were 367 cases of malicious damage and 133 of arson; and over 300 families, mainly Catholic, were driven from their homes. In a later inquiry into the riots, the city coroner commented that those involved were aroused almost entirely by the public speeches of men in high and responsible positions. He stated that 'people were easily led and influenced'. It was the fiercest eruption of civil unrest in Northern Ireland since 1922.

Nevertheless, the extent of the deterioration in community relations could be overstated. One month after the riots had ended, Linfield, the Belfast Protestant football club, played Derry City in the Catholic Bogside, and Belfast Celtic travelled to Ballymena, Co. Antrim: no incidents of a sectarian nature were recorded at either match. Six weeks later, when Linfield hosted Celtic at Windsor Park in Belfast, both teams came out together and got a splendid reception. On the eve of World War II, J.J. Campbell, lecturer and writer, could detect the growth of a more moderate mood and, in consequence, cherished 'great hopes for the future of the city'.

Certainly the years 1932 and 1935 were exceptional; to focus attention exclusively on the events which occurred then is to give a distorted impression of the normal levels of violence in Belfast. On 7 October 1937, John Clarke Davison, the newly appointed parliamentary secretary to the Minister of Home Affairs, informed the Commons that over the previous six years only eighteen murders occurred there, for which no one was found guilty and convicted. Eleven of these took place during the 1935 riots and in seven of these cases, 'there is no evidence to show that there was any actual intention to assassinate the particular victim'. In Northern Ireland as a whole, 147 people were murdered between 1922 and 1955. Ninety-seven of these attacks were politically motivated, almost all of them taking place in 1922 or 1935. In most years no more than two or three murders occurred, a level which compares favourably with Britain's experience. In England and Wales, for example, with a population thirty times larger, the figure was 150 per year. During the inter-war years, society in the North was afflicted by deep sectarian divisions but within the UK context, the region was far from being exceptionally violent.

Nor was life irredeemably bleak for the poor in an undernourished city. A wide range of amusements was available, often at the keenest of prices and each eager to compete for custom. Patrick Shea noted the popularity of pitch-and-toss and bingo, and that everywhere, 'in entries, and small parks and muddy side streets, shabby, down-at-heel men played marbles until the evening light had gone'. Association football, however, had long established itself as the major source of entertainment for men and boys in working-class districts. Irish League games were fully attended and Belfast Celtic was in the ascendancy. Jimmy Penton can remember, as a child, the excitement in Ballymacarrett when Glentoran won the Irish Cup in 1932. The team arrived at Dee Street on the back of a lorry and was fêted by the entire neighbourhood. Later, when he worked as a message boy for a local engineering firm, he was paid 10s.0d. (50p) weekly, with an extra 2s.6d. (12½p) on Saturdays to 'go and support the Glens'. Greyhound racing was also beginning to attract increasing interest and support. In 1928 it made its first appearance in Belfast at Celtic Park – the second track to open in the United Kingdom. Dunmore Stadium was added shortly before the outbreak of war.

However, the cinema had become the most popular form of recreation, appealing to both sexes, and all classes and ages, with prices as low as 3d. (1½p) for matinee performances. In *Fading Lights, Silver Screens: A History of Belfast Cinemas*, Michael Open noted that already in the mid-1920s 'perhaps one-quarter of the population of Belfast went to the cinema in any one week'. By 1935 audiences could choose from any one of thirty-five cinemas. With a total of 28,200 seats then available, one for every fifteen of the population, the city was almost as well endowed as London, which had one for every fourteen. Yet the climax of the cinema-building boom was still to come: in 1936–7 the Ritz, Curzon, Park, Broadway and

Donegall Place in 1937.
(Arthur Campbell)

Stadium were opened. Audiences could escape from the drudgery and worry of city life with some of the best-remembered stars of the big screen – Clark Gable, Greta Garbo, James Cagney and Humphrey Bogart. These, and performers such as Charlie Chaplin, Laurel and Hardy, and the Marx Brothers, were the true opiate of the people. At some establishments admission could be gained by 'paying' with a jam jar. One cinema offered hearing-aid facilities, another had a 'tea lounge' within viewing range of the screen. Less opulent conditions, however, prevailed elsewhere: at the New Princess on the Newtownards Road on Wednesday nights, patrons were given a packet of Keating's powder to discourage the resident flea population. At the Clonard on the Falls Road, toilet facilities were lacking and youngsters were known to just 'do it on the floor'.

Gresham Street, Smithfield: a favourite haunt for generations of Belfast people. (Arthur Campbell)

Inevitably other forms of entertainment suffered from the universal appeal of the new medium. Although not necessarily related, drinking declined in the inter-war years and convictions for drunkenness fell by more than one-third. With the coming of 'sound' during the years 1930–1, the Hippodrome closed its doors as a theatre and opened as a cinema. Dancing, on the other hand, retained its widespread appeal and even increased its popularity with the advent of the Big Band era. It was not unusual to queue for an hour to gain entrance to the more popular dance halls and tickets normally cost no more than 2d. (1p) for women and 3d. (1½p) for men.

Much of Belfast's social activity took place close to home, within the numerous separate villages of which the city was composed. Local communities were more isolated then; people travelled less to different parts of the city. This lack of integration helped sustain sectarian sentiment. In west Belfast Winifred Campbell observed that 'the rival factions lived a completely segregated life, each convinced that his cause was just'. This was also instrumental in preserving regional differences in dialect between the dif-

York Street–Donegall Street area of Belfast, several months before the outbreak of war. The buildings beside St Anne's Cathedral (bottom right-hand corner) were to be obliterated during the blitz. (Ulster Folk and Transport Museum)

ferent districts. In *Belfast in the Thirties* Florrie Addley, from north Belfast, recalls that she knew nothing of Ballymacarrett in east Belfast:

> Well, the Shankill now, you had a wee bit of leaning towards and the Falls and Grosvenor Road, but once you crossed the bridge, you went in fear and trembling. I didn't know anyone that lived over there, and anyone that went over there, we thought it was like going to America: you would never see them again.

Within these urban villages, the Churches and the political organisations promoted much of the social life. For Winifred Campbell on the Shankill, everything 'centred around the church; there I met my school friends and we attended the Girl Guides and other organizations'. Jimmy Penton met his wife at the regular dance held in Painters' Hall on Dee Street – it was the local Unionist Party headquarters. He also remembers vividly his boyhood pleasures at collecting for the bonfire on the 'eleventh night', walking to the Field with the Orange lodge, LOL 1200, holding the strings of the banner, and later that evening enjoying a free fish supper from 'Ma Dempsey's' fish-and-chip shop, off the Newtownards Road. Another highlight was the annual children's party held under the auspices of Captain Herbert Dixon, Unionist MP, in his East Belfast constituency: 'two buns, an apple, an orange and a picture show' were the main attractions.

Jimmy Penton was just fourteen when German troops invaded Poland in September 1939; he had left school earlier that fateful summer. He recalls with amusement that when he heard soon afterwards that a scheme of food rationing was going to be introduced by the Government, he was at first well pleased. He anticipated that the rations would be distributed free of charge to those who needed them and that 'at last, I would have something to eat'. This naïve expectation was at least partially fulfilled. After all, World War II brought work and a measure of prosperity to Ballymacarrett and beyond, which had not been known for twenty years. It also generated a keener public awareness of the scale of social deprivation, and a resolve, even at official level, to build a better world. Some would even suggest that, in the short-term at least, the war helped heal the bitter sectarian conflict which had for so long darkened the lives of both communities.

2
PREPARING FOR WAR
1935–1939

Belfast civil defence report centre, 1 district, in a state of readiness. (Ulster Museum)

During the late 1930s, the political tensions in Europe deepened and preparations for inevitable war steadily accelerated. Britain was slow to respond, Winston Churchill describing the early period of the decade as 'years that the locust has eaten'. But from 1935, rearmament began in earnest. When Prime Minister Stanley Baldwin had expressed the widely held view that the 'bomber will always get through', he had thus predicted that there would be 'tens of thousands of mangled people, men, women and children, before a single soldier or sailor suffered a scratch'. Air raid precautions planning followed, the pace quickening during and after the Czechoslovakian crisis in 1938. Progress in Northern Ireland was minimal despite Prime Minister Lord Craigavon's reassuring boast: 'Ulster is ready when we get the word and always will be.' Even during the final days of peace, it is evident that his government's most pressing concern was not the

Belfast Auxiliary Fire Service men pose with som of their equipment. (Ulster Museum)

imminence of Britain's intervention in Europe but rather the 'serious danger of IRA outrages' at home. Unfortunately, Belfast was as ill-prepared for war as it had been ill-governed in the years preceding it. It was already emerging as the most unprotected major city in the United Kingdom.

In spite of the fact that for some months imperial defence experts had predicted that over 650 aircraft would cross nightly from Germany to attack Britain during the first weeks of hostilities and had recently informed the Ministry of Home Affairs that Belfast was a definite Luftwaffe target, few steps had been taken to provide for civil defence. In addition, the city was, in the words of Air Commodore C. Roderick Carr, 'easy' to locate and identify, 'situated at the head of a lough' (water cannot be blacked out), and with 'many prominent landmarks on the coast, including lighthouses'. Nevertheless, when the conflict began, Belfast had no fighter squadrons and no balloon barrage and was dependent for its defence on just twenty anti-aircraft guns. By November 1939 most of its searchlights had been transferred to England along with the brigades that manned them, and the whole region had yet to be integrated into the air-raid warning system operating in Great Britain.

The city's passive defences, which included firemen, rescue workers, air raid precautions wardens and casualty staff, were also underequipped, understaffed and in an acute state of unreadiness. A civil defence plan, belatedly approved by the Belfast Corporation in June 1939, required sixteen thousand volunteers in order to operate efficiently. Three months

Members of Waterside Auxiliary Fire Service in Londonderry during a training session. (*Londonderry Sentinel*)

later, just ten thousand had been enrolled, and of these barely one-fifth had been trained. The only available public air-raid shelters were four, constructed with sandbags, in the grounds of the city hall, the underground toilets in Donegall Square North and similar subterranean accommodation at Shaftesbury Square. Meanwhile, the authorities had failed to provide a single domestic air-raid shelter anywhere in Northern Ireland.

The causes of this lamentable lack of progress are complex but much blame undoubtedly attaches to both the Westminster and Stormont governments. Throughout the 1930s, the response of Northern Ireland ministers to the emerging threat of war was hesitant, uninformed and ineffective. Initially the prospect appeared to be remote and they were predictably absorbed by more immediate domestic issues, in particular, rising unemployment. In any case, they persistently assumed that Northern Ireland was a highly unlikely target. None more so than Craigavon, who considered that it would 'hardly be possible to find' in the United Kingdom an area less exposed to attack from the air. He suggested reassuringly that while enemy aircraft made their hazardous journey across Great Britain and the Irish Sea, 'valuable time for defensive preparations would be gained'. Until the last few months of peace, this viewpoint was shared in all essentials by British ministers and officials. They regarded the possibility of gas attacks on Northern Ireland as so 'negligible' as to be 'almost grotesque', and the likelihood of any form of attack on Belfast as 'too remote to receive serious

PUBLIC NOTICES

A.R.P. BELFAST.

INSTRUCTION OF PUBLIC.

A LECTURE ON AIR RAID PRECAUTIONS FOR THE GENERAL PUBLIC will be given in the following CINEMAS at 3-30 p.m. on the dates shown below. The subject will be

WHAT TO DO IN AIR RAIDS— HOW TO DO IT

ADMISSION FREE.

The Public are advised to attend at the Cinema in this list which is nearest to their homes, and to come early to be sure of admission. DOORS OPEN at 3 p.m.

N.B.—CHILDREN UNDER THE AGE OF 15 YEARS WILL NOT BE ADMITTED UNLESS ACCOMPANIED BY AN ADULT.

"A"	DISTRICT—	RITZ CINEMA, FISHERWICK PLACE	JULY 14th
,,	,,	CLASSIC CINEMA, CASTLE LANE	JULY 21st
"B"	,,	(CINEMA TO BE PUBLISHED LATER)	JULY 21st
,,	,,	BROADWAY	JULY 14th
"C"	,,	STADIUM, SHANKILL ROAD	JULY 14th
,,	,,	PARK, OLDPARK ROAD	JULY 21st
"D"	,,	CAPITOL, ANTRIM ROAD	JULY 14th
,,	,,	LYCEUM, ANTRIM ROAD	JULY 21st
"E"	,,	ASTORIA, UPPER NEWTOWNARDS ROAD	JULY 21st
,,	,,	STRAND, HOLYWOOD ROAD	JULY 14th
,,	,,	NEW PRINCESS, NEWTOWNARDS ROAD	JULY 14th
,,	,,	AMBASSADOR, CREGAGH ROAD	JULY 21st
"F"	,,	MAJESTIC, LISBURN ROAD	JULY 14th
,,	,,	CURZON, ORMEAU ROAD	JULY 21st
"G"	,,	TROXY, SHORE ROAD	JULY 14th
,,	,,	DUNCAIRN, DUNCAIRN GARDENS	JULY 21st

Belfast News-Letter, 11 July 1940

consideration'. There was also a predictable and justifiable tendency at Stormont to regard the whole question of defence as a Westminster government responsibility. Therefore, in 1937, when British ministers introduced the Air Raid Precautions Act, detailing the duties of GB local authorities, Craigavon and his colleagues pleaded passionately that Northern Ireland should be included in its terms. Their arguments were, however, uncompromisingly rejected; Charles Markbreiter, a Home Office official, even suggested that, in his opinion, the region 'should be asked to look after itself in time of war'.

On 24 November 1938 the Stormont parliament passed a measure of its own, the Air Raid Precautions (Northern Ireland) Act, which was very similar to that adopted at Westminster; responsibility for preparing and implementing civil defence schemes was laid on the North's local authorities, with the Ministry of Home Affairs acting in a supervisory capacity, making grants available and providing necessary equipment. But there was one vital difference. For Northern Ireland councils, this new function was to remain strictly voluntary, whereas in Britain it had been made compulsory. This decision by Stormont ministers not to force councillors to take appropriate action in so vital an area as civil defence was primarily due to political weakness. Minister of Home Affairs Dawson Bates expressed a fear, shared

Residents of Argyle Terrace, Londonderry, fitted out with gas masks. (*Londonderry Sentinel*)

by his cabinet colleagues, that the Government might have been defeated in the House if the additional duties had been imposed. As a result, the legislation was ignored. The response of Belfast Corporation was typical. Although cajoled and offered generous financial reassurances, it initially failed to take any steps whatsoever. This lack of progress stemmed not just from the incompetence and irresponsibility of its members, but also from their assumption that civil defence was a function of central government and, in any case, they thought it to be a waste of time, money and energy. At Stormont, Independent Unionist Tommy Henderson declared: 'We are as backward as they are in the wilds of South Africa.'

The Czechoslovakian crisis in the late summer of 1938 temporarily generated a greater sense of urgency. On 10 August, Belfast's first scheme of civil defence was completed by the corporation's newly appointed, full-time air raid precautions officer, Major Frank Eastwood. Simultaneously, he appealed for sixteen thousand volunteers, under the slogan 'train while there is time', warning that 'this is not a joke'. He predicted that 'thousands of fire bombs will be thrown from planes like apples out of a basket', causing fires 'beyond the control of our regular fire brigade'. During the tense weeks leading up to the Munich Conference in September 1938, with war apparently imminent, air raid precautions wardens patrolled the city's streets and the fire service was put on full alert at the docks and the city centre. Trenches were dug at public parks and at the harbour estate, where it

Preparations for war: *Building an air-raid shelter* by William Conor. (Ulster Museum)

was hoped that they would provide protection for up to ten thousand workers; Craigavon had apparently been advised by friends that they were effective during the Spanish Civil War. In addition, the Ministry of Home Affairs ordered and began to distribute one million sandbags to help protect public buildings from blast damage. It also requested almost one and a half million respirators, enough for the entire population of Northern Ireland, but it eventually received just 420,000 to meet the estimated needs of the Belfast area. However, this rush of activity proved to be short-lived, subsiding once the crisis in Europe appeared to have ended. On 30 September, with British Prime Minister Neville Chamberlain claiming 'peace in our time', the *Belfast News-Letter* confirmed the popular belief that the world had been 'saved from war'. Local enthusiasm for air raid precautions gave way once more to apathy. By December 1938 Major Eastwood had succeeded in raising a mere three thousand recruits for his scheme. The enrolment of adequate personnel, using solely voluntary recruitment, was to be a perennial problem.

In the meantime the Westminster parliament was proceeding with a civil defence bill which extended the provisions of the earlier Air Raid Pre-

Munitions workers at James Mackie and Sons, 1940. (Ulster Folk and Transport Museum)

cautions Act. Its main purpose was to ensure that appropriate measures were being taken by the local authorities, particularly with regard to the provision of shelters. During negotiations between the two governments, which continued until the spring of 1939, Craigavon and other Northern Ireland ministers again argued forcefully that the six counties should be included in Westminster's legislation. Once more this request was 'absolutely turned down'. British officials stressed the 'very great difficulties' in their accepting responsibility for civil defence in Northern Ireland. They urged that it would involve 'interfering' with councils there and 'cutting across' Stormont departments. Privately they expressed uneasiness about assuming the additional financial liability likely to be involved. Again it was emphasised strongly by some of the British representatives towards the end of the discussions that they regarded Northern Ireland as a highly improbable target. Sir Wilfrid Spender, head of the Northern Ireland civil service, recorded that in the opinion of Major-General Sir Hastings-Ismay, secretary of the Committee of Imperial Defence, 'There was very little likelihood of any attack being made upon us. He instanced that Northern Ireland was rather in the position of a Woolworths Store, of which the only entrance was through Carringtons, the biggest jewellers in London.' Spender also noted that Charles Markbreiter was similarly reassuring, commenting that the North was 'so sheltered that he did not think we need worry very much about war measures' and that Belfast was 'of insignificant importance from the military point of view'.

In mid-1938 comments like these would have had considerable justification. The city had then only a very modest share of Britain's rearmament programme, and no one at Westminster, let alone at Stormont, could have been expected to foresee that in little over eighteen months Germany would occupy the whole north European coastline from Norway to Brittany. But the remarks were actually made in March 1939. At precisely this time, imperial defence experts were beginning to regard Belfast as a very definite target, partly because the number of arms contracts being completed there had so greatly increased. The Northern Ireland negotiators were of course unaware of the experts' changing opinions and were clearly impressed by the confident observations made by their British counterparts during the talks. Soon after the negotiations had ended, Sir Wilfrid Spender noted that the chances of a raid were 'so remote that although certain precautions might be required in the harbour area, [elsewhere they] were scarcely necessary'. John M. Andrews, Minister of Finance, also considered that they were in 'very large measure. . . unnecessary, owing to our sheltered position'.

Although British ministers had refused to include Northern Ireland in their legislation, they did of course provide it with equipment, financial support, and the advice of air raid precautions experts. The pace of local progress, however, remained glacially slow, with the Stormont government continuing to rely on voluntary co-operation from the local authorities, and itself providing hesitant and uninformed central direction. None the less, Dawson Bates and his parliamentary secretary at Home Affairs, Edmond Warnock, faced genuinely daunting problems in devising and implementing an effective policy. At first, there was uncertainty on the question of financial liability for civil defence in Northern Ireland. In fact up to spring 1941, some ministers felt that 'the monetary provision allowed us is not at all in the proportion which would be incurred in Great Britain, in cities of comparable size to Belfast'. A further major difficulty was the grossly inadequate supply of civil defence material made available by Westminster departments. Although respirators, at least enough to meet the needs of Belfast, were dispatched, no Anderson shelters for use by private households had been received by April 1939, and the quantity of fire-fighting equipment provided did not approach the level which British officials had themselves estimated was urgently required.

Most alarming of all was the failure to locate sufficient active defences – anti-aircraft guns, fighter planes or searchlights – in Northern Ireland. In fact, the Committee of Imperial Defence did not even begin to consider what defence facilities should be allocated to the North until early February 1939. During the following months, a detailed examination of its liability to aerial attack was at last undertaken. The inquiry concluded that though the area 'received considerable security by virtue of its position to the Westward of the general defence system', it was, nevertheless, definitely 'within bombing range'. It also noted that Belfast was beginning to emerge as a possible enemy target, having recently 'assumed increased importance both as regards shipbuilding and aircraft production'. It therefore advised that, 'with the least possible delay', some provision for the city's docks and harbour should be made, as this was 'where all the vital points are situated'.

Lord Craigavon (second from left), Northern Ireland's first Prime Minister, standing on the steps of Stormont beside John M. Andrews (second from right), who was to succeed him in 1940. (Public Record Office of Northern Ireland)

In April the committee specified precisely how much military equipment it considered should be sent to Northern Ireland. Its list of recommendations included one regiment of 3.7-inch mobile batteries (modern, heavy anti-aircraft guns), two mobile light batteries (approximately twenty-four guns), one fighter squadron and two radar stations. In total it would have cost over £2.5 million. However, Edmond Warnock had to inform his cabinet colleagues of the stark truth that owing to the shortage of essential supplies in Britain, it would be 'some months' before a 'reasonable number of anti-aircraft guns' or any fighter aircraft would be available. He stated candidly that his department had, therefore, 'no plans for the direct protection of the people'.

During the late spring of 1939, Stormont ministers had clearly become confused by the conflicting information about the vulnerability of Northern

Ireland which they had recently received from Westminster. Consequently, before proceeding with any further civil defence legislation of their own, they decided that they would first seek the advice of imperial defence experts. Accordingly, Edmond Warnock and Sir Wilfrid Spender were nominated to cross over to London and ask for clarification on the precise 'steps that should be taken to protect the civilian population'. Unfortunately, during the months which followed, the Stormont government repeatedly failed to act upon the very clear recommendations which it was then receiving from Britain. In late June, Warnock outlined to the cabinet the results of his talks with British ministers and officials. At the outset he stated categorically that he had received 'no support for the view that Belfast was likely to escape attack'. Indeed he was informed that if the British Civil Defence Bill had applied to the whole of the United Kingdom, Belfast would have been scheduled as a 'vulnerable area', as it was a 'probable target' and its entire population would have been given protection. It would have become an 'absolute duty' for all large factories and commercial premises to provide air-raid shelters for their employees; the Belfast Corporation would have been obliged to erect public shelters throughout the city and the Government similarly compelled to distribute Anderson shelters, free of charge, to all householders with incomes of less than £250 per year. In the course of his remarks, Warnock also made a harrowing though realistic estimate of the possible effect of an enemy air raid on Belfast, suggesting that it could cause as many as eight hundred casualties.

Despite these considerations, Warnock advised strongly against including some vital provisions of the British bill in his proposals for civil defence legislation at Stormont. Instead, he stated his conviction that Belfast would 'not be subject to frequent attack or to attack by large concentrations of enemy aircraft'. He defended this opinion on the grounds that, to reach the city, Luftwaffe bombers would have to fly over one thousand miles, negotiate on two occasions the 'active gun, searchlight and aeroplane defences of Great Britain' and, in the process, pass over 'targets which appeared to be more attractive'. He therefore concluded that the level of risk was 'not sufficiently great' to justify the Government in imposing on local industry and commerce the heavy financial burden of compulsorily providing shelters for their work force. If it was agreed not to exert compulsion on factory owners even in vulnerable areas, Warnock argued that it would be 'illogical for the Government to provide Anderson shelters for private houses' in those locations either. In the event of a raid, he claimed, 'people would not have time' to reach them anyway, as it would 'probably all be over in a matter of minutes'.

No final decision on these urgent issues was made until almost two months later, when the Stormont cabinet once again considered the terms of a civil defence bill for Northern Ireland. On this occasion, it was Dawson Bates who updated his colleagues on the most recent opinions expressed by imperial defence experts. He reported that Belfast was now regarded as 'a very definite target', and was classified as a 'vulnerable area' on a par with Plymouth. He had also been advised that though it was more distant for enemy aircraft than GB cities and ports, at speeds of 240–300 m.p.h. this was of 'no great moment'; in any case, much of this additional mileage was over sea, which bomber crews 'much preferred to land'. However, he strongly recommended that the Stormont government should not extend to Belfast the protective measures which were being applied to comparable areas of the United Kingdom by the Westminster government. He explained that it was his intention instead to 'rely on opinions expressed to the effect that raids on [the city would not] be of the same frequency or intensity as those on similar towns in Great Britain'. He proposed to proceed on the

> assumption that air raids would take place at night or at dawn and that the object of such raids would be the destruction of definite targets in the Harbour estate rather than the general objective of undermining civilian morale.

This totally unjustified assumption, made within weeks of the German invasion of Poland on 1 September 1939, was accepted by the cabinet without discussion. As a result, the ministers then agreed to restrict the compulsory provision of shelters at factories to the harbour area alone. This decision was not taken solely on security grounds. Some expressed strong fears that to do otherwise would impose a 'crushing burden on [Belfast] industry' and would arouse the 'strongest possible opposition from industrial interests'. The Belfast Corporation was given the parallel obligation of constructing public shelters to protect the 'number of people expected to be in the vulnerable part of the city at night or at dawn'. It was also decided that the Government should provide householders with domestic shelters, free of charge, 'beginning in certain limited areas near the danger zone'. The precise terms under which they would be available was still being debated when the war began.

During the long period when the Northern Ireland Civil Defence Bill was under consideration, several other civil defence measures were taken. After prolonged pressure from the Ministry of Home Affairs, in June 1939 Belfast councillors at last discussed and adopted the city's first comprehensive and detailed scheme of civil defence, the Hamill Plan (called after Major G. Hamill, Eastwood's successor as air raid precautions officer). Meanwhile the Stormont government itself took further measures as a preliminary to war. Preparations were made to increase the capacity of hospitals, to evacuate the city's seventy thousand elementary school children, and to receive air-raid warnings from Britain and transmit them to the public, using sirens at factories and police stations. Blackout plans for the whole of Northern Ireland were also set in motion, partly to prevent the Luftwaffe from using the lights of the North to identify its target in Great Britain. Clearly the steps taken were not fully effective. During the early weeks of the

war, local newspapers reported that lights still glowed on the southern side of villages bisected by the border and that, in Belfast itself, no masking precautions had been taken at telephone kiosks or at a number of shops and public houses. (On 10 April 1941, two days after the first air raid, the Air Commodore in Northern Ireland, C. Roderick Carr, drew attention to the fact that the lighthouses on Belfast Lough were still functioning as in peacetime and continued to do so even after the alert had been given.)

There was a belated flurry of activity in the city during late August and early September. Trenches in parks and at schools, closed over after the Munich crisis, were reopened, and many business premises were sandbagged against blast damage. Belfast Corporation workers coated kerbs, lampposts, telephone poles and trees with bands of white paint in preparation for the blackout. Transport vehicles were shrouded in a dull blue and their lights were dimmed. A number of buses were converted into mobile casualty posts and cars made into makeshift ambulances. The distribution of respirators was completed by wardens, most of them still without uniforms and with only badges and arm bands to indicate their status. Many even bought children's rattles to warn the public in case of gas attack; official rattles had not yet been issued. One warden recalled the sense of foreboding on Sunday, 3 September, as he reported for duty after Neville Chamberlain's mournful broadcast that morning, indicating that the 'long struggle to win peace' had failed. On arrival at his post, he was informed: 'You are just in time, they are bombing London. Someone from headquarters has just been through on the phone and heard the sound of the sirens.' Personnel in Belfast listened, expecting bombs to erupt at any time. Two days earlier, William McCready, a post office worker, recorded dolefully in his diary:

All street-lights in Belfast were out tonight, tramcars carried minimum lights

HINTS TO MOTHERS
★ Learn to put on baby's gas helmet quickly, while wearing your own mask. Your Health Visitor will show you how. If you don't know her address ask at Town Hall or at the Child Welfare Centre.
★ With more than one baby you need help. Arrange with a neighbour, or find out if your local W.V.S. has a Housewives' Service.
★ Toddlers soon learn to put on their own masks. Let them make a game of it and they will wear their gas masks happily.
In a gas attack, first put on your own mask, then you will be better able to help baby.
MAKE SURE YOUR FAMILY HAVE THEIR GAS MASKS WITH THEM NIGHT & DAY

> and the mail at the GPO was pushed through so that the office could be left in darkness. Two thousand years of Christianity and now we face this enormous tragedy.

Northern Ireland government ministers must bear much of the blame for the extent to which the North faced the tragedy unprepared and unprotected. They did of course labour under immense difficulties. They had, after all, been forced into making decisions, with extreme reluctance, on issues which arguably ought never to have been delegated to them. They suffered persistently from a lack of clear information on which to base policy, from financial uncertainty and from acute shortage of the most vital equipment, ranging from fire hoses to anti-aircraft guns. None the less, the fact remains that the response of Craigavon and his colleagues to the growing prospect of war had been indecisive and feeble, even irresponsible. It had certainly been characterised by political weakness. It was partly for this reason that the cabinet chose not to impose on local authorities the legal obligation to prepare air raid precautions schemes or decided not to compel those large industrial firms outside the harbour estate to provide shelter accommodation for their workers. It, yet again, ignored Westminster's precedent when it refused to assume the power to direct individuals to join the civil defence services; it preferred instead the politically easier option – voluntary recruitment. Kingsley Wood, Chancellor of the Exchequer, was to describe the public response in Northern Ireland to the call for personnel as the most 'disappointing' of any region in the United Kingdom. The Stormont cabinet's consistent record of inadequate leadership contributed significantly to the widespread apathy that was evident both at the outbreak of war and when the German air raids actually occurred less than two years later. The *Northern Whig* had for long complained that people were 'abysmally ignorant of the very elements of ARP'.

Sir Wilfrid Spender had become 'greatly perturbed' at the 'very unsatisfactory' level of local defence preparedness, and he laid the blame squarely on the incompetence of the regional administration. He was particularly critical of the Minister of Home Affairs, Dawson Bates, and had referred to him in August 1938, as 'more ill than is generally known [and] incapable of giving his responsible officers coherent directions on policy'. However, Spender was by then not just concerned with the inadequacy of one individual minister but rather with the inept performance of the whole Northern Ireland cabinet. When surveying the broad political scene that autumn, he felt profoundly dejected; he was acutely aware that the Government was 'losing ground' with public opinion. This he attributed mainly to its inability to stop unemployment from mounting and its poor record on housing and civil defence. He considered that the actions of the Prime Minister and his colleagues, their 'lack of prudence and forethought', their 'disregarding of their responsibilities' and their 'mistakes' constituted a 'grave danger to the system of democratic government' in Northern Ireland.

Spender regarded Craigavon as a vital source of this administrative weakness, describing him bluntly as 'too unwell to carry on' and incapable of doing 'more than one hour's constructive work' per day; a leader whose 'true friends would advise to retire now'. In Spender's view, Craigavon was remaining in office mainly out of financial necessity, even though he was in receipt of a salary larger than the British Prime Minister, and also because he was under very strong pressure from his wife not to relinquish his position. Lady Craigavon seemed unaware either of the extent of her husband's physical deterioration or of its disastrous impact on the overall competence of the Stormont government. Instead she cocooned him from reality, stating that in her opinion, his 'present life gave [him] plenty of leisure and just sufficient interest to occupy his mind'. But she stated firmly, 'on no account was he to be worried'. Indeed Craigavon's doctor spoke in similar vein, warning that the 'worry' of his leaving the premiership 'might prove fatal'.

The Prime Minister's casual and careless leadership was, in Spender's view, the major reason for the collapse of the cabinet system at Stormont. He observed that ministers met 'seldom', and that the Government was characterised by 'quick and hasty decisions, its members unaware of what was happening until an announcement was made in the press'. He was, in

A BLACK-OUT TIME-TABLE TO CUT OUT AND KEEP.

These are the official Northern Ireland black-out times for April, May and June. It should be noted that the times given are those on which the black-out *ends* and *starts* each day

APRIL

Apr.	Ends a.m	Starts p.m.	Apr.	Ends a.m.	Starts p.m.
1	6-27	8-29	16	5-50	8-58
2	6-25	8-31	17	5-48	9- 0
3	6-23	8-33	18	5-46	9- 2
4	6-20	8-35	19	5-43	9- 4
5	6-18	8-37	20	5-41	9- 6
6	6-15	8-39	21	5-39	9- 8
7	6-12	8-41	22	5-36	9-10
8	6-10	8-43	23	5-34	9-12
9	6- 7	8-45	24	5-32	9-14
10	6- 5	8-46	25	5-30	9-15
11	6- 2	8-48	26	5-27	9-17
12	6- 0	8-50	27	5-25	9-19
13	5-57	8-52	28	5-23	9-21
14	5-55	8-54	29	5-21	9-23
15	5-53	8-56	30	5-19	9-25

MAY

May	Ends a.m.	Starts p.m.	May	Ends a.m.	Starts p.m.
1	5-16	9-26	17	5-45	10-55
2	5-14	9-28	18	5-44	10-57
3	5-12	9-30	19	5-42	10-59
4	6-10	10-32	20	5-40	11- 0
5	6- 8	10-34	21	5-39	11- 2
6	6- 6	10-36	22	5-37	11- 3
7	6- 4	10-38	23	5-36	11- 5
8	6- 2	10-40	24	5-34	11- 7
9	6- 0	10-42	25	5-33	11- 8
10	5-58	10-44	26	5-32	11- 9
11	5-56	10-45	27	5-31	11-11
12	5-54	10-47	28	5-30	11-13
13	5-53	10-49	29	5-28	11-14
14	5-51	10-51	30	5-27	11-16
15	5-49	10-52	31	5-26	11-17
16	5-47	10-54			

JUNE

June	Ends a.m	Starts p.m.	June	Ends a.m	Starts p.m.
1	5-25	11-18	16	5-16	11-32
2	5-24	11-20	17	5-16	11-32
3	5-23	11-21	18	5-16	11-33
4	5-22	11-22	19	5-16	11-33
5	5-21	11-23	20	5-16	11-34
6	5-21	11-24	21	5-16	11-34
7	5-20	11-25	22	5-16	11-34
8	5-19	11-26	23	5-16	11-34
9	5-18	11-27	24	5-17	11-34
10	5-18	11-28	25	5-17	11-34
11	5-17	11-29	26	5-18	11-34
12	5-17	11-30	27	5-18	11-34
13	5-16	11-30	28	5-19	11-34
14	5-16	11-31	29	5-19	11-34
15	5-16	11-32	30	5-20	11-34

any case, scathingly critical of almost all Craigavon's colleagues, considering them to be too incompetent or too unwell or simply too often absent to cope with their responsibilities. The end result of this apparently infinite catalogue of collective inadequacy was that the 'whole weight' of administration fell on the ageing shoulders of John M. Andrews, who not only served as Minister of Finance but also acted as Prime Minister when 'anything unpleasant' had to be done, and periodically as Minister of Commerce and Minister of Labour as well. Spender concluded: 'I think another year of [the Government's] loosc conduct of affairs may do irretrievable harm to Ulster and the Unionist cause.' In fact, almost exactly one year after these words had been written, the same ministerial team, which had been so critically dissected, had to confront the challenge of World War II.

Belfast Telegraph

THIRD SPECIAL

70th YEAR [REGISTERED AT THE G.P.O. AS A NEWSPAPER] SUNDAY, SEPTEMBER 3, 1939. THREE-HALFPENCE

BRITAIN AND FRANCE AT WAR WITH GERMANY

FORMAL DECLARATION OF HOSTILITIES

"The following official communique was issued from 10 Downing Street: On September 1 His Majesty's Ambassador in Berlin was instructed to inform the German Government that unless they were prepared to give His Majesty's Government satisfactory assurances that the German Government would suspend any aggressive action against Poland and were prepared promptly to withdraw their forces from Polish territory, His Majesty's Government would without hesitation fulfil their obligations to Poland.

At nine this morning His Majesty's Ambassador in Berlin informed the German Government that unless not later than 11 a.m. to-day (British Summer Time) satisfactory assurances to the above effect had been given and had reached His Majesty's Government in London a state of war would exist between the countries from that hour.

Shortly after eleven the Prime Minister said "This country is at war with Germany."

France delivered a final ultimatum to Germany demanding that German troops withdraw from Poland. The ultimatum expires at five p.m. (B.S.T.).

The British and French Ambassadors formally bade goodbye to von Ribbentrop.

3
'LIFE IS REASONABLY NORMAL'
SEPTEMBER 1939–MARCH 1941

On Sunday, 3 September 1939, at 11.15 a.m., Neville Chamberlain informed the nation that a state of war existed between Britain and Germany. Both the sadness in his voice and his choice of words betrayed his own feelings of deep personal grief; he had held out the hand of friendship and it had been bitten to the bone. Mary Wallace can remember that beautiful sunny morning well. She was nine years old and lived off Bloomfield Avenue in east Belfast. In the street outside she could hear neighbours shouting excitedly: 'There's a war! There's a war!'; she 'didn't know what it meant'. Billy McNeill, then a young police constable, recalls that, after hearing the broadcast, he immediately cycled into Mountpottinger police station; there, he and his colleagues sat, 'waiting for the sirens to go and the bombers to come over anytime'.

On Monday, 4 September, under the headline 'Hitler Plunges the World into War', the *Belfast News-Letter* expressed a measure of relief that at last the apparently interminable sequence of international crises had ended. That day the Northern Ireland parliament met; it had been recalled one month early from its summer recess. The outbreak of war dominated its proceedings. Some of the Opposition members present injected a note of caution, even of fear, into the debate. Tommy Henderson, Independent Unionist, responding to a colleague, queried, 'Does [the honourable

The usual FRONT PAGE advertisements appear to-day in Page 3.

Daily Mail

FOR KING AND EMPIRE

NO. 13,529 — MONDAY, SEPTEMBER 4, 1939 — ONE PENNY (2d. EIRE)

CHURCHILL IN BRITAIN'S WAR CABINET

BRITAIN & FRANCE AT WAR WITH GERMANY

member] realize that these fast [enemy] bombers can come to Northern Ireland in 2¾ hours?' John Nixon, another Independent Unionist, expressed concern about the mood outside the chamber, stating: 'I am afraid there is some panic abroad. People ask me what they should do or where they should go in order to be safe.' Craigavon's speech dominated later newspaper headlines. He affirmed:

> We here today are in a state of war and we are prepared with the rest of the United Kingdom and Empire to face all the responsibilities that that imposes on the Ulster people. There is no slackening in our loyalty. There is no falling in our determination to place the whole of our resources at the command of the government in Britain.

One month later he returned to this theme, declaring: 'We must share and share alike with our fellow citizens across the water.' In fact, from the earliest stages of the war, a stark contrast rapidly and dramatically emerged between the experience of Northern Ireland and other parts of the United Kingdom: in Northern Ireland, attitudes, behaviour and the overall pace of life were uniquely static and unchanging. Even its official war history, *Northern Ireland in the Second World War* by John W. Blake, describes the period after the outbreak of hostilities as 'monotonous', a time when there was 'little progress towards victory' and 'inactivity persisted'.

This continuity with the pre-war years was not unwelcome to the local civilian population. With justification and obvious relief, Moya Woodside, a surgeon's wife living in south Belfast and reporter for the Tom Harrisson Mass Observation organisation, noted in her diary during the spring of 1940 that she was then living in 'probably the pleasantest place in Europe'. Changes had of course taken place which she lamented. There was rationing, and the inevitable wartime shortage of a variety of goods from hairclips to tinned grapefruit. Shopping had steadily become more time consuming and laborious. Unfamiliar purchases had to be made and diet modified accordingly. Pig's feet, knees and cheeks, for example, traditionally the preserve of the poor, now made their first appearance in the shop windows of smart downtown butchers and onto the tables of the middle class. However, food was more readily available than in most parts of Britain. Cross-border smuggling was rife, there was an active black market, and, in

STOP PRESS NEWS

LITHUANIA HOLDS A GERMAN PILOT

Damaged German pursuit 'plane came down on Lithuanian territory, says Reuter Kaunas message. Pilot has been interned.

NEW ZEALAND IS READY, TOO

Telegram has been received from New Zealand Government supporting British Government in war, and stating they will give fullest consideration to any suggestion from British Government as to methods by which they could best assist in the common cause.

Proclamation issued at Canberra empowers calling-out for war service of Australian naval, military, air, and civil defence forces.

PETROL TO BE RATIONED

Petrol rationing will be introduced as from September 16, and public will be told to-day how to secure ration books. Government appeal to motor vehicle owners to use them only for essential purposes.

Daily Mail, 4 September 1939

MAXIMUM RETAIL PRICES

JAM AND MARMALADE (Made in the United Kingdom)

	½ lb. s. d.	1 lb. s. d.	2 lb. s. d.	7 lb. s. d.
GROUP I				
Strawberry ...	0 8	1 3	2 5	7 11
GROUP II				
Blackcurrant Jelly ... / Apricot ... / Blackcurrant ... / Bilberry ... / Elderberry Jelly ...	0 7½	1 2½	2 3½	7 6
GROUP III				
Strawberry and Gooseberry / Blackberry Jelly ... / Plum and Blackcurrant / Apricot and Peach ...	0 7	1 1½	2 2	7 0½
GROUP IV				
Raspberry ... / Raspberry Jelly ... / Cherry ... / Plum and Strawberry / Loganberry Seedless / Apple and Blackcurrant / Blackberry ... / Pineapple ... / Redcurrant Jelly ... / Greengage ... / Damson ...	0 7	1 1	2 1	6 9
GROUP V.				
Plum and Raspberry / Peach ... / Apple and Strawberry / Gooseberry and Raspberry / Gooseberry ... / Raspberry and Redcurrant / Plum Jelly ... / Loganberry ... / Rhubarb and Raspberry / Special Marmalade ...	0 6½	1 0½	2 0	6 5½
GROUP VI				
Apple and Raspberry / Apple and Loganberry / Apple and Damson ... / Apple Jelly and Quince Jelly / Rhubarb and Blackberry / Plum ... / Ordinary Marmalade / Apple and Blackberry / Apple and Plum ... / Rhubarb ... / Any other Jams ...	0 6½	1 0	1 10½	6 0½

IMPORTED CANNED JAMS

	12 oz.	16 oz.	24 oz.	32 oz.
Cape Gooseberry or Apricot	1/-	1/2	1/9	2/3
Green Fig ...	11d	1/1	1/7	2/1
Strawberry ...	1/1	1/3	1/10	2/4
Blackcurrant ...	11d	1/2	1/8	2/2
Loganberry, Raspberry, Pineapple, Peach, or Peach and Pineapple ...	11d	1/1	1/6	2/-
All other Jams ...	10d	1/-	1/5	1/10
	1 lb.	1½ lb.	2 lb.	
Imported Canned Marmalade	1/-	1/5	1/10	
Points for Canned Marmalade	4	6	8	

SYRUP AND TREACLE (8 Points per lb. net)

In Tins or Cartons—1 lb., 8½d. 2 lbs., 1/4; 4 lbs., 2/7½.
In Glass Jars—1 lb. or less, 9d. per lb.; over 1 lb. to 4 lbs., 8½d. per lb.
In any other container—8½d. per lb. net.

	No. ½ size.	No. 1 size. s. d.	No. 2 size. s. d.
MINCEMEAT	7d.	1s. 1d.	2s. 1d.
FRUIT CURD	6½d.	1s. 0½d.	1s. 11d.

HOME PRODUCED HONEY

Extracted Heather—½ lb., 1/10; 1 lb., 3/6; Larger, 3/- per lb.
Other Honey—½ lb., 1/6; 1 lb., 2/9; Larger, 2/3.
Honey in Comb—Heather—2½d. per oz.; Other, 2d. per oz.

PLUMS

	s.	d.	
Group 1—Czar, Yellow Egg, Gisborne, Purple Pershore, Kent Bush, Blaisdon Red, and Mogul	–	5	per lb.
Group 2—Dessert Victoria Plums, Greengages, and Gages ...	–	9½	do.
Group 3—Damsons ...	–	6½	do.
Group 4—All other varieties ...	–	7	do.

PEARS

Group 1, 1/6½d. per lb.; Group 2, 1/1½ per lb.; Group 3, 8½d. per lb.

ORANGES ... 7½d per lb.
LEMONS ... 6½d. per lb.
RHUBARB ... 3d. per lb.
ONIONS ... 4½d. per lb.
CUCUMBERS 10d. per lb.
LEEKS ... 4½d. per lb.
BANANAS ... 2d. each
CARROTS PER 2 LBS. Until Oct. 7, 4d.; Oct. 8 to Jan. 31, 3½d.

TOMATOES PER LB.
Until Oct. 15, 1s. 3d.; Oct. 16 to Dec. 3, 1s. 6d.

GREEN WALNUTS 1 3 per lb.

GREEN ONIONS

Less than 1½ in. in diameter, 5d. per lb.; larger, 3½d. per lb.

GREEN VEGETABLES PER LB.

Autumn Cabbage and Cabbage Greens, 2¾d.
Savoys and Savoy Greens, 2¾d.
Brussells Sprouts, 5d.
Sprout Tops, 3½d.
Kale and Sprouting Broccoli, 3 d.
Broccoli (heading types) and Cauliflower, trimmed, 4½d.
Sub-standard Green Vegetables, 2¼d.

BEETROOT AND PARSNIPS PER LB.

2½d. per lb.
2½d. per lb. may be added when they are sold cooked.

POTATOES PER 7 Lbs. Until Oct. 5, 6d.

From Oct. 6, Golden Wonder, King Edward, Red King, Gladstone—in District 1, 6d.; in District 2, 5½d. Kerr's Pink, Redskin, Up-to-date, Dunbar Standard, Arran Peak, Arran Victory—in District 1, 5½d.; in District 2, 5d. Any other variety—in either district, 5d.

DRIED BEANS 1 Point per lb.

	s.	d	
Kenya, Kenya Rose Coco, Rangoon hand picked, Chilean Coloured, French Brown Haricots, American Coloured ...	–	4	per lb.
Burma Butter, Large French Haricots, South African White, East African White, Brazilian White, Persian White, Canadian Pea Beans, American White, Chilean Crystales, Chilean Arros ...	–	6	do.
Madagascar and Maintarano ...	–	8	do.

PEAS

Wrinkled ...	–	7½	per lb.
Wrinkled, soaked in water ...	–	4	do.
Other Dried Peas (1 Point per lb.) ...	–	10	do.
Hand Picked, soaked in water 1 Point per 2 lbs.)	–	5	do.
Yellow Split Peas (2 Points per lb.) ...	–	5	do.
Green Split Peas (1 Point per lb.) ...	–	9½	do.
Pea Pickings sold for human food ...	–	4½	do.

LENTILS CHILEAN GREEN (no points) – 9 per lb.

RICE (Loose) 4 Points per lb

	s	d	
Patna, Egyptian, Brazilian, and U.S.A. ...	–	7	per lb.
Empire Japan, Sughandi, Burma round grain	–	6	do.
Parboiled Rice ...	–	6	do.
Board of Trade Rice ...	–	7	do.
Burma XX ...	–	4½	do.

PEARL BARLEY 7½d. per lb.

TAPIOCA (Loose) 4 Points per lb.

U.K. Flakes, 8½d.; Singapore or Java, 7d.; any other, 6½d.

SAGO (Loose) 4 Points per lb ... – 6½ per lb.

MACARONI, SPAGHETTI, AND VERMICELLI

Pre-packed, 1 lb. net, 8½d.; ½ lb. net, 4½d.; Loose, 7½d. per lb.

SOYA FLOUR (less than 28 lbs), 5d. per lb.

FLOUR

PLAIN.—3 lbs. or less, 2¾d. per lb.; over 3 lbs. and under 20 lbs., 2½d. per lb.; 20 lbs. to 112 lb., 2¼d. per lb.; 140 lbs., 22s. 6d.
SELF-RAISING.—Under 3 lbs., 3¾d. per lb.; 3 lbs. to 6 lbs., 3⅝d. per lb.; over 6 lbs. to 112 lbs., 3½d. per lb.; 140 lbs., 25s. 6d.

BREAD

	4 lb.	2 lb.	1¾ lb.	1 lb.
In Northern Ireland ...	9½d.	4¾d.	4¼d.	2¾d.

BISCUITS

CLASSIFIED PRODUCTS.—Prices range from 9d. to 2/6 per lb. The product group number and price must be clearly indicated

PEPPER (Loose)

Whole—picked or cleaned, Black, 2s. 0d.; White, 2s. 8d.
Ground—Black, 2s. 8d.; White, 3s. 4d.

PEPPER (Prepacked)

	Ground White.	Ground Black.
1 oz. and less than 4 oz. ...	4½d.	3½d.
4 oz. „ „ 5 oz. ...	1/-	8½d.

CANNED SALMON

		s.	d.		Points
GRADE 1:	1's Flats or 1's Talls ...	1	10½	per tin	32
	½'s ...	1	0½	do.	20
	¼'s ...	–	8½	do.	10
GRADE 2:	1's Flats or 1's Talls ...	1	5½	do.	32
	½'s ...	–	9½	do.	20
	¼'s ...	–	7	do.	10
GRADE 3:	1's Flats or 1's Talls ...	1	0	do.	6
	½'s ...	–	7½	do.	4
	¼'s ...	–	5	do.	2

HOME PRODUCED CANNED FISH

Brisling, Sild and Sprats, ¼'s, 6½d. (3 Points); ⅛'s, 5d. (2 Points); 1/16's, 3½d. (1 Point).
Perch and Perchines, ½'s American, 10½d. (6 Points); ¼'s Dingley, 6½d. (3 Points).

CANNED SARDINES PER LB. (Points in brackets)

1/10th club	20 m/m	8d	(2)	⅛th club	25 m/m	9½d	(3)
⅛th club	30 m/m	10d	(3)	⅛th flat	24 m/m	11½d	(3)
¼'s special	25 m/m	11d	(3)	¼'s club	30 m/m	1/-	(4)
¼'s club	40 m/m	1/4½	(5)	¼'s oval	30 m/m	1/5	(5)
¼'s reduced	18 m/m	10d	(3)	¼'s usual	22 m/m	1/-	(4)
¼'s usual	24 m/m	1/2	(4)	¼'s usual	30 m/m	1/4½	(5)
¼'s American	30 m/m	1/7	(7)	Large ½'s	40 m/m	2/7½	(12)
4/4	80 m/m	5/6	(24)				

American and Canadian ¼'s (3¼ or 3½ ozs.) ... 4½d (2)
For Boneless and Skinless or Boneless Sardines the above prices may be increased by 1d. per container for 40 m/m and ½d. per container for other sizes

IMPORTED CANNED FISH

			s.	d.		
Pilchard Fillets ...	8 oz. oblong		–	8½	each	6 Points
Silvets ...	½s oval		–	5½	do.	3 do.
Silver Fish ...	½s round		–	5	do.	0 do.

Other Pilchards, Herrings, and Mackerel—

1's oval	1's tall	8 oz. oblong	½'s oval	½'s round	5 oz.	6 oz.
10d.	9d.	7½d.	7d.	6d.	5d.	5d.
POINTS—						
(2)	(2)	(1)	(1)	(1)	(1)	(1)

Crawfish (Crayfish), including Cape, Rock and Cape Spinney Lobster and Langouste du Cap, ½'s round, 1s. 2½d. (12 Points); ¼'s round, 9d. (6 Points).
Cod, Haddock, Catfish, Cod Roes, 1s, 1/6 (12 Points); 2s, 2/8 (24 Points)
Fish Balls and Fish Cakes, 1's, 1/4½; Curried Fish, 1's, 1/3 (4 Points); Fried Fish in Sauce, ½'s, 9d. (2 Points).
Kipper Snacks, ¼'s, 7d. (0 Points)
Shrimps and Prawns, 1's, 1s. 9d. (12 Points); ½'s, 1s. (6 Points)

POINTS VALUES

	1's	½'s	¼'s	⅛'s	1/16's
Lobster and Crab ...	16	8	4	–	–
Tuna Fish ...	–	8	4	–	–
Anchovies ...	–	–	–	–	1

SOUPS IN TINS 10 ozs. net, 6½d. 16 oz. net, 8½d.

CANNED MEAT IN TIN OR GLASS

	s.	d.		Points
Corned or Boiled Beef, Pork or Mutton	1	4	per lb.	
Luncheon Meat, Pork Loaf or Ham Loaf,	2	2½	per 1 lb.	15 per lb.
Luncheon Meat, Pork Loaf or Ham Loaf, 12 oz. tins ...	2	2½	per lb.	11 per tin
Brisket ...	2	3	do.	32 per lb.
Pressed Beef ...	2	3	do.	32 do.
Pork Fillets ...	2	3	do.	
Chopped Lunch Tongue ...	2	8	do.	32 do.
Other Lunch Tongue ...	3	0	do.	32 do.
Ox or Calf Tongue ...	3	6	do.	32 do.
Canned Boneless Chicken or Turkey	3	6	do.	20 do.
Minced Meat Loaf ...	–	10	12 oz. tin	12 per tin
Stewed Steak ...	1	8	per lb.	20 per lb.
Pork Sausage Meat ...	2	6	1½ lb. tin	12 per tin
Sheep's or Lamb's Tongue (imported)	1	9	12 oz. tin	24 do.
Canned Rabbit—				
2 lb. tin, including bone ...	2	6	per tin	16 do.
1 lb., including bone ...	1	5	do.	8 do.
1 lb., boneless ...	1	10	do.	8 do.
Ready or Prepared Meals ...	–	11½	16 oz. tin	4 do.
SLICED—				
Ox or Calf Tongue ...	4	0	per lb.	32 per lb.
Lunch Tongue ...	3	4	do.	32 do.
Chopped Lunch Tongue ...	3	0	do.	32 do.
Pork Loaf or Ham Loaf ...	2	6	do.	16 do.
Luncheon Meat, Pork Loaf or Ham Loaf ...	2	6	do.	16 do.
Brisket ...	2	8	do.	32 do.

Wartime food prices. (Ulster Folk and Transport Museum)

CANNED FRUITS

HOME PRODUCED	E1 Can	A1T Can	A2 Can	A2½ Can	A10 Water Packed	A10 Syrup Packed
Plums (Golden, Red, Purple, Yellow Egg, Gisborne, Czar, Kent Bush & Mogul)	7½d	8½d	10d	1/2	3/4	3/7½
Other Plums and Damsons ...	9d	9½	1/–	1/4	4/–	4/2
POINTS VALUES ...	(4)	(4)	(6)	(8)	(20)	(20)

CANNED VEGETABLES

	E1	A1	A1 Tall	A2	A2½	A10
Macedoine ...	6½	5½	7½	9	1/1	3/11
Peas	—	5½	7	8½	11½	3/1
POINTS for Peas	(2)	(2)	(2)	(3)	(3)	(12)
Baked or Steamed	8 oz.	A1	A1 Tall	A2	A2½	32 oz.
Beans in Tomato	4	5½	7	8½	11½	1 1
Spaghetti in Tomato	4	5½	7½	—	—	—
Cooked Macaroni in Cream Sauce with Cheese ...	4½	—	8½	—	—	—
Vegetable Salad with Mayonnaise ...	7	8½	1 1	—	—	—
POINTS for Beans: In Sauce ...	(2)	(3)	(4)	(5)	(8)	(8)

CONDENSED MILK

SPECIAL FULL CREAM SWEETENED

	s. d.			s. d.	
1¾ pints	1 0½	8 Points	⅞ pint ...	– 6½	4 Points

FULL CREAM SWEETENED

	s. d.			s. d.	
1¼ pints	– 11½	6 Points	¾ pint ...	– 6	3 Points

FULL CREAM UNSWEETENED

	s. d.			s. d.	
2 pints	– 9½	4 Points	¾ pint ...	– 4½	2 Points
14½ oz.	– 9	4 Points	American 14½ oz.	– 8½	4 Points

SKIMMED

	s. d.			s. d.	
2¾ pints	– 6	4 Points	1⅞ pints	– 5	4 Points
1⅜ pints	– 4	2 Points			

SUGAR PER LB.

Granulated, 4d.; Preserving, Grocery Crystals, Demarara, 4½d.; Cubes or Castor, 4½d.; Pieces or Soft Brown, 3½d.

CHRISTMAS PUDDINGS

1 lb., in returnable basin, 2/–; in other basin, 1/9.
2 lb., in returnable basin, 3/7; in other basin, 3/4.

SACCHARIN TABLETS PER 100

Standard Saccharin, 10d. Sweetening Tablets, 9d.

APPLES (home produced) PER LB.

Group I.—1/-. Group II.—7d. Group III.—3½d.

APPLES (imported) PER LB.

Group I.—1/1; Group II.—6½d. Group III.—3½d.

SOFT FRUITS PER LB. NET

	s. d.		s. d.
Dessert Gooseberries	1 7	Loganberries ...	1 1½
All other Gooseberries	– 7	Cherries ...	1 9½
Raspberries ...	1 2½	Blackcurrants ...	1 9
Cultivated Blackberries	– 10½	Red and White Currants	– 10½
Wild Blackberries ...	– 8	Bilberries ...	1 2
Strawberries ...	1 3½		

COFFEE PER LB.

Raw, 1s. 6d.; Roasted or Ground or Coffee Mixture, 1s. 8d.

Roasted or Ground Coffee may be sold at a price not exceeding 2s. 8d. per lb., and Coffee Mixture at a price not exceeding 2s. 4d. per lb., provided that Roasted or Ground Coffee or Coffee Mixture is available at a price not exceeding 1s. 8d. per lb., and a notice is displayed accordingly.

NATIONAL BUTTER in bulk must be labelled "National Butter."
SAUSAGES must have descriptive label on or close to them.
APPLES must be labelled with the group number and the price.

UNMIXED BROKEN BISCUITS.—Prices must not exceed half the maximum price of the product group.

POINTS—For Whole Biscuits: Chocolate, 16 per lb.; Sweet or Semi-Sweet, 8 per lb.; Plain, 4d. per lb. For Broken Biscuits: Chocolate, 8 per lb.; Sweet or Semi-Sweet, 4 per lb.; Plain, 2 per lb.

CAKE AND FLOUR CONFECTIONERY

Containing less than 14 per cent. fat and sugar, 8d. per lb.; containing more than 14 per cent. fat and sugar, 10d. per lb.; but where ingredients cost more than 3½d. per lb. the maximum retail price is to be three times the cost or 1s. 6d. per lb., whichever is lesser.

SEMOLINA

PRE-PACKED.—½ lb., 3½d.; 1 lb., 6½d.; over 1 lb. but less than 28 lbs., 6d. per lb.; 28 lbs. and over, 4d. per lb.

LOOSE.—Less than 7 lbs., 5d. per lb.; 7 lbs. and under 28 lbs., 4½d. per lb.; 28 lbs. and over 4d. per lb.

OAT PRODUCTS (not Prepacked)

	s. d.
Oatmeal, including Brown Groats	– 3½ per lb.
Oat Flakes, including White Groats and Rolled Oats (not pre-packed) and Oat Flour ...	– 3¾ do.

OAT FLAKES (Prepacked) 1 Point per 8 oz. or less.

2 lb. or less, 4½d. per lb.; more than 2 lb., 4¼d. per lb. (White Groats are points free.)

CEREAL BREAKFAST FOODS

		s. d.
Brown & Polson's Corn Flakes ...	8 oz. ...	– 6½
,, Wheat Flake ...	8 oz. ...	– 6
Force	8 oz. ...	– 6
Kellogg's Wheat Krispies	8 oz. ...	– 5½
,, Corn Flakes	8 oz. ...	– 5
,, All Bran	10 oz. ...	– 7½
Quaker Malted Corn Flakes ...	8 oz. ...	– 5
Shredded Wheat	12 oz. ...	– 8
Weetabix	16 oz. ...	1 1
,, ...	8 oz. ...	– 7½
Briskies	8 oz. ...	– 6½

POINTS VALUES—8 ozs. or under, 2 points; 12 ozs. and over 8 ozs., 3 points; over 12 ozs, 4 points.

HARD SOAPS (Factory net weight)

	s. d.		s. d.
A.R. Hand Pumice ...	– 8	Jeyes' Primrose	– 7½
A.R. Hand Pumice (Lysol)	– 9½	Kay's White Windsor	– 7½
Boaler's Patent ...	– 7½	Kilty	– 9
Bodyguard	– 8	Lifebuoy	– 9
Bolton's White Windsor	– 7½	Magdov Kosher ...	– 9½
Boots' Pumice ...	1 0	Minster White Windsor	– 7½
Borolic	– 9	Nimrod	– 9
Calvert's No. 5 Carbolic	– 11	Nuway	– 11
Caurnie Self Cleanser	1 0½	Peerless Carpet ...	2 1
Chiver's Carpet ...	3 0	Petobolic	– 8
Croftol Disinfectant ...	– 8½	Play	– 7½
Dr. Lovelace's ...	– 7½	Pompey Hand ...	1 0
Dr. Lovelace's Carbolic	– 7½	Pumit Pumice ...	1 1
Dr. Lovelace's Floating	– 9	Rexall Pumice ...	1 0
Family Health ...	– 9	Royal Primrose	– 7
Field's Pumice ...	1 1	Sanitas Disinfectant ...	– 11
Finlay's Finbel Pure Curd	– 10	Schoolboy	– 9
Fleet-Wing Health First	– 7½	Scotsman Paraffin ...	– 7½
Furmoto Universal Cleaner	2 0	S.C.W.S. Finest White Windsor ...	– 7½
Gleniffer White Windsor	– 8	Springfield Sanitary Carbolic	– 7½
Gordon Kosher ...	– 9	Thistle	– 7
Gorney Kosher ..	– 9½	Thom's Finest Castile	– 7½
Hanson's Carpet Shampoo	1 8	Thom's Pure Pink Carbolic	– 7½
Harrod's Primrose	– 7	Timothy White's and Taylor's White Windsor	7½
H.B.T. Aseptic ...	– 8½	Volvolutum	– 8½
Hedley's Lava ...	– 10	Young's Glycerine and Cucumber ...	– 8½
Home Guard ...	– 8½	Zixt	1 4
Isdale & McCallum's Finest White ...	– 7	OTHER HARD SOAPS— Except Carbolic ...	– 6½
Isdale & McCallum's Lysol A.1. ...	– 8	Carbolic	– 7
Izal	– 8	SOAP FLAKES, loose— Per 3 oz. net ...	– 1¾
Jeyes' Household ...	– 8	SOAP SUBSTITUTES—	Prices on labels
Jeyes' No. 1 Carbolic ...	– 7½		
Jeyes' No. 1 White ...	– 8		

SOFT DRINKS

Lemonade, Orangeade, Limeade, Appleade, Ginger Ale, Ginger Beer, Sparkling Special, Fruit Cup, Soda Water, Spa Sparkling, Herbal Beverage, Botanical Beverage, Hop Bitters:—Bottles—40 ozs., 6½d.; 24—28 ozs., 4½d.; 18—23 ozs., 4d.; 9—12 ozs., 3½d.; 6—8 ozs., 3d.; 3½—4½ ozs., 2½d.; Syphons—36—40 ozs., 10d.; 26—35 ozs., 9d. Jars—1 gallon, 2s. 4d.; ½ gallon, 1s. 2d.

Lemon Squash, Orange Squash, Grapefruit Squash, Lemon Barley, Lime Juice Cordial, Blackcurrant Cordial, Elderberry Cordial:—Bottles—26 ozs., 2s 6d.; 1-gallon jar, 10s.

Lemon Flavour Cordial, Lime Flavour Cordial, Orange Flavour Cordial, Blackcurrant Flavour Cordial, Elderberry Flavour Cordial, Specialty Flavour Cordial, Ginger Cordial, Peppermint Cordial:—26-oz. bottle, 2s.; ½-gallon jar, 8s. 6d.

container is over 1 lb. capacity, and not more than 1 lb. is sold on the occasion of one sale. Only the contents of 2¼ lb. or 3 lb. tins of Home Produced Meat Roll or Galantine may be used for slicing.

MEAT ROLL OR GALANTINE

10 ozs., 7½d. (1 Point); 16 ozs., 11d. (2 Points); 2¼ lbs., 1s. 11½d. (4 Points); 3 lbs., 2s. 7d. (5 Points). Sliced, from 2¼ lb. or 3 lb. tins, 1s. per lb. (2 Points).

MEAT OR FISH PASTE

In Glass—2¾ oz., 8d.; 2 oz., 6½d.; 1¼ oz., 5d.; ¾ oz., 3½d.
In Tins—3 oz., 3¾d.; 1½ oz., 2¼d.; 1 oz., 1½d.

SAUSAGES AND MEAT PRODUCTS PER LB.

Produced in U.K., other than in airtight containers.

	s. d.		s. d.
Pork Sausages ...	1 2	Beef Sausage ...	– 8
Pork Sausage Meat	1 1	Beef Sausage Meat ...	– 7
Liver Sausage ...	1 4	Meat Roll or Galantine ...	1 0
Brawn (including Potted Head) ...	1 1	Meat or Fish Paste ...	1 6
		Haggis ...	1 4
Luncheon Sausage, Breakfast Sausage of Polony ...	1 0		

Additional 1d. per lb. may be charged for Sausages filled in Sheep's casings and sold at not less than 10 to the lb.

PRESSED OR COOKED MEAT

(Produced in U.K., other than in airtight containers)	s. d.
Beef, Veal, Mutton, Lamb or Pork (Unsliced)	2 3 per lb.
do. do. do. (Sliced) ...	2 8 do.
Ox or Calf Tongues (Unsliced)	3 6 do.
do. do. (Sliced)	4 0 do.
All other Tongues (Unsliced)	3 0 do.
do. do. (Sliced)	3 4 do.
Cooked Tripe	– 9 do.

CURED MEAT

	s. d.
Uncooked Chaps	– 11½ per lb.
Cooked Chaps, bone in, 1s. 6d. per lb. Boneless,	1 8½ do.
Eyepieces, cooked or uncooked	– 5 do.
Uncooked Ox or Calf Tongues	1 2 do.
All other Tongues	1 0 do.

COOKED HAM OR GAMMON 3 4 per lb.

BACON— BONELESS

	Unsmoked. s. d.	Smoked. s. d.
MIDDLE	2 0 per lb.	2 1 per lb.
BACK	2 3 do.	2 4 do.
STREAK OR BELLY—Thick	1 8 do.	1 9 do.
STREAK OR BELLY—Thin	1 4 do.	1 5 do.
GAMMON OR HAM ...	2 3 do.	2 3 do.
PRIME COLLAR ...	1 9 do.	1 9 do.
FORE END OR SHOULDER	1 8 do.	1 8 do.
BACON TRIMMINGS ...	– 10 do.	– 10 do.

	Unsmoked other than Pale Dried. s. d.	Smoked or Pale Dried. s. d.
ULSTER ROLL—Shoulder End	1 8 per lb.	1 8 per lb.
ULSTER ROLL—Middle Cut	2 0 do.	2 1 do.

UNCOOKED OR COOKED, per lb.—

Hind-leg Knuckles ..	8d.	Sheet Ribs ...	6d.
Fore-leg Knuckles ...	6d.	Bones	1d.

POULTRY (per lb.)

Turkeys (dead weight)—Plucked, Undrawn and Untrussed, 3/- per lb.; Drawn and Trussed, including Giblets, 4/3 per lb.

Poussins (young chickens)—Plucked, 3/6 per bird.

Other Poultry (dead weight)—Plucked, Undrawn and Untrussed, 2/- per lb.; Drawn and Trussed, including Giblets, 2/10½ per lb.

FISH CAKES

Pieces—Fried, 2½d.; Unfried, 2¼d. each.
Slab—Fried, 1/4; Unfried, 1/2½ per lb.

FATS PER LB.

	s. d.		s. d.
Butter ..	1 8 per lb.	Cooking Fat ...	– 9 per lb.
Special Margarine	– 9 do.	Dripping ...	– 8 do.
Standard Margarine	5 do.	Lard ...	– 9 do.

Suet—(Pre-packed), price marked on container; (Loose), 1d per lb. less than price of same brand in ½ lb. packets.

CHEESE PER LB.

Soft and Curd (less than 35% fat), 10d. All other, 1s. 1d.

EGGS PER DOZEN

CATEGORY I. 2s. 0d. CATEGORY II. 1s. 9d.
Spray Dried or Flake Dried Whole Egg, 1/3 per 12 egg container.

EDIBLE EXTRACT OR SOUP MIXTURE

Price on label, or price charged on 2nd December, 1940.

GRAVY PREPARATION—Price on label

DRIED FRUITS (Loose) PER LB.

Figs, Currants, Dates, Muscatels, Raisins, Sultanas, Apples, Plums or Prunes, 9d. Apricots, Nectarines, Peaches, Pears, 1/-. Prices of pre-packed Dates (stoned or unstoned) may be increased by 2d. per lb. Prices of Stoned Raisins may be increased by 1½d. per lb. Points per lb.: Currants, 16; Apples, Figs or Prunes, 6; other Fruits, 8.

any case, Northern Ireland was a major exporting region. Local farmers, under threat of losing their holdings, responded well to the call for increased production. In Belfast vegetable allotments proliferated. Even the manicured lawns at Queen's University were divided up and allocated to staff. A keen golfer in the city recalled that at her favourite course 'cattle grazed on the rough', fenced off from the sheep which 'roamed on the immaculate fairways'. The alternative was having both ploughed up under government tillage orders.

Three of Belfast's most opulent centres of popular entertainment – the Grand Opera House, the Hippodrome, and the Ritz. Theatres, cinemas and dance halls continued to flourish throughout the war (Ulster Folk and Transport Museum)

There were numerous other sources of irritation which Moya Woodside noted: the scarcity and cost of domestic servants; the slowness of the mail service; the growing evidence of censorship of letters, of telephone calls and of the press; and 'the narrowing and impoverishment of cultural life'. Entertainers and visiting lecturers were generally unable to get travel permits from Britain and those from Éire disliked the blackout and the risk of bombs. She also felt some resentment at the very considerable military invasion of Northern Ireland – not from Nazi Germany but from Britain. Over seventy thousand British troops had arrived by November 1940, overwhelming some small towns, stretching available accommodation to the limit, and pulverising road surfaces with their heavy vehicles. In addition, there was an influx of several thousand evacuees into Northern

Belfast News-Letter

MONDAY, SEPTEMBER 4, 1939

THEATRES, CINEMAS, ENTERTAINMENTS, &c.

NOTICE TO THE PUBLIC

CINEMAS & THEATRES

THE GOVERNMENT OF NORTHERN IRELAND do not consider it necessary at present to apply the Order closing Cinemas and Theatres to Northern Ireland. ALL CINEMAS AND THEATRES WILL, THEREFORE, REMAIN OPEN AND PROGRAMMES WILL BE SHOWN AS USUAL.

ISSUED BY THE AMUSEMENT CATERERS' ASSOCIATION, N.I.

Ireland from Britain, many of them expectant mothers, and a fair proportion of the remainder had settled unofficially. Nevertheless, Moya Woodside was correct in her claim that war had caused much less disruption in Northern Ireland than anywhere else in the United Kingdom and in much of the rest of Europe. She wrote: 'We are unbombed, we have no conscription, there is plenty to eat and life is reasonably normal.'

Much of the North's traditional cultural activity survived relatively untouched by the European conflict. Although the normal 12 July Orange demonstrations in 1940 were replaced by religious services, at least the church bells continued to ring; in Britain they had been banned except to announce invasion. Football suffered less than across the water: no limits were ever placed on crowd attendances; without conscription, there was no need to cancel players' contracts; and even though gates fell, public interest was maintained by a range of regional, even national, competitions and by the army of guest players available from locally based military units. No six-foot trees grew on the terraces of Windsor Park stadium at the end of the war – unlike Old Trafford. Northern Ireland's cinemas also prospered – unique in the United Kingdom, they remained open during the autumn of 1939 and in Belfast their capacity was stretched to the limit and beyond. They offered warmth and entertainment and, apart from the newsreels and the profusion of uniforms in attendance, there was little to suggest that Northern Ireland was at war. On a typically crowded Saturday night, one film-goer recalled hearing 'a North Country voice shouting in the middle of the big picture, "This is the first time I've ever paid to sit on t'floor."'

The contrast between the experience of Northern Ireland and of Great Britain in wartime was pervasive. It struck informed English visitors most forcefully. One of them was Harold Wilson, later Labour Prime Minister, who arrived in Belfast in December 1940. As joint secretary of the British war cabinet's Manpower Requirements Committee, he was sent over to investigate the use being made of local labour resources for war production. He was shocked to discover that after fifteen months of hostilities, Northern Ireland, far from emerging as an important munitions centre, had become

AIR RAID WARNINGS

In the event of an Air Raid *"Alert"* being received, and in case any member of the audience wishes to leave the Theatre, a *red light* will be shown on the right hand side of the proscenium during which time the Play will proceed. This *Red Light* will be extinguished on the *"ALL CLEAR."*

The nearest Air Raid Shelters are in Clarence Street West, Ormeau Avenue, and Linenhall Street.

progressively more and more depressed. During this period, not a single new factory had been constructed in the region and, apart from shipbuilding, orders placed with existing firms were 'exceedingly meagre'. At a time when British unemployment had halved, it had risen locally to reach seventy-two thousand – a level similar to that found in Britain during 1932, the blackest year of the Depression. Wilson suggested that the result was a disappointed and disillusioned work force; others claimed that it had caused an increase in political extremism and juvenile delinquency. Leading local politicians feared that if unemployment reached one hundred thousand, it would have 'terrific repercussions for the Government'. When Winston Churchill was informed of the North's negligible contribution to the war effort, he ordered an immediate investigation and called for action to ensure that fuller use was made of its resources.

Other aspects of local life, which are less easily quantified, also diverged starkly from British experience. Even as late as 1942 it was obvious to a professional wartime investigator of public attitudes and behaviour, who was sent over by the Mass Observation organisation. The observer came to Belfast during June of that year, having just completed extensive enquiries

Even after conversion to sound cinema in the early 1930s, the Hippodrome could still host spectacular live wartime entertainment (Arthur Campbell)

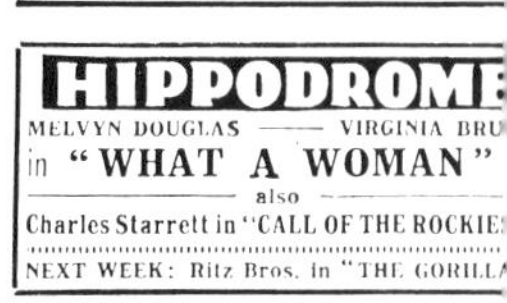

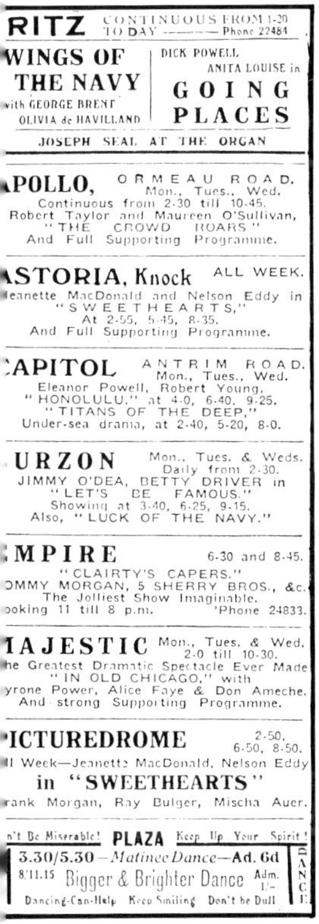
RITZ CONTINUOUS FROM 1-20 TO DAY — Phone 22484
WINGS OF THE NAVY with GEORGE BRENT OLIVIA de HAVILLAND
DICK POWELL ANITA LOUISE in GOING PLACES
JOSEPH SEAL AT THE ORGAN

POLLO, ORMEAU ROAD. Mon., Tues., Wed.
Continuous from 2-30 till 10-45.
Robert Taylor and Maureen O'Sullivan,
"THE CROWD ROARS"
And Full Supporting Programme.

STORIA, Knock ALL WEEK.
eanette MacDonald and Nelson Eddy in
"SWEETHEARTS,"
At 2-55, 5-45, 8-35.
And Full Supporting Programme.

APITOL ANTRIM ROAD. Mon., Tues., Wed.
Eleanor Powell, Robert Young.
"HONOLULU," at 4-0, 6-40, 9-25.
"TITANS OF THE DEEP,"
Under-sea drama, at 2-40, 5-20, 8-0.

URZON Mon., Tues. & Weds. Daily from 2-30.
JIMMY O'DEA, BETTY DRIVER in
"LET'S BE FAMOUS."
Showing at 3-40, 6-25, 9-15.
Also, "LUCK OF THE NAVY."

MPIRE 6-30 and 8-45.
"CLAIRTY'S CAPERS."
OMMY MORGAN, 5 SHERRY BROS., &c.
The Jolliest Show Imaginable.
ooking 11 till 8 p.m. 'Phone 24833.

IAJESTIC Mon., Tues. & Wed. 2-0 till 10-30.
he Greatest Dramatic Spectacle Ever Made
"IN OLD CHICAGO," with
yrone Power, Alice Faye & Don Ameche.
And strong Supporting Programme.

ICTUREDROME 2-50, 6-50, 8-50.
ll Week—Jeanette MacDonald, Nelson Eddy
in "SWEETHEARTS"
rank Morgan, Ray Bulger, Mischa Auer.

n't Be Miserable! PLAZA Keep Up Your Spirit!
3.30/5.30 — *Matinee Dance* — Ad. 6d
8/11.15 Bigger & Brighter Dance Adm. 1/-
Dancing-Can-Help Keep Smiling Don't be Dull
DANCE

on Merseyside and in the Humber area. He observed that 'the lack of war urgency and relative lack of anxiety are most striking in Ulster, [in fact] unmistakeable'. It appeared to him that the whole 'atmosphere is entirely different. Though Ulster is in the war, psychologically it is not fighting it.' He claimed that in Northern Ireland, 'things taken for granted by the average Englishman, or Scotsman, or Welshman, like clothes rationing or transport difficulties, are still the source of considerable resentment'. To illustrate this he described as 'typical' an incident which took place in one of the city's restaurants. He asked a waitress for some sugar. She brought it but complained bitterly and loudly:

> Getting the sugar, getting the sugar! All day long I am going from table to table getting this ruddy, rationed sugar. I am sick to death of the whole damned business. When will the war end and finish this rationing? Oh God, I wish it would end and I won't have to go around for the sugar.

The overall 'slackness' in public attitudes was so 'noticeable' that in this reporter's opinion, 'anyone who is keen on the war effort is liable to feel uncomfortable in Ulster'. He himself constantly experienced 'a curious feeling of guilt at being here at all. It seemed somehow as if one was getting out of the war and having too easy a life.' He noted, for example, that

> people thought nothing of asking one to lunch and talking the whole afternoon. Being half an hour late for an appointment did not matter in the slightest and perhaps the most curious shock of all is seeing men lying about in the morning on the grass outside the City Hall or sleeping with their feet up in the backs of cars.

The visit heightened his awareness of just how much 'the whole tempo' of life had changed in Britain since peacetime. He concluded by speculating that if anyone were to behave in London or Liverpool as they were continuing to do in Belfast, they 'would at once be noticeable and might even start a riot'.

There is no lack of evidence to corroborate these observations. On occasion Stormont ministers themselves spoke of Northern Ireland as being 'only half in the war'. So far as they were concerned, an embarrassing symptom of this apathy was the disappointingly small number of volunteers for military service from the North, which, it was felt, 'placed the Government in a very unfavourable light'. During the early months of the war, recruits had come forward at a monthly rate of twenty-five hundred, but rapidly this had fallen to less than one thousand. In March 1940 these returns prompted a private initiative by Lindsay Keir, the vice-chancellor at Queen's University, who wrote to both staff and students advising them that if they were physically fit, they should enlist. Two months later, Craigavon, who was also very concerned at the figures, convinced a reluctant War Office to launch a recruitment drive. This was aimed primarily at young men living in country districts and on Craigavon's suggestion,

NEWS-LETTER, TUESDAY, JULY 16, 1940

BELFAST RECRUITING RALLY

Ulster Hall Crowded: Men Enrol On The Spot

stress was laid on tactful presentation in order to lessen the risk of civil disorder.

The outcome was a series of twenty rallies, held throughout Northern Ireland, starting in mid-July 1940. They had, however, little or no success. Although the number of volunteers returned briefly to higher levels, unknown since the beginning of hostilities, the upsurge was short-lived, and due mainly to the wave of patriotic sentiment aroused by the evacuation of over three hundred thousand Allied troops at Dunkirk. The appointment of the Minister of Agriculture, Sir Basil Brooke, a politician with a demonic reputation within the minority community, to spearhead the recruitment campaign and his decision to use the Unionist Party machine for publicity purposes must have weakened the response among Catholics. However, the essential problem was the all-pervading apathy which the Mass Observation reporter later identified 'amongst both religious groups'. The failure forced Craigavon to consider desperate alternatives. For a time he favoured withholding unemployment assistance from those men of military age who had failed to enlist. This potentially explosive approach was in the end rejected because of acute uneasiness as to likely Unionist reaction. John Fawcett Gordon, the Minister of Labour, warned the Prime Minister very forcefully that it would be 'impolitic', as it would 'affect our position as a government. . . We would find it very difficult to get the party to stand behind us.' Meanwhile, by December 1940, monthly recruitment levels had dropped to just over six hundred, and the long-term trend was downwards.

Further powerful evidence of a lack of urgency in Northern Ireland is provided by the performance of its major industries: collectively, they had the worst production record to be found in any region in the United Kingdom. Soon after the outbreak of war, ministers both at Westminster and at Stormont became acutely concerned at their unsatisfactory levels of output and productivity, prolonged delays in completing contracts, and hostile relations between management and labour. When Sir Basil Brooke, the newly appointed Minister of Commerce, sought contracts from British departments, he was immediately advised to resolve these problems and he 'would get work'. From the outset, he found Harland and Wolff totally unco-operative in its attitude towards his department, uninterested in the welfare of its labour force, and unwilling to subcontract to neighbouring engineering works. Brooke became convinced that the root cause of the firm's failings was incompetent management. The British Minister of Labour and National Service, Ernest Bevin, regarded its overall per-

The Mayor Sets a Fine Example

PREMIER'S APPEAL

LORD CRAIGAVON issued a clarion call to the youth of Ulster last night to enlist in the three new Ulster battalions.

Speaking at a recruiting rally at Bangor, the Premier declared that Ulster's youth had a high reputation to live up to.

"The need for bringing all our fighting services up to maximum strength is urgent," he emphasised. "The enemy is on our doorstep. At any time he may drench our countryside with bombs, soil it with parachutists, and try to smash his way into our very homes. Are we going to let him do it? No! Never!"

Sir Basil Brooke, Bt., Minister of Agriculture, spoke of the country's great history and added: "Don't live on traditions: live up to them."

The Mayor of Bangor (Mr. W. H. M'Millan), who presided, announced, amid cheers, that he had joined the Royal Inniskilling Fusiliers.

Proud Distinction

Lord Craigavon pointed out that Northern Ireland had earned the proud distinction of being one of the finest recruiting grounds for the fighting forces. The records of their famous regiments, he said, abound with deeds of valour that had become part of their national history. There were few more glorious chapters in military annals than the one which told of the heroism of the 36th (Ulster) Division in the last Great War. The fame of the men who responded so nobly to the call of King and Country during those fateful years would never perish. Ulster's youth had, consequently, a high reputation to live up to.

"To-day we see Continental Europe overrun by Hitler's hordes, with the British Empire alone carrying on the fight against the forces of agression, tyranny and brutality. At the outbreak of hostilities I pledged, on your behalf, our fullest support to the Imperial authorities in the waging of the war. I said, 'All our resources are at your disposal—our man-power, our industrial capacity, our agriculture, everything that will help to bring victory to our arms.' Whatever the Imperial Government called upon us to do we have done.

Belfast News-Letter, July 1940

Leslie Burgin, Minister of Supply at Westminster, ıecking munitions during a :our of inspection at James Mackie and Sons in the ɔring of 1940. (Ulster Folk and Transport Museum)

formance as 'significantly inferior' to that achieved by comparable producers in Britain.

It was Short and Harland, however, which had the worst strike record of any major manufacturer in Northern Ireland, whether gauged by the frequency of disputes, their duration or the numbers involved in them. Already in December 1940 and January 1941, Sir Wilfrid Spender observed that the company was 'giving us a bad name across the water' and was a 'great disappointment'. Owing to the firm's persistent failure to achieve output targets, the minister responsible for aircraft production, John Jestyn Llewellin, favoured placing the foundry, James Mackie and Sons, at that time manufacturing munitions and Stirling and Sunderland components for the war effort, in charge of all aircraft production in Northern Ireland. Mackies' wartime performance was widely regarded as being exemplary. After due consideration, the proposal was in the end rejected because of fears that it would, at least in the short-term, disrupt local production levels and further aggravate labour relations at Short and Harland. In addition, Stormont ministers shrank from the political consequences of such an unpopular decision.

Public attitudes towards air raid precautions provide another illustration of the contrast in 'atmosphere' between Northern Ireland and Great Britain;

Patriotic citizens collectin[g] scrap metal for the war effort in Londonderry. (*Londonderry Sentinel*)

a further example of 'things taken for granted' in Britain and yet deeply resented locally. Within Northern Ireland, civil defence was widely regarded with indifference, even hostility. A few days after war was declared, Lady Londonderry wrote to her husband: 'All sorts of rot are going on here. Air-raid warnings and blackouts! As if anyone cared or wished to bomb Belfast.' The diary comments and asides of Moya Woodside during the first eighteen months of hostilities were written in similar vein. Although their author was intelligent, articulate, unionist, and middle class, from south Belfast, she was most reluctant to co-operate willingly with the growing volume of government orders and instructions that she received. She dismissed the blackout as nothing more than 'a political stunt', on the grounds that it had not worked in England and that the Luftwaffe would experience no difficulty in locating Northern Ireland, especially since three-quarters of Ireland continued to be brightly lit. Blackout preparations took up ten minutes each evening and she observed: 'How we grudge the time spent!' She was also totally unsympathetic to official appeals that private householders should volunteer to provide temporary billets for those who might be made homeless as a result of enemy action. She even felt uneasy about the holding of a war weapons week in Belfast to raise money for the construction of mine destroyers because, she claimed, cities in which they had been organised were soon afterwards attacked by German bombers. However, her deepest loathing and contempt was reserved for her 'officious' local air raid precautions warden. She watched with haughty disdain as he 'rushed aimlessly up and down the street, clad in his mac, tin helmet, gas mask and other paraphernalia'. She regarded both his attempts and those of the Royal Ulster Constabulary to enforce the various wartime regulations as 'meddling and interference', and observed: 'I only comply with the bare minimum. . . not from any conviction. . . but because I shall be fined if I don't.' She considered, no doubt correctly, that this response was widespread within Northern Ireland and acknowledged that her English guests found such attitudes simply incomprehensible. Harold Allen, a warden in Ballyhackamore in east Belfast, still vividly recalls how much local people 'resented the uniform'.

The glaring contrast in outlook and behaviour which emerged between Northern Ireland and the rest of the United Kingdom is more easily described than explained. The Mass Observation reporter suggested that it was in part due to 'the cut-offness of Ulster', which had resulted from delays in communication, 'censorship difficulties', and the interruption of the 'free exchange of culture and personalities between Ulster and Britain'. In his opinion these developments had 'astonishingly wide effects, working through more intelligent people downwards'. Whatever the accuracy of

Scrap metal being loaded at Londonderry docks. (*Londonderry Sentinel*)

such a claim, undoubtedly most local people were convinced that Northern Ireland would never be attacked precisely because they considered it to be too remote and unimportant and at the same time hoped that it might benefit from Éire's neutrality. Rita McKittrick, who lived on the Shankill, remembers the feeling that it was 'England's war. Germany was not fighting us. They would hit London.' When the conflict began, John Oliver, who was to become private secretary to the Minister of Public Security, heard a leading Stormont civil servant remark: 'Damn the English politicians for getting us into this!'

Some local ministers eventually became convinced that the absence of conscription was the key determinant of local attitudes. The Mass Observation reporter shared this view. He considered that 'by studying the Ulster situation one is able to see the enormous part' which conscription had 'played in influencing Britain psychologically' both by 'increasing war awareness' and by heightening 'psychological frictions and anxieties'. He related it closely to 'the other outstanding factor' in the North – 'the religious dichotomy which divides the country into Catholics (mainly Nationalist), and Protestants (mainly Unionist)'. This division had influenced the Westminster government decision not to extend conscription to Northern Ireland. In addition, the observer's enquiries indicated that 'politically fostered dissatisfaction' was contributing to labour indiscipline at such firms as Short and Harland. Also, 'the constant fear of IRA activity' helped to account for the surprising efficiency of security at the ports and elsewhere in Belfast and Londonderry, an efficiency which was 'not essentially related to the war'. However, although he drew attention to the importance of the sectarian cleavage in Northern Ireland, this observer was convinced that the 'lack of war urgency' was common to both sides of the religious divide. He considered that a vital root of this shared characteristic was the complacency of local politicians. In his opinion, the laxity of public attitudes was 'noticeable at all levels – from the cabinet minister to remote peasant dwellings on the Antrim coast'.

Until his death on 24 November 1940, Craigavon continued to lead the Northern Ireland government in characteristically dictatorial and whimsical fashion, major decisions being taken hastily by the Prime Minister himself, or after consultation with a select inner clique. Robert Gransden, his newly appointed cabinet secretary, resented, as much as his predecessor had done, running such errands for the Craigavon household as buying cigarettes and ordering marmalade from Fortnum and Mason's in London. By 1940 the party leadership was having to adopt some quite extraordinary tactics for controlling parliament. For example, when the Prime Minister's excessive salary came before the House for review, the chief whip sought to reduce the time available for debate by providing Unionist back-benchers with points on other matters with which they might criticise the Government's record. And he also arranged for Independent Labour MP Jack Beattie, a voluble and effective Opposition member, to be detained in the

Commons' bar.

Sir Wilfrid Spender doubted that such a government could survive the demands and pressures of war for long. Soon after the outbreak of hostilities, he was confidently predicting that Westminster would be forced to consider introducing martial law into Northern Ireland, with the permanent secretaries of local departments being asked to take over some of the functions of Stormont ministers. He thought this possible partly because of the complete lack of co-operation between some members of Craigavon's cabinet and the military authorities based in the North. The Minister of Home Affairs, Dawson Bates, for example, apparently refused to reply to army correspondence. Lieutenant-General Sir Hubert J. Huddleston, who had served as General Officer Commanding in Northern Ireland, actually raised the whole question directly with George VI, and the king subsequently discussed it with John M. Andrews, as soon as he became Prime Minister of Northern Ireland. Huddleston, in common with a number of other senior officers, favoured martial law, and Spender considered it unlikely that 'the British War Office or government would interfere with his discretion in the matter'.

Craigavon's death provided an obvious opportunity to remove at least some of the 'old guard' from the Government. However, John M. Andrews stubbornly resisted any such pressures. Days after becoming premier, he informed Spender that he had 'found it necessary to move' one of Craigavon's ministers (James Milne Barbour), 'who had been subjected to a great deal of criticism'. Spender was utterly bewildered when it transpired that the 'move' was not to the back-benches, rather Andrews was 'promoting him'. Andrews's administration contained just one new member, Lord Glentoran, and was if anything more incompetent and directionless than its predecessor. In March 1941 it suffered the humiliation of losing the by-election in North Down, a seat which Craigavon had held unopposed since the foundation of the Northern Ireland parliament in 1921. Andrews himself was just one year younger than Craigavon; his health had already begun to fail and he proved incapable of providing the leadership that was so urgently required. Spender wrote of him that he had 'no idea of the war situation' and that it was 'very difficult for a man of his upbringing and outlook to realize. . . the relative importance of matters of local interest and those of European concern'.

Without question, the 'lack of war urgency' in Northern Ireland was in large measure due to the inertia and laxity of Stormont departments during the premiership of both Craigavon and Andrews. Although ministers had displayed some enthusiasm for air raid precautions when hostilities began, their earlier negligence rapidly returned. Unlike the pre-war period, this was not due to lack of finance; the Government's revenue trebled between 1939 and 1945. Rather, it reflected their fundamental conviction that Northern Ireland would not be attacked, despite expert advice to the contrary. Acting on this assumption in December 1939, the cabinet decided that it was quite

A unit of the Local Defenc
Volunteers, the Northern Ireland home guard, recruited from Mackies work force. (James Macki
and Sons)

unnecessary to instruct Belfast citizens to carry their gas masks. In the same spirit, Edmond Warnock, parliamentary secretary at the Ministry of Home Affairs, arbitrarily cancelled orders for fire-fighting equipment which had been recommended by the Home Office. (Indeed John MacDermott, soon after being appointed Minister of Public Security, was 'horrified to discover' that Warnock had actually returned material to Britain as he was so certain that Northern Ireland lay beyond the range of German bombers.) It is hardly surprising that when Craigavon was preparing a statement on war preparations for the reassembling of parliament in early February 1940, he was advised by an official in the Ministry of Home Affairs: 'there is very little we can contribute', adding that there had been 'no developments and even in Belfast the less said about this at the moment the better'. Far from being alarmed by such inactivity, Sir Wilfrid Spender praised 'the considerable courage' of ministers in exercising 'discretion in air raid policy'. He even justified it privately on the grounds that the 'civilian population should be willing to share a small proportion of the risks which men in the fighting forces are subjected to'.

From May 1940, the Government's interest in and commitment to civil defence increased. This was caused less by any sudden realisation that action was necessary than by increased pressure from critics following the Fall of France and attendant fears of invasion. On 10 May the German offensive in the West had begun. By 27 May, Belgium and the Netherlands had capitulated and the British and French troops had been pushed back on to the beaches at Dunkirk. During the next eight days, 338,226 men were evacuated across the English Channel. German troops entered Paris on 14 June, their high command confident, in the words of General Alfred Jodl, that 'final German victory over England is only a matter of time'.

The dramatic deterioration in the Allied military position in Europe, and the emergence of a new and more dynamic British administration under Winston Churchill on 10 May 1940, made the fumbling ineptitude of Craigavon and his ministers appear all the more indefensible. Two junior ministers resigned. Edmond Warnock, whose own record was not without blemish, relinquished his post on 25 May 1940. After his resignation, he accused his former colleagues of being 'slack, dilatory and apathetic', adding with justification that when a person became a member of the Northern Ireland government, he became a 'tenant for life. Nothing but death, illness or promotion removes anybody.' Less than three weeks later Lieutenant-General Alexander Robert Gisborne Gordon, parliamentary secretary at the Ministry of Finance, followed suit. He also bitterly condemned the cabinet for its 'lack of drive and initiative and utter lack of what the war means', and demanded that it 'resign and be reconstituted immediately'. These criticisms had the support of many back-benchers and even sections of the unionist press.

Craigavon responded with measures which were in part determined by developments at Westminster but were mainly designed to ensure the survival of his government. On 28 May he followed Britain in creating a home guard in Northern Ireland. Its formation drew heavily on the membership of the Ulster Special Constabulary, and was officially called the Local Defence Volunteers but was soon nicknamed the 'Look, Duck and Vanish' brigade. Gerry Hannah, then a child, recalls seeing volunteers train in the Cregagh Hills, throwing hand grenades and practising bayonet charges. The Prime Minister's extravagant claim in the House that the force had been enlisted, armed and placed on duty within one week of his personal appeal for recruits was the immediate cause of Gordon's resignation.

Soon afterwards, Craigavon, acting on impulse as usual, agreed to establish a parliamentary committee at Stormont to advise on civil defence. It was one of his favourite stratagems for silencing critics and as committee members were generously remunerated, it was always likely to be effective. Minister of Home Affairs Dawson Bates, whose ministry would now come under the scrutiny of this new body, was outraged. In cabinet he drew attention to the alarming prospect of MPs now gaining access to information which showed that 'we had not distributed gas masks on the scale proposed' and that 'our shelter programme was far behind Britain'. However, these objections were overruled. Ministers accepted the Prime Minister's view that 'circumstances had radically changed in the last few weeks', due to what Craigavon described as the increased 'danger of promiscuous attack by German parachutists'. As a result, it was agreed that 'the Government's policy to the present could be justified'.

Pressure from the new Commons committee, combined with threats by Warnock and Gordon to move a motion of no confidence in the Government, forced Craigavon to make a further and more vital concession. He agreed to create a Ministry of Public Security. It was to be responsible for public security, civil defence and the 'protection of persons and property from injury or damage in the present emergency', taking over these responsibilities from the Ministry of Home Affairs. Appointed Minister of Public Security, John MacDermott was given this unenviable task on 25 June 1940. He was a lawyer and King's Counsellor and until being approached by Craigavon, he had been serving as an officer with the Royal Artillery, having enlisted in August 1939. He was also Unionist MP for Queen's University Belfast. He considered himself fortunate to have this seat as he was not a member of the Orange Order and he believed therefore that no other Unionist Association in Northern Ireland would have been willing to adopt him as their candidate. His promotion owed much to the fact that his father knew the Prime Minister well.

John Oliver, who became his private secretary, remembers MacDermott as a 'dignified, competent, conscientious minister, who was hard working and in many ways the right man for the appointment. He gave a sense of stability and the public liked him.' However, he had weaknesses. He was somewhat 'ponderous and slow to reach decisions'. Also, he was 'rather dull and lacked the human touch; he had no way with him'. Oliver recalls travelling with him to inspect an air raid precautions post in Banbridge, Co. Down, and MacDermott spending much of his time counting the number of stirrup pumps and other fire-fighting equipment there, to check whether they matched departmental figures. (In contrast, during a later visit, MacDermott's successor, William Grant, chatted to personnel informally and casually about football and matters of mutual interest, and created a much more favourable impression.) William Iliff, who had also served with the Royal Artillery, became permanent secretary at the new department. He was an energetic, impatient, and ill-tempered man – in Oliver's words, a 'ball of fire'. That he should later have become vice-president of the World Bank is a measure of his abilities.

With a deepening sense of urgency, MacDermott sought to accelerate the pace of war preparation and make up for the months, even years, that had been squandered. British service chiefs left him in no doubt that Northern Ireland was likely to be attacked. He watched anxiously and sought to learn from the 'indiscriminate bombing' of British cities during the autumn of 1940. On 7 September, Hermann Goering assumed direct command of the German air offensive against Britain; that same evening the London blitz began. The decision to attack the capital, and later, other British cities, changed the course and possibly the outcome of the war. The new offensive almost certainly saved the Royal Air Force, because, unknown to the Germans, the Luftwaffe's earlier attacks on British airfields had Fighter Command reeling. Without serious opposition from the air, the intended German invasion would undoubtedly have succeeded.

Meanwhile, MacDermott encouraged civil defence workers, local authority officials and his own civil servants to visit blitzed areas in Britain, partly for training purposes but also to heighten their appreciation of the

Young Belfast evacuees with their conductors at a dispersal centre in Co. Londonderry. (*Londonderry Sentinel*)

vital significance of their work. Undoubtedly, his enterprise, courage and commitment bore fruit. He benefited from the tense and expectant atmosphere which prevailed at the time of his appointment. Even the Belfast Corporation caught, at least temporarily, some of the patriotic spirit inspired by Dunkirk, and displayed more realism and energy. The awakening of greater public interest in air raid precautions is indicated by a sharp rise in the number of volunteers – from fifteen to twenty-two thousand between June and December 1940, with more recruits continuing to enrol. During these months, all the essential services in Belfast emerged better able to cope with an aerial attack than ever before.

None the less, the preparations taken remained woefully inadequate. Too much required to be done; the time available was too short. The obstacles in the way of effective action proved to be insurmountable, even in such vital areas as the evacuation of children from Belfast, the building of shelters and the strengthening of the fire service. MacDermott's best endeavours were thwarted by lack of adequate support from ministerial colleagues for whom financial considerations remained more important than the security of the people; by the incompetence and insufficient commitment of local authority officials who retained the power of decision in crucial areas; and by his legacy of deep-rooted public apathy. In addition, with major British cities increasingly under attack, there was an acute shortage of vital supplies from Britain. Overall, the record of the Ministry of Public Security was one of brave but inevitable failure.

MINISTRY OF PUBLIC SECURITY

EVACUATION OF SCHOOL CHILDREN

The Evacuation of School Children from Belfast will begin on **SUNDAY NEXT, JULY 7th**

Further announcements will be made in the Press and by Posters outside Schools on SATURDAY

ONLY REGISTERED EVACUEES WILL BE DEALT WITH ON SUNDAY. They should assemble at the Places and Times stated on their personal Assembly Instruction Sheets.

UNREGISTERED CHILDREN in the Area covered by the Schools named below will be Evacuated on MONDAY JULY 8th:—

BEECHFIELD
BELVOIR HALL
BLYTHE STREET
CURRIE JUNIOR
DUNCAIRN
EARL STREET BOYS'
GIRLS'
INFANTS'
GROVE
HILLMAN
LANCASTER STREET
LINFIELD SENIOR
JUNIOR
MABEL STREET
MAGDALENE
MARINERS
McQUISTON

MEGAIN MEMORIAL
MEMEL STREET
MERSEY ST. SENIOR AND JUNIOR
MOUNTCOLLYER
MOUNTPOTTINGER
NEW ROAD SENIOR
JUNIOR
PORTER
QUEEN VICTORIA
ST. ANTHONY'S (MILLFIELD)
BOYS' AND GIRLS'
ST. BARNABAS
ST. COLMAN'S
ST. COMGALL'S BOYS' AND GIRLS'
ST. GEORGE'S
ST. JOSEPH'S BOYS' (YORK ROAD)
GIRLS' " "

ST. MALACHY'S
BOYS' (NEW LODGE ROAD)
GIRLS " " "
ST. MALACHY'S
C.B. (OXFORD STREET)
CONVENT (SUSSEX PLACE)
ST. MATTHEW'S BOYS'
GIRLS'
ST. PATRICK'S
BOYS' (DONEGALL STREET)
GIRLS' " "
C.B. " "
ST. PAUL'S (CANNING STREET)
SANDY ROW
SEAMEN'S
STRAND
TEMPLEMORE AVENUE
WORKMAN
YORK STREET

Assembly Instructions for UNREGISTERED CHILDREN will be given by Poster outside the Schools named above.

NO OTHER UNREGISTERED PERSONS WILL BE EVACUATED FOR THE PRESENT.

Stormont Castle, Belfast, July 4th, 1940.

MacDermott rapidly became aware of these insuperable difficulties. At his first cabinet meeting on 1 July 1940, he won cabinet approval for the immediate voluntary evacuation of all Belfast school children, arguing that this was essential 'in the light of the present military position'. At that time large British cities such as Liverpool and Glasgow had not been evacuated and Westminster ministers, fearing the repercussions from their own urban populations, strongly opposed the initiative. They suspected that it was a 'political manoeuvre' hatched by the Stormont government. From the outset, the prospects of the Belfast evacuation being successful were not encouraging. Out of a total school population in the city of seventy thousand, fewer than eighteen thousand had been officially registered for evacuation. On the appointed day, 7 July, only seven thousand of these turned up; a further eighteen hundred arrived when a second opportunity was offered six weeks later. In the words of the ministry's own officials, it was a 'flop', a 'fiasco', an 'absurdity'. Failure was partly due to the fact that the attempt had been made during school holidays, but a more fundamental reason was the all-pervading assumption among citizens that Belfast would not be bombed. Also, working-class people were not used to travelling far. As Winifred Campbell recalls in 'Down the Shankill', they went at most for 'a tram ride to Bellevue or an occasional day trip to Bangor. The annual Sunday school excursion was a tremendous treat.'

EVACUATION PLAN "FLOPS"

THE UNREGISTERED CHILDREN

Only 10 Per Cent Taken From Belfast

Belfast News-Letter, 7 July 1940

MacDermott's endeavours to accelerate the pace of shelter construction in Belfast met with no greater success. The need was self-evident: in June 1940 only four thousand households (out of over sixty thousand) in the city, which were eligible for free domestic shelters, had actually received them. Many of those that had been built interfered so badly with the cramped back yards of the terraced houses where they had been located as to render the yards useless for anything else. It was later established that they actually contravened public health by-laws. MacDermott's first initiative was to

Belatedly the Belfast Corporation had public shelters constructed in the city centre, like these in Donegall Square East. (Ulster Folk and Transport Museum)

encourage local authorities to advise and assist householders on ways of strengthening their own houses, using materials provided free of charge. Some took the 'Your house as an air raid shelter' appeal very seriously. One occupier could vividly recall clearing the attic and lining it with asbestos, then installing steel pillars in the dining room and erecting a second ceiling made of corrugated iron. But by December 1940, the minister had abandoned this approach as being inadequate. Having seen at first hand the results of aerial attack on London, he was convinced that effective protection could not be provided in this way. Instead, he favoured a crash programme of public-shelter construction, hoping that this would provide a simple, quick and inexpensive solution to the problem.

However, the unsightly brick structures that were now erected at high speed in Belfast were far from being wholly successful either. Gerry Hannah remembers that even to work on their construction was looked down on as a 'menial job; people would ask was it all you could get?' They were built on the edge of narrow pavements, barely three feet wide in poorer districts, and as a result, they blocked out light and air from adjacent houses. In practice, they were used for almost every purpose other than that for which they were intended. Moya Woodside, who gave public lectures on birth control, had already noted with concern the effect of the blackout. She recorded the case of a 'woman who had to move [house] because her former rooms were reached through a public yard and every night after blackout, men and

Possibly the best-equipped shelters in Belfast were thos[e] constructed at Gallaher's tobacco factory. (Gallaher Limited)

women were to be found having intercourse there. The children were afraid of them.' She describes the shelters as being used by courting couples, or as providing opportunities for 'ill-disposed' men, but most generally as being used as public conveniences. Rita McKittrick recalls how local women would 'walk down the middle of the street past them, because of the fear of being molested. Their entrances were on the pavement side.' A belated attempt by the Government to prevent their improper use and to make them more attractive by installing doors and lights was an abject failure. Air raid precautions wardens reported that these fittings were the object of 'senseless destruction', electric cable being 'torn out as quickly as it was put in'. Partly because of their filth and squalor, when the blitz came, the shelters were underused. In any case they were too few in number and physically incapable of providing adequate protection against heavy bombs.

MacDermott was not just concerned with the safety of Belfast citizens in their own homes. In December 1940 he secured reluctant cabinet approval for the extension of compulsory shelter provision by factories and commercial interests. This had only applied to the harbour area but was now to 'cover the whole city'. Also, the Belfast Corporation was empowered to increase the number of public shelters from the 200 that had been constructed by June 1940 to 750 by the end of that year. They were to be erected in places where substantial numbers of people were expected to be during the daytime. Nevertheless, overall, the construction programme was

Roomy, well-lit and omparatively comfortable, Gallaher's shelters were primarily intended for the tobacco workers but also attracted large numbers of people from the underprotected neighbouring streets. (Gallaher Limited)

a failure. When the Luftwaffe attacked in April 1941, most of the people of Belfast were without any physical protection. Even if all the shelters in the city, domestic and public, had been filled to capacity, they would have accommodated at most 25 per cent of its population. No provision had yet been made for thirty thousand of the workers employed in vital war production. Three hundred thousand people living in houses which were eligible for free shelters had still not received them even though the Government had promised to provide them during the first week of the war under conditions which were substantially less generous than in Great Britain.

In this instance public apathy was not the reason for failure; rather it was due at least in part to the apathy of the Northern Ireland government. It had consistently refused to provide anything like sufficient funds to enable the Ministry of Public Security to fulfil its statutory obligations. Also, despite MacDermott's pleading, Stormont ministers did not regard his scheme as their most pressing building commitment during these critical months. Instead, from June 1940, they gave precedence to the provision of over twenty military airfields, scattered throughout Northern Ireland, which starved the shelter programme of sufficient bricks, labour and transport.

This order of priority was imposed from Westminster. Herbert Morrison, the Home Secretary, personally requested Craigavon 'to give every possible assistance' to the construction of airfields. By 1 April 1941 even Spender was recording his 'relief' on hearing that the relevant Westminster department was at last going to make building materials available for shelters, and was, in his words, 'recognizing that we are entitled to take precautions'. But his sense of relief was premature. The high level of military demands continued unabated for two more months. In early May, when the fourth and final air raid on Northern Ireland was just over, William Iliff complained angrily and bitterly to Westminster about the utterly impossible position in which his department had been placed. It had simply not proved feasible to satisfy the requirements of the military personnel based in Northern Ireland and at the same time to adequately protect the citizens of Belfast from aerial attack.

An acute shortage of essential supplies also helped to stultify John MacDermott's efforts to revitalise the city's fire service. In response to blunt advice from imperial defence experts that drastic action was required, he had immediately reinstated and expanded the orders that had been cancelled earlier by Edmond Warnock, and had authorised the Belfast Corporation to increase substantially the number of full-time firemen in Belfast. Unfortunately, additional fire engines, pumps and steel pipe fittings had, in the meantime, become extremely difficult to obtain. Large British cities, now under constant threat of attack, were seeking desperately to augment their fire-fighting provision and received priority from British officials. A further vital source of the minister's difficulties was the incompetence and inertia of the corporation. It continued to have little interest in air raid precautions, and its leadership was weak, composed of men who, in John Oliver's phrase, had been promoted 'far beyond their ability'. By April 1941 it had recruited roughly 230 full-time firemen, even though it had been empowered to raise four to five times that number. Urban areas of comparable size in Great Britain normally had a full-time establishment of eleven to thirteen hundred, and some officials at Westminster had suggested that Belfast ought to have had as many as five thousand, given its remoteness from any large neighbouring force capable of giving support in case of emergency.

The city did of course have sixteen hundred part-time auxiliary firemen, but the inadequacy of their training had given rise to public criticism, even scandal. Jimmy Mackey, a member of the regular service, recalls members of the Auxiliary Fire Service being 'taught to pour water on fires, but not real fire-fighting'. On 20 September 1940 the *Northern Whig* reported that the force attended their posts week after week and did nothing other than clean and polish brasswork, and the newspaper orchestrated a campaign to pressurise the Government into action. Ministry officials considered that such allegations were 'not an overstatement'. One report, written by a Westminster official in March 1941, attributed much of the blame to

Switchboard of the Belfast Fire Brigade Ambulance Service, January 1940. (Ulster Folk and Transport Museum)

Belfast's chief fire officer, John Smith. It claimed that he had made 'no serious effort to co-operate with the AFS'. He had refused to consult its officers and had made no use of its men on fires, as a result severely impairing their training and also sapping their morale and subverting their enrolment. The report concluded that he had neither the 'inclination' nor the 'ability to amalgamate the two services' and was 'incapable of realizing how serious the situation' had become. He had not visited any of the bombed areas in Britain, nor had he ever requested any additional fire-fighting equipment, even though it was obviously required. The inquiry recommended that he be retired and replaced immediately.

Belfast Corporation displayed a similar lack of foresight in relation to other vital aspects of civil defence. The high death rate caused by the attacks on Britain compelled councillors to review local mortuary and burial facilities. As a result, an amicable and reasonable arrangement was made with four of the city's leading undertakers. They were to hold one thousand coffins in reserve on which the corporation would have an option but would be liable only for depreciation if they were not needed. However, on 28 March 1941, when a leading civil servant discussed with Belfast's mortuary superintendent 'every phase [of a raid] from the dropping of bombs to the

The Hack, 1 September 1942

internment' of the dead, he was shocked to learn that the city's mortuary service could only accommodate two hundred bodies. It was 'hardly enough', he suggested. But at such a late stage nothing could have been done in time to rectify this gross underestimation of probable future casualities.

Preparations for the care of those made homeless through enemy action were based on a similar degree of miscalculation. By February 1941 the corporation had earmarked almost seventy rest centres, mainly church halls and schools, and equipped them with sufficient food and bedding to meet the needs of ten thousand people. This proved to be hopelessly inadequate; houses occupied by ten times that number were made temporarily uninhabitable over the next three months. That the service did not collapse completely says much for the improvisation and competence of some of its members. However, as with other branches of civil defence, such qualities could not hope to compensate for their lamentable lack of staffing, equipment and organisation.

The Hack, 1 January 1943

Clearly, in this crucial period, the corporation manifested a tragic lack of vision and energy, and in some instances the sheer incompetence of its officials was mercilessly exposed. Unfortunately, these characteristics were

Sir Crawford McCullagh, Belfast's Lord Mayor during the war years. The Belfast Corporation's inadequate response to the crisis led to its suspension by the Northern Ireland government in 1942. (Belfast City Council)

shared in almost equal measure by most members of the Stormont cabinet. Even MacDermott was totally unprepared for the scale of the panic evacuation from Belfast once the blitz had begun and it was an official from his own ministry, Alan McKinnon, who predicted on 4 February 1941: 'It is highly unlikely that more than a fraction [of the seventy rest centres] will be needed at any one time.'

MacDermott made some effort to improve the organisational structure of civil defence in Belfast by modifying the role of the city's councillors. In order to speed up the decision-making process, in December 1940 he transferred all of the corporation's powers in relation to air raid precautions to a three-man council committee, the Civil Defence Authority. This new body was to be responsible for providing the various services, with his ministry continuing to give support through grants, the supply of equipment and advice from officials. However, very soon afterwards, he became convinced that more far-reaching initiatives were required. Early in the new year he received a report from Rear Admiral Richard King, the Royal Navy's Flag Officer in Charge in Belfast, describing the impact of the German attack on Coventry on Thursday, 14 November 1940. It contained 'none of the comforting, censored prose' which he had read in the press. Having attacked London nightly since 7 September 1940, the Luftwaffe suddenly switched targets and assailed this middle-sized Midlands city in force. Hitler had been infuriated by a Royal Air Force raid on Munich on the night of 8 November; this was his act of retaliation. A force of 449 bombers participated in the attack, and in the course of over eight hours, they dropped 503 tons of high explosives and almost 32,000 incendiary bombs.

Never before had an attack of such weight and intensity been unleashed against a centre of population, and even the most experienced German airmen were staggered at the holocaust they produced. A new word, 'coventration', entered the English language. The anti-aircraft barrage was inadequate and the night-fighters totally ineffectual. More than 50,000 houses were destroyed or damaged, many factories were gutted, 554 people died and 865 were seriously hurt. MacDermott described King's account as a 'pen picture of what a city looked like after a raid. It made my hair stand on end because I realized that this was what Belfast would be like.' At the same time, William Iliff, MacDermott's permanent secretary, said: 'I'm almost appalled at the magnitude of the task with which we shall be confronted if Belfast has its turn.'

On 3 February 1941 MacDermott outlined to his cabinet colleagues in graphic detail the probable scene after an attack; normal life brought to a standstill; extensive casualties; people shocked and dazed; multiple fires raging uncontrollably; buildings collapsing; widespread damage to private property; industry dislocated; conditions 'bordering on the chaotic'. The Civil Defence Authority, he suggested, would be unable to cope with these circumstances unaided. He therefore advocated a plan, the Hiram Plan, which had been prepared by officials at his department and been named by one of them, William Iliff, after the biblical King of Tyre. This provided for the formation of an emergency government which would take full charge of Belfast immediately after a raid. An advance headquarters was to be set up, composed of three commissioners (the town clerk and two civil servants), which it was hoped would be able to act quickly, co-ordinate the efforts of all departments, public authorities and utilities and give clear instructions to the civilian population. It was to function until the machinery of government could again operate effectively and then, as the secretary at the Ministry of Home Affairs, Adrian Robinson, wrote rather frivolously, 'hand back the city with the fires nicely under control, streets cleared, emergency transport system running. . . and all the sick and mangled tucked away in hospital beds'.

The cabinet accepted this suggestion but insisted that MacDermott should himself take control at advance headquarters. Sir Wilfrid Spender alone fervently opposed the proposal throughout. He predicted that the administrative arrangements would end in chaos and that the public would be outraged with the Government for devolving so much authority to MacDermott and his commissioners. It revived Spender's earlier dread that if ministers did not face up to their responsibilities, martial law would be imposed. His worst fears did not materialise; none the less, when the blitz came, these plans collapsed in utter confusion and the whole scheme had to be extensively redrafted.

The inadequacy of Northern Ireland's preparations for aerial attack went far beyond the appalling weakness of its civil defence services or the impracticality of the Hiram Plan. Its active defences were also woefully deficient. It had entered the war almost totally undefended. During the autumn of 1939, its protective screen actually became weaker as locally recruited anti-aircraft regiments crossed to Britain and were soon joined there by the North's entire searchlight provision. In June 1940 Belfast was protected by seven heavy guns, some light machine-gun-fire and the batteries of whatever warships and merchant ships happened to be anchored in the lough. No other city or town in the six counties had any defences, not even the headquarters of British troops in Northern Ireland at Lisburn, Co. Antrim, which would have had sole 'responsibility for active operations in Eire' had they been regarded as necessary.

Northern Ireland's continuing vulnerability was mainly because defence equipment was still in such short supply in Britain. Also it was still widely assumed that the region would benefit from its geographical position to the west of Britain's active defences. In addition, prolonged immunity from attack encouraged the illusion among Stormont ministers that no raids would ever occur and probably lessened the urgency of their appeals for more material. Even Westminster officials thought it possible that 'the Nazis are trying to ingratiate themselves with the Irish, North and South', particularly after their aircraft had begun to use Irish airspace to reach British targets.

However, after the Fall of France in 1940, both the likelihood of Northern Ireland being attacked and its strategic significance had increased dramatically. Its importance was rooted in much more than its growing industrial output. Once Germany had established control of the north European coastline, the north-west British ports became vital to the United Kingdom's survival. They were natural conduits for the food and weapons which it sorely needed and, at the same time, they provided vital military bases in the battle of the Atlantic. In *The Blitz Then and Now*, vol. 1, Winston G. Ramsey quotes Hitler's November 1939 directive against Britain: 'In our fight against the Western powers England has shown herself to be the animator of the fighting spirit of the enemy' and he declared that its defeat was 'essential to final victory'. He suggested that if the German army succeeded in 'seizing and holding a sector of the coast of the Continent opposite England', the Kriegsmarine and Luftwaffe should then attack the principle English ports, its shipping and industrial plant. Belfast was one of the cities which he predicted should be attacked. Robert Fisk's *In Time of War* indicates that he had also come to believe that 'the occupation of Ireland might lead to the end of the war', precisely because it could be used as a base to carry out these intentions more effectively.

In mid-1940 imperial chiefs of staff recommended that Northern Ireland defences be virtually doubled, and the Governor, Lord Abercorn, wrote personally to Churchill asking that this be 'given priority' by the War Office, as an invasion of Éire 'now seems certain'. During the months which followed, all three of Britain's armed services built up their presence in Northern Ireland. By April 1941 the number of troops based there had reached one hundred thousand and detailed plans were prepared for the North's defence as well as for the occupation of Éire. Chiefs of staff regarded it as essential to deny the enemy access to Belfast's port and its aerodrome facilities nearby. They considered that the most likely German landing places in the six counties were the beaches along the Antrim and Londonderry coasts. At this time Moya Woodside recalled her amazement when driving through a Co. Antrim village thirty miles from Belfast:

> The preparations along the roads are fantastic. . . Barriers of concrete and railway sleepers 3 and 4 deep bar the exit from [the city] and entrances and exits of every village en route, usually with pill-boxes as well. All the bridges, even on small secondary roads are mined and a cross-roads in the heart of the country is fortified as if to hold up an advancing army. [Small towns] are crammed with several thousand troops; my in-laws report that the men are bored stiff while the officers throng the hotel bars to drown their boredom in drink. There is absolutely nothing else to do.

At the same time Northern Ireland also emerged as a naval-operations centre with the vital functions of helping to prevent possible invasion and of protecting the west Atlantic shipping routes. Belfast became the headquarters of an ocean-going escort force near which great convoys assembled and dispersed. Larne in Co. Antrim was an important armed-trawler base, and Londonderry, a safe haven for destroyers and corvettes, as well as Britain's most westerly fuelling port. In December 1940 MacDermott described the latter as 'much more vulnerable than had once been thought'. He considered that the danger of it being a target was 'little if any less than Belfast'. Meanwhile, local shelter construction had been in large part sacrificed to facilitate the building of airfields for the Royal Air Force. These housed bomber squadrons ready to act in support of the army if Germany invaded. They also served as bases for reconnaissance, air-sea rescue, meteorological research and training drills. But their most important function was to support the long-range Liberators and flying boats which operated from them; in *Action Stations*, David J. Smith concluded that their activities 'turned the tide of the U-boat war'.

Although such a concentration of military might in Northern Ireland inevitably increased the risk of aerial attack, its active defences were only very slightly improved. In September 1940 both Belfast and Londonderry were provided with a light balloon barrage which was marginally reinforced six months later. By spring 1941 the strength of the anti-aircraft barrage in Northern Ireland had risen to twenty-four heavy guns and fourteen light guns. Twenty-two of these were located in Belfast (six light and sixteen heavy). This allocation represented less than half of the strength approved earlier by the Committee of Imperial Defence. It afforded fairly effective cover for the harbour area but left the rest of the city more or less unprotected. Perhaps the most significant new development was the transfer, on 20 July 1940, from Turnhouse, near Edinburgh, to Aldergrove of a

An anti-aircraft gun emplacement being mounted in Londonderry. (Charlie Gallagher)

Royal Air Force squadron (number 245), equipped with Hurricane fighters. Unfortunately these could only operate fully under daylight conditions. If a raid took place on a bright moonlit night, it was thought that they might be able to function but not in sufficient numbers to make their influence felt. When the blitz occurred, there were still no properly equipped night-fighters, nor were there facilities for operating them. There were no search-lights until 10 April 1941, though they had been recommended by imperial defence experts, and there was no provision for a smoke screen. The arrival of just one bomb-disposal unit can hardly have been reassuring.

In the meantime, the radar network in Northern Ireland had been extended but local service chiefs and civil servants doubted whether it would provide sufficient warning in the event of an attack. Air Commodore C. Roderick Carr feared that enemy aircraft would be able to approach 'outside the effective scope of the fighter command intelligence organization' and the cabinet secretary at Stormont was also worried that 'we may be

subject to aerial bombardment without any preliminary warning at all'. When the first raid did occur, on the night of 7–8 April 1941, eyewitnesses recorded hearing the Luftwaffe overhead first, then the deafening roar of the anti-aircraft guns and only after that the sirens. Writing of Northern Ireland's overall defence position, its official war historian, John W. Blake, concluded that 'the position was not much better' in April 1941 than it had been ten months earlier, and that ministers thought it best to keep this 'situation hidden from the public'.

Royal Air Force squadron number 245, equipped with Hurricane fighters, arrived at Aldergrove on 20 July 1940; they were later based at Ballyhalbert, Co. Down. (Short Brothers)

The Stormont government in spring 1941 was requesting protective equipment from Great Britain with a growing sense of desperation. In MacDermott's view, Belfast was less well-defended than 'any comparable city or port in the United Kingdom'. He encouraged Northern Ireland Prime Minister John Andrews to ask for night-fighters, searchlights and more guns, brushing aside the opinion of some leading civil servants at Stormont 'to trust the Committee of Imperial Defence to allocate available anti-aircraft defences'. However, the enemy struck before these negotiations had produced any tangible results. With Britain's major cities under constant attack since the autumn of 1940, military supplies remained scarce, and at Westminster, neither Belfast nor Londonderry were considered to be in 'the most vulnerable category'.

Too late John Andrews's cabinet had begun to realise that an aerial attack on Belfast was extremely likely, and to appreciate that if one did occur, there was little hope of avoiding tragedy. By January 1941 Andrews was reported to be 'very concerned at our anti-aircraft defences' and at the 'position which might arise in Belfast after a severe air attack'. He had therefore regarded the Hiram Plan as 'of the utmost significance'. His close confidante, Sir Wilfrid Spender, had also become more despondent, even fatalistic: in May 1940 he had observed: 'I admit that I expect at some time a serious [raid] on our ports.' Nine months later he anticipated that 'within the next two months Belfast will be severely attacked'. By early April 1941 he was predicting that the Luftwaffe would strike the city within the next nine days. MacDermott had been convinced, probably from his first day as minister, that Belfast had 'a place on the enemy's bombing programme'. He had constantly striven to awaken his complacent colleagues to this prospect and had justified his requests for additional equipment on this assumption. On 29 March 1941 he concluded a letter to Andrews with comments that are almost unnerving in their prophetic accuracy:

> Up to now we have escaped attack. So had Clydeside until recently. Clydeside got its blitz during the period of the last moon. . . The period of the next moon, from say, the 7th to the 16th of April, may well bring our turn.

In part such a prediction was based on an awareness of the changing pattern of German aerial attacks on Britain. In September 1940 the Luftwaffe had begun its huge night-time raids. Initially these were directed mainly against London and the South-east. However, from November onwards, apart from a temporary disruption caused by bad weather during December 1940 and January 1941, other major centres of industry and commerce were repeatedly attacked. The most alarming feature of the enemy's tactics was a growing concentration on the ports. Increasingly the emphasis was on the blockade aspect of the offensive rather than a direct assault on the industrial war effort. By the end of March more than twenty-eight thousand civilians had died in Great Britain since the bombing began and over forty thousand had been injured and detained in hospital.

At the same time there was a growing recognition that Belfast was not only a vulnerable target but also a worthwhile one. This was stressed by British service chiefs and officials. One imperial defence expert, who visited the city in March 1941, predicted that it would be attacked because 'work of National importance takes place there', adding that 'the vital importance of [Belfast's] undertakings must be seen to be appreciated'. Subsequent events were to demonstrate that its emerging role had not escaped the attention of the German general staff. In mid-April 1941, after the Easter Tuesday raid (15–16 April), Belfast was described on German radio as 'a harbour and arms centre of decisive importance for the English war economy'. It also broadcast the observation that 'since all the important British western ports had been affected by German air attacks, Belfast has assumed more and more the role of central storage port'.

Moreover, there was unmistakeable evidence that enemy activity over Northern Ireland was increasing from the autumn of 1940 and this provided further justification for concern. By then the Ministry of Public Security was receiving quite frequent reports of explosions from the Royal

Ulster Constabularly and from civilians, particularly in eastern parts of the North. On enquiry some proved to have been caused by British planes jettisoning their bombs before attempting a forced landing, but not always. Occasionally, after major attacks on Glasgow, Liverpool and other cities in Britain, returning German pilots unloaded their surplus explosives, usually at some point along the coast of Co. Down or Co. Antrim. On 20 December 1940, for example, police reported that two large parachute mines had fallen on open moorland near Larne in Co. Antrim. After their craters and shrapnel had been examined by naval and Royal Air Force experts, they were identified as being of the latest and largest type being produced in Germany.

Opposite
Aerial photograph of the dock area taken by a Luftwaffe reconnaissance aircraft in November 1940 (Imperial War Museum)

The most serious single incident, however, had occurred two months earlier. On Friday, 13 September, a lone Luftwaffe bomber, which had unsuccessfully attacked some ships in Belfast Lough, flew low over Bangor, Co. Down, and dropped about twenty incendiaries, mostly on Main Street. Next morning David Davidson vividly recalls hurrying to catch the 7.15 a.m. train for Belfast from Bangor station. He had just turned the corner from Bingham Street into Hamilton Road when he noticed an unfamiliar object lying in the street opposite St Comgall's Church. Although he had never seen one before, from its shape and aluminium colour, it was unmistakeably a bomb. He remembers well his feelings of fear and his immediate instinct to 'run like hell' until he had reached the railway platform. When he later told friends in the city of his experience, 'they simply refused to believe it'.

From July 1940, there are also quite regular reports of Belfast Lough and harbour being mined. The mines were dropped from bombers; once they were immersed in the water, a soluble plug dissolved, which in turn activated a magnetic device. On at least two occasions the Luftwaffe aircraft involved in these mine-laying sorties crashed – one ditched into the Irish Sea fifteen miles north-east of Belfast, and the other exploded at Kirkcudbrightshire in Scotland, probably because of engine failure. The Ministry of Public Security diary of incidents even records that three enemy frogmen were found diving in Belfast Lough and were promptly detained by British servicemen. As a necessary precaution, every week a minesweeper cruised down to Bangor, clearing the waterway for merchant ships moored off the Copeland Islands.

There were other less closely observed but more ominous indications that the German high command was directing more of its attention towards Northern Ireland. From August 1940, high-ranking civil servants at Stormont were concerned at mounting rumours and reports of enemy reconnaissance planes being sighted over the six counties and it was suspected that they were constantly using the southern Irish coast to escape detection. The day-fighter squadron at Aldergrove could neither confirm nor deny this speculation. It did not identify a single German aircraft in local airspace until early February 1941 when it glimpsed a Heinkel HeIII,

GB 21 26 b

Nur für den Dienstgebrauch

Bild Nr. F 228/40/II/117 (Lfl. 5)

Aufnahme vom 18. 10. 40

Belfast

Tankanlage am Conns Water

Länge (westl. Greenw.): 5° 53′ 45″ Breite: 54° 36′ 20″

Mißweisung: – 14° 18′ (Mitte 1940) Zielhöhe über NN 10 m

Maßstab etwa 1 : 15 000

Genst. 5. Abt. November 1940

Karte 1 : 100 000

Irl. 5

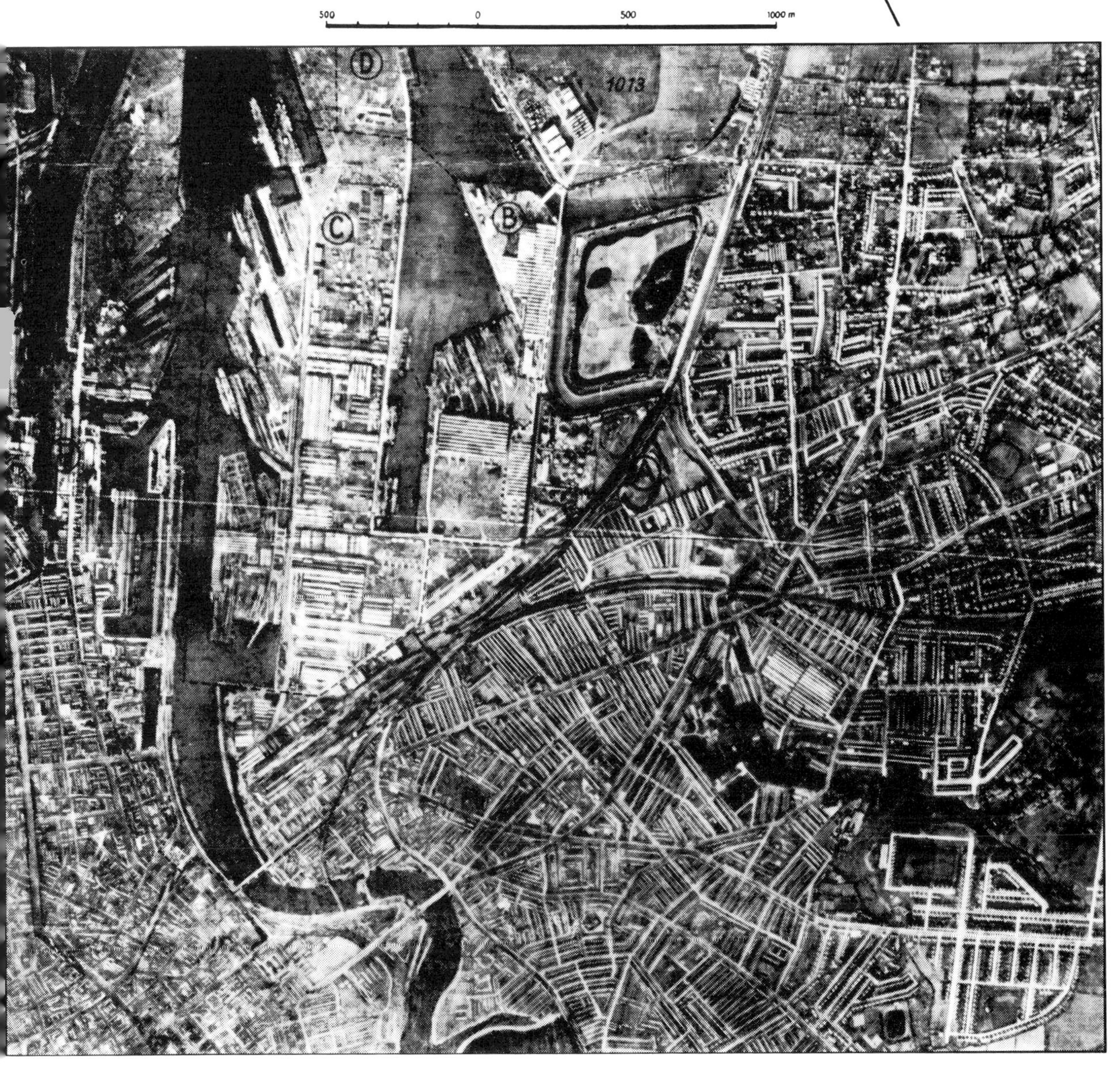

Ⓐ GB 2126 Tankanlage am Conns Water

Ⓑ GB 7413 Flugzeugwerk Short u. Harland

Ⓒ GB 835 Schiffswerft Harland u. Wolff Ltd.

Ⓓ GB 5049 Kraftwerk Belfast

Ⓔ GB 45182 Hafenanlage

Ⓕ GB 5677 Großmühle Rank u. Co.

twenty-eight thousand feet above Islandmagee in Co. Antrim, too high and too distant for its Hurricanes to intercept. None the less, from as early as July 1940, a section of the Luftwaffe, operating from northern France, was gathering detailed intelligence about Northern Ireland. It used Heinkel He111s and Dornier Do17s, equipped with superb Zeiss cameras. A typical and highly successful reconnaissance flight occurred on Friday, 18 October 1940, entirely unobserved by Northern Ireland's defence system. The German crews returned to base having taken a series of vividly clear photographs of Belfast's most important industrial and strategic sites, including *'das Flugzeugwerk'* (Short and Harland), *'die Schiffswerft'* (Harland and Wolff), *'das Elektrisches Hauptkraftwerk Nordirlands'* (the harbour power station), *'die Grossmühle'* (Rank's flour mill), and *'die* Victoria *Kaserne'* (Victoria barracks). A surprising inclusion was *'das Wasserwerk'* (Belfast Waterworks). This pictorial record was dispatched to the appropriate branch of the German general staff – Section 5. There it was analysed and used in the preparation of detailed target files to guide and instruct Luftwaffe crews on their bombing missions to Belfast six months later.

A number of these dossiers were captured by Allied troops after the war; most of them had been completed on 28 November 1940, four days after Craigavon's death. They would have given little cause for comfort to his successor, John Andrews. They gave the precise position, size and layout of the various targets using Ordnance Survey maps. In addition, photographs showed what each target looked like, either at ground level or from an elevation of a few hundred feet. Their locations were pinpointed both by giving precise grid references and by detailing their distance and direction from other strategic sites and major landmarks. The files stressed the ease with which objectives could be identified. Luftwaffe pilots searching for Harland and Wolff were informed: 'On the North East coast of Ireland, towards the South West lies a recessed bay [Belfast Lough]. At the end of the bay, where the River Lagan joins it, lies the harbour, in the middle of which lies [the shipyard].' The German general staff also drew attention to Belfast's vulnerability. The only active defences which their analysis had revealed were the anti-aircraft batteries at Victoria barracks, at the Custom House, to the north-west of Clarendon Dock and 'near the coastal town of Holywood'. Finally, squadrons detailed to attack targets in the city were left in no doubt as to the strategic significance of their mission. Harland and Wolff was described as 'the fourth largest repair yard in Great Britain' for naval and merchant ships, with, in addition, 'an annual building capacity of 200,000 tons'; the harbour power station was designated as 'the main electricity station for Northern Ireland' (it actually generated 80 per cent of the North's electrical power), and Rank and Company as 'the largest flour mill in Ireland'. By the spring of 1941, additional strategic sites in Northern Ireland had been identified and photographed, and for these detailed target files had also been prepared. Predictably, the proliferation of military airfields had become the major focus of German interest. They would almost certainly have been the next objective had the blitz continued after the raids on Belfast in early May. There is also some evidence to suggest that airfields at Long Kesh, Aldergrove, Langford Lodge and Nutt's Corner would have been among the first areas attacked in any airborne enemy invasion during this period.

Although, in general, the files prepared by the German general staff showed diligence and care, they were not without error. In one file Victoria barracks was wrongly located on the Antrim Road rather than on North Queen Street. More curious, and potentially tragic, was the fact that a complete target card was produced for Belfast Waterworks, the reservoirs of which, it was claimed, provided Belfast with its 'main water supply'. In fact the waterworks had been put out of commission in the 1860s, the Oldpark stream even then unable to meet the needs of the expanding city; the Silent Valley in Co. Down, officially opened on 24 May 1933, eventually became the main source of water supply to Belfast. This mistake was probably caused by enemy analysts relying too heavily on Luftwaffe reconnaissance photographs and, more especially, on Ordnance Survey maps. The latter still marked the old 'Belfast City and District Waterworks', with its filter beds, straining wells and pumping stations. There was nothing to indicate that for seventy years the area had been used for nothing other than recreation – the hiring of pleasure boats, fishing, fireworks displays and musical concerts. The misinterpretation of its function may have contributed at least in part to the Luftwaffe's heavy concentration on north Belfast during the 1941 Easter Tuesday raid (15–16 April), in which so many people died. (At the time of the attack it was popularly believed in Belfast that enemy aircraft had mistaken this whole area of the city for the commercial docks and shipyards at the head of the lough.)

Although imperial defence experts had come to recognise Belfast's growing vulnerability, there is little evidence to indicate that the increasing level of enemy activity over the United Kingdom from late 1940 did much to rouse Northern Ireland civilians from their apathy. Locally, the ominous German presence had been too unobtrusive and too little observed to make much impact. It had not been on such a scale as to suggest that a series of determined attacks was about to be launched on the North. None the less, a diary entry by Emma Duffin, who had served as a nurse near the Western Front during World War I, does suggest some feeling of apprehension. Reflecting back on this period, she wrote:

> We wondered if Belfast's turn would come next. We knew its ARP arrangements were far from ready. There were rumours that the Germans had said on the wireless that they would reduce [the city] to a ploughed field for not having stayed neutral like Eire.

Belfast's first public air-raid warning, on Friday, 25 October 1940, brought the war dramatically nearer home and provided its citizens with their first

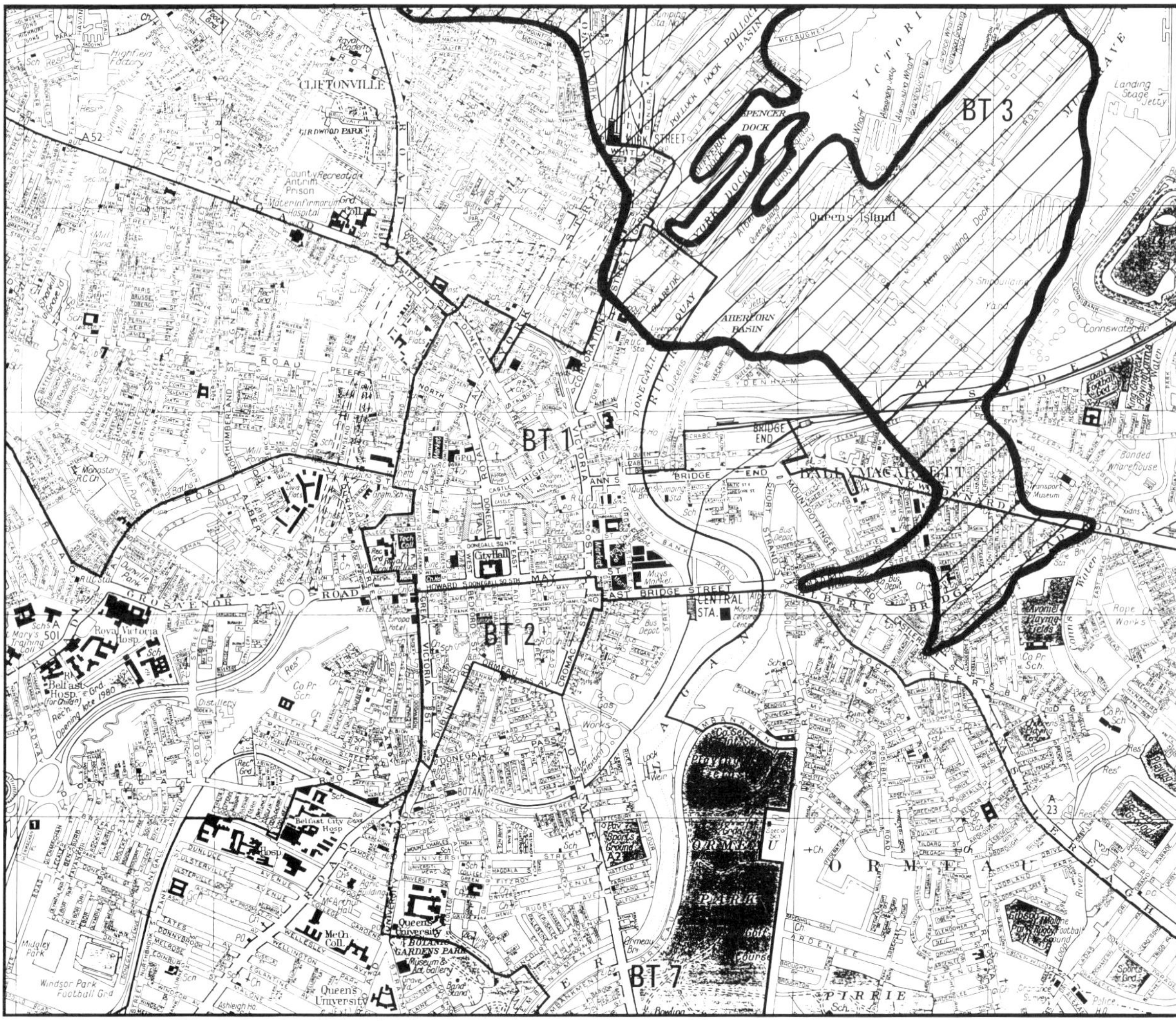

4
THE DOCKSIDE RAID
7–8 APRIL 1941

Based on official records, this map indicates the area in Belfast principally affected during the Luftwaffe raid on 7–8 April 1941.

At around midnight on 7 April William McCready was completing his income tax returns forms at his home in north Belfast's Keadyville Avenue, off the Shore Road. He recorded in his diary:

> Suddenly I heard a long roaring whine and next moment a hell of a thud. . . I knew at once it was something out of the ordinary. . . and went upstairs to the attic and standing on a box, opened the skylight. Something in my stomach seemed to drop, for the whole length of the shipyard was ablaze with stark white light. . . The guns all over the city began to roar. I knew it was our first raid.

Fortunately for its citizens, Belfast was not the Luftwaffe's main target. On this same night every single civil defence region in the United Kingdom experienced bombing; the attack was among the most extensive and widespread of any in the whole course of the war. German records indicate that a total of 517 aircraft were involved and that they concentrated mainly on their by now familiar objectives – Glasgow, Liverpool, Bristol, Great Yarmouth, and of course London. Belfast had seven distinct but minor assaults by aircraft, most of which were on their way to or back from targets in Great Britain. The raid was of a pin-pricking, exploratory nature, concerned to probe and test local defences and to unnerve the local population. It began just after midnight and ended three and a quarter hours later, with never more than eight enemy bombers overhead at any one time.

The leading Luftwaffe group flew up the Northern Ireland coast between Ardglass and Bangor in Co. Down, and then travelled westwards down Belfast Lough. It included at least one aircraft, a Heinkel He111 from Kampfgruppe 26, one of the force's two pathfinder squadrons whose specific skill was to identify targets and act as fire-raisers for the waves of bombers coming behind. Although equipped with sophisticated radio instruments to enable it to pinpoint its objectives, the Heinkel delivered its bombs on the Belfast docks by sight. This was due in part to the fact that the area was so easy to identify from the air. It was illuminated by flares and the weather was fine, the moon half-full, winds light, and visibility good, though it became more overcast towards dawn.

Throughout the raid, the enemy airmen displayed a total disdain for Belfast's anti-aircraft defences. They attacked mainly from seven thousand feet – just above the level of the city's balloon barrage – but occasionally they came in at half this height. Admiralty officials also noted, almost disbelievingly, that some kept their navigation lights on during part of the attack, apparently unconcerned that this would make their identification easier from the ground. In reports, completed after they had returned to their bases in northern France, the bomber crews described the city's defences as 'inferior in quality, scanty and insufficient'. In stark contrast, the defences of Glasgow and Liverpool were considered to be 'heavy and well-positioned', and consequently they attacked these targets from higher altitudes.

People in Belfast were stunned by the raid; their sense of confusion, disbelief and shock was heightened by the fact that they received no preliminary warning when this first attack occurred. In south Belfast Moya Woodside was, like many others, 'just falling asleep' when she 'heard thuds, and bumps and a loud bang'. Only then did she hear the sirens. Sir Wilfrid Spender recorded with surprise and concern that he 'heard the planes before the guns and the guns before the alert'. The first official casualty of the blitz was an air raid precautions warden, who was injured by shrapnel from the first burst of gunfire which preceded the siren. He had been making his way towards his post.

Undersized, shoddily built shelters added to the terro[r] of the air raids. (*The shelte[r] warden* by Thomas A. Crawley, courtesy of the Ulster Museum)

erupted in their immediate vicinity. It was fortunate that none of the shelters was struck as some of the bombs dropped weighed as much as five hundred kilograms – twice the strength that the shelter walls were built to withstand. When at last the all-clear sounded, local people returned to find streets and pavements in places knee-deep in slate, glass and rubble.

Incendiary bombs and high explosives also fell on the Shore Road and York Road in north Belfast. At least half a dozen small bombs fell on the Grove playing fields near an anti-aircraft gun emplacement, where they churned up the soil and impaled bowling-green seats on railings. Some failed to explode and, as a result, the first-aid post at Grove elementary school had to evacuate hurriedly during the raid to Mountcollyer school, half a mile away. At Alexandra Park Avenue quite a large bomb exploded, causing a crater fifteen feet wide and two feet deep in the middle of the road. Yet, Jimmy Mackey recalls in amazement that not a single window was broken or slate removed from the roofs of the adjacent terraces. After visiting the scene, an official commented that it was 'freakish'. Others were less fortunate – 'two to three streets away, a man in his bath was blown out of his house into the middle of the road by the force of the blast'. A civil defence worker recorded a small bomb falling on a group of four flimsy working-

218TH DAY OF WAR'S SECOND YEAR BELFAST TELEGRAPH, TUESDAY, APRIL 8, 1941.

ULSTER AT CLOSE QUARTERS WITH WAR

North's First Blitz: Night Of Thrills

MANY H.E. AND FIRE BOMBS DROPPED

Two A.F.S. Men Victims

NORTHERN IRELAND SUFFERED ITS MOST SEVERE RAID OF THE WAR THIS MORNING, WHEN A NUMBER OF ENEMY PLANES DROPPED MANY INCENDIARY AND HIGH EXPLOSIVE BOMBS.

Damage was done to industrial, commercial, and residential buildings.

Two members of the Auxiliary Fire Service were victims of the attack, and there were other casualties.

RAIDER BROUGHT DOWN.

Ground defences were in action and one of the raiders was brought down by a night fighter.

A family of four residing in one area had a narrow escape when a bomb landed in the front garden, blowing the entire front out of the house.

The husband had brought his two children down to the kitchen for safety and they were underneath a table, while his wife was in the scullery when the bomb exploded.

When A.R.P. workers hastened to the scene they found that the husband had succeeded in getting his wife and children clear and they were immediately taken to a rest centre.

UNSCATHED CHURCH WINDOW.

Incendiary bombs fell in many places in another area and a well-known church was badly hit.

There are gaping holes in the roof and a transept and gallery were burned. A window showing Christ and the Apostles was unscathed and there was little damage to the altar.

DAMAGE CAUSED BY A DELAYED ACTION BOMB IN THE STREET OF A NORTHERN IRELAND TOWN.

class houses on York Road, virtually demolishing them. When soon afterwards the occupants emerged, shaken but without serious injury, they were 'treated like heroes. . . congratulated by all and sundry', and 'thousands' later flocked to the area to see the damage for themselves.

Some high explosives fell on the east side of Belfast, around the Newtownards Road, Templemore Avenue and Albertbridge Road. However, the most vivid impression left there by the raid was of 'incendiary bombs raining down like hailstones' and of 'flames sprouting up everywhere'. Officials estimated that about eight hundred incendiaries fell on this part of the city alone, some containing explosives which spread the devastation and acted as an anti-handling device. Most fell into streets or empty back yards, where they burned themselves out harmlessly. Frightened people cautiously picked their way around them on their way to shelters, or caught glimpses of their fierce glow from coal-hole retreats under stairs. Upwards of 150 incendiaries smashed their way through the roofs of houses, in some cases as many as five to a single dwelling. But even these were generally extinguished quickly with sandbags, stirrup pumps and buckets of water, the damage being usually restricted to broken roof tiles, and scorched ceilings, floors and bedding.

The worst of approximately fifteen fires that sprang up was at St Patrick's the area, and stated merely that 'a big raid by several German planes took place on this night, lasting some hours. . . We went to the cellar. Big damage was done by bombs in the Docks and a great conflagration could be observed from the monastery windows.' Similar comments were entered in the parish diary of St Paul's on the Falls Road by Father James Dean Hendley. In south Belfast Emma Duffin could hear the anti-aircraft guns and explosions in the distance, and took refuge in a shelter which, she writes, was 'dripping with damp. . . a cold chill struck through to my bones'. Moya Woodside, who lived close by, refused to believe that it was a raid. When her husband attempted to waken her, saying, 'they are dropping bombs, better come to the kitchen', she records:

The Harland and Wolff aircraft factory suffered th biggest fire of the 7–8 Ap raid, with serious disrupti of its production of Stirlin fuselages. (Harland and Wolff)

> I stayed where I was. . . We have had so many false alarms that in my drowsy state I muttered something about it being only anti-aircraft fire. . . I could not hear planes and came to the conclusion that this was some sort of practice. . . [Next] morning I was astonished to hear from my husband that there had been a genuine raid and that he had been called to the hospital as additional staff to aid with the large number of injured. . . We only live about 1½ miles away [from the docks]. . . It seems amazing that all this can have happened so near while I lay calmly in bed.

On the morning of 8 April the Ministry of Public Security claimed in a confidential report that all fires had been extinguished, all roads had been cleared, all unexploded bombs had been dealt with, and all bodies had been

CITY OF BELFAST

FIRE WATCHERS ORDERS

APPEAL FOR VOLUNTEERS

UNDER ORDERS OF THE MINISTRY OF PUBLIC SECURITY THE DUTY is placed on the citizens either through the occupiers of business premises or the Belfast Civil Defence Authority to see that all buildings in the City are watched with a view to preventing fires from incendiary bombs.

All male persons between the ages of 18 and 60 who are not engaged on A.R.P. work for 48 hours each month or who are not Local Defence Volunteers may be required to undertake fire watching either on their own business premises or elsewhere in an unpaid capacity.

The need is very great and I appeal to all citizens who have the safety of the City at heart and who have not already enrolled with their own business firms not to wait but to come forward at once as volunteers.

Volunteers will be entitled to the benefit of the Personal Injuries (Civilians) Scheme, 1940, for " war service injuries."

Forms of enrolment which will be accepted from women as well as from men may be filled up at the A.R.P. Headquarters, Academy Street, or at the City Hall.

CRAWFORD McCULLAGH,
LORD MAYOR.

Northern Whig, 9 April 1941

recovered. In fact the bodies were not all identified until forty-eight hours later. The final casualty figures were thirteen dead, and eighty-one injured, twenty-three of them seriously. Meanwhile the Government sought to reassure the public and to maintain morale. Official statements emphasised how well people had 'stood up to the test', and applauded the 'energy and efficiency of the civil defence services'. The heavily censored local press echoed and sought to reinforce these sentiments. Reports stressed: 'We can take it'; 'Everyone is going to work normally'; 'It is business as usual.' A typical account described how the dust had scarcely settled on a row of demolished houses, than Union Jacks appeared at the windows and fluttered proudly in the breeze. There were numerous stories of individual heroism and of narrow escapes from death. Readers were assured that the anti-aircraft regiments formed 'a cordon of steel around the province', that air raid precautions members 'acted with promptitude and resource'; in fact that 'everything had gone like clockwork'.

Such inaccurate and unrealistic claims can only have lessened the urgency of simultaneous press appeals for women and children to evacuate, for more fire-watchers, for volunteers to join anti-aircraft regiments and civil defence forces, and for a more efficient blackout. The effect of such reports may also have been counterproductive in other ways – in heightening distrust of 'official' news and statements, in feeding rumour, and in bringing home the stark reality that the first casualty of war is truth. William McCready noted 'how disgusting' he found a *Belfast Telegraph* article which stated: 'We are now in the front line with England, Scotland and Wales; our people would not have it otherwise.' 'Not bloody likely,' he observed. 'All the people I know disliked it a hell of a lot and don't want a repetition. . . [They are] *not* proud of being in the front line.'

Moya Woodside felt a similar sense of outrage, writing:

> Local newspapers read almost as if [the raid] occurred in Timbuctoo – 'some damage to houses', interview with rector of bombed church (unspecified), write-ups of heroism in dealing with incendiaries. No suggestion anywhere that anything of importance was hit or that anyone was unpleasantly wounded. . . I suppose it is 'keeping up morale' for the general public to be lulled in ignorance and for them not to know about men with both legs blown off, backs broken, half their faces gone or worse. . . But it makes one wonder how much is not being told all over England and Scotland when for once we know the truth ourselves.

Workers forlornly survey the damage at the Harland and Wolff aircraft factory after the 7–8 April raid. (Harland and Wolff)

During the following week, she recorded some of the rumours in circulation locally, each of them 'supposed to have been authenticated by eyewitnesses'. These included, for example, claims that the 'Nazis' had attempted to invade the Isle of Wight but had been 'repelled by a wall of fire on the water', that the centres of large British cities, such as Southampton and Bristol, were 'in ruins', and that aircraft factories in Britain had been 'so damaged that it is no longer possible to produce a complete plane anywhere'.

Newspaper statements that everything had gone 'like clockwork' were pure fantasy. The small number of Luftwaffe bombers involved in the attack treated Belfast's active defences with contempt. Local anti-aircraft guns threw up a total barrage of about three hundred rounds. Compared with that being used increasingly in Britain, their equipment was outdated, they scored no hits and indeed suffered one unreported reverse: at Balmoral post a shell burst prematurely, killing one soldier outright; four others required hospital treatment. Overall, governmental anxiety at the extent of Belfast's vulnerability was significantly increased. Sir Wilfrid Spender, a veteran of World War I, described the sound of the guns as 'very slight'. This

The remains of the Harlan[d] and Wolff aircraft factory after the 7–8 April raid – jigs, machine tools and Stirling fuselages have bee[n] reduced to rubble. (Harland and Wolff)

was less obvious to the public partly because over a dozen vessels at the port, including trawlers and smaller craft, initially joined in the firing, some using machine guns. As none of this action was integrated by any means to the shore batteries, they shot more or less indiscriminately in the general direction of the barrage. This was contrary to standing orders under which ships were not to fire unless the harbour was being dive-bombed. It ceased altogether when those involved were reprimanded by Rear Admiral King, the Flag Officer in Charge, for wasting scarce ammunition 'against invisible targets'.

The Hurricanes based at Aldergrove registered the night's only success. They were not equipped for night-fighting but, none the less, conducted three single aircraft patrols during the raid. The second of these was by the squadron leader, J.W.C. Simpson DFC, an experienced airman who had already shot down ten Luftwaffe aircraft during their raids on Britain. At about 1.30 a.m. miraculously he made contact with two of the enemy planes. He closed in and fired through the deepening haze from a distance of about fifty yards. A police constable later reported seeing the bomber, a Heinkel He111, exploding in mid-air, plunging downwards from seven thousand feet, and disappearing 'like a meteor' into the sea off the Co. Down coast near Downpatrick. Neither the five-man crew nor the debris of

Workers explore the rubble at the Harland and Wolff aircraft factory after the 7–8 April raid. (Harland and Wolff)

the plane were ever recovered.

Local press reports had praised with greater justification the courage and devotion to duty of the city's civil defence services; in part this was evident from the night's casualties among wardens. One report described a warden who remained at his post on the top of a three-storey building, though its windows were blown out, its ceilings brought down and it contained a one-thousand-gallon petrol tank. None the less, all of the services were hampered even in this small raid by the legacy of official and public indifference towards civil defence matters. Shelters, where available, were sparsely used and in some cases locked, with the keys lost or unobtainable. As a result, doors had to be smashed down to gain entry. Houses, even in the most strategically vulnerable areas, continued to be occupied by large numbers of women and children. However heroic these may have been in coping with incendiaries and explosives, it is clear that they ought to have been evacuated from the city months before. Members of the fire service recorded their frustration at finding, all too often, industrial and business premises closed, empty and ablaze, their owners having failed to introduce even elementary fire-watching precautions. Crucially, some of the reports

The Hack,
1 September 1942

from the dock area, a vital strategic centre of war production in Northern Ireland, were deeply disturbing. The fire services, though undoubtedly distracted by many calls on their slender resources, were in a number of cases remarkably slow in arriving at the scene of incidents. Even more ominous was the fact that at some of the larger fires in this area firemen were unable to raise sufficient quantities of water to quench the flames. This was because many of the local earthen water pipes had been fractured by high explosives and also because the supply of hose was inadequate. The owner of MacNeill Limited in Corporation Street, whose premises had been gutted, complained with bitterness and in disbelief: 'It is evident that there is an insufficient water supply in this area.' With Belfast now clearly identified as a Luftwaffe target, such a conclusion was far from reassuring.

Although the Government showed a greater sense of urgency over civil defence in the aftermath of the raid, this could easily be overstated. The attack does not appear either on the agenda or in the conclusions of the cabinet meeting held at the Prime Minister's room at Stormont eight hours after the Luftwaffe had gone; recorded discussions centred on drainage and fisheries. Nor indeed was the matter raised in the House later that day. However, during the afternoon, Minister of Commerce Sir Basil Brooke, at the request of the Prime Minister, personally urged on Westminster ministers and officials the necessity of strengthening Belfast's inadequate defences. In fact very little was actually achieved before enemy aircraft returned on 15–16 April. This was due to the lack of time available and also to the acute shortage of strategic equipment in Britain. The profoundly unsatisfactory outcome was that, on 10 April, Northern Ireland's first and only searchlights arrived at Larne, Co. Antrim, followed next day by one single additional anti-aircraft battery.

In these unhappy circumstances, alternative methods of protecting the city had to be considered. For a time defence officials discussed setting up an elaborate system of decoy lighting in Northern Ireland, its purpose being to confuse and hopefully deceive enemy bombers as to the true location of their targets. Although this technique had been applied with apparent success in parts of Britain, it was finally decided not to introduce it into the North. The port of Belfast was thought to be so easily recognised from the air that it would be impossible to disguise or camouflage effectively in this way. In addition, the Air Ministry was concerned at the existence of 'subversive elements' in Northern Ireland and the presumed likelihood that

The Harland and Wolff aircraft factory after the 7–8 April raid. (Harland and Wolff)

'information on the scheme [would be] disclosed' to the enemy. However, one new initiative was agreed on. It was decided to initiate experiments into the creation of a smoke screen for the dock area of Belfast. This would take advantage of the fact that the city lay in a depression between hills where there was a natural tendency for smoke and fog to concentrate. Also, military personnel had already established a smoke-producing unit in Northern Ireland, which had been studying this approach for some months and had sufficient capacity to provide cover for the square mile of the port. William McCready was soon aware of 'an infernal machine at the end of the street. . . producing heavy, black, smelly smoke'. He recorded standing, bemusedly, at his front door, watching it 'for two or three minutes' and as a result, 'the kitchen and scullery were soon full of the damned stuff'. The area covered by this screen was nicknamed locally 'the blue circle', a clearly identified, vulnerable zone. Its existence cannot have helped either the morale or the health of those citizens affected by it, but sooner than they would have hoped, they had reason to be grateful for the inconvenience it caused.

It is not easy to assess the impact of this first aerial attack on the people of

The Northern Whig
and Belfast Post

NORTHERN IRELAND SHOWS IT "CAN TAKE IT"

Skill and Courage in Nazi Blitz

EIGHT people are known to have been killed in Northern Ireland's first severe air raid. Six bodies were recovered from debris at an industrial building, and two A.F.S. men lost their lives.

Northern Whig, 9 April 1941

Belfast. Although some eyewitnesses recorded incidences of panic and hysteria while it was in progress, symptoms of the preceding months of public complacency were also obvious. One official report concluded that the civilian population was 'simply not aware of the horrors of an air-raid, nor did the necessity of taking cover appear to concern the majority'. Most people acted as if they were 'front seat spectators at a gigantic Brock's carnival put on especially for their benefit'. At the city centre, the report claims that while a few of those 'thronging homewards from theatres, cinemas and dance-halls' at first scurried for shelter, most 'quickly recovered from their surprise and lined the shop-fronts looking skywards'. In industrial areas families generally clustered around their front doors 'to exchange remarks', and to speculate on the object of the attack.

Sidney Coleshill, a Falls Road public baths attendant, recalled how 'we were all peering into the sky to try and see [the planes], not realising the danger'. Moya Woodside later discovered that she was 'unique in having spent the entire night in bed in ignorance'. Many of her friends had 'stayed up. . .watching the illuminations'; towards the latter stages of the raid some had even climbed up neighbouring hills 'to get a better view'. William McCready at first observed the scene from the skylight of his home in Keadyville Avenue. He was 'fascinated, I had never seen anything like this before. The sky was ablaze. It was not only an unusual spectacle, but a tremendously big one. I found myself engrossed. . .' After walking to the top of Premier Drive for a better vantage point, he recorded his reactions: 'It was frightening, it was exciting, it was wonderful. . .very high in the sky I could see the balloons, they looked tiny and lovely. . .I could see a solitary seagull.' However, in retrospect, after the elation had passed, McCready recorded his last and most enduring impressions of the attack. It seemed then 'like a sort of nightmare. . .a terribly bad dream. . .during the night I

NEMY RAID ON ULSTER

/ICTIMS' BODIES RECOVERED

Vomen Fight Fire Bombs

HILDREN EVACUATED

ODIES of a number of the victims of the air raid on thern Ireland, the first big ck on the Province, were vered yesterday.

he raid was carried out by a ll force of enemy bombers— of which was shot down by fighters—and continued inter-tently during the small hours he morning.

Damage to property was com-aratively slight. Women in one ea in which showers of incen-aries were dropped tackled the mbs as they fell and thus saved eir homes.

s a precaution many people 1 small children living in the bed areas left during the rnoon to stay with friends in country districts. Groups of se voluntary evacuees were to een waiting at bus stops Most he children carried their gas ks slung over their shoulders. 1e majority of these people had e private arrangements with ions to accommodate them. It is

Belfast News-Letter, 9 April 1941

found it difficult to read. . . every sound drew my mind back to the possibility of another raid'.

There is some evidence that the experience did serve to shake public complacency. At least, it did so more than earlier government appeals and propaganda had succeeded in doing or indeed the reports of raids on British cities. With an acute sense of guilt, Emma Duffin had come to regard these reports as 'monotonous and boring'; she felt 'numbed by the repetition of horrors'. The black pall of smoke over the docks, the demolished houses and gutted businesses that were viewed by thousands of curious onlookers during the following week, the loads of salvaged furniture, the funeral cortèges of the victims – all these were tangible proof that Belfast's long immunity from aerial attack really had ended. The opinion that the Luftwaffe would never attack the city or Northern Ireland because of its assumed military insignificance, or remoteness, or out of some peculiar regard for the feelings of neutral Éire, had been shattered. In the words of one official, J.B. Meehan, 'the curiosity of the early hours [of 8 April] sobered down to a new anxiety', at least temporarily. Some people seemed almost to have been haunted by the spectre of a further raid. Billy Boyd, a shipyard worker, recalled vividly how his father removed some of the interior doors from their home, off the Shankill Road, and used them to strengthen and support the dining table in the scullery for use as a domestic shelter. His father told the family of a dream which was clearly causing him some concern. In it he saw a parachute floating silently down, with two coffins ominously suspended beneath it. No one then could have imagined that within days this unnerving premonition of death would be translated into grim reality.

The 'new anxiety' was to some extent evident from changes in the pattern of public behaviour. Moya Woodside, who was downtown on the morning after the raid, noted that though 'everything seemed normal, no visible damage anywhere, there were many more gas masks'. In the space of half an hour she saw 'two men and eight women carrying them'. She also noted that the blitz had become

> the sole topic of conversation. . . In streets, shops, trams, phone-calls, even perfect strangers start talking about it. Everyone anxious to recount their reactions and experiences and to cap the other fellow's story of the damage done.

Some declared, 'not apologetically, but as a matter for congratulation, "I hate all foreigners". . . anti-Hitler slogans were painted on boarded-up shop windows'. Similarly, William McCready reflected on 'the impossibility of loving your enemy'.

A further indication of the heightened consciousness of danger was the noticeable exodus of people from the city, mainly women and children, that began on the morning after the attack. Queues appeared at bus stops, railway stations reported that they were busier than anticipated, even including the trains bound for Dublin, and at seaside hotels and boarding houses, bookings for the Easter holidays rose sharply. At the time, this movement was treated sympathetically in the local press on the grounds that the 'workers deserve a respite' and would 'doubtless return refreshed and ready to go all out'. Meanwhile, in St Paul's parish on the Falls Road, an area not directly affected by the raid, Father Hendley noted a significant surge in the numbers coming to confession, greater than the predictable increase over the Easter period. At Clonard Monastery nearby the night adoration of the confraternity for Holy Thursday was cancelled 'owing to the risk of bombs'. However, the conclusion of John Blake's official history of the war, that the raid had been a 'chastening as well as harrowing' experience and that, as a result, 'apathy and complacency disappeared', is an overstatement. There is unmistakeable evidence that while public complacency may have been shaken it none the less persisted and revived. This was most apparent when the Government launched its third evacuation scheme on Saturday, 12 April. Despite intensive advertising directed at women, children and the homeless, and repeated warnings that the Luftwaffe would return, only three thousand had bothered to register before the Easter Tuesday attack on 15–16 April. By then most of those who had voluntarily evacuated themselves, even from areas such as the docks, had filtered back again to their homes.

On reflection, almost a week after the event, Moya Woodside identified 'three main types of reaction' to the raid. Firstly, there were

> those whose [lives are] conditioned by the possibility of a [further] attack, who are constantly thinking about it, unable to sleep or sleep badly, won't go out in the evenings, run around at night filling baths and buckets and turning off taps, talking about the certainty of more or worse raids with a sort of eager gloom, build hideouts under the stairs and [pack] trunks ready for evacuation. Secondly, those who do not bother about raids or precautions in the daytime but become hysterical or lose their nerve [in the event of an alert]. . . Lastly, those who adopt a fatalistic attitude towards the whole thing, who take no precautions and remain calm, resolutely quelling what imagination they possess.

The writer herself fell into the third category along with most of her fellow citizens. After all, in many respects, Belfast's first raid had been reassuring to the Government, the civil defence services and the public. Although it had been on a very small scale, many people seemed to have convinced themselves that the city had been subjected to a blitz, comparable in its severity to the November raid on Coventry. For the moment they could enjoy the dangerous illusion of being able to cope with the worst that Hitler had to offer without great effort or anxiety. In addition, the attack had followed a predictable pattern. In Moya Woodside's view, it had been 'confined, in truth, to military objectives' in the docks, the sector long regarded as the most vulnerable in Northern Ireland with 'other damage,

Fears for children's safety intensified throughout Northern Ireland after the elfast Dockside raid: in this photograph children from .ondonderry Model School wait evacuation to country billets. (*Londonderry Sentinel*)

apparently incidental'. Hence it was popularly referred to afterwards as the 'Dockside raid'. At the time officials estimated that twelve of the thirteen deaths which it had caused occurred in this area.

Thus, for most people, the normal pattern of life, which in any case had never been seriously disrupted, rapidly returned as Easter approached. Yet on any rational calculation a further attack on Northern Ireland was highly probable. Between 7 and 14 April, the Luftwaffe launched massive offensives against major industrial centres and west-coast ports in Britain, including Birmingham, Coventry, Tyneside, Liverpool, Glasgow and Bristol. It required little imagination to conceive that, as novelist Brian Moore put it in *The Emperor of Ice Cream*, at the 'Reich chancellery in Berlin, generals stood over illuminated maps plotting Belfast's destruction', and that 'Hitler

Northern Whig, 13 April 1941

EVACUATION OF CHILDREN

A FURTHER OPPORTUNITY IS NOW OFFERED TO PARENTS of children residing in the County Borough of Belfast to bring them within the Government's Evacuation Plans. These Plans cover:—

1. CHILDREN OF SCHOOL AGE.
2. CHILDREN UNDER SCHOOL AGE ACCOMPANIED BY THEIR MOTHER OR OTHER RESPONSIBLE FEMALE RELATIVE.

Mothers who wish to accompany their children who are of school age may, however, be accepted if one or more of the children is under school age OR if they have definite arrangements to be received by friends.

Parents who wish to take advantage of this offer and who
HAVE MADE DEFINITE ARRANGEMENTS FOR THE TRANSFER OF THEIR CHILDREN TO FRIENDS IN THE COUNTRY WHO ARE ABLE AND WILLING TO RECEIVE THEM;

OR

ARE PREPARED TO HAVE THEIR CHILDREN READY AT THE TIME AND PLACE FIXED FOR THEIR ASSEMBLY FOR TRANSFER TO THE RECEPTION AREAS;

AND

ARE, IN EITHER CASE, PREPARED TO ALLOW THEIR CHILDREN TO REMAIN EVACUATED UNTIL GOVERNMENT DECIDES THAT IT IS NO LONGER DESIRABLE,

should make application to the Welfare Department of the Belfast Civil Defence Authority at

MUNICIPAL COLLEGE OF TECHNOLOGY

on SATURDAY, 12th April, or on any week-day following until further notice between the hours of 10 A.M. AND 4 P.M.

himself smiled in glee'. Rumours persisted that Northern Ireland would be attacked again. Some of these originated with the redoubtable Lord Haw Haw, who taunted his listeners with the prediction that there would be 'Easter eggs for Belfast'. On 12 April 1941 the *Northern Whig* felt moved to counter these alarming transmissions by ridiculing their source, stating: 'Traitor Joyce. . . How does Joyce know?. . . It would be eccentric to say the least of Goering to broadcast his intentions.' Meanwhile in Belfast the sirens howled with such frequency that in the words of Frank Skillen, a young shipyard worker, 'you could have set your kettle by them'. However, all of them passed without serious incident. Although enemy aircraft were occasionally sighted, no bombs fell. Less than a week after the Dockside raid, when the alert sounded, Moya Woodside observed that 'no one appeared to pay any attention'.

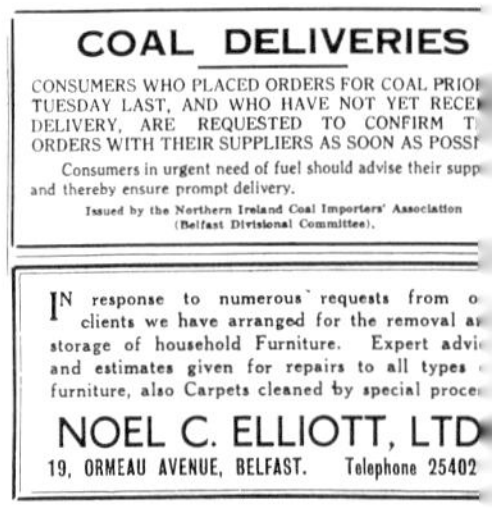
COAL DELIVERIES

CONSUMERS WHO PLACED ORDERS FOR COAL PRIO
TUESDAY LAST, AND WHO HAVE NOT YET RECE
DELIVERY, ARE REQUESTED TO CONFIRM T
ORDERS WITH THEIR SUPPLIERS AS SOON AS POSS

Consumers in urgent need of fuel should advise their supp
and thereby ensure prompt delivery.

Issued by the Northern Ireland Coal Importers' Association
(Belfast Divisional Committee).

IN response to numerous requests from o
clients we have arranged for the removal a
storage of household Furniture. Expert advi
and estimates given for repairs to all types
furniture, also Carpets cleaned by special proce

NOEL C. ELLIOTT, LTD
19, ORMEAU AVENUE, BELFAST. Telephone 25402

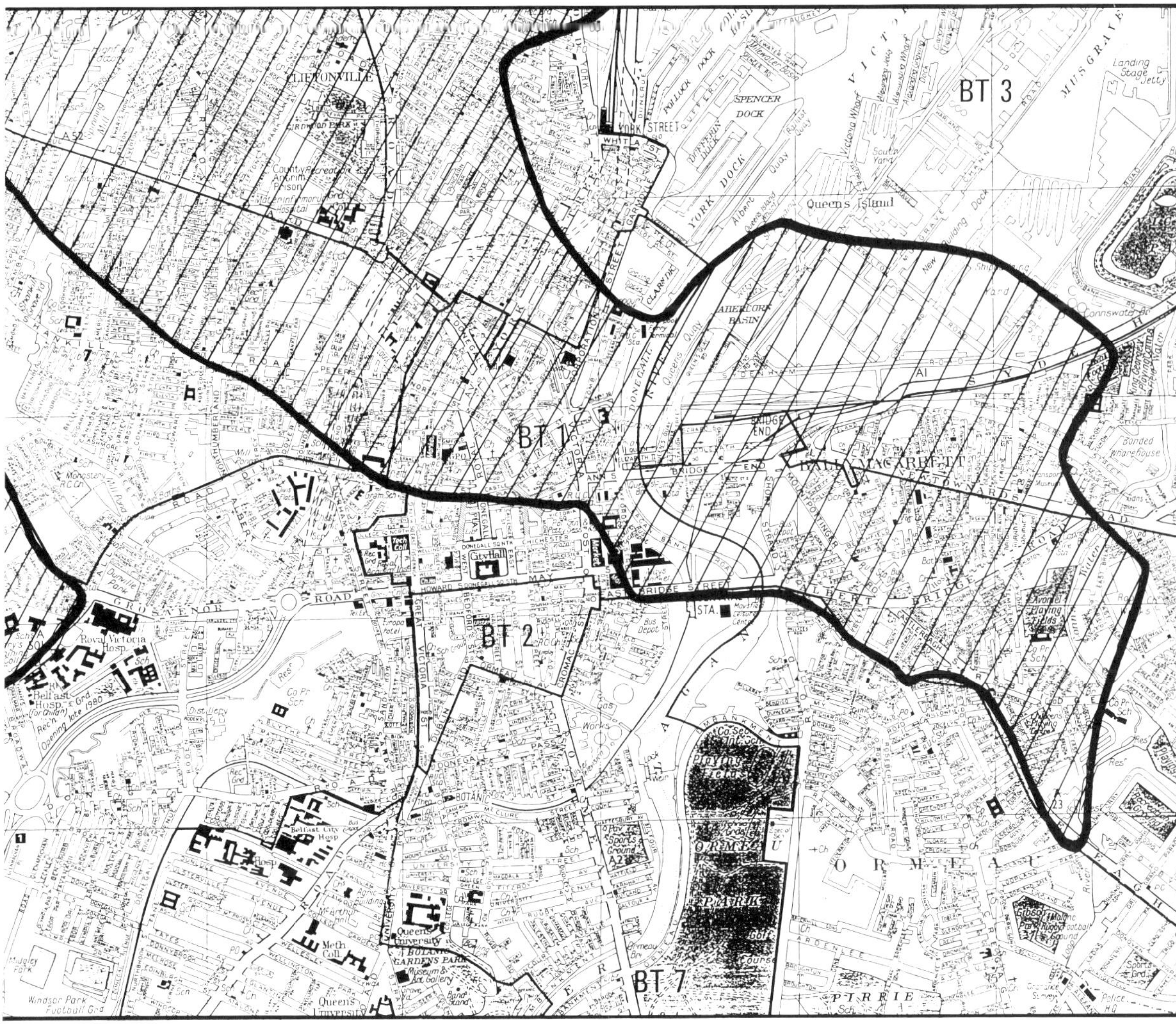

5
THE EASTER TUESDAY RAID
15–16 APRIL 1941

Based on official records, this map indicates the areas in Belfast which suffered most severely during the Luftwaffe raid, 15–16 April 1941.

Occurrences which at the time appear to be more or less trivial and insignificant are often etched deeply into human memory when they are succeeded by traumatic events. So it was with the Easter Tuesday raid on Belfast. Mary Taggart, a young teacher, can still recall vividly how after Mass on Good Friday, 11 April 1941, as the congregation left Holy Family Church on the Limestone Road, a plane swooped so low over the building that she and her companions felt constrained to duck their heads. They were convinced that the aircraft was German. Nellie Bell was married in Sinclair

Greencastle in north Belfast or Bangor in Co. Down. The Ulster Transport Authority offered rail transport 'to Bangor and back for a bob'. David Davidson from Bangor recalls walking along Queen's Parade, dressed as fashion required in sports jacket and flannels, and watching bemusedly Belfast youths sitting on the rocks, eating willicks which they scooped into their mouths using a pin. Moya Woodside had gone that afternoon to a suburban cinema. However, the experience was slightly less relaxing than she had anticipated, owing to an incident that suggests the authorities were somewhat more tense and expectant than usual. On entering the foyer, she and her companions were challenged by a policeman who demanded to see their identity cards. On their surprised response, he explained that 'a bomb might fall on the picture-house and it would be difficult sorting out bodies afterwards if they had no identification'. It was, she observed, 'rather a macabre preliminary to our afternoon's pleasure'.

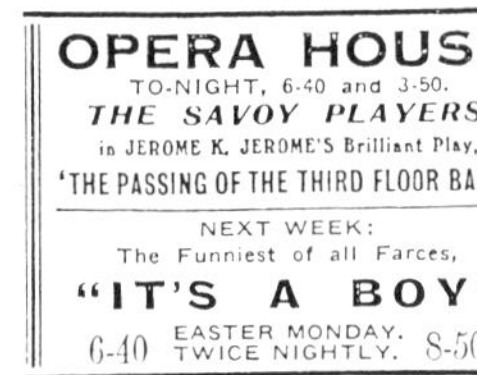

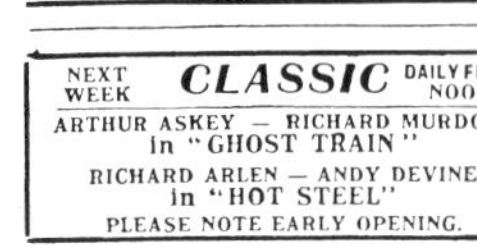

The events of the night that followed would never be forgotten by any of those fortunate enough to survive them. The evening was mild and bright with a light south-westerly wind. The low cloud from earlier in the day had gradually broken up and had disappeared completely by 10 p.m. The moon was three-quarters full, its pale light being regarded as a welcome relief from the oppressive darkness of the blackout. At about 10.40 p.m. the sirens sounded again. Civil defence workers and troops took up position. The anti-aircraft gunners on the Castlereagh Hills were at their posts from 10.30 p.m.; by then the crude smoke-screen machines were already belching out thick black smoke over the area of the port.

Doubtless many people felt reassured by the prolonged period of silence that followed the alert. However, after about half an hour the unsynchronised drone of approaching aircraft could be heard over Carlingford Lough in south Down. To the knowledgeable ear they were unmistakeably German bombers – Heinkel He111s and Junkers Ju88s. Minutes later, in the old cathedral city of Dromore, Co. Down, people thronged onto the streets to listen to the convoy passing over in ominously large numbers. Stumbling in the moonlight, some scrambled up the adjacent low-lying hills to gaze helplessly and expectantly in the direction of Belfast. Journalist James Kelly had left his Belfast newspaper office and was going up the Glen Road. He had begun to suspect that the alert was a false alarm, but now he heard the low humming sound coming from the east and the fire of the anti-aircraft guns.

Luftwaffe reports indicate that after leaving their bases in northern France, most of the bombers flew north over Cherbourg to Cardigan Bay on the west coast of Wales. There the convoy broke up; some swung eastwards to inflict sharp diversionary raids and scattered minor attacks on English ports and cities, including Tyneside, Merseyside, Hull and Great Yarmouth. The main force, however, veered west and moved *en masse* towards Belfast, its primary target, which, as the BBC later reported, 'bore the brunt of the attack'.

Georg Deininger, a Luftwaffe pilot who took part in the raid on Belfast, 15–16 April 1941. A member of the élite pathfinder squadron, Kampfgruppe 100, he is en here at the controls of a Heinkel He111. (Kenneth Wakefield)

Among those in the first wave were aircraft from Kampfgruppe 100, one of the élite pathfinder squadrons, now involved in its first bombing mission over Northern Ireland. Two of its pilots, Paul Wiersbitzki and Georg Deininger, later vividly recalled their precise route. Both left from their base at Vannes airfield in Brittany and used radio beacons to track a course for Bishop's Rock in the Scilly Isles; distance precluded the use of their x system signal equipment, their aid to target identification, throughout the entire journey. From the Scilly Isles, they followed a track to a point twenty miles off Ardglass in Co. Down, 'with a visual check passing Dublin'. (They returned from Belfast, via Holywood in Co. Down, to Penzance in Cornwall, once again keeping close to the coast of neutral Éire.)

Their account is of considerable interest as it indicates the Luftwaffe's growing respect for the British night-fighter force and its consequent fear of interception. It also serves to confirm the suspicions of the Stormont government that the unmasked lights of Southern towns and cities helped guide enemy aircraft to their destinations in the North. However, although many enemy pilots, unlike Wiersbitzki and Deininger, may have returned via Donegal and the west coast, on their outward journey they most probably kept to the prescribed route over south-west England, despite the greater risk of being shot down. One crewman, Heinrich Schmidt, recalled urging his pilot to deviate from this route and to take an alternative track up the Irish coast. Their bomber was over the Bristol Channel at the time and had been held by searchlights virtually from the moment that it had crossed the English Channel. It was so bright that Schmidt found it 'possible to read a newspaper in the aircraft'. However, his request was dismissed. Soon afterwards, their Heinkel was attacked and he was ultimately forced to bale out into captivity. It would seem then that the Luftwaffe did not routinely use the lights of the South as an aid to locating targets in Northern Ireland.

At about 11.30 p.m. the first groups of enemy aircraft approached Belfast from the direction of Belfast Lough, flying at a height of seven thousand feet, just above the level of the balloon barrage. Local estimates of the total number of bombers involved in the raid vary as bomb damage caused a failure of telephone circuits during the attack, making it impossible for the anti-aircraft-operations control room to plot the later waves. On the basis of the tonnage of bombs dropped, Royal Air Force intelligence estimated that over ninety bombers were involved. Rear Admiral King, Flag Officer in Charge at the port, put the figure at between one and two hundred. German air ministry records indicate that a total of 327 aircraft were dispatched on the night of 15–16 April and that of these, 180 were active over Northern Ireland. Most of those which failed to reach Belfast diverted course because of weather conditions. During the early stage of the raid, the city was more or less free of clouds but subsequently local conditions deteriorated significantly and German crews reported complete cloud cover until late in the night when once again it began to clear.

The sirens sounded at 10.40 p.m. Sarah Nelson, a young civil servant who lived opposite the waterworks on the Antrim Road, remembers, after supper, looking out through her kitchen window and seeing the dark, brooding outlines of German aircraft hovering above the city. She never for a moment imagined that bombs would soon be pounding down on the streets outside or that by dawn her mouth would be 'dry with praying and with countless repetitions of the rosary'. At approximately 10.45 p.m. the actual Luftwaffe attack began somewhat slowly but its first phase left an indelible impression on those who witnessed it. It was not one of deafening explosions or showers of incendiaries but rather of a ghostly silver glow cast by flares. It was at once breathtakingly beautiful and profoundly unnerving.

The early raiders dropped an estimated three hundred illuminants, each suspended from small white silk parachutes. They fell mostly on the north side of the city and as they drifted downwards they spread out horizontally at varying heights. An air raid precautions warden at Whitewell in north Belfast recorded

> hearing the drone overhead and [then] looking up defenceless and impotent at [the] brilliantly glowing magnesium flares. At first, drifting North-Easterly, they plunged harmlessly into Belfast Lough, around Whiteabbey. Later, however, they fell in the area of the port, causing a light brighter than at noon in Summer-time. I looked along the street and could recognize clearly two wardens one hundred yards away. I felt as if I was standing in the street stark naked.

In Keadyville Avenue, William McCready had gone 'upstairs to the attic and opened the skylight right over against the roof'. He continues:

> Then looking out I saw something like the powerful head-lights of a car shining straight down from the sky. I couldn't understand it and inside I had a sinking feeling. I realized that on this occasion the Germans meant business.
> More and more flares, intensely white, appeared in the sky and soon the

whole sky was as bright as day. During this time one could hear the steady drone of planes high overhead. In the streets, cars were being driven at high speed; ARP and fire-fighting men dashing to their posts, whilst others, civilians, were getting to hell out of the city and into the country. The steady almost monotonous drone of the planes went on and on; more and more brilliantly white flares came gliding down. Some of them looked like huge lights suspended from overhead wires. They didn't appear to lose height. It was now after midnight and so bright that I could very easily read the small print on a Woodbine packet. The barrage guns had not yet opened fire and the only sound came from the planes high over the city. I didn't see a plane.

In south Belfast Emma Duffin had been awakened by the sirens and had dressed with 'trembly fingers'. She could also see the glow from the flares through cracks in ill-fitting kitchen blinds. 'It was as light as day outside,' she writes and like William McCready, she 'realized that this was a real blitz'. Jimmy Doherty was near the centre of the city and remembered feeling despondently, 'What good is your blackout?' Certainly the Luftwaffe pilots overhead had a spectacularly clear aerial view of Belfast. One pilot in this first wave was subsequently shot down and captured during a raid on Britain. While recuperating in hospital, he described to one of the nurses attending him his sense of surprise and shock when the first of his flares highlighted with dramatic clarity the crucifix at Beechmount in west Belfast.

However, the pilot's overall vision would not have been an unimpeded one. Owing to the operation of the smoke screen, much of the dock area was obscured by thick black smoke. Frank Skillen was on the night-shift at the shipyard, carrying out repair work to the boilers of HMS *Furious*, an aircraft carrier. He was working on a jetty about one hundred yards away from the ship and beyond earshot of the sirens. He only became aware of the raid when the harbour power station, on a prearranged signal, flashed the electric lights which he worked by. Because of the smoke screen, he was unable to see the flares and found his way to the marginally greater safety of the supply ship by following the voices of those who had gone on a little ahead of him. Joe Dodds, an engineer on HMS *Furious*, first realised that a raid had begun when the ship's guns suddenly erupted into action in support of the city's anti-aircraft barrage.

A Luftwaffe pilot later described for German radio the mood of his colleagues on the eve of the attack:

We were in exceptional good humour knowing that we were going for a new target, one of England's last hiding places. Wherever Churchill is hiding his war material we will go. . . Belfast is as worthy a target as Coventry, Birmingham, Bristol or Glasgow.

Each of these British cities had been attacked during the preceding week. He concluded with words, spoken perhaps by way of exculpation, 'We are sorry for each bomb which may miss its target now and then.'

Some of the devastation in Thorndyke Street, off Templemore Avenue, east Belfast, after the 15–16 April raid. (Ulster Museum)

In fact almost from the outset it was the predominantly residential areas to the north and east of the city that suffered most damage rather than the harbour, the shipyard or the aircraft factory. The Government had correctly foreseen the likely pattern of the raid, familiar since Coventry – flares followed by incendiaries and high explosives. But they had not foreseen the target. Some twenty-nine thousand incendiaries showered down on mainly working-class districts. They were dropped in containers which blew open at a predetermined height. In Robert Fisk's *In Time of War* one eyewitness remembers that they made 'a crackling sound when they hit the ground, like sparks from tramwires. Then little sparks of flame would spring up.' Each incendiary generated a heat sufficient to melt steel. In addition, Luftwaffe records indicate that 674 bombs fell at an average rate of over two per minute over the five hours of the raid. Many had steel plates fitted to their noses to prevent excessive penetration of the ground so that maximum blast effect would be obtained. The bombs tore down whole streets, blowing them to dust, rupturing gas and water mains. Over greater distances, the blasts entered chimneys and scattered live coal from grates in all directions. The whistling bombs, William McCready noted, 'were the most terrifying. Each seemed to be directed at the roof of the house.' Tubes, shaped like organ pipes, were fitted to tail units; as the bomb dropped the wind blew through the tubes causing them to shriek. Apart from their destructive potential, their purpose was also to help break military and civilian morale.

Seventy-six land mines were also dropped, suspended from green, artificial silk parachutes. The fuse was activated by the impact of the mine with the ground. Their existence was not publicly acknowledged by the British government until 1944. They were designed to smash through metal defences and pre-stressed concrete of industrial targets in built-up areas. Instead, well over half of them glided down onto fragile, decaying Victorian slums. Sir Perceval Brown, chairman of the Civil Defence Authority, said that on impact each bomb caused an 'enormous crimson cloud, followed by a rumbling roar and then the blast'. A total of over two hundred tons of high explosives landed; much of it on back-to-back terraces, 'where the poor of Belfast lay unprotected', from the docks at York Road near the London, Midland and Scottish Railway Station to the Antrim Road and Cavehill. The ground vibrated as explosions ripped across the little houses and tiny streets. In some instances shelters were also destroyed; in others, though they remained intact, they were blown by as much as three inches along pavements. Jimmy Doherty later recalled human bodies being 'cooked by the heat from the blast of bombs'.

At Greencastle the raid erupted with dramatic suddenness and ferocity. After the siren had sounded, local air raid precautions wardens had been warning residents to take cover during the delay. Then suddenly they caught sight of a parachute mine coming down nearby. They had just time to fling themselves to the ground when it fell in the middle of Veryan Gardens with a vibrating crash that seemed to shatter the neighbourhood. Almost immediately afterwards, it was followed by another, coming from the direction of the Whitewell Road. In a matter of seconds the whole area had been devastated. Almost 130 homes in Vandyck Gardens and Veryan Gardens were demolished or severely damaged. A woman who was taking a bath was blown thirty feet into the Serpentine Road and died from her injuries. At number 45 Veryan Gardens eight members of the Danby family were killed instantly by the first blast; twenty-five residents in the street died. James Makemson, a member of the Local Defence Volunteers, remembers bricks from houses 250 yards away being hurled through the roof of his home in Whitewell Park.

Scarcely had the wardens recovered their faculties when they witnessed an 'appalling sight'. Several hundreds of terrified, screaming people came rushing from their wrecked houses, and began running down the Whitewell Road. Some of them were seriously injured. Police Constable James Hawthorne later recalled: 'All had one objective – to get away from it.' Unfortunately there was nowhere safe to go: no shelter had been built in an area so remote from any identifiable target. There were 170 casualties, 46 of them fatal. They were tended wherever cover could be found – houses with rooms still intact, fields and ditches; many, a warden recorded, 'were too dazed or distracted to understand instructions'.

On the Shore Road William McCready observed:

The Whitewell Road in the suburbs of north Belfast wa extensively damaged durin the course of the 15–16 April raid. (Ulster Museum

> About 1.15 it really started. A roar followed by a heavy dull thud and then the sound of vibrating windows and doors and I knew we were in for a bad night. Then the sound of anti-aircraft guns and, intermittently, the sound of heavy guns stationed all over the city. . . I came down from the attic to the kitchen and dressed in my overcoat and hat sat down on the settee. The girls [his daughters] were on the floor underneath the heavy oak table. . . Bombs [were] falling every few minutes. Suddenly one much closer than the others blew the kitchen window in with tremendous force. . . The drone of the German planes high in the sky went on and on.

One of the explosions that William McCready would have heard was at York Road police barracks. Donald Fleck was barrack orderly that evening. He was sitting in the day-room when he was informed that a neighbouring furniture shop had caught fire. He remembers commenting: 'It will kill the old man' – a reference to the shop owner, Mr Kelly. Fortunately he decided to go out into the street to inspect the extent of the damage. On opening the front door of the station, he saw a breathtaking sight. Just at that precise moment a huge parachute mine had landed on the road opposite and its silk parachute was still in the process of nestling over it. From training, Fleck knew that in about another twenty seconds the mine would detonate. As he remarked later, 'Fear lends you wings.' He dashed back inside and yelled to his colleagues to clear to the rear of the building; 'one hell of an explosion' followed, which created such a vacuum that the front wall of the station was sucked out into the road along with those of several shops and houses, and the spire of Alexandra Presbyterian Church. Not all of his colleagues were fortunate enough to escape injury. James Macklin, who had been answering the telephone, was buried beneath the rubble and killed, and a special constable, whose back was broken and legs were crushed, died later in hospital. But for Fleck's warning, however, the number of casualties would have been much greater: there had been fifteen men in the day-room until seconds before the blast. Nellie Bell lived in Crosscollyer Street, near the station. At an early stage in the raid, after a bomb had blown in her back door and kitchen window, she and her family had gone to the nearest shelter which was in Deacon Street. She remembers well that

> it was packed. . . we were all very quiet I think. I holding my father's hand and my new husband's. We stood, we could not sit down, it was pitch dark. I don't know who all was there only I remember one wee man at the door of the shelter every time we heard the screeching of the falling bombs and the planes seemed to be just roof high, he always shouted: 'Don't worry, it's one of ours.' Some wit at the back shouted: 'Tell them we are here.' Well I had no feeling in my feet and legs and I don't know what time it was but a landmine just missed the shelter and struck [the police station] and a row of houses in the street we were in. Well the smoke and the debris all landed on our shelter and we thought we had had it. However, when it was realised we were all 'safe', somebody started singing 'Nearer my God to Thee' and from then on it was hymns.

Some of the poorest and most densely populated areas of working-class housing in the city were situated close by the police barracks. Bryce Millar was born and bred near York Street flax spinning mill. He lived in Michael Street which was then near the interface between Catholic and Protestant communities. For much of the raid he remained at home, comforting his dog and later trying to sleep in the attic bed he shared with his brother. He covered himself, as he always did, in a threadbare sheet and the greatcoat his father had returned in at the end of World War I. Outside he could hear and see local people gathering hurriedly in nearby shelters while the bombers circled overhead. Their front doors were left unlocked – as he explained, 'nobody had anything to lose'. He can vividly recall listening to the rival groups of youths in the shelters, taunting one another, chanting slogans, and singing provocative party songs. But as the bombs began to fall ancient hatreds were, for the time being, cast aside and mutual provocation faded. Both sides joined in the familiar strains of 'Oh God our help in ages past' and 'Nearer my God to Thee'. As he observed: 'Fear took over. They combined together in an attitude of prayer. They made an integrated appeal to the Almighty to protect them.'

One of the worst incidents in the entire raid occurred at York Street mill. The mill dominated the area, towering over the dwellings of the poor which encircled it. It was reputedly the largest of its kind in the world and was a likely Luftwaffe target. It had suffered several early hits before being struck, at about 1 a.m., by a land mine. This caused a rear wall, six storeys high and over sixty yards long, to collapse without warning. Forty-two houses in Sussex Street and Vere Street were demolished, a further twenty-one were damaged, and a number of small shelters were pulverised by the massive pieces of falling debris. Later, officials were unable to say for certain whether the widespread devastation had been caused solely by the disintegration of the wall or had also been due in part to smaller bombs falling at more or less the same time. Even as the raid continued, rescue work began. Bryce Millar remembered people, in despair and desperation, digging for relatives with their bare hands. Their mood was one of anger as well as of fear. Two policemen, Alfred King and Robert Moore, helped organise and lead the search. Moore recalled that although fifty to sixty people were rescued from the rubble, by dawn dozens of dead bodies lay on the footpath. The final death toll was thirty-five.

Meanwhile a parachute mine and several bombs fell nearby on the closely packed houses and terraces in and around Duncairn Gardens. Arthur Jackson lived in Hogarth Street. Its name became almost synonymous with the death and destruction caused by this raid. He recalls that between 2 and 3 a.m., both top and bottom ends of the street suffered direct hits simultaneously. From the coal hole under the stairs, he felt the whole floor of the house ripple and rise up beneath him; its roof and walls collapsed. Stunned and shaken, he and his family dragged themselves from the rubble and followed the surge of people picking their way towards the dubious safety of the basement in Mountcollyer public elementary school. They ran past burning houses and churches; incendiary bombs were 'falling like confetti'. The immediate area was devastated. In Hogarth Street alone over seventy houses were destroyed and forty-five people died. Ruth Street, Upper Canning Street and Mervue Street also suffered extensive damage.

Josephine Downey lived in Hillman Street, one hundred yards away on the opposite side of Duncairn Gardens. That evening she had gone to a dance at the Paradise Club on Donegall Street when suddenly the manager interrupted the entertainment to make an announcement. He stated that there had been an alert and that 'they could stay or go'. She decided immediately that she must try to reach home. As the trams were not running, she walked briskly, her path lit by the moonlight, the flares and the brilliant shafts of light streaming up from the newly arrived searchlights at Victoria barracks. She had scarcely turned into Hillman Street when the bombs began to fall and, still in her dance clothes, she joined her family in their vigil under the stairs. During occasional lulls in the attack, they could hear close by a neighbour singing gently to her children in a vain effort to console them.

After a short time the Downeys became aware of the acrid smell of smoke coming from an upstairs bedroom. Unheard, an incendiary bomb had crashed through their roof. Josephine's brother and Mr Duff, a friend who happened to be in Belfast overnight, went upstairs and quite quickly succeeded in extinguishing it. Fatefully, on their way back down again, Mr Duff paused to look out through a window. At that precise instant the parachute mine struck Duncairn Gardens, the gable of the house disintegrated and he was buried and killed by the falling masonry. The family was initially stunned, silent, and uncertain about what had happened. Then they 'began to yell to see who was alive and who wasn't', Josephine's sister becoming hysterical. Amid the debris, dust and darkness, she 'didn't know whether the others were there or not'. Josephine herself had ribs broken and a shoulder dislocated and she remembers her father stating later that at the moment the bomb detonated, he 'felt that his heart would burst' from the force of the blast. Soon afterwards, when the wardens had led them to a shelter, her mother suffered a heart attack. Josephine recalls that her mother was a 'very modest woman', and when the doctor indicated that he would have to undo her clothes, she replied: 'No, not in front of all these people.' Even after the all-clear their nightmare continued. They passed the ruins of a shelter on the corner of Atlantic Avenue and the Antrim Road. It had been demolished by a direct hit from a bomb which later expert analysis revealed

Rescue and salvage work in progress on the Antrim Road, opposite Eia Street, after the 15–16 April raid; some buses are already back in action. (Imperial War Museum)

it was 'a terrible night. . .All night the hum of planes overhead, the firing of AA guns, bombing, flares. . . [but] the parish escaped more or less unscathed. . .nothing very serious occurred.' The people appeared to be 'quiet' generally, but 'frightened in the neighbourhood of Mackies' foundry' on the Springfield Road, where many incendiaries had fallen. He concluded: 'Providence has watched over us this night. Deo Gratias'. Mackies was actually hit by a number of incendiaries which were dealt with promptly by an alert team of fire-watchers, and only minor damage resulted. High explosives also fell in the Eastland Street–Conway Street area nearby, killing two air raid precautions wardens. James Gracey, the senior warden on duty there, was later recommended for his bravery. An official report stated that while bombs and debris were still falling, he entered burning houses 'in response to cries and screams' and on 'practically every attempt brought people into the street'. Five hours after the all-clear, a bomb that had fallen at the corner of Springfield Avenue and Cavendish Street exploded, destroying eight houses.

Wilton's Funeral Parlour (right), Crumlin Road, reduced to a shell after the 15–16 April raid. (Wilton Funeral Service)

The Shankill Road largely escaped the worst of the night's devastation, but for one major incident that resulted in appalling carnage and that scarred itself indelibly into popular recollections of the raid. Standing on the flat roof of a mill on North Howard Street, Kenneth Taylor, a lorry driver and member of the Auxiliary Fire Service, saw a dark object drifting silently

Interior view of Wilton's Funeral Parlour, showing the extent of the devastation after the 15–16 April raid. (Wilton Funeral Service)

past, about twenty feet above his head. Initially he mistook it for a Luftwaffe pilot who had baled out – until it struck the ground. In fact it was a very large parachute mine and it fell within fifteen feet of a crowded public shelter in Percy Street. The suction created by the explosion seconds later was greater than its walls were built to withstand. They crumpled and those inside were left exposed to the fury of the blast. Simultaneously, the shelter's huge concrete roof was blown almost two yards sideways before hitting the ground, killing some people and pinning others beneath the wreckage. An official report describes 'a great deal of confusion and hysteria', as people in adjacent, damaged houses 'ran into the danger of the open street'. Rescue work began at once, though at first no medical help was available. With the aid of jacks from a local builder's yard, the concrete roof was eventually wedged up enabling some of those trapped beneath to crawl or to be pulled to safety. Mary Agnes Mercer recalls a local doctor, Dr Jameson, having to amputate the legs of some of those still trapped by the debris in order to release them. Casualties were treated on the pavement, the bombs still falling. The final death toll was thirty. Joe Barrett was among those who

Ewart's weaving mill, Crumlin Road, the object a serious incendiary attacl in the 15–16 April raid. (Ulster Folk and Transport Museum)

helped in the rescue effort; he recalled that in some instances he was carrying out the limbs of occupants, so badly had they been crushed by debris and torn by the blast. Next morning, eyewitnesses saw 'pieces of human body lying' across the road; water from broken mains was running down the street like a river in spate; and an entire block of buildings beside Percy Street Gospel Hall was on fire. At least two householders from Westmoreland Street, who had gone on holiday over Easter, returned to find decaying corpses in their back yards.

After the Dockside raid, Billy Boyd's father had experienced an ominous dream in which two coffins had floated downwards, suspended from a parachute. The dream was now transformed into horrifying reality. During the early part of this second attack, the whole family had remained together at their home in Percy Street. There was insufficient room under their reinforced dining table and as the bombing became more intense, on their father's suggestion, two of Billy's brothers went to Percy Street shelter; when they arrived there, it was full. They were standing at the corner of Percy Street and the Shankill Road when the parachute mine landed. Both were killed instantly by the blast; 'there was no sign of injury to them of any kind'. At the same time the force of the explosion caught the end house of the row in which the Boyds lived. The whole terrace collapsed and folded under the impact. When Billy regained consciousness, he was 'up to [his] neck in bricks, surrounded by flames and smoke, and feeling numbed, but no fear'. Just one gable of his house was still standing. Eventually he was rescued, along with his father and the rest of his family, by firemen wearing gas masks.

Only some parts of east Belfast experienced death and destruction comparable in extent to the stricken areas north of the city. During the early part of the raid, Jimmy Penton's most vivid memory was of the roar of anti-aircraft fire from gun turrets at Victoria Park, the top of Mackies' textile mill, the HMS *Furious* and, more distantly, from the Castlereagh Hills. The shrapnel, he recalls, 'was falling like raindrops'. His first concern was to assist his grandmother, then in her nineties, to the nearest public shelter, which was located on Dee Street. It was hot, humid and filled to overflowing. After standing near its entrance for a short time, he observed an awesome spectacle – a large parachute mine floating gently down. It was, he believed, 'meant for' Mackies, but narrowly skimmed over the top of its assumed target. Seconds later it landed on the vulnerable, poor but well-kept terraces of Tamar Street and Carew Street. Jimmy Penton recalls 'the ground erupting like an earthquake, the immediate area blown to pieces, the houses flattened'. A shower of bricks hurtled over and crashed into the shelter; fortunately, because of its position behind a railway embankment, it suffered only minimal blast damage.

However, on the other side of the Newtownards Road, near Templemore Avenue, public shelters were hit by high explosives. Billy McNeill, a police constable based at Mountpottinger station, described the scene afterwards as 'a shambles, total devastation, ambulance workers bringing people and parts of bodies out, legs, bits of torso'. Billy McNeill had himself been fortunate on two occasions earlier in the raid. He had been off duty, at his home in Loopland Avenue, off the Castlereagh Road, when the first bombs fell. One of them landed directly outside his house, blowing railings through his windows, bringing down ceilings and blasting doors off their hinges. A little later, as he worked to rescue neighbours from their shattered houses, he was informed of serious high-explosive damage in the Woodstock Road area and of 'tramlines jutting thirty feet into the air'. Before proceeding in this direction, he urinated in the newly formed crater outside his home, quite oblivious to the fact that it contained a delayed-action device, one of almost thirty dropped during this raid. After a few minutes, it violently erupted; by then he had walked barely two hundred yards up the road.

Damage throughout this area of the city was extensive. At the Oval football grounds the stand was demolished, the pitch was severely cratered and the entrance gates and parts of the perimeter fence blown away. A wing of the Ulster Hospital on Templemore Avenue was destroyed. The floor of the swimming pool of the public baths nearby was littered with incendiaries which had crashed through the glass roof and spluttered out harmlessly in the water. Fires had broken out in the more distant Stormont estate;

incendiaries had ignited timber transferred there from the port for security reasons after the Dockside raid. Houses close by, some of which belonged to leading civil servants, were wrecked by high explosives.

The fires throughout much of east Belfast were intense. Mary Wallace, who was then just eleven years old and lived beside the ropeworks, off Bloomfield Avenue, spent much of the night with her family in the coal hole under the stairs of her home. Her brother had diarrhoea and was vomiting with fear. She remembers her amazement when she glimpsed briefly out through a window: 'The sky was red, pure red. You would have thought that someone had set fire to the world.' Some time later they went to the nearest shelter which 'stank', despite her mother's weekly efforts at scrubbing and cleaning it. There they prayed and sang hymns and choruses. The words of one chorus remain fresh in her mind, though she is uncertain of its origins:

God is our refuge,
Be not afraid,
He will protect you
In an air raid.
Bombs may be falling
Danger is near,
He will protect you
Till the all-clear.

Despite the operation of the smoke screen, the major industrial sites in Ballymacarrett and Sydenham did not escape the attentions of the Luftwaffe. German crews reported as many as thirty to forty good-size fires in the eastern portion of the dock. At 11.35 p.m. the Harland and Wolff shipyard was hit by large high-explosive bombs, which affected the Queen's yard in particular. A government report said of one mine, almost the last dropped in the area, that 'from a damage point of view [it] could not have been more perfectly placed'. The boiler factory was struck, and many cranes and roofs collapsed, which caused serious blackout problems later. The buildings were flimsy and afforded little protection either to men or equipment. Although the resulting fires were extinguished in less than one hour, there were over forty casualties, and in the short-term war production for the Admiralty was halved. Meanwhile at Short and Harland four almost complete Stirling aircraft were ignited by explosions as they sat on the final erection line of the main factory, adjacent to the runway. Firemen had the grim task of freeing the charred and broken bodies of fire-watchers from the twisted wreckage. Here also, output was significantly disrupted; two weeks after the raid it was still 25 per cent below the normally anticipated level.

Partly through sheer good fortune, the port itself escaped virtually unscathed. There were no direct hits against any vessels, though the HMS *Furious*, the only ship to join in the anti-aircraft barrage, experienced a number of near misses which damaged its lifeboats, hull and superstructure.

Reconstruction work beginning at the Ulster Hospital, Templemore venue, east Belfast. (Public Record Office of Northern Ireland)

Elsewhere within the area of the harbour, no fewer than ten parachute mines failed to explode. In most cases they dropped into a cushion of mud and when uncovered at low tide, they were demolished where they lay. The highly vulnerable harbour power station was a vital Luftwaffe target as it met most of Northern Ireland's electricity needs. The bombers succeeded in striking it with high explosives early in the attack but the resulting small fire was quickly extinguished. However, at E.T. Green's, the flour mill on Donegall Quay, a delayed-action bomb exploded five hours after the all-clear and caused extensive damage.

An official report of the raid stated that it left 'the main centre of the city and shopping area practically unaffected'. It was fortunate, therefore, that at the Ulster Hall in Bedford Street, Delia Murphy, a popular singer, should have encouraged her large and appreciative audience to remain in their seats and sing on throughout the attack. Of course not all did so. Jimmy Magee, the gardener at Clonard Monastery, left hurriedly, convinced that he would be safer in the monastery's grounds. On his arrival he was amazed to find a number of the priests sitting calmly in the garden and he mildly rebuked them, commenting that 'this was a quare carry-on'. Soon afterwards, all retreated to the safety of the cellar. For others, leaving the concert was a prelude to tragedy. Jimmy Doherty recalls that some of his colleagues in the air raid precautions service had also attended it. As they returned home, he last heard them walking up Clifton Street, still singing to keep their spirits up. They failed to notice a parachute bomb which came down and struck a church on Trinity Street. All of them died in the subsequent explosion. The bodies of the Hill family, who lived beside the church, were never recovered; they were later declared dead in a coroner's court. Yet, incredibly, wardens found two other people, shaken but still alive, at the bottom of the bomb crater. The worst single incident in the history of the air raid precautions service occurred nearby when the post at Unity Street was hit. Twelve deaths resulted, five of them wardens.

Although much of the city centre survived unscathed, a number of its familiar landmarks were damaged in the course of this attack. The Victoria barracks, another important Luftwaffe target, received a direct hit and was

Damage at the boiler shop Queen's Works, Harland and Wolff, after the 15–1 April raid. (Harland and Wolff)

gutted by fire. The nurses' homes, both at Frederick Street and the Mater Hospital, suffered severely from fires caused by incendiaries. The Free Library in Royal Avenue was pockmarked by shrapnel and sustained considerable blast damage. Jimmy Mackey, a regular fireman, remembers well one of the explosions which occurred in this vicinity. He was 'suited out' and on his way to attend fires in York Street in a seven-ton fire tender which was travelling down Donegall Street when high explosives fell adjacent to the library. On impact the vehicle was blown more than twelve inches into the air, without serious injury to the firemen. Unfortunately, around the corner, a car and trailer pump being manned by two Auxiliary Fire Service men, A.P. Castle and G. Spence, caught the full force of the blast; both were killed. They were the final casualties suffered by either the regular or auxiliary service during the German air raids on Belfast.

In Academy Street, the air raid precautions headquarters was destroyed by fire. A nurse's report from the neighbouring casualty post, which was itself fortunate to escape the bombing, provides a vivid insight into the terrible events of this night. It describes those who arrived for treatment. Casualty number seven was carried in by two policemen early in the raid:

> Both his legs were fractured and were almost severed and he was bleeding profusely. The Medical Officer decided that an amputation was necessary and this was performed. The patient was a warden and did not realize the extent of his injuries and kept urging us to hurry and put a bandage on as he had work to do and his helmet was blown off and he was anxious to find it.

Soon afterwards, a mother and baby were brought in from the ruins of their home. The baby was covered with blood and 'was clasped so tightly in her mother's arms that we had to gently force the arms apart. . . On examination the little one was found to be without a scratch, the mother having protected her with her own body. The blood was from her own serious injuries. Her eyes were destroyed.' Later, when the raid was at its height, a child appeared, supported by a policeman. He had found her 'wandering in York Street. Unable to give her name and address, she was recorded as "little girl, blue eyes, carried in by policeman, found in York Street".' Her father was later admitted and he claimed her. Their house, he explained, had been demolished and somehow she had got out and 'wandered away'.

During the raid, many casualty posts were stretched beyond their capacity, some dealing with up to 150 cases and with as many as 40 patients at any one time. Also, in the stricken areas the posts themselves risked bombing. A number were forced to evacuate to different premises as the raid progressed. Telephone and electricity failure were common. Overcrowding was endemic; it was caused not only by the growing number of injured needing treatment but also by people fleeing in panic from their homes, damaged or otherwise, in search of rest and comfort.

The hospital service faced problems which were possibly even more acute. At an early stage the Mater Hospital on the Crumlin Road was so overwhelmed that it could not accept further stretcher cases and, as a priority, its surplus was transferred elsewhere next morning. Soon after the attack began some members of staff and those patients who were sufficiently mobile attended Mass in the chapel. Many then huddled into shelters in the hospital grounds. Later, with bombs falling throughout the immediate area and death apparently imminent, a priest gave general absolution. Joseph Crilly, a medical student, was fire-watching on the roof when the first of the dead began to arrive. He was called down and helped to carry in the almost unmarked bodies of some uniformed soldiers, and women from the Auxiliary Territorial Service. They had been based at Eglinton Street school nearby and were killed by the blast from a torpedo bomb which had devastated the street. Already the capacity of the hospital morgue, which contained just three slabs, had been exhausted.

There were similar scenes at the Royal Victoria Hospital on the Grosvenor Road. Agnes Campbell, who was a nurse there, observed that the 'injuries to victims were not as severe as you might expect', as so many were 'killed outright' or survived unhurt. Most were suffering either from burns or from shock. In their panic, others had injured themselves by bumping into lampposts or each other as they sought safety in the blacked-out streets during the attack. Many were so badly traumatised that 'they did not know their names'. Nora Carse, then a trainee nurse, well remembers the confusion caused by the unexpected influx of casualties, aggravated by having to work by torchlight. People were admitted without name tags and their clothes were piled under beds. She can still recall her sense of horror when

Opposite
In the foreground, a bomb crater, and behind it the twisted stern-framing of a corvette under construction at Harland and Wolff, after the 15–16 April raid. (Harland and Wolff)

she walked past an empty surgical theatre and saw a recently amputed leg still lying on the operating table, in full view of patients.

After about four hours of constant attack and with apparently no end to the raid in sight, William McCready became quite fatalistic about his chances of survival. Many must have felt as he did. He was sitting on the settee at his Keadyville Avenue home and he wrote:

> Feeling shaky. I was belching wind every few minutes but sometime after 3.00 a.m. I became reconciled to the worst. I thought for a few minutes of our bodies being dug out next day. I thought of all my friends and wondered if I would ever see them again. For a moment I imagined their faces next day in the office and some one saying: 'Did you hear about old McCready? he was killed in the air raid last night.'

South Belfast once again escaped with minimal damage. When the raid started, Patrick Shea records in *Voices and the Sound of Drums* that he was at his 'fiancée's home in the southern suburbs. No bombs fell near us, but from an upstairs window I watched fountains of debris from exploding bombs rising through the beams of the searchlights in the Crumlin/Oldpark/Antrim Road area.' In Elmwood Avenue Moya Woodside recorded her impressions 'dazed and mentally battered after 5½ hours of blitz'. She was having a bath when the sirens had erupted and had then gone to bed hoping to sleep as she had done during the Dockside raid. But this proved to be impossible:

> After about an hour or so, one started listening and waiting for the bombs. . . The Nazi planes kept coming back for all the world like some gigantic swarm of insects whose drone was only ineffectually interrupted by bangs and crashes.

Like William McCready, she also adopted an air of resignation:

> At 3.00 am I could stand it no longer and feeling desperately frightened and somewhat hysterical, I put on my dressing gown and went down to join my husband in his vigil below the stairs. I grabbed the whiskey decanter and with shaky hands drank off about a quarter tumbler neat to try and pull myself together (usually I dislike whiskey and never touch it). We then sat down in the pantry and just waited. After a while I recovered my self control and began to reflect mournfully that this was civilization in 1941 – sitting shivering, bored and frightened in a cubby hole at 3.30 am. I thought too of Madrid and how the Spanish people had neither defences nor the sympathy of the outside world. Well, now it was our turn!

As she listened, 'trying to analyse peculiar sounds', one feature of the raid increasingly puzzled and disturbed her. Even after 'an hour or so', she began 'wondering why the [anti-aircraft] barrage was not louder'. She noted: 'For lengthy periods no noise could be heard but the planes kept flying about. One fretted: Why don't they fire at them? and where are our fighters?'

CASUALTIES FEARE HEAVY IN ULSTER

Raid Extended Ove Most of Province

"VICIOUS, INDISCRIMINATE

THE FOLLOWING COMMUNIQUE W ISSUED THIS MORNING BY T MINISTRY OF PUBLIC SECURIT NORTHERN IRELAND, AND HEA QUARTERS R.A.F., NORTHERN IRELAN

"A HEAVY FORCE OF ENEM BOMBERS CARRIED OUT AN ATTAC LASTING SEVERAL HOURS OVER A AREA COMPRISING PRACTICALLY TH WHOLE OF NORTHERN IRELAND.

"THE INTENSITY OF THE ATTAC VARIED. IN SOME AREAS IT WA VICIOUS AND INDISCRIMINATE.

"DAMAGE HAS BEEN SUSTAINED B SOME INDUSTRIAL PREMISES, BU MANY OF THE BOMBS FELL ON RES DENTIAL PROPERTY.

"FROM PRELIMINARY REPORTS IS FEARED THAT CASUALTIES MAY B HEAVY.

"FURTHER DETAILS WILL B ANNOUNCED LATER."

IT IS UNDERSTOOD THAT THE WIN OF A HOSPITAL AND NURSES' HOM HAVE BEEN DAMAGED.

GUNS ROARED FOR MANY HOUR AND ON SEVERAL OCCASIONS THER WERE BURSTS OF MACHINE-GUN FIRE.

Public transport services continued runni until their usual hour of stopping.

PEOPLE TRAPPED

Numerous craters were left in roadways. A bomb in one street failed to explode and families in neighbouring houses were evacuated.

The occupants of a car are believed to hav been killed.

Northern Whig, 16 April 1941

HEAVY RAID ON ULSTER

INDISCRIMINATE BOMBING

CASUALTIES MAY BE HEAVY

NORTHERN IRELAND experienced the full fury of German frightfulness last night.

The following communique was issued this morning by the Ministry of Public Security, Northern Ireland, and headquarters, R.A.F., Northern Ireland:—

"A heavy force of enemy bombers carried out an attack lasting several hours over an area comprising practically the whole of Northern Ireland.

"The intensity of the attack varied. In some areas it was vicious and indiscriminate. Damage has been sustained by some industrial premises, but many of the bombs fell on residential property.

"From preliminary reports it is feared that casualties may be heavy. Further details will be announced later."

Hundreds of Bombs

Hundreds of bombs, including high explosive and incendiaries, were dropped.

Ground defences put up a strong barrage and night fighters were also in action, but the attack was kept up intermittently for several hours.

The raiders, who seemed to come in waves, dropped flares and then released high explosive bombs. Anti-aircraft defences employed machine guns to extinguish the flares. At one time the whole sky was lit by the flares drifting to earth.

Considerable damage was done to commercial premises as well as dwelling-houses.

Defences kept the enemy at a good height but occasionally a machine came quite low in search of a target.

Civil defence services mobilised smartly and operated smoothly and efficiently in exceptionally trying circumstances.

As the raid progressed, bombing became indiscriminate. A library, a hospital and a church were damaged.

Belfast News-Letter, 16 April 1941

When shopping in the city centre next morning, she observed that these questions monopolised much of the conversation: 'Everyone is asking: "Why didn't we hear a proper barrage?" "They just did as they liked", is being said on all sides.' The feeling that they had been left to endure the attack more or less unprotected burned deeply into people's memories of the Easter Tuesday raid. Many years later eyewitnesses recalled that 'The Luftwaffe took control of Belfast, picking their spot at will'; 'They had the whole town to themselves'; 'They attacked without let or hindrance'; 'One felt that they were there by right'. It was also widely assumed, at the time and since, that but for the aircraft carrier, HMS *Furious*, Belfast would have suffered even greater devastation. It was in communication with the anti-aircraft-operations control centre and the roar of its guns reverberated around the city. Such was the recoil caused by the discharge of its shells that the ship sheared loose from its moorings. None of the other vessels in the port opened fire except with machine guns aimed at the parachute flares.

Only contemporary press reports of the raid praised the role of the local active defences, some even claiming that the barrage had kept the German bombers at a good height. But such suggestions could not mask the reality. From the outset, as both the Northern Ireland government and the Luftwaffe appreciated, Belfast was extremely vulnerable. In *The Blitz, Then and Now*, vol. 2, Kenneth Wakefield comments that it was 'the most unprotected major city in the United Kingdom'. Using their inadequate supplies of outmoded equipment, the anti-aircraft batteries fired without success until 1.45 a.m. At that moment a large parachute mine fell at the junction of Oxford Street and East Bridge Street. Fortunately, though it landed within fifteen yards of a shelter crowded with over one hundred people and sucked a four-and-a-half-inch outer skin of bricks from its walls, no one inside was injured. However, the explosion did cause substantial blast damage to surrounding buildings and in particular to the central telephone exchange, where telephone cables were ripped asunder. The repercussions of this were dramatic: the main switchboard was abandoned and soon afterwards, trunk lines out of the city to Liverpool, Manchester, Glasgow and London were severed and many local lines cut. As a direct result, Belfast was left virtually without protection. The proper co-ordination of defences became impossible once anti-aircraft command headquarters had lost its most vital means of communication. It was for this reason that the barrage practically ceased, and not, as was widely rumoured at the time, because the anti-aircraft guns had overheated or ammunition supplies had become exhausted. Damage to the telephone exchange also resulted in Royal Air Force fighter sector cross-channel operational circuits being severed. The radar direction lines between Aldergrove and the filter station at Preston were broken. The sector controller of Hurricane fighters could only guess at the number of enemy bombers and at their directions. Consequently, he instructed his pilots not to approach within five miles of Belfast.

Some time around 1.45 a.m. appears to have been a turning point in the development of the raid. Not only did the local active defences virtually collapse then, but also, more or less simultaneously, the fires in Belfast began to rage out of control. At this vital stage in the attack the water supply in some of the worst-affected areas of the city dropped to critically low levels. This was due to many factors – the tide turning, the rupturing of conduits and mains, and the large number of firemen drawing on the volumes of water available. The supply of hose was also insufficient and by now much of it had been damaged, so making the necessary 'deep lifts' impossible. When Victoria barracks sustained a direct hit, nearby hydrants were found to be 'totally ineffective'. According to military authorities, local firemen had the situation 'well in hand' until 1.45 a.m., but thereafter, 'the task was beyond their capacity'.

By 2.30 a.m. many of Belfast's main arterial roads had become impassable because of extensive fires and fallen debris; they included: York Street; Shore Road; Antrim Road; Crumlin Road; North Queen Street; Corporation Street; Albertbridge Road; and Newtownards Road. Progressively, by 3.15 a.m., help had been summoned from each of the civil defence regions in Northern Ireland. Yet little over an hour later, at 4.30 a.m., officials confirmed there were 4 'conflagrations' in the city, spreading and out of control, 19 'serious' fires, requiring 11 to 30 pumps, and 116 smaller fires. In these circumstances and with the Luftwaffe continuing to attack virtually at will, the Ministry of Public Security sought further assistance. At 4.25 a.m. an urgent telegram was sent to the Home Security War Room in London requesting fifty trailers from Glasgow and Liverpool. A Westminster government report, written at about 6 a.m., indicates that its officials then knew little about the raid on Belfast 'owing to the break-down in communications'. Thus it underestimated the scale of the Luftwaffe attack, assuming just sixty bombers were involved. None the less, it was already clear that there had been 'heavy casualties', with perhaps two hundred dead, and that there were a 'large number of fires, many serious', some of which 'would show light tonight'. Help was dispatched promptly: twenty-seven large pumps with crews came from Glasgow by Admiralty ferry and special train out of Larne, Co. Antrim, ten came direct from Liverpool, aboard a destroyer, and more from Preston by Heysham steamer; a total of forty-two pumps and four hundred firemen.

Meanwhile, a further and more momentous decision had been taken. At about 4 a.m., R.D. Harrison, City Commissioner of the Royal Ulster Constabulary, sent an urgent message by dispatch rider to the War Room at Stormont, suggesting that assistance be requested from Dublin. Based at the police barracks in Chichester Street, Harrison was ideally placed to observe and absorb the alarming deterioration in local conditions. Also, the civil defence control room was housed in the same building and it received a constant stream of messages, delivered by hand, updating it on the scale of the night's devastation. Soon afterwards, the commissioner's suggestion was transmitted to John MacDermott at the Ministry of Public Security,

The Northern Whig and Belfast Post, April 17, 1941

'CO-OP' MILK
PASTEURISED
—the Milk the Doctors order
BELFAST CO-OPERATIVE SOCIETY, LTD
DAIRY DEPT., FEDERATION STREET
Tel. 57451

BLACK-OUT: To-night, 9.0—To-morrow Morning, 5.46

The Northern Whig
AND BELFAST POST

No. 41,373 BELFAST, THURSDAY, APRIL 17, 1941 ONE PENNY.

BELFAST'S
Balance Your Budget
MURPHY
With a Pre-Tax Set.
ROSEMARY RADIO & ELECTRICAL Co.
31, ROSEMARY ST. Phone 24771
RADIO CENTRE

200 FEARED DEAD IN NORTHERN IRELAND BLITZ

Germans Claim Attack Heavy As Any Launched On British Ports

"HUNDREDS OF BOMBERS" LEAVE BELFAST STREETS IN RUINS

A HEAVY DEATH-ROLL—POSSIBLY 200—IS EXPECTED AS A RESULT OF YESTERDAY MORNING'S GERMAN AIR RAID ON NORTHERN IRELAND. RESIDENTIAL DISTRICTS IN BELFAST WERE THE MAIN TARGETS, AND SECTIONS OF THE CITY FAR REMOVED FROM MILITARY OBJECTIVES WERE LAID IN RUINS.

WORKERS' HOMES WIPED OUT

The enemy claim that hundreds of bombers pressed home the attack, and declare it was in every way as heavy as those directed against armaments centres and ports in Britain. But although industrial premises were damaged, working-class districts took the heaviest battering.

OUR HEROES

People there withstood the ordeal in a way which has drawn praise from English evacuees and military alike. Deeds of marvellous endurance and heroism were performed by Civil Defence services and ordinary civilians.

Young Men Rush to Join Up

British Government Tells Ulster
ALL WE CAN SEND IS YOURS!

Belfast Hospital Blitzed

A corner of a hospital shows the nature of the Nazi attack on Northern Ireland, which was described as vicious and indiscriminate.

5 ENEMY SUPPLY SHIPS, 3 DESTROYERS ANNIHILATED

TRIPOLI CONVOY FIGHT

THE ADMIRALTY STATES:—

"BRITISH NAVAL FORCES ON TUESDAY NIGHT INTERCEPTED AND ANNIHILATED A SOUTH-BOUND ENEMY CONVOY BETWEEN SICILY AND TRIPOLI. THE CONVOY CONSISTED OF FIVE SUPPLY SHIPS, ESCORTED BY THREE DESTROYERS.

"Two of the supply ships were vessels of about 5,000 tons, heavily laden with motor transport. These were sunk.

"Another was an ammunition ship of about 4,000 tons, which blew up with a terrific explosion.

"The other two ships were vessels of about 3,000 tons, probably transports. These were also blown up.

"The convoy escort consisted of the Italian destroyer Luca Tarigo, of 1,628 tons, and two smaller destroyers. All three were sunk.

BRITISH DESTROYER TORPEDOED

NAVY SHELL LIBYAN COAST

THE Admiralty announced last night:—

"The C.-in-C., Mediterranean, reports that the enemy's operations on the Libyan coast are being constantly and successfully

No Immediate Threat To Egypt

LAST night's communique from British G.H.Q. in Cairo reported that vigorous action by our patrols in the Sollum sector on the Libyan and Egyptian borders had again caused the enemy losses in men and vehicles and prisoners had been taken. The communique added that the situation was unchanged in the Tobruk area.

Push Not Yet Exhausted

---

who had been telephoning the War Room every fifteen minutes throughout the raid. He responded favourably. From his home in east Belfast, MacDermott could see for himself the red glow growing ever brighter in the night sky; explosions had already blown his windows in and the shrapnel clattered onto his roof tiles. While making some of his telephone calls, he had thought it advisable to crouch for cover below the desk in his study. At 4.15 a.m. he telephoned Sir Basil Brooke, who was staying near Stormont, and asked 'for authority to order fire engines from Eire'. Brooke noted in his diary: 'I gave him authority as it is obviously a question of expediency.' At 4.35 a.m. the telegrammed request was sent to the town clerk in Dublin using the railway telegraph service, as telephone lines between Belfast and the South had been severed.

Eamon de Valera, the Éire Taoiseach, was awakened and informed of the urgent nature of the telegram. He agreed to provide the assistance required, and within two hours, the War Room at Stormont had been advised of his intentions. Seventy men and thirteen fire engines were assembled and dispatched from Dublin, Dundalk, Drogheda, and Dun Laoghaire, arriving in Belfast at about 10 a.m. It is possible, though improbable, that the Taoiseach's reaction was influenced by Cardinal Joseph MacRory, Primate of All-Ireland. Patrick Finlay, one of the Dublin firemen, had vague recollections of his chief fire superintendent, Major Comerford, an ex-army officer, appealing for volunteers at Tara Street, saying: 'The Primate has

spoken to de Valera and "Dev" is asking us to help.' It was certainly a technical breach of Irish neutrality and therefore a courageous and generous response. Robert Fisk in *In Time of War* states that the German minister to the Irish Free State, Eduard Hempel, observed: 'We could have protested, but... nobody from Germany protested.' It was indeed fortunate for Ireland that the German authorities should have adopted this viewpoint. Southern leaders subsequently defended their action. During a visit to Boston, Frank Aiken, the long-standing Fianna Fáil cabinet minister, justified the decision before the American press, stating: 'They are Irish people too.' On 21 April 1941 the *Irish Times* reported that two days earlier, at Castlebar in Co. Mayo, de Valera himself spoke of the raid as a 'disaster', as though it fell within the category of natural calamity rather than a premeditated act of war. He also indicated that help had been given 'whole-heartedly... they are all our people'.

FIREBOMB FRITZ
will come again —
Are you ready
to put him out?
YES! Britain's Fire Guard — we men and women of Britain — are resolved and ready to save our factories, our railways, our food, our homes. Fire Guard work is often dull, sometimes dangerous, but it's a job that's got to be done. Our heart and soul is in it. We train and we practise. We know our sectors like the backs of our hands — every corner, every roof top. We watch. We climb ladders, work pumps, wield sandbags. We will shatter Firebomb Fritz and all the Nazi horrors he stands for.
Fire Guard Tips No. 1.
Firebombs that fall in the street are usually harmless unless they are close to something inflammable, like a motor vehicle. Look for bombs on buildings first.
BRITAIN SHALL NOT BURN!
ISSUED BY THE MINISTRY OF PUBLIC SECURITY

Shortly before contact with Dublin had been made, it was decided, at 4.25 a.m., to put the Hiram Plan into operation immediately, using Belfast City Hall as headquarters. In effect, a state of emergency had been declared. As a consequence, MacDermott and the Ministry of Public Security became solely responsible for restoring, 'if not normality itself, at least a semblance of normality' as quickly as possible. At once dispatch riders were sent to inform Wilfrid Spender, who was a strong critic of the scheme. He and his family had spent the night in the 'strong room' of their home on the Belmont Road, his wife knitting, while his daughter attempted to read *Anna Karenina*. After the raid, they discovered that two huge sections from the bomb-releasing equipment of a German aircraft had dropped into their garden.

Set in its context, the decision to implement the emergency plan was manifestly justified. Even while it was being taken, a number of large parachute mines fell, shaking the city to its foundations; high explosives had already fallen in most districts, innumerable fires were raging, and no end to the raid seemed in sight, beyond hopes that the light of dawn might bring relief. However, predictably and rapidly, events were to prove that the task of restoring normality lay far beyond the competence of a single local ministry or any combination of them. All of the Government's plans had been utterly overwhelmed by the scale of the attack; as John Oliver, MacDermott's private secretary, observed, 'it made our schemes look woefully inadequate'.

'Well, it was a long night,' William McCready noted, 'but, at last, the dawn came and there was quietness.' At 4.55 a.m. the all-clear sounded, air raid precautions wardens ringing handbells in those areas where the electricity had failed. It came over six hours after the initial alert and just one hour before sunrise. But, in Ulster writer Joseph Tomelty's words, 'I don't think any of us noticed the dawn, for in a sense it had never been night.' A reporter on one of the Luftwaffe bombers described on German radio his final impressions of Belfast towards the end of the raid. He spoke of 'huge

fires. . . tremendous devastation, flashes of lightning from exploding bombs coming up towards us some hundreds of yards into the air, whole blocks of buildings on fire and pouring out smoke'.

We could lose the war by Fire! Be ready for FIREBOMB FRITZ
We could lose the war by fire! We could. But we WON'T. We men and women of Britain's Fire Guard will see to that. Fire Guard work is often dull. Sometimes it's dangerous. But it's work that's got to be done. So we put into it every ounce of enthusiasm we've got. We watch unceasingly! We train till we're really good! We know all the awkward places and how to get there. We won't be caught off guard as Firebomb Fritz will find.
FIRE GUARD TIPS. No. 2
It's not the fire-bomb that's important as a rule but the fire it starts. Deal with that fire first of all.
BRITAIN SHALL NOT BURN!
ISSUED BY THE MINISTRY OF HOME SECURITY

His account was by no means apocryphal. Much of Belfast was enveloped by flames which swept from the Cavehill Road and Crumlin Road down towards the docks and the commercial centre and spread across into Ballymacarrett. Although firemen worked beyond exhaustion, the task massively exceeded their resources and many fires were left to burn themselves out. An official report spoke of 'quiet residential areas enveloped in fire, torn apart by bombs'. It referred to 'marching ranks of flame spreading along main shopping areas towards the heart of the city, [eating] their way from street to street'. On the north side of the city, it described 'ruin-fringed roads, blocked by great heaps of smoking debris and acrid smelling craters, water [running] through the rubble', gas mains sprouting 'fountains of flames', people returning from 'hideouts', standing 'silent and numbed before the wreckage of what was once their homes'. The whole city was cloaked in a cloud of dust and ash. It permeated the streets and houses, and settled in a fine layer on trees and fields up to ten miles away. Smoke and fire spiralled hundreds of feet into the air, clearly visible from as far distant as the Carlingford hills on the border with the South. In Dromore, Co. Down, people, stunned and tense, watched for a time the great glow in the night sky, before making their way back to their homes, 'wondering what had taken place and what news [they] would hear when morning came'.

6
COUNTING THE COST
16 APRIL–3 MAY 1941

At the military hospital on the Stranmillis Road, Emma Duffin heard 'bit by bit' news of the night's devastation. Some of the accounts sounded exaggerated but 'it was obvious [to her] that a good deal of damage had been done'. She could see for herself lorries bringing the dead to the infirmary mortuary, 'the civilian hospitals being very full'. Next morning, like many others, she went into the city to survey and assess the extent of the destruction at first hand. With obvious relief, she noted that 'the centre was

Opposite
oldiers begin the grim task of rescue work on the Antrim Road after the 5–16 April raid; Duncairn Gardens is in the background. They were eventually to recover 240 bodies in Belfast after the ttack, 22 of them still alive. (Imperial War Museum)

alright'. After walking a little further, she met growing evidence of Luftwaffe activity; she saw a large crater in Royal Avenue, the Free Library 'pitted all over', and people boarding up windows, every pane of glass in 'the big Co-op' smashed, and 'only the shell' of Frederick Street nurses' home still standing. On her way up to Carlisle Circus 'ruins' fringed the footpaths. But it was only when she reached the Antrim Road that she began to realise the true extent of the damage. There she found 'side streets in ruins, houses reduced to dust'; a shelter where, she was informed, 'most of the occupants had been killed'; buses running at long intervals 'and so crowded'. In the blitzed area 'not a window was left unbroken'. Glimpses along the crumpled terraces 'showed demolition squads and military digging frantically'. She considered how 'awful it is to think that people might still be alive in those heaps of rubble' and that those who had died had been so 'unlikely. . . to die in the front line fighting Hitler'. Soon afterwards, she accepted the offer of a lift in a car and listening to the despairing tones of fellow passengers, she 'heard the voice of a woman asking for a child, a little boy in velvet trousers'.

To Moya Woodside, who was also downtown that morning, the bombed districts

> looked like photographs of Spain or China or some town in the last war, houses roofless, windowless, burnt out or burning, familiar landmarks gone, and in their place vast craters and mounds of rubble, the desolation indescribable. . . thousands and thousands must be homeless and as for the death toll – I shudder to think of the ghastly injuries and death which have occurred.

On this occasion she sensed that the atmosphere was 'completely different' from the morning after the Dockside raid. People, many with faces blackened and heads bandaged, were 'quiet and look harassed and weary. There is much less tendency to dilate on personal experiences'; though as the days went by, she found that they would talk of little else. Among the 'many soldiers', she noted feelings of anger and of impotence, they were swearing: 'If we could only get at them.' World War I veterans argued with passion that 'to be in the trenches was preferable. You had a rifle in your hand and could do something. In the house, it's like being a rat in a trap.' Even local newspaper reports, though constrained by censorship and considerations of public morale, could not fail to acknowledge the widespread mood of shock and despair. Reporters described: 'tear stained, mourning faces'; people 'wild-eyed' and 'dazed'; 'small bundles lying on pavements opposite the blackened, scarred walls of houses. . . all that many families had had time to retrieve'.

After their wedding on Easter Monday, the only honeymoon that Nellie Bell and her husband Bob could afford was a trip to Bangor next day. Much of the night that followed was spent in an air-raid shelter, close to York Road police station and about one hundred yards from her family's home in

The lower Antrim Road after the German air raids; in the foreground, McLaughlin's public house, in the background, the Phoenix. (Ulster Museum)

Crosscollyer Street. Many years later she could vividly recall her emotions and experiences immediately after the raid was over. She wrote:

> I will never forget when the all-clear went and we came out, the sky was pink. I don't think it was just dawn. There were fires everywhere and ambulances and fire engines roaring all over the place. Hundreds were killed that night. We could hardly walk we were so stiff and cold and of course shocked. We were afraid to look round the corner as we came to our house. We couldn't imagine it would still be there, but there it was. The whole gable end was cracked and windows all broken and inside was awful. The few presents we had got were buried under the glass and dirt from the bay window which was caved in. Anything breakable was broken. . . Anyhow we went to bed but it was automatic, I think, for we were up again and trying to get some tea made. I am kind of vague about that. I know I was very cold. . . the kitchen was full of soot and broken glass. . . Bob was very anxious about his mother. . . who lived top of Springfield Road. [We] set off to walk there. There was no transport of course. The whole way along it was terrible. At the top of Duncairn Gardens there had been a direct hit on a shelter. . . As we passed, the dead and injured were being brought out. . . The Phoenix bar was standing, no doors or windows on it. . . We went in and had a drink and then on our way right across to Springfield. . . They were all safe. . . I had not shed a tear the whole time but when we got to Springfield, after all the things I had seen on the way and the whole trauma of it all I was physically sick and cried and cried. Mrs Bell [her mother-in-law] really scolded me and said I should be glad we were all alive and I suppose she was right but I felt she was very unkind. . . I took a long time to forgive her for barging me as she did. I was only married after all. All my dreams and hopes and we didn't know what more was going to happen.

For William McCready also 'that day [Wednesday] was a nightmare'. He had witnessed similar scenes on the Whitewell Road where he cycled past 'men digging out dead women and children, who had been killed in their homes'. On York Street and North Queen Street 'ambulances and fire engines were seen and heard everywhere', and the roads were 'covered with broken glass and debris'. At the head post office in Royal Avenue 'hundreds of people were lined up waiting to withdraw money and send telegrams to relatives'. The air was thick with smoke and the lingering stench of burning, which permeated clothing, was inhaled with every breath. Stunned by what had happened during the night, John MacDermott went first to the city hall, headquarters of his emergency government set up under the Hiram Plan. There he was quietly greeted by Tommy Henderson, Independent Unionist MP for the Shankill, who assured him he could not be blamed, and taking him by the arm, said: 'How can you stop these things falling anyway?'

It was not until 2 p.m. on Wednesday, 16 April, that the fires were finally brought under control, many by then having burned themselves out. Even at 11 a.m. next day, a number still required a good deal of watching and cooling down. A military assessment after the attack stated bluntly that the local fire brigades had been completely overwhelmed by the task. These tragic circumstances were entirely predictable. During the previous month, a Home Office inquiry had recommended that the number of regular firemen in Belfast should be quadrupled and that there should also be a drastic increase in their supplies of hose, ladders and appliances. Reggie Briggs, who was then new to the service, recalls that he and his colleagues fought the fires as best they could throughout Easter Tuesday night and all next day. When exhausted, they snatched a few hours' sleep at headquarters, still wearing their uniforms.

New Belfast Fire Brigade Chief

Mr. John Smith, Chief Officer of Belfast Fire Brigade, has resigned, and Mr. Ben White, commandant of the Belfast Auxiliary Fire Service, has been appointed to the post.

Mr. Smith, who is a Scotsman, was for 16 years chief officer of Bootle Fire Brigade before coming to Belfast in 1931.

Mr. White led two parties of Belfast A.F.S. men who travelled to the South of England to acquire some actual fire-fighting experience under "blitz" conditions.

Northern Whig, 19 April 1941

Their morale cannot have been helped by widespread reports that the nerves of John Smith, Belfast's chief fire officer, had crumbled. He was an ageing Scot whose leadership had been severely censured in Westminster government reports even before the raid. After it, numerous eyewitnesses, including members of Southern crews, claim to have seen him, frightened and weeping, under a table at Chichester Street Fire Station, never having left his headquarters throughout. Some would argue that such accounts were deliberately exaggerated by leading figures within the Auxiliary Fire Service who were anxious to discredit officials from the old regular Belfast force and replace them with men from their own branch of the service. The matter was later raised at Stormont where Jack Beattie, Independent Labour MP, suggested that the whole episode graphically illustrated the 'folly that is pursued in bringing here people from outside who know nothing about the country and nothing about what they are doing'. In any case, Smith resigned on 17 April on grounds of 'ill health', submitting the appropriate medical certificate, but a Home Office official observed that his decision had been made 'apparently under pressure'.

BELFAST FIRE CHIEF'S RESIGNATION

Request on Medical Grounds

In the Northern House of Commons yesterday **Mr. MacDermott, K.C.**, Minister of Public Security, told **Mr. Beattie** (Soc., Pottinger) that he was informed that the Chief Officer of the Belfast Fire Brigade had requested to be allowed to resign his appointment on medical grounds and had furnished medical evidence in support of his request.

This request was agreed to and the officer's resignation accepted by the Belfast Civil Defence Authority.

Under an Order made by his Ministry on December 6, 1940, the Minister continued, the functions of Belfast Corporation relating to extinction of fires, whether exercisable under the Civil Defence Act or otherwise, had been transferred to Belfast Civil Defence Authority.

Northern Whig, 2 May 1941

Overall, Wilfrid Spender considered that the local fire services had put up

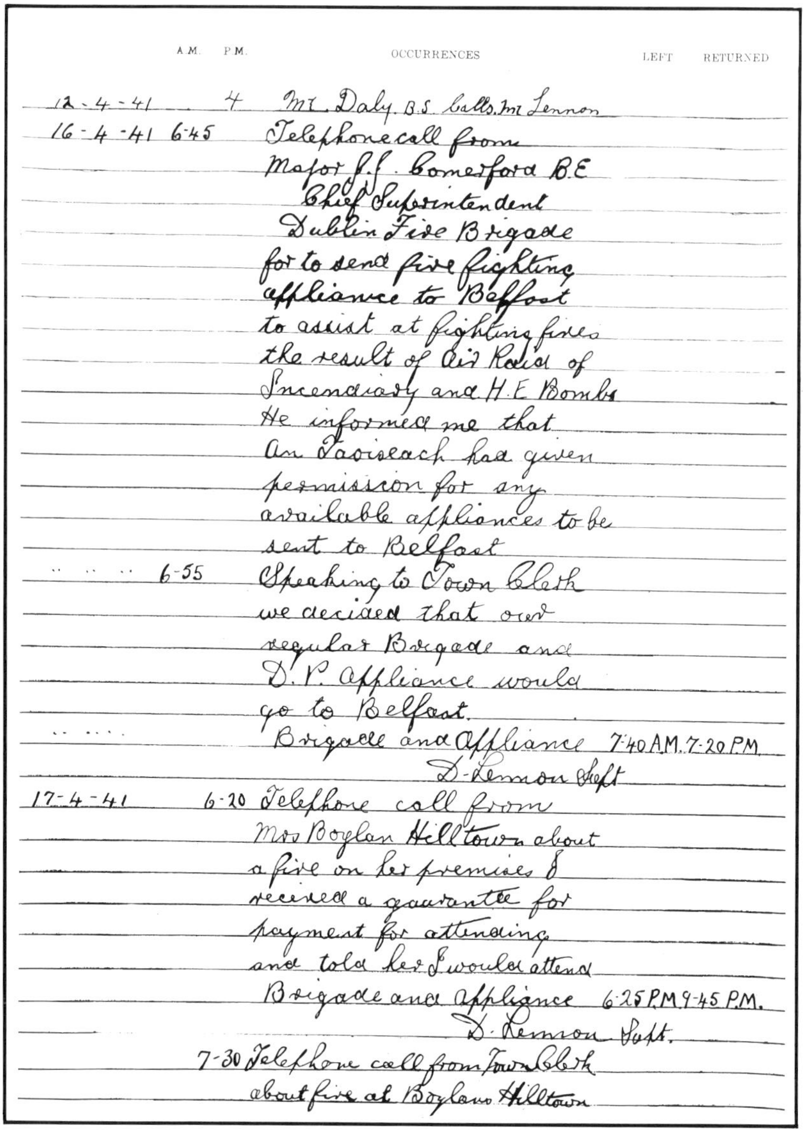
A.M. P.M. OCCURRENCES LEFT RETURNED

12-4-41 4 Mr Daly B.S. calls Mr Lennon
16-4-41 6.45 Telephone call from
Major J.J. Comerford B.E
Chief Superintendent
Dublin Fire Brigade
for to send fire fighting
appliance to Belfast
to assist at fighting fires
the result of Air Raid of
Incendiary and H.E Bombs
He informed me that
An Taoiseach had given
permission for any
available appliances to be
sent to Belfast
" " " 6.55 Speaking to Town Clerk
we decided that our
regular Brigade and
D.P. Appliance would
go to Belfast.
" " " Brigade and Appliance 7.40 A.M. 7.20 P.M.
D. Lennon Supt
17-4-41 6.20 Telephone call from
Mrs Boylan Hilltown about
a fire on her premises &
received a guarantee for
payment for attending
and told her I would attend
Brigade and Appliance 6.25 P.M. 9.45 P.M.
D. Lennon Supt.
7.30 Telephone call from Town Clerk
about fire at Boylans Hilltown

The call to assist with the fires in Belfast as recorded in the incident book on 16 April 1941 at Drogheda Fire Station. (Drogheda Fire Brigade)

a 'poor showing' and had given a 'poor impression of our organization' to units from Éire and Great Britain. However, such comments would appear to be unfair, given the fire services' lamentable deficiencies in resources and the lack of adequate co-operation from the public; there was, for example, a noticeable absence of fire-watchers in the blitzed area. In contrast, both the military authorities and Home Office experts considered that local fire-fighting personnel 'behaved splendidly'. This was also the view of Edward Lennon, a member of the Dun Laoghaire brigade, who stated emphatically that 'they did a great job'.

The thirteen Southern crews began to arrive in Belfast at 10 a.m. on the morning after the raid. With lights unmasked, they had sped north across the border, rushing through Lisburn, Co. Antrim, at 60 m.p.h., their path being cleared by local air raid precautions men who had been posted at each crossroads to wave them through. They were 'frozen to the bone', travelling

TOP PRESS

' was confirmed in Dublin this rning that units of fire-fighting ambulance services from ne towns in Eire assisted to put fires resulting from Northern land's blitz.

Northern Whig, 17 April 1941

in open engines, without protective clothing, but they must have been heartened by the crowds who 'wildly cheered in towns and villages in Ulster as they passed through'. Their reasons for volunteering to attend fires in Belfast were varied and to some extent unpredictable. Edward Lennon agreed to go partly for the experience – he was young, as most of them were. Also, he was aware that de Valera had given his approval for the appliances to be sent and that their families would be provided for in the event of injury or death. Others had additional motives. Patrick Finlay from Dublin harboured dark suspicions that Northern firemen 'might only concern themselves with Protestant areas'. Sean Kelly, an ardent republican also from Dublin, who had participated in the Easter Rising of 1916, went to Belfast out of a deep sense of nationalist identity; as he said, 'the people of Belfast were Irishmen too'. While fire-fighting, he was appalled to meet British soldiers with strong Dublin accents. Their speech betrayed their origins. To Kelly their actions betrayed their country.

On arrival, Tom Kenny from Dundalk was struck forcibly by the extent to which the 'whole organization in Belfast had fallen apart'. He and his men, along with others from Dublin, had immediately reported to Lisburn Road police barracks. There, he claims, they waited for a period of time approaching two hours 'without receiving instructions of any kind'; few of them had any knowledge of the geography of the city. A further symptom of the chaos, which Kelly and some others also complained of, was the fact that no meals were provided for them by the Northern authorities throughout the entire course of the day. In addition, as they had no ration books, they experienced considerable difficulty in purchasing anything, whether food, 'Aspros' or even petrol. Members of the Drogheda brigade, which was working in the Albert Memorial Clock area, were therefore deeply grateful when local dockers offered them their lunches, which in many cases consisted of two thick slices of bread filled with raw onion.

When eventually the Southern firemen were turned-out from Chichester Street headquarters to the docks, east Belfast and the Crumlin Road, they faced fires incomparably worse than most would experience for the rest of their careers. Edward Lennon can still vividly recall his sense of apprehension from the moment they reached the foot of the Mourne Mountains and he could see 'a huge pall of smoke hanging over the city'. He was temporarily attached to an Auxiliary Fire Service station near the ropeworks in east Belfast. It was a traumatic experience. Many years later he recalled: 'I could not believe the scale of the destruction in east Belfast and could never get it out of my head.' Patrick Finlay was sent to the Leopold Street–Flax Street area. He had been to Belfast just once before, passing through on his way to Bangor, Co. Down, for his honeymoon, and had noted then that 'everything seemed bright and clean'. On this occasion 'fires blazed everywhere', and at Ewart's weaving mill, in particular, he was conscious of 'an acute shortage of oxygen, making it difficult to breathe' (the conditions which exist in the vacuum preceding a fire storm). Initially, he and the rest of his crew fought to confine the flames and prevent them from spreading. It was hazardous work: he recalls setting a ladder up against a wall and when he attempted to mount it, the whole wall was swaying out and then easing back. Shortly afterwards, when the ladder was removed, the entire gable collapsed. In another incident, a colleague close by had climbed to the top of a turntable when an unexploded bomb was discovered beside the wheels of his fire tender. He made a rapid descent. At the docks William Allen, a fireman from Drogheda, can remember his frustration at trying to extinguish fires so intense that it was impossible to gain entry into buildings in order to quench them. An additional and unforeseen difficulty was that some of the fire appliances were equipped with two-and-three-quarter-inch hoses, whereas the English standard was two and a half inches. The gravity of this incompatibility was compounded by the fact that Belfast's fire-fighting equipment had never been standardised; coupling sizes varied even within the area of the port. However, brass adaptors could be fitted and, in any case, much of the Southern equipment had been bought in England and so conformed to English specifications. Overall, the additional hose lengths brought up from the South did supplement effectively the supplies available locally and enabled the ample water supplies of the River Lagan to be tapped more successfully.

At about 6 p.m. the same day, two hours before sunset, the Southern brigades left for home. By then, all of the fires were well under control, though a number were still showing light. No doubt, concern was felt at governmental level that Éire's relationship with Germany might be complicated if their firemen were killed during a further raid on Belfast. The men themselves certainly feared further bombing, a fear heightened for some by an eerie incident earlier in the day. Shortly before noon, two German reconnaissance planes flew high above the city, 'like specks in the sky'. In east Belfast, Edward Lennon watched 'people scattering in panic towards shelters'. There was no siren as the electricity supply had not yet been restored. He recalls that the 'hair stood on the back of my head'. William Allen also spotted the aircraft and as he was in the docks, he felt particularly vulnerable. He remembered feeling an acute sense of being 'lost, I didn't know where to hide. It was a very frightening experience.' The return journey was itself a 'nightmare', not only due to the freezing cold but also because the tenders were not equipped with blackout covers for their headlamps and had to be driven in the dark for much of the way. Having reached the border, the Dun Laoghaire units were further delayed by the Royal Ulster Constabulary at Newry, Co. Down, as apparently there had been another alert in Belfast. However, after a short time spent waiting in an Ancient Order of Hibernians hall, an all-clear signal was received and they proceeded home.

Apart from the unrelenting flames which they had courageously fought to contain, the most enduring memory of their journey north, still shared by many Southern firemen, is of the hitherto unimagined scale of physical

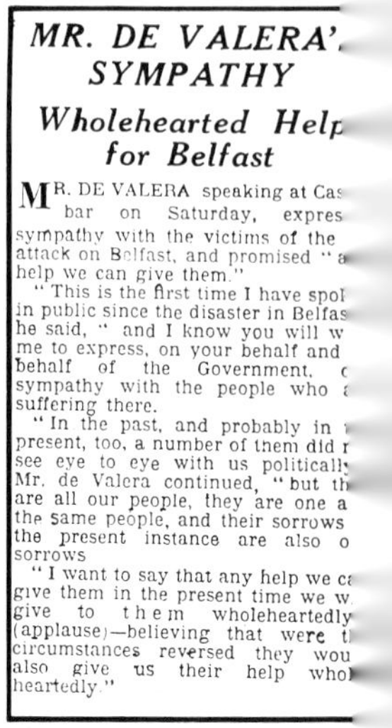
MR. DE VALERA'
SYMPATHY
Wholehearted Help
for Belfast

MR. DE VALERA speaking at Cas
bar on Saturday, expres
sympathy with the victims of the
attack on Belfast, and promised "a
help we can give them."
"This is the first time I have spol
in public since the disaster in Belfas
he said, " and I know you will w
me to express, on your behalf and
behalf of the Government,
sympathy with the people who
suffering there.
"In the past, and probably in
present, too, a number of them did
see eye to eye with us politicall
Mr. de Valera continued, "but th
are all our people, they are one a
the same people, and their sorrows
the present instance are also o
sorrows
"I want to say that any help we c
give them in the present time we w
give to them wholeheartedly
(applause)—believing that were t
circumstances reversed they wou
also give us their help whol
heartedly."

Northern Whig,
21 April 1941

BLACK OUT
FOR EIRE
Special Signs to be
Banned

EIRE is to have a unified black-ou
and from Wednesday next, Apri
23 no sky sign, facia, or advertise
ment may be illuminated during th
hours of darkness—from half an hou
after sunset to half an hour befor
sunrise—nor may any light be dis
played outside or at the entrance t
any premises or on any hoarding o
similar structure for the purpose o
advertisement or display.
This is the effect of an Emergency
Powers Order made by the Minister
for Industry and Commerce.
It is further provided that during the
hours of darkness no lights shall be
displayed on the exteriors of cinemas
theatres, or other places of public en
tertainment.
Lights may be displayed in a shop
window only so long as the shop is
open to the public, and customers may
be served in the shop.

Northern Whig,
17 April 1941

BOIL ALL WATER!

Belfast householders on the Co. Antrim side of the Lagan are warned to boil all water required for drinking purposes.

Northern Whig, 17 April 1941

devastation in Belfast. For the citizens of Belfast, its impact was almost overwhelming. To William McCready it seemed that 'the whole city had been dislocated'. He proceeded to list some of the damage: 'entire rows of houses had been flattened; huge buildings burnt out; water and gas pipes blown up; tramcar lines no longer on the main roads'. William Ward, the caretaker at St Ninian's parish church on the Whitewell Road, recorded similar sentiments, writing that 'the tragedy of these awful nights of terror and death was intensified by the great havoc and destruction spread over all the district'. Even Northern Ireland's official war history by John Blake suggests that 'citizens wondered how the life of the city could be renewed'; the question was also raised by some local newspapers.

It appeared that virtually nothing had escaped the destructive powers of the Luftwaffe. After the raid, the amount of electricity generated was reduced to half normal volumes because of damage to power stations, cables and insulators. Gas production, which was distributed to 75 per cent of the houses in areas such as Sandy Row, Ballymacarrett and the Shankill Road, was heavily disrupted by fractured and flooded pipes. Due to broken conduits and mains, water pressure over much of the city was at less than half pre-blitz levels and in some areas supplies had been cut off entirely. Public notices carried stark warnings that 'all water on the County Antrim side must be boiled' and stressed the danger of typhoid fever. As a consequence, Jim Jenkins, an assistant in a wholesale grocers, remembers people armed with containers, scrambling up the Cavehill in search of fresh springs. The telephone system was seriously dislocated. Tramway services suffered from the bombing of two depots, damaged lines and blocked roads, and on average, trams were running at 60 per cent usual frequency. Due to the combination of Easter holidays and the impact of the blitz, shops had little to sell. Perhaps, most crucial of all, industrial output for the war effort dropped to 25 per cent below pre-blitz figures.

None the less, the disruption of both essential services and production could so easily have been infinitely more severe. Both the harbour power station and the central telephone exchange had actually escaped with relatively little structural damage. The gasworks itself was unaffected by the raid. On examination it was found that there was just one major break in the sewage system and that the water supply was not in fact contaminated. Although the transport system had been seriously disrupted, at least the three main bridges across the River Lagan remained intact. By 21 April, gas and water supplies were again available 'to most citizens', transport services were running 'fairly smoothly', and damage to telephone exchanges had been repaired. In truth, as Thomas J. Campbell KC, leader of the Nationalist Party, said in the House, the 'toll was greatest in the narrow streets, where life crowds thick and fast and where the struggle for existence never ends

HOMES FOR BELFAST'S HOMELESS

Clearing Wreckage from the Bombed Areas

BELFAST is recovering from the effects of the air raid on Tuesday night. Considerable progress was made yesterday with the clearing of debris from the bombed areas.

Belfast News-Letter, 18 April 1941

from the cradle to the grave'. As a result of the attack, thirty-five hundred houses had been demolished or severely damaged, and a further ten thousand needed urgent repairs to windows and roofs. An estimated twenty thousand people had been made homeless and there was widespread speculation that the final death toll would also be measured in thousands. The devastation was spread over five hundred streets. Some of them, like Veryan Gardens, Hogarth Street, Eglinton Street, Tamar Street and Carew Street, had been virtually obliterated. In addition, two hospitals, one nurses' home, two schools and eleven churches were at least partially destroyed. The suffering and anguish caused by such extensive destruction, affecting as it did so many innocent victims, aroused a deep sense of shock and outrage. Prime Minister John Andrews reflected the popular mood when he described the raid as a 'very vicious and brutal attack by a cruel, oppressive and inhuman foe'.

Rescue work and the clearance of debris were inevitably slow and hazardous owing to the extent of the devastation and the innumerable fractured gas pipes and exposed wires associated with it. Unexploded mines and bombs created additional difficulties. Air raid precautions wardens frequently lacked any adequate knowledge of the number of people occupying each house or of where they would shelter during an attack, and their activities were continuously disrupted by a constant stream of enquiries from those looking for relatives and friends. In these very difficult circumstances Stormont ministers considered that the whole civil defence organisation 'stood up remarkably well' and showed 'great devotion' to duty. Such claims had obvious justification: three members of its constituent services were awarded the George Medal, six received the British Empire Medal and a further four were commended. Twenty-one wardens had died as a result of this raid.

Home Office officials and the armed forces based locally also shared the view that Belfast's passive defences had carried out 'magnificent work'. However, the military authorities in particular expressed the most profound dissatisfaction with some aspects of their performance. For example, they criticised their lack of co-ordinated planning. Also, they regarded the numbers of police, wardens, rescue workers, fire-fighters and first-aid personnel as derisorily inadequate and the quantity and quality of their equip-

Eglinton Street, near Carlisle Circus, was virtually obliterated by the 15–16 April raid. (Ulster Museum)

ment as similarly deficient. Consequently, after twenty-four hours' duty, members of these services, 'however willing. . . were physically exhausted', and without any shift or rota to relieve them, 'a critical situation arose'. As a result, a very heavy reliance was placed on Northern Ireland's military establishment to carry out rescue work, fight fires, control traffic, operate medical services, and supply ambulances, lorries and blankets. After the Easter Tuesday raid, British soldiers expended the equivalent of 10,500 working days in attempting to restore normal life to the city, and in the process they helped to remove 240 bodies from the debris. In parliament at Stormont, John MacDermott gratefully acknowledged 'their ready response and good work', stating that it would 'never be forgotten'. In some areas Churches erected commemorative tablets as a gesture of public appreciation. However, local military leaders were themselves extremely uneasy, even resentful, at being required to play so pervasive a role. They consistently warned that such assistance could not and should not be relied upon, especially if a blitz was accompanied by enemy invasion. They were totally unimpressed by the small amounts of labour provided by the civil authority. Above all, the army regarded the 'attitude of large numbers of able-bodied young men, who spent their time sight-seeing and refused to lend a hand, [as] disgusting'.

SIGHTSEERS UNWANTED

The following statement was issued by the Ministry of Public Security yesterday :—

"Owing to the large number of sightseers, in cars and on foot, who have been touring the bombed districts of Belfast the work of the civil defence services has been much impeded. An urgent appeal is made to all citizens not to visit the damaged areas except for imperative reasons.

"It is of the greatest importance that rescue and demolition work should proceed unhindered and that the streets should be kept clear for essential traffic."

Belfast News-Letter, 18 April 1941

Of course the military command was well aware that not all of those who gathered in the bombed areas, from around day-break after the raid, were there solely to spectate. Looting was widespread, if not universal. This was

FURNITURE REMOVAL

MANY CASES HAVE OCCURRED WHERE REMOVERS HAVE GONE TO COLLECT FROM HOUSES AS A RESULT OF REQUEST FORMS THROUGH WARDENS' POSTS AND FOUND THEM LOCKED. OWNERS WHO ARE ABSENT AND HAVE MADE SUCH REQUESTS MUST AT ONCE DEPOSIT THE KEYS AT THE NEAREST WARDENS' POST.

In all cases, Owners filling in forms must in future insert the address of the nearest Wardens' Post to the damaged house, where the Keys, properly labelled, must be deposited.

The Removers have been instructed not to remove any furniture from houses considered weatherproof.

BY ORDER.

Northern Whig, 19 April 1941

despite the presence of police and army anti-looting patrols, the roping off of damaged streets, and the prompt issue of permits to legitimate householders. On the morning after the raid, Josephine Downey, whose home on Hillman Street had been badly damaged, remembers searching the garden of her house for articles that might have been blown there by the blast. As she lifted a green dress, which belonged to herself, a complete stranger came over and pulled it from her, saying: 'I saw it first.' He sped off rapidly when she informed him that she held a permit. Later that day, her brother, who was a barman at McLaughlin's public house on the Antrim Road, was asked if he wished to purchase twelve glasses. He glanced at them, realising immediately that they belonged to his parents. When he pointed this out, the customer, who had offered them for sale, promptly turned and ran out, leaving the glasses behind. On the Shankill Road, Rita McKittrick saw chairs and settees being carried from bombed furniture shops and a

NATIONAL MILK SCHEME

NOTICE TO PERSONS HAVING CUSTODY OF EVACUEES UNDER FIVE YEARS OF AGE.

THE MINISTRY OF AGRICULTURE ANNOUNCES THAT PARENTS OR HOUSEHOLDERS HAVING CUSTODY OF EVACUATED CHILDREN UNDER 5 YEARS OF AGE SHOULD APPLY TO THE NEAREST EMPLOYMENT EXCHANGE IF THEY WISH TO RECEIVE MILK UNDER THE ABOVE SCHEME. PARENTS WHO ARE ALREADY PERMIT HOLDERS UNDER THE SCHEME SHOULD, WHEREVER POSSIBLE, TAKE THEIR PERMITS WITH THEM TO THE EXCHANGE IN ORDER THAT THE NECESSARY AMENDMENTS THERETO MAY BE EFFECTED.

Application should be made as soon as possible by those persons who propose to remain for some time at their new address in a reception area, but permits will not normally be issued if their stay is likely to be of short duration.

Stormont, Belfast,
19th April, 1941.

Northern Whig, 19 April 1941

chemist's shop being looted. In Percy Street, Billy Boyd returned home from hospital to find that his cash-savings box had disappeared and that a family heirloom – a sword dating back to the Indian Mutiny – had been stolen from his bedroom wall. As Police Constable Billy McNeill commented: 'The forces could not be everywhere.'

Meanwhile rescue workers proceeded with the harrowing task of sifting through the debris. Those involved were immediately conscious of the very considerable number of dead. For Joseph McCann, who was an air raid precautions warden, 'the shock was the number of people killed, not the buildings'. This had also struck some of the Southern firemen. On the

'he terraces of Tamar Street
ripped apart by the force of
an explosion during the
15–16 April raid.
(Ulster Museum)

Crumlin Road, Patrick Finlay recalled: 'I was totally unprepared for seeing so many dead and mutilated bodies. We could do nothing for them.' In east Belfast Edward Lennon was horrified to see so many bodies being loaded on to military vehicles for transport to temporary morgues. Even the *Belfast Telegraph* reported on 18 April 1941: 'Bodies being recovered from heaps of rubble all over the place'. When touring the city with his permanent secretary, William Iliff, John MacDermott noticed that a 'benevolent white dust had settled on the faces of the corpses'. Bodies were found in the streets, amid the rubble, spread-eagled over pavements, even collapsed over roofs and buildings and trees, blown there by explosives. In houses in north Belfast Jimmy Doherty remembers finding 'the blonde head of a girl and a boy's sock on a foot' – all that remained to be identified. At York Street mill Bryce Millar witnessed the slow frantic process of combing through the massive pieces of debris, men clawing with bare hands, and women and children weeping as growing numbers of dead were recovered and placed along the roadside. Arthur Jackson watched the bodies being laid out side by side at the top and bottom end of Hogarth Street, most of them covered by blankets. Among them he remembers 'a child called Moore, brought out without a scratch'; eight members of the Gordon family were killed; and at one house, where neighbours had gathered for mutual comfort during the raid, well over a dozen bodies were removed. They included those of a mother and her children, who had just come from Glasgow to escape the blitz there.

In some cases the remains of occupants were never recovered; number 142 Duncairn Gardens received a direct hit and seven members of the Warwick family were later recorded as missing, presumed dead. In other instances those thought to be safe were found buried beneath the debris. Gerry Hannah recalled the particularly tragic experience of a night-shift worker who returned home to find his house in ruins, but consoled himself with the belief that his wife and children had evacuated to the country and were therefore unhurt. However, as he examined the rubble he stumbled upon some of their personal belongings, including his wife's dentures. Immediately, rescue workers were called in and a search began. One by one the members of his family were dug out; all of them had been killed.

LORRIES WANTED FOR CLEARAN
OF DEBRIS

A LARGE NUMBER OF MOTOR LORRI (carrying capacity 2–6 tons) is requi at once for the clearance of debris.

Would all owners of motor lorries, suita for this purpose, offer their vehicles on hire (w drivers) immediately to the **EMERGEN TRANSPORT COMMITTEE.**

Northern Whig, 19 April 1941

When the Downeys went back to Hillman Street, they informed the local air raid precautions warden that a friend was buried underneath the collapsed gable wall of their house and that they 'would not be satisfied' until an effort had been made to rescue him. They were concerned that, if alive, he might be burned by the flames spouting up from broken gas pipes. Josephine vividly recalls that when the dead body was uncovered and the final bricks were being removed, its 'arms rose automatically into the air'. A doctor explained that it had been a last despairing reflex action made by their friend, as he tried in vain to protect himself. A considerable sum of money which he had been carrying was never recovered. Their next-door neighbours had also been killed by the same blast. Further along the Antrim Road, Dr F.M. MacSorley returned home from hospital where he had been working throughout the night. He found that his house had been demolished and was on fire. But on arrival, he stated with total certainty that his wife was still alive, appealing to air raid precautions wardens: 'I know she is still alive because she is calling to me. I want you to dig for my wife.' The wardens did not believe it possible that she could have survived, but with military help, Dr MacSorley's wife, her maid and a dog were released, without serious injury, from underneath a downstairs table.

The harrowing scenes at Veryan Gardens that morning mirrored those at any of the bombed residential areas of the city. On one side of a crater stood an ambulance and on the other, a lorry. Rescue workers were loading these vehicles with dead bodies, which would then be taken to a local felt works where a temporary mortuary had been established. On a tree in a garden hung part of a green parachute and some silken cord. Yet despite the almost overwhelming evidence of death and the atmosphere of terror and gloom which permeated this whole district, there were occasionally heartening moments. At approximately 2 p.m. the senior warden on the nearby Whitewell Road was asked if he was satisfied that no one had been left on the site of a bomb-damaged house. A parachute mine had fallen beside it, blasting it to pieces and devastating the neighbourhood. He replied that he was not fully satisfied. At that moment, he noticed that the ground just below foundation level had a churned-up appearance. Work was immediately restarted and after about a quarter of an hour, the head of a child was uncovered. Feverishly the digging proceeded. In a few minutes the hood of a Tansad appeared and, moments later, a little girl of about fifteen months was lifted out unhurt. Another warden who witnessed the rescue wrote:

> The hearts of those who stood around, which had been frozen in our breasts throughout the long hours preceding, seemed to melt in a glow of joy and for the first time that day we felt like cheering. We had, however, to restrain our feelings on account of the desolation and grievous loss surrounding us.

Later that week, on Friday, 18 April, it was possible to hold a 'stocktaking' of all those known to have been present in the Veryan Gardens–Whitewell Road area at the time of the raid. All were accounted for apart from one child, and this mystery was quickly resolved. A photograph appeared in the local press next day, stating that an unidentified child had been found sleeping on his own in one of the city's hospitals. On enquiry it proved to be the missing boy.

In the city the death toll rose inexorably day by day. On 17 April a ministry official stated that 173 people had been killed and predicted that

Parts of the city centre came through the entire blitz with little damage. This photograph of Donegall Square North and Donegall Place was taken on 15 September 1942. (Ulster Folk and Transport Museum)

this figure might yet rise to 300. Two days later the figure quoted was 363 and the same official now anticipated that it could reach 450. He explained: 'I do not feel that there can be more persons recovered alive from the sites that I visited.' One week after the raid, John MacDermott spoke for the first time publicly about the level of fatalities. He informed parliament: 'The dead is at present known to number 500 based on the number of bodies removed to date.' He then added, with unjustifiable optimism: 'I fear that there are more to be recovered and that there are a number missing to be added but I think I may say that I have told the House the worst.'

The scale of the tragedy was most horrifyingly revealed at the city's mortuaries. Accommodation for the dead at hospitals and undertakers was utterly overwhelmed. Joseph Crilly recalls that at the Mater Hospital, within two to three days, the number of corpses had risen to about eighty. In the latter stages they were arriving in an extremely mutilated condition – dismembered limbs and fragments of human remains. They overspilled from the morgue into an open back yard at the rear of the hospital and into the area around the boiler house. After a time, Jeyes Fluid was used to help contain the smell of decomposing flesh. A steady stream of people came to the hospital desperately hoping to identify missing friends and relatives. Crilly also remembers a visit by the head of the city's casualty service, Professor T.T. Flynn, a father less famous than his son Errol, who called to see for himself how they were coping with the deluge of death. He brought with him two bottles of rum which were opened and consumed there and then by those looking after the bodies. Ulster author Brian Moore was an air raid precautions warden attached to the Mater Hospital and he helped coffin the dead. In *The Emperor of Ice Cream* he wrote:

> In the stink of human excrement, in the acrid smell of disinfectant these dead were heaped, body on body, flung arm, twisted feet, open mouth, staring eyes, old men on top of young women, a child lying on a policeman's back, a soldier's hand resting on a woman's thigh, a carter still wearing his coal-slacks on top of a pile of arms and legs, his own arm outstretched, finger pointing, as though he warned of some unseen horror. Forbidding and clumsy, the dead cluttered the morgue room from floor to ceiling.

As the death toll mounted, additional mortuary accommodation had to be improvised within hours after the raid. On Wednesday, 16 April, the town clerk issued instructions to staff at the public baths on the Falls Road and Peter's Hill, advising them that coffined bodies would be arriving from about midday. Soon afterwards, Joseph McCann, a warden and an attendant at Falls Road public baths, remembers the first hearses arriving and the coffins being unloaded. At the beginning they were laid out around the side of the pool with their lids removed to facilitate identification by members of the public. He vividly recalls his feeling of shock and horror when he opened the first one. It contained the bodies of a mother and beside her, an infant; both had been stripped naked by the blast. In another there was 'a young girl in her confirmation robe, with blue silk ribbon and long black hair', and nearby, 'a child, unmarked and never claimed'; it was believed that her entire family had been killed. At one point volunteers struggled to carry in a large, heavy, awkwardly shaped parcel. It bore a tag which read: 'Believed to be a mother and five children.' Disembodied arms, legs and heads were brought in on planks. Soldiers arrived with a stretcher, piled high, its grim contents covered by a sheet – a mound of human remains, pieces of bodies that had been gathered up. As the army sergeant accompanying the stretchers waited for a receipt to be signed, he looked round and commented: 'They call this war.'

The number of dead brought to the baths continued to rise steadily, increasing eventually to 150. They were conveyed to the baths in ambulances, military vehicles, furniture vans, coal lorries, even Belfast Corporation bin lorries; most were from the area of York Street mill and Percy Street. When the sides of the pool had filled up, the water was drained so that they could be laid out on its white tiled floor. There were soon no more coffins, and the bodies, mostly of women and children, came wrapped in blankets or in the clothes that they had died in. 'They were,' wrote Joseph Tomelty, 'the homeless poor lying in their own shabby blankets, blankets that had known the rough face of the wash board for years, thin and devoid of fleece.'

Jimmy Doherty was one of those who volunteered to work at the Falls baths. His most lasting recollection is of the smell of decomposing bodies and of the disinfectant used to spray those entering and leaving the building. There was a constant flow of people looking for relatives and friends who were dead or missing. One of them, Artie Corr, was a republican internee, imprisoned in Londonderry. He was brought down to Belfast under police escort to identify his mother and brother. Their two bodies had been recognised earlier by neighbours of the Corr family; they had then notified their Catholic bishop, who immediately had informed the civil authorities.

After three days, those bodies that had still not been claimed were transferred from the various mortuaries in the city to St George's Market. On 18 April reports appeared in the press advising the public that they would have a final opportunity to identify bodies there from 18 to 20 April. They were also informed that after a period of two days, those still unclaimed and those that could 'never be recognized' would be buried together in a common grave. Although the market was large, covered and central, it was far from ideal for the purpose proposed, mainly because it lacked adequate washing facilities, and because bodies could not be left there uncoffined overnight owing to the presence of rats. Due to the severity of the injuries that the victims had sustained and to their advancing stage of decomposition, the identification of the dead was difficult. Also, in the chaos of removing them from bomb sites and transferring them to mortuaries, information indicating where they had been found was often mislaid or not recorded. It was equally unfortunate that no record had been made of where each of the bodies had been found and that the retention of clothing and personal belongings with bodies had often been neglected. There were even cases of corpses that had been successfully identified in one mortuary being removed to another and 'lost', while relatives were making arrangements for burial. In some cases body counts were duplicated as mortuaries became filled and bodies were removed to emergency mortuaries. At St George's, rough notes were written in chalk on some of the coffins, stating the name of the street from which the body had been recovered. Where available, these were regarded as a valuable identification aid by both the public and the staff.

The queue at the market is among the most enduring memories of the Easter Tuesday raid. From the Saturday afternoon, Emma Duffin was one of the nurses on duty there and she graphically recorded her impressions of the scene:

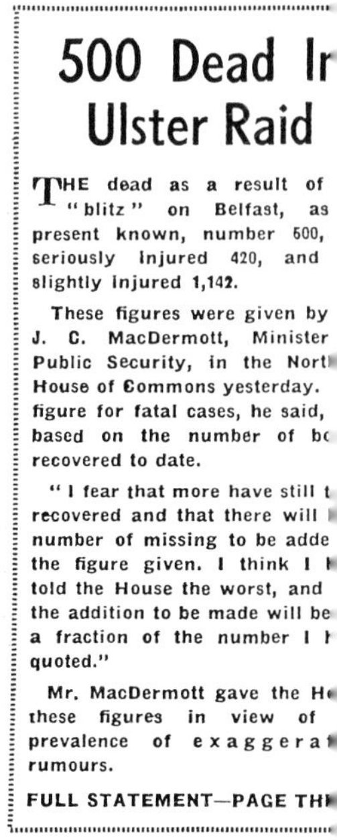
500 Dead Ir
Ulster Raid

THE dead as a result of "blitz" on Belfast, as present known, number 500, seriously injured 420, and slightly injured 1,142.

These figures were given by J. C. MacDermott, Minister Public Security, in the Nort House of Commons yesterday. figure for fatal cases, he said, based on the number of bc recovered to date.

"I fear that more have still t recovered and that there will number of missing to be adde the figure given. I think I told the House the worst, and the addition to be made will be a fraction of the number I quoted."

Mr. MacDermott gave the H these figures in view of prevalence of exaggera rumours.

FULL STATEMENT—PAGE TH

Northern Whig, 23 April 1941

> It was a job for an older woman and my experience at the hospital should have prepared me to some extent. I say *should* have. . . The gates were guarded by police but at the sight of my uniform, they opened them. . . The place was full of coffins, some varnished but the majority plain deal. At the end of the hall was a Salvation Army mobile canteen and beside it was a rough table where some men with papers took particulars. Red Cross and St John ambulance nurses and some civilians met and went around with relatives. Two men went around with each group and opened the coffins, lifting the lids. There were two doctors in attendance. A man watered the floor with disinfectant from a watering pail; a wise precaution as the place smelt. It was a hideous nightmare. All the way to the place I had told myself I was bound to see horrible sights but only when seen could the full horror be realized. I had seen death in many forms, young men dying of ghastly wounds, but nothing I had ever seen was as terrible as this. . . [World War I casualties] had died in hospital beds, their eyes had been reverently closed, their hands crossed to their breasts. Death had to a certain extent been. . . made decent. It was solemn, tragic, dignified, but here it was grotesque, repulsive, horrible. No attendant nurse had soothed the last moments of these victims, no gentle reverent hand had closed their eyes or crossed their hands. With tangled hair, staring eyes, clutching hands, contorted limbs, their grey-green faces covered with dust, they lay bundled into the coffins, half-shrouded in rugs or blankets or an occasional sheet, still wearing their dirty, torn, twisted garments. Death should be dignified, peaceful, Hitler had made death grotesque. I felt outraged. I should have felt sympathy, grief, but instead feelings of revulsion and disgust assailed me.
>
> The men who were removing the coffins. . . were of the roughest, coarsest type; one was disfigured by a skin disease. They shouted to each other as they worked. God knows they had a distasteful enough job and they had been at it for five days – enough to stifle finer feelings in more sensitive people. A young girl stood in a group, in Red Cross uniform. She was chewing sweets. . . fed up. I was sorry for her but shuddered to think of grieving relatives searching amid those gruesome remains for some one they loved, being accompanied by

500 DEAD IN BELFAST

Minister Reviews Results of the Raid

QUESTION OF PROFITEERING

IN the Ulster House of Commons yesterday Mr. J. C. MacDermott, Minister of Public Security, reviewed some of the effects of the air raid on Belfast.

He revealed that at least 500 persons were killed, 420 seriously injured and 1,142 slightly injured, and added that these were not final figures.

Several members alleged that exorbitant rents were being charged to refugees, and the Parliamentary Secretary to the Ministry of Home Affairs, said that the Government was examining the position. If sufficient powers did not exist to deal with the situation fresh legislation, which would be retrospective, would be sought.

Belfast News-Letter, 23 April 1941

> a girl of that type. It was no job for a girl and no one should have been kept at it for more than a few hours.

Others who were present can recall seeing one of the men on duty spraying bodies with cold water while eating a ham sandwich.

Turning her attention to the constant stream of people coming to the mortuary, Emma Duffin continued: 'Only small groups were allowed in at a time, mercifully. I went with a man and his wife, they looked desolate, exhausted, with red-rimmed eyes and haggard faces.' They were looking for a sister-in-law and had seen all the coffins 'but more were being brought in and they hung around waiting'. Another was a woman 'looking in vain for her mother and sister. She had been up from the country on this awful quest three days running. Her brother was. . . in a terrible state. . . his face twisted, and his hands trembling.' However, Emma Duffin felt much less sympathy for some of the others:

> One group seemed to be touring the line of coffins over and over again [and a woman], her hat on top of her head, twisted hands clasped in front of her, mumbled and murmured words I could not catch, retailing horrors, and, I

could not help feeling, perhaps unjustly, enjoying a certain amount of satisfaction from being included in the drama and the tragedy.

Of the 255 bodies taken to St George's Market, 151 were successfully identified and 92 of these were taken away by relatives and friends for burial. The remainder shared a common grave. The private funerals were so numerous that eyewitnesses said they 'lost count' and watched 'in a dazed silence', as the hearses went by. Belfast had never experienced anything like it before. Lists of names of citizens killed by enemy action filled three columns in the *Belfast Telegraph* on 19 April 1941. The public funeral of the unclaimed dead took place, as arranged, on Monday, 21 April. Its organisation raised some unique difficulties. The authorities first searched the unidentified corpses for personal effects, such as beads or crucifixes, in an attempt at least to establish their religious identity. If these artifacts were found the body was placed with the Catholic victims. After separate Catholic and Protestant services at the market, the dead were taken in five covered military vehicles to Milltown cemetery or to the city cemetery nearby. Regarding the organisation of the funeral, Lord Mayor Sir Crawford McCullagh remarked that it would be 'difficult indeed to decide who or how many [the chief mourners] may be'. Those people with relatives missing, presumed dead, followed behind the coffins. Thousands lined the streets and as the cortège passed by, both men and women wept without restraint, and civilian and military rescue squads stood with heads bowed.

Meanwhile the number of known dead, which stood that Monday at five hundred, was continuing to rise. The bodies and the limbs of victims, green with corruption, were still being discovered amidst the debris of buildings, in derelict and vacant houses, even in roof gutterings. Many weeks after the mass burial, Joseph McCann recalls repairing the slates of a house in Cambrai Street and finding a disembodied head. It had been blown through a ceiling and had become trapped in the eaves. On 23 April the town clerk appealed in the local press for information about those still missing and unaccounted for. In early June further public notices gave details of a coroner's inquiry into the death or presumed deaths of a list of named persons killed during the Easter Tuesday raid.

Controversy still surrounds the final death toll. Official statistics, first made available to the public by the Northern Ireland government in October 1944, indicated that 745 civilians were killed and over 430 seriously injured. Similarly, both the *Ulster Year Book* for the year 1947 and John Blake's official history of the war state that at least 700 died; Blake also states that there were some 420 serious casualties. However, Westminster government files would suggest that the number was significantly higher. Although one Ministry of Home Security document contains an anonymous handwritten note stating that there were 758 fatalities, subsequently, the department produced another more detailed analysis. This provided a breakdown of the total which included 310 men, 237 women, 148 children and 163 unclassified, which provides a final figure of 858. Assuming that this sum did not include over twenty deaths suffered by military and naval personnel, it would seem that an estimate of at least 900 is justified. Northern Ireland Fire Authority figures state that 950 people died and that 600 were seriously injured. One thing at least is certain, in John Blake's words: 'No other city in the United Kingdom, except London, had lost so many of her citizens in a single night's raid. No other, except possibly Liverpool, ever did.' It was an unenviable and lamentable distinction.

No single factor can account for Belfast's exceptionally high mortality rate but an indisputably vital element was the nature of the German attack and specifically the high proportion of Luftwaffe bombs which fell on residential areas. Northern Ireland government statements referred to explosives having been 'dropped at random'. Some local press reports went further and claimed that the fundamental objective of the attack had been 'to break down civilian morale'. Indeed since the Coventry raid in November 1940, John MacDermott himself had become deeply concerned

Memorial erected to the unidentified victims of the German air raids, buried at Belfast city cemetery. (Ulster Museum)

that residential property appeared to be regarded as a legitimate target by enemy bombers. However, recent research suggests that the essential aim of the blitz on Coventry was to cripple the armaments industry there and to strike at a number of specifically military locations. Also, the main thrust of Germany's bombing campaign from late 1940 had been directed towards the destruction of the western ports. These were playing an increasingly vital role in the defence of the North Atlantic and as points of entry for supplies of war material for Britain from the United States. They were easily located and highly vulnerable; after the Fall of France, the United Kingdom's anti-aircraft defences were at first completely out-flanked as they had been deployed to meet attacks from aircraft based in western Germany.

In addition, German sources relating to the Easter Tuesday attack on Belfast would suggest that the destruction of the harbour area, with its concentration of war industry, was its primary purpose. German radio accounts of the raid stressed that the city was a 'harbour and arms centre of decisive importance for the English war economy' and the 'meeting and starting place for numerous convoys', especially as other 'west coast ports had been affected by earlier bombing'. They proceeded to claim that the first waves of bombers had scored direct hits on 'the port and arms works', and even three weeks later they persisted with assertions that the shipyards had been 'completely destroyed. . . not even emergency work can be undertaken'. Also, virtually all the target files for Belfast, carefully prepared by the Luftwaffe from late 1940, related to strategically important sites in and around the docks. After the raid, most of the bomber crews claimed in their written reports that their bombs had exploded 'in the vicinity of the port' and 'in the target area of Harland and Wolff shipyard'. That they should have returned again in force three weeks later, suggests in itself that the Easter Tuesday attack had been poorly executed rather than predominantly concerned to kill civilians.

If the port was the main Luftwaffe target, given the apparent ease with which it could be identified, it is difficult to explain why it should have sustained such relatively little damage. Northern Ireland government figures indicate that just seventeen of the bodies identified after the raid were recovered from the dock area. None of the eighteen smoke-screen-producing trailers located there was hit, nor did any of the personnel operating them suffer any injury, and there were no fatalities among the work force at Harland and Wolff.

Popular explanations for the pattern of the attack and, in particular, the extensive devastation which occurred to the north and west of the city vary and conflict. Some suggest that the extent of the destruction on the Antrim Road was not accidental but was related to the presence there of a significant Jewish population. Others noted at the time that there was substantial new road development in the Greencastle area of north Belfast and suggested that this may have been mistakenly identified by German aircraft as the runways of an airport. But the most widely held view of the raid is that the Luftwaffe did not just misinterpret the nature of a specific target but rather that they totally misread the whole topography of the city. It is claimed that they mistook the old Belfast Waterworks for dock basins and therefore assumed that the vital industrial sites lay south and east of its reservoirs. The presumption is that the heavy concentration of the attack on the Antrim Road, Cavehill Road and Crumlin Road was a direct and tragic consequence of this fundamental error.

Although it is now clear that the Luftwaffe had actually prepared a target file on the waterworks, present-day expert opinion, none the less, assumes that the port area was the primary objective of their attack. It would stress, however, that errors in a night blitz during 1940 and 1941 were normal and inevitable, especially as distance precluded the use of radio-aided bombing in attacks on Belfast. As a result, more rudimentary techniques had to be employed: these involved identifying targets by 'dead reckoning', relying on aeronautical instruments without sight of the ground, or dropping bombs blindly when flak or searchlights or the glow of fires indicated to crews that they were in the broad vicinity of a target. Even when targets could be seen clearly, mistakes were still likely to occur as bombsights provided only a very restricted view of the ground. Crews were of course aware that their 'mistakes' could in any case further their military intentions. After all, production was bound to suffer if workers were made homeless or fled to the countryside as a result of an attack. In addition, unfavourable weather conditions over Belfast greatly increased the probability of bombing error during the Easter Tuesday raid. Luftwaffe reports indicate that clear skies early in the attack quickly gave way to very extensive cloud cover, though this broke up again in the latter stages of the attack. Consequently, the early waves of bombers and the later arrivals were able to bomb visually. But other crews, throughout most of the raid, were forced either to bomb blindly or to divert to targets in England. Fortunately for Northern Ireland, many adopted the latter course, fifty of them attacking Liverpool for two hours early on Wednesday morning.

Informed sources at the time believed that other factors combined with variable cloud density to contibute to Luftwaffe error. It was the opinion of the local military authorities that the early attackers, in clear light, succeeded in striking the assumed target area – the docks and shipyards – causing a number of fires which were dealt with promptly. At the same time other bombs were dropped which caused further outbreaks to the north of the city but, unlike those at Queen's Island, they were not extinguished quickly. As a result, the army report concluded: 'It is probable that the enemy considered that [north Belfast] was the real target area. Almost all of the attacks were west of the Lagan.' If this analysis is accurate, as seems likely, the harbour area was extremely fortunate that so many of the mines dropped there failed to explode, so minimising the scale of the fires during a crucial phase in the attack.

Overleaf
e controversial Luftwaffe target file for Belfast aterworks with Ordnance rvey map in which the key strategic objectives are ighlighted. (Imperial War Museum)

Nur für den Dienstgebrauch	Ort: Belfast	Ziel-Nr. G.B. 53 75
Zielstammkarte	(Nähere Lage): 3½ km nordwestlich Stadtmitte (City Hall)	Kartenbl.-Nr. Irl.5/1:126000 Irl.36/1:63360
Land: Grossbritannien Nord-Irland	Geogr. Werte: 5° 56' 55" W 54° 37' 20" N	E. B. Nr.

1. Bezeichnung des Zieles: Wasserwerk Belfast.

   Vgl. mit Ziel-Nr.

2. Bedeutung: Hauptwasserversorgung von Belfast.

3. Beschreibung des Zieles:

   a) Verkehrsanschlüsse: Strassenanschluss.

   b) Ausdehnung insgesamt: Etwa 350000 qm   Bebaute Fläche: Etwa 1000 qm

   c) Bauweise, Bauausführung, Luftempfindlichkeit, Brandgefahr:

   Das Wasserwerk besteht aus 4 Rohwasserbassins und 6 viereckigen Klärbassins. Am Rande der Rohwasserbecken ist je eine Pumpanlage.

   d) Erzeugnisse:

   e) Erzeugungsmenge im Monat:
   Maximal und normal,
   bei wieviel Schichten und Arbeitern?

   f) Belegschaft:
   Männer, Frauen, Volkszugehörigkeit,
   politische Einstellung, Unterbringung.

   g) Lebenswichtige Teile, Wasser- und Kraftversorgung, Sabotage:

   4 Pumpenhäuser.

   h) Reservenversorgung:

   i) Lagerung:

   k) Sonstiges:

Etwa	20 km	im WNW	Belfast Stadtmitte (City Hall) liegt	der Flugplatz Aldergrove		(G.B. 10 6)
Etwa	17 km	im ONO	liegt	der Flugplatz Newtownards		(G.B. 10 158)
"	5 km	" NNO	"	der Flugplatz Belfast		(G.B. 10 13)
"	3,5 km	" SO	"	die Werft Harland & Wolff Ltd.		(G.B. 83 5)
"	4,2 km	" SO	"	die Tankanlage Conns Water		(G.B. 21 26)
"	4,2 km	" OSO	"	die Flugzeugfabrik Short & Harland		(G.B. 74 13)
"	2,4 km	" SO	"	die Grossmühle Rank & Co.		(G.B. 56 77)
"	3,9 km	" OSO	"	das Kraftwerk Belfast		(G.B. 50 49)
"	4,2 km	" SSO	"	das Gaswerk Belfast		(G.B. 52 49)
"	2,3 km	" SSO	"	die Kasernenanlagen Victoria Barracks		(G.B. 13 800).

4. Aktiver und passiver Luftschutz, örtl. Bewachung:

   Etwa 4,5 km im SO Victoria Park mit Flakbatterie.
   " 3 km " SSO dicht nordwestlich des Clarendon Docks und nordwestlich der Queensbrücke Flakstellungen.
   " 6 km " O bei dem Küstenort Holywood 2 Flakbatterien.

5. Orientierungspunkte zur Zielerkennung:

   Belfast Lough, die Bucht an der nördlichen Ostküste Irlands endet im Hafen von Belfast.
   Im Norden der Stadt 1,8 km westlich der Bucht liegen die Becken, Kläranlagen und Pumpwerke des Wasserwerks.
   Vom Hafen-Mittelpunkt etwa 3 km in NW-Richtung.

6. Bild- und Kartenunterlagen vom Ziel und vom Zielraum:

   1) Anliegend:
   a: Kartenausschnitt
   b: Bild mit Einzeichnung
   ~~Bild ohne Einzeichnung~~
   c: Auswertung

   b) Außerdem vom Zielraum vorhanden:

7. Zielunterlagen hat:

Genst. 5. Abt. (Z) [signature]
Bearbeitet: 28.11.40.

GB 5375 c

Nur für den Dienstgebrauch

n. Bild Nr. F 228/40/11/111 (I II. 5)

Belfast

Wasserwerk Belfast

Länge (westl. Greenw.): 5° 56′ 55″ Breite: 54° 37′ 20″

Mißweisung: 14° 19 (Mitte 1940) Zielhöhe über NN 50 m

Genst. 5. Abt. Dezember 1940

Karte 1 : 100 000

Irl. 5

500 1000 m

Maßstab 1:10 000

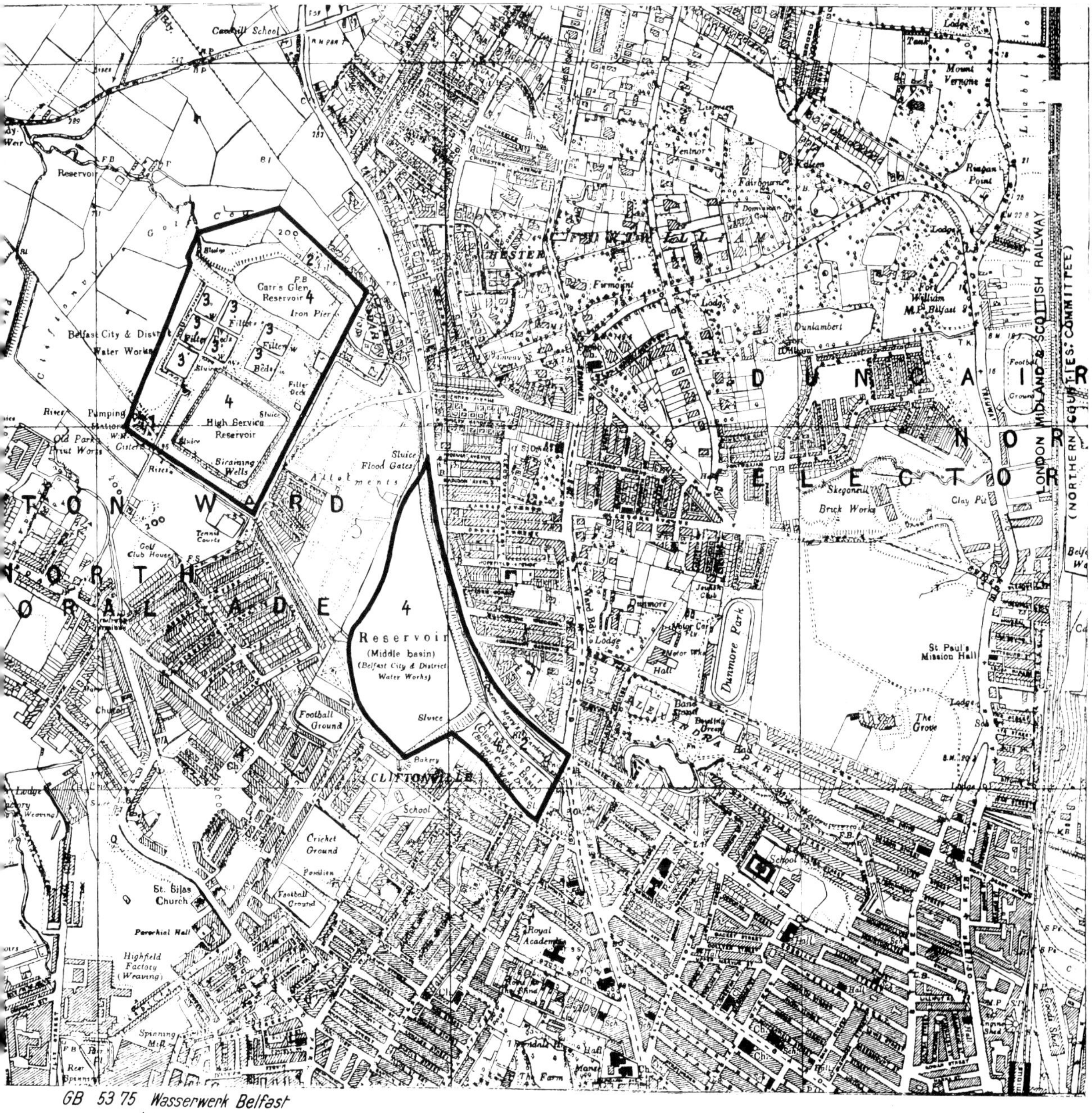

GB 5375 Wasserwerk Belfast

1) Pumpanlage etwa 550 qm
2) ansch. Pumpanlagen etwa 400 qm
3) 7 Filterbecken
4) 4 Rohwasserbecken

bebaute Fläche etwa 950 qm

Gesamtausdehnung etwa 350 000 qm

Air Commodore C. Roderick Carr, at Royal Air Force headquarters in Belfast, put forward a rather different explanation for the main features of the German raid. He considered that the smoke screen, which covered an area of about one square mile, adjacent to Sydenham airport, was the key factor in 'diverting the weight of the enemy attack away from the vital area'. He noted that by the time the German bombers had arrived 'the eastern portion of the town and docks were under cloud'. They proceeded to drop bombs that 'started fires in residential property and small industrial concerns in an area of clear visibility immediately west of the smoke screen'. He also observed that 'subsequent attacks were confined mainly to this area'. W.P. Kemp, manager at Short and Harland aircraft factory, agreed with this conclusion wholeheartedly, stating: 'There is little doubt in my mind that this screen had the effect of limiting the amount of damage done to Queen's Island to a very great extent.'

Almost certainly a combination of factors caused the Luftwaffe to make errors in identifying the target area. These included the heavy cloud cover for much of the raid, the speedy elimination of the first fires within the area of the port, and the operation of the smoke screen. Having made their mistake, probably at an early stage in the attack, there was little or nothing to prevent subsequent enemy aircraft from delivering their blitz of bombs, mines and incendiaries, with full fury. Their crews' reports were utterly dismissive of Belfast's active defences, commenting on the scant provision of searchlights, the small number of barrage balloons, and the lack of night-fighters – they had noticed just one aircraft on patrol during the entire course of the raid. They also described the anti-aircraft guns as 'very badly positioned', though this criticism may simply confirm the view that they had totally misread the topography of the city. Overall, they suffered no losses of bombers over Northern Ireland, whereas a possible fourteen were shot down that night over Britain.

However, Belfast's high death toll was not due solely to the distribution or the ferocity of the Luftwaffe's attack. The population of the city had woefully little protection on the ground, when the bombs actually fell. The devastated area was dominated by closely packed, densely populated, working-class housing. The report, written by Dr Carnwath in December 1941, at a time when twenty-six thousand people had been officially evacuated, stated that in 'bad areas' the typical number of occupants in the larger terraced houses was fifteen. These ageing, fragile, decaying slums were least able to provide adequate cover or a secure hiding place for householders. Newspaper reports described bombs ripping through gable walls and the occupants inside being 'hurled over the tops of houses' into neighbouring streets. Even on the newer estates in Greencastle, an air raid precautions warden expressed his 'surprise' at how quickly 'the entire fabric' of dwellings could 'be turned over'. The shoddy quality of housing is reflected in the relatively high number of people killed outright in these poorer areas. The Reverend J. Woodburn, a Presbyterian cleric, who

The burnt out shell of Frederick Street nurses' home after the 15–16 April raid. (Ulster Museum)

had gone 'around some of the devastated places' felt constrained to approach John MacDermott later. He wrote: 'I hope and trust that they will never be rebuilt again. . . A minister said to me, whose congregation had been bombed. . . if he could get the people entirely out of the way, he would be happy if the Germans would come and bomb the place flat.'

Possibly in these circumstances the death rate would have been lower had the population been more shelter conscious. A Home Office report commented after the raid on the 'marked tendency' among civilians to congregate together in each other's houses rather than utilise such shelters as existed. In some cases up to nineteen bodies were recovered from a single house. However, the provision of shelters was uneven and inadequate. In suburban areas, such as Veryan Gardens or the Whitewell Road, which were remote from centres of vital industry, none whatever existed. As a consequence of this raid, the Reverend W.J. Finlay Maguire of St Ninian's parish church in Greencastle placed his boiler house at the disposal of the local community. But even in York Street, which lay well within the danger zone, the military authorities considered that the shelters were 'too few and too packed'. They regarded this as a major cause of 'panic' at Vere Street after York Street mill was struck. One army officer reported that soon afterwards 'a rush was made for my car', but that he 'persuaded them to stay in shelters'. Following the raid, Jim Jenkins recalls people climbing up the Cavehill, armed with spades. They were hoping to unearth tunnels, believed to exist behind Bellevue Zoo, and to use them for the protection of themselves and their families.

The performance of existing shelters during the attack had been uneven. On occasion they had been spectacularly effective, as when a huge parachute mine had fallen near the telephone exchange in Victoria Street. But in other instances, notably at Percy Street, Thorndyke Street and Atlantic Avenue, they had collapsed. They had been constructed to withstand blast damage from bombs of up to five hundred kilograms; the heaviest of the German bombs dropped in the course of this attack, aptly named the 'Satan bomb', had weighed eighteen hundred kilograms. As a result of the raid a government inquiry therefore recommended that the walls of shelters should be strengthened and also that they should be of equal height to surrounding buildings. Overall, confidence in their effectiveness was not enhanced by the attack and, in areas such as Percy Street, there was subsequently an increased resistance to entering them. Generally, however, the public had never warmed to their use; they were dark, dirty, cold and stinking. There was also a widespread attitude, expressed by Nellie Bell's father, that 'If there was a bomb with his name on it, he would take it at his own fireside.'

DOGS AND CATS FRO[M]
BOMBED PREMISES.

THE DOGS' AND CATS' HOM[E] BALMORAL will receive and kee[p] Dogs at owners' risk, free of charge, f[or] a period not exceeding 14 days. Dogs [or] Cats can be lethalised free of charg[e]. All Dogs or Cats can be left at 28, Ma[…] Street, Belfast, for transmission to th[e] Home.

Belfast News-Letter, 19 April 1941

Whether or not the increased use of shelters would have lowered the death toll significantly is unclear. It is certain, however, that the evacuation of more people from the densely populated areas of Belfast would have reduced it substantially. Westminster government figures indicate that of the 695 classified deaths resulting from the Easter Tuesday raid, no less than 385 of them were of women and children. When it took place, fewer than five thousand people had evacuated from the city under official schemes, even though three of these had been launched since the summer of 1940. In essence this derisively inadequate response was due to a widespread disbelief in the possibility of a serious attack, and a total lack of imagination as to the resulting conditions should one occur. Both of these circumstances were utterly eradicated during the night of 15–16 April. As a result, the Government was confronted in dramatic fashion with a new and completely unforeseen problem, the mass exodus of tens of thousands of citizens from the city.

This outward migration began even before a bomb had been dropped, with people trekking on foot to parks, fields and hills, while others, in cars and bicycles, headed towards the assumed safety of the open countryside. Above the noise of planes still circling overhead, William McCready could hear vehicles 'being driven at high speed. . . civilians getting to hell out of the city and into the country'. This initial impulse gathered pace throughout the raid; after the all-clear, it rapidly assumed the proportions of a mass movement. The traumatic psychological impact of the five-hour bombardment not just on the districts which bore its full ferocity but on the whole community was immediately evident.

On 16 April eyewitnesses noted a constant surge of traffic along the

Suburban houses in Sunningdale Park, off the Cavehill Road, also bore the scars of the 15–16 April raid. (Ulster Museum)

Antrim Road, vehicles were full to overflowing with evacuees and others on foot. In west Belfast Joseph McCann saw 'streams of people moving up the Falls, the women and children with mattresses and bedclothes strapped to prams and handcarts'. On 'one road leading out of town', Moya Woodside watched 'an exodus on foot, trams, lorries, trailers, cattle floats, bicycles, delivery vans, anything that would move was utilized. Private cars streamed past. . . all sorts of paraphernalia roped on behind. Hundreds were waiting at bus-stops. Anxiety on every face. . . where they are going and what they will find when they get there, nobody knows.' On 17 April 1941 the *Northern Whig* reported that the scenes 'were like the pictures of American pioneers'; on the same day the *Belfast Telegraph* described 'a man cycling towards the country, on his back all he had managed to save, his head swathed in bandages. . . a grim reminder of the horrors of the night'. At the city centre, Emma Duffin found 'everywhere, people with parcels or suitcases struggling to get away'. Major H. John F. Potter, who had been evacuated to Portstewart, Co. Londonderry, was sixteen years of age when he noted in his diary: 'People have been scared. They are streaming out of the city, some camping in the Holywood hills, others even flying south. . . And these evacuee people say it was cruel to put up a smokescreen over the aerodrome and docks, as it meant that their houses were bombed.' Railway and bus stations were overwhelmed; passengers demanding to be taken somewhere into the country, not caring where, but just desperate to get out of Belfast.

At the Great Northern Railway Station, the only rail terminus left undamaged by the attack, the mood of panic was evident. Soldiers observed 'men elbowing women away in order to secure seats on trains'. Mr S. Hill, a ticket clerk, recalled that 'they would just back a train down, put it out, and go away, and you didn't know where the train was going until they decided where most people were for'. Moya Woodside described the station forecourt:

> I have never seen any thing like it. . . thousands of people crowding in cars, buses, carts, lorries, bathchairs, women pushing prams and go-carts with anything up to six children trailing behind, belongings in blankets, pillow-boxes, baskets and boxes. [Later, at 5 p.m. that afternoon] the station doors had been shut. Crowds were waiting outside on the pavement all around, a constant stream of people arriving on foot or on buses, many looking exhausted. It was a heartbreaking sight.

By Saturday, 19 April, Great Northern Railway officials estimated that twenty-five thousand passengers had left the city from their platforms. On 20 April, Jean Stewart, a Women's Voluntary Service worker, recorded her forlorn attempt to place an 'old woman of seventy, who couldn't walk' on to a bus for Newcastle, Co. Down. The bus station was

> a seething mass of people laden with cases, trunks, children of all ages, prams piled high with luggage, parcels tied up and coming undone, blankets, etc. One woman was clutching a large clock, a garish affair, evidently very dear to her. We tried without success to get [the old woman] on a bus but the minute a bus nosed its way into the entrance to the bus station it was mobbed. We realized the hopelessness of getting a woman who required two strong men to lift her on board and decided to take [her] by car.

Day after day the outward migration continued. It included not only many of the estimated twenty thousand homeless, but also those from houses still habitable and from areas undamaged by the raid. They sought refuge not just in surrounding towns and villages but throughout Northern Ireland and beyond – in the Glens of Antrim, the Mourne Mountains, the area around Lough Neagh, in counties Fermanagh and Tyrone, and in Éire. Roughly three thousand went to Dundalk, the first of them arriving by train at noon on 16 April. On 19 April 1941 the *Dundalk Democrat* reported that the coaches were 'crammed with haggard, weary women, and frightened children, a number of them still wearing their night-clothes' and that crowds of curious onlookers thronged the approaches to the town's station threatening to 'embarrass the evacuees'. By 26 April a further five thousand had fled to Dublin, many travelling by three special trains which had run on Wednesday, 16 April, and into the early hours of Thursday morning. At least half of them were adults, mostly women, who according to local newspaper reports were 'inadequately clad and drawn from the poorer classes'. The majority were going to friends and relatives, others would take rooms in hotels for as long as they could afford and the rest would rely on the charitable support of the Irish Red Cross. On that Wednesday morning Mrs E.M. Sweeney had been married in Carlisle Road Methodist Church in Londonderry and later that day she and her husband caught the train for Dublin, where they had arranged to spend their honeymoon. In the course of their journey they were amazed at the huge number of refugees from Belfast who boarded at Portadown, Co. Armagh; the carriages became so crowded that passengers had to stand shoulder to shoulder in the aisles. However, the full horror of the attack only became apparent to them when they noticed that some of the women were clutching dead infants in their arms.

The Northern Ireland government estimated that by Tuesday, 29 April, at least one hundred thousand of Belfast's citizens had evacuated from the city and were remaining in accommodation scattered throughout the country. The fundamental cause of this crash evacuation was fear – the fear of further bombing and an urge to escape from homes which were manifestly so vulnerable. 'There is a strong feeling,' L. Eardley-Wilmot, a Home Office official, commented, 'that they are going to be subjected to another attack.' It was his opinion, shared also by Stormont ministers, that this was 'not at all improbable'. Widespread alarm was fuelled by rumour and speculation. Moya Woodside noted: 'Everyone is quoting Lord Haw Haw: "He will give us time to bury our dead before the next attack"; "Tuesday was only a sample"; "People living in such and such an area will have their turn".' In these circumstances the attraction of the surrounding countryside proved irresistible for almost one-quarter of the population; it was both accessible and likely to remain, as it had been until now, virtually immune from the attentions of the Luftwaffe.

However, not all chose to migrate so far or so permanently out of Belfast. 'There was,' Minister of Home Affairs Dawson Bates informed the cabinet, 'an additional problem to be solved.' He was referring to 'the ditchers', the many thousands who, though they did not necessarily live in danger areas, none the less refused to sleep in their own houses at night. Instead, they sought safety in the outskirts of the city – in hills, fields, barns, woods and roadsides – some staying out until dawn, others returning when they considered that the likelihood of a raid had passed. Jimmy Doherty first became aware of the phenomenon soon after leaving the 'morgue' at Falls Road public baths during the evening after the Easter Tuesday raid. He remembers feeling 'amazed at the floods of people still streaming out of the town', even from areas totally unaffected by the attack. At Carlisle Circus he met a number who were 'frantic to get out' and, to their profound relief, he was able to arrange military transport for them to Glengormley. As they went they sang 'over and over again' a modified version of a Belfast street song, which now contained the refrain: 'Hitler thought he'd beat us with his ya, ya, ya.' Moya Woodside also recorded travelling into the city that evening 'through the gathering darkness'. It was, she wrote, 'a horrible

UARD AGAINST TYPHOID

Advice by City Medical Officer

S a safeguard against the possibility of typhoid Belfast Medical icer of Health advises that all nking water should be boiled and s those resident in badly bombed as to present themselves for culation.

he recent raid on the city may e damaged the sewage system, h the result that germs may have nd their way into the drinking ter.

here are no signs that the drinking ter has been affected, yet the medi- authorities are taking all precauns by dealing with it at the source supply. To make certain, however, Medical Officer of Health asks the zens to have protective inoculation.

Only Sure Method

noculation is the only definite ans of preventing spread of the ease

lthough typhoid can easily be dealt h in normal times the risk of an demic is so great following events h as Belfast suffered recently, that s the duty of everyone to guard inst it.

he Medical Officer points out that ess the citizens take personal pretions the city's medical staffs may inundated in the event of an demic, with a resultant heavy th roll.

Northern Whig, 28 April 1941

INFECTIOUS DISEASES

Two Deaths From Typhoid in Belfast

According to a return by the Medical perintendent Officer of Health, 57 of e 200 deaths in Belfast during the eek ended April 19 were cases of fectious disease. Of that number, two re of typhoid fever, 13 of scarlet fever, of diphtheria, two of acute primary eumonia, nine of cerebro-spinal fever, o of acute poliomyelitis, two of puerral pyrexia, five of measles, and nine whooping-cough. At the Tuberculosis stitute eight persons were diognosed as ffering from tuberculosis of the notible type.

The deaths from all causes registered the ten principal towns of Northern eland (exclusive of non-residents) mbered 251, representing an annual te of 22.0 per 1,000 of the population. e deaths from certain epidemic seases registered in these towns were uivalent to 0.5 per 1,000. The births mbered 164, representing 14.4 per 1,000. The deaths in Belfast numbered 200 presenting 23.5 per 1,000., The average te for the second quarter of each the previous ten years was 13.4 r 1,000. Included in the 200 deaths re five from epidemic diseases. Deaths om tuberculosis, numbered 12. The rths registered numbered 120, or 14.1 r 1,000.

Belfast News-Letter, *April* 1941

BELFAST AIR RAID

OFFICIAL NOTICES

The following notices are issued by the Ministry of Public Security, Northern Ireland, and the Belfast Civil Defence Authority:—

(1) ACCOMMODATION FOR THE HOMELESS.

Arrangements are being made by the authorities to billet homeless people as quickly as possible.

It is the imperative duty of householders to receive the homeless into their houses. *THE AUTHORITIES WILL TAKE A SERIOUS VIEW OF ANY REFUSAL TO DO SO.*

(2) STAY AT HOME IF YOU CAN.

PEOPLE WHOSE HOMES ARE STILL HABITABLE SHOULD CONTINUE TO LIVE IN THEM, and so relieve the pressure on the authorities, who are fully engaged in providing accommodation and transport for those whose homes have been destroyed.

17th April, 1941.

BELFAST AIR RAID EMERGENCY

IF YOU have changed your address since Monday please send a postcard to CASUALTY ENQUIRIES BUREAU, CITY HALL, BELFAST. Your friends are anxious to know your whereabouts.

ISSUED BY THE BELFAST CIVIL DEFENCE AUTHORITY.
17th April, 1941.

experience and I admit to feeling rather frightened. . .parties of people were still trailing towards the country'. Almost two months later she received a chilling insight into the mood of panic which was still widespread in Belfast when she visited a woman in hospital who had given birth to 'a five months' child' on 16 April, the day after the raid. That same night the woman had 'got up and trailed out to the fields with her other children'. She continued doing this 'night after night' and now she had just been informed by the medical authorities that 'her health will never be the same again'.

The nocturnal migration affected all parts of the city. Frank Skillen, a shipyard worker, observed that people moved to 'where they felt safe, they kept to their own area, they didn't venture'. In east Belfast they went to Dundonald, and the Castlereagh and Cregagh Hills; on the Shankill Road, to Woodvale Park and beyond; on the Falls Road, to Falls Park, to the grounds of Clonard Monastery and Hannahstown; on the Grosvenor Road, to Bog Meadows; on the Antrim Road, to the Cavehill and Glengormley. Suspected Luftwaffe targets were avoided, such as the neighbourhood around Mackies' foundry on the Springfield Road, or much of the Holywood Road because of its proximity to Sydenham airport. A contemporary Royal Ulster Constabulary inquiry estimated that ditchers generally walked to a distance of about two miles beyond the city boundary, and that at first most of them slept in the open, under hedges, or they scooped out dugouts for themselves in steep slopes or hillsides. Gradually, however, because of the time of year, more found shelter in sheds, byres, or barns, the animals being in the fields. There they slept on stone, concrete or earthen floors, establishing a 'sort of squatter's right' to their place. There were no sanitary arrangements, and therefore there was obviously a considerable risk of epidemic, especially by milk contamination spreading from dairy farms. None the less, local police encouraged farmers to make their property available, as otherwise, they feared that widespread outbreaks of rioting would have occurred. Clearly, the ditchers were impelled mainly by fear; the incidence of an alert, a Haw Haw rumour, or the phasing of the moon, helping to determine their precise number during the weeks following Easter Tuesday. But there was also a widespread feeling that there was safety in numbers and people who lived close to demolished buildings and deserted and empty city streets were demoralised.

It is clear that the ditchers, and those who evacuated more permanently into the countryside, were not two separate and distinct categories. The police report indicated that evacuees from Belfast continued to ditch even in safe and remote rural areas and indeed introduced the habit of ditching to other parts of Northern Ireland. It noted that wherever inquiries had been made ditching was going on:

> It happens in Kilkeel, Ballyclare, parts of Tyrone and Fermanagh. It has been caused undoubtedly by the presence of evacuees in these areas. The people come down from Belfast and the country people see them go out at night and they say to themselves that the Belfast people know what's what in regard to air-raids and if they think it is worthwhile going out into the fields at night, then it must be.

The consequences of the mass exodus from Belfast were felt throughout all districts. Sarah Nelson, a young civil servant, recalls that the Antrim Road and the Shore Road were so quiet 'it was like a plague had come'. At many schools on the Falls Road pupil attendance dropped to below 50 per cent normal levels when the summer term began, nine days after the raid. A priest in the dockside parish of St Joseph's, which he stated 'had suffered very severely from the raid', reported that 'his people had left'. Even in south Belfast many began to commute to work in the city from neighbouring seaside towns and villages. Moya Woodside noted: 'Everywhere one hears remarks: "Oh, I am living out at so and so now, I have to get up at 6.00 to be in on time at the office."' House maids had also become scarce, as so many had returned to their rural homes; and rooms and flats, which had previously been unobtainable throughout the area, were soon being advertised in substantial numbers. City-centre cinemas and theatres were virtually empty in the late evening and in suburban areas many closed doors completely, so accentuating the air of desolation. Even hospitals like the Royal Victoria were affected, with country people anxious to end their treatment and leave, or reluctant to enter it at all and avail themselves of its specialist medical services.

The scale and persistence of this elemental popular migration went far beyond anything that the Government had foreseen. Early in 1941, John MacDermott had provided the cabinet with an apocalyptic vision of conditions in Belfast on the morning after a blitz. He had predicted many fires raging, public buildings crumpled and in ruins, the city centre reduced to a charred skeleton, rows of streets flattened, rumours pervasive, workers uncertain whether their place of employment was still standing, and thousands of homeless people wandering about 'aimlessly and dazedly'. It contained one glaring omission: there was no hint or suggestion of a possible crash evacuation out of the city. In fact government ministers never seriously envisaged having to deal with more than ten thousand evacuees – the maximum number considered likely to be made homeless in the event of an attack. It had been arranged that they would be looked after temporarily at thirty or so rest centres in the city, before being evacuated directly to billets in the country.

These modest plans appeared to be fully justified. After all, the three previous government evacuation schemes had each foundered utterly on the bedrock of general complacency and disinterest. Also, as John Oliver, MacDermott's private secretary, accurately observed, 'many people living in Belfast had never been beyond the tramlines'. Such deep-rooted public attitudes and patterns of behaviour seemed unlikely to change, even as a consequence of the Easter Tuesday raid. There had of course been some reports of panic and confusion while the bombs were falling and of people rushing from their houses towards the open country. But others recorded their surprising fortitude and calmness; a confidential military analysis concluded that civilian 'behaviour was generally very good'. Only gradually did ministers and officials become aware of the scale of the subsequent mass exodus from Belfast. Even after the attack it was at first widely assumed that popular morale was unshaken, that the Government's emergency machinery was working well, and that no crash evacuation was taking place. By Friday, 19 April, however, it was evident that morale was not high, that people were leaving the city in tens of thousands and that consequently official plans and provisions had been absolutely overwhelmed. MacDermott condemned the 'blitz-quitters' and despondently acknowledged that more were 'leaving Belfast in proportion to population than any other city in the United Kingdom'. He held Craigavon at least partially responsible. Many years later MacDermott recalled that the Prime Minister had made an extremely injudicious remark in 1940: while discussing air raid precautions measures for the protection of the people, he had said: 'The country is near and they can take to the ditches.'

In the event, the mass evacuation certainly raised a number of critical problems for the Northern Ireland government. It helped to reduce communications to chaos by blocking and overloading arterial roads, and it would have impeded a military response had the blitz been accompanied by enemy invasion. The removal of debris and completion of rescue work were delayed because so many army and civilian vehicles were employed in moving people and furniture, often from undamaged houses. In addition, the exodus eroded further the strength of Belfast's civil defence services, which were already short of personnel and had been depleted by recent casualties. MacDermott spoke of air raid precautions men 'sloping off'. One senior warden was seen, helmet in hand, walking out of Amiens Street Railway Station in Dublin with hundreds of refugees hours after the attack. However, the performance and commitment of the wardens and other services varied. Emma Duffin wrote of 'wardens leaving their posts, of panic, [and also] of incredible bravery'. Similarly, the military authorities reported that though some had left the city, others were 'carrying out their duties admirably'. This was also Jimmy Doherty's experience. He recalls that 'a number were in it for the badge, they had no idea what to expect and flew in buses and trains. But most stayed, though they had lost homes, relatives, jobs, clothes. The organization had broken down, the men worked on, there was nothing else for it.' In the wardens' service alone twenty-one members died in the course of this attack.

The evacuation also contributed to a slackening off in Belfast's industrial production which for weeks stubbornly remained at 25 per cent pre-blitz levels. On 3 May, output at Harland and Wolff shipyard was 70 per cent normal and at Short and Harland aircraft factory as little as 30 per cent. This was due in fact to the migration of workers from the city, which directly caused absenteeism and loss of hours through late arrival for work. Other major causal factors included the physical damage to factory plant, the disruption of essential services and the much greater unwillingness of employees to work night-shifts in the area of the port after the raid.

However, the Government's most acute problem was the extent to which its own post-blitz plans had been reduced to utter chaos and confusion. Newspapers reported 'endless queues' at the city's thirty-three rest centres. These were mainly comprised of church halls and schools. Some of them had already filled up while the raid was in progress; all were subsequently overwhelmed, even being compelled to close their doors temporarily. They had been intended to provide short-term emergency support for up to ten thousand homeless. On 16 April they fed seventy thousand people and forty thousand slept in them overnight. Knock Methodist Church was not untypical. Harold Allen, an air raid precautions warden, recalls it being used to provide sleeping accommodation for several days after the raid and the particular care taken to 'select a clean family for behind the communion rail, people who would respect it'. The centres attracted many whose homes were undamaged but who were in desperate need of food, warmth and comfort. But the threat of further tragedy loomed as a number of centres were located in vulnerable districts without adequate air-raid shelter provision nearby.

In the countryside, billets which the Government had earmarked for the genuinely homeless under the official evacuation scheme were overrun by self-evacuated refugees. As a consequence, quiet rural areas became acutely overcrowded. Their housing facilities and services, which were already strained by the presence of such large numbers of troops in Northern Ireland, now approached and in some cases surpassed saturation point. There were reports of unscrupulous landlords inflating their rents to five and six times pre-war levels or cramming small, poor quality houses with billetees and then claiming substantial government allowances, 'without themselves providing anything'. By 17 April, officials were receiving information that food supplies had been exhausted in villages even forty miles and more from Belfast. Minister of Commerce Sir Basil Brooke expressed acute concern about the health risks resulting from the flood of refugees into a county as remote as Fermanagh. Minister of Home Affairs Dawson Bates informed his colleagues that within a fortnight of the raid two thousand had settled in Dromara, Co. Down; its normal population size was five hundred.

'It is not difficult,' he concluded, 'to imagine what conditions there are like', and he predicted very serious criticism both in Northern Ireland and in Great Britain 'unless the Government found a solution' to this increasingly urgent problem.

Because of its close proximity to Belfast, Lisburn in Co. Antrim inevitably also faced a massive influx of refugees coming by bus, car, train and military lorry. Miss M. Barnes, a full-time member of the Women's Voluntary Service, recalls that most of them were panic-stricken, fleeing from undamaged homes but simply 'too terrified to spend another night in Belfast'. All needed to be 'fed, housed, deloused, marshalled, bathed, clothed, pacified and brought back to normal'. In this unforeseen emergency, temporary accommodation was improvised at four local schools, though at the time no one knew where to obtain government assistance or information about families that had become separated. The nearby army base provided a mobile bath unit which proved to be 'extremely necessary'. She recorded that 'the men had their baths quickly enough' but many women objected on the grounds that they 'would catch cold'. She found that the overall reaction of the evacuees to their treatment varied. A number 'tried to pay someone for the food and care' received; others were less responsive. One old lady from Ardoyne maintained that it was 'little enough we were doing in return for all the Ardoyne ones did the time Lisburn was burnt'. An endemic problem at the various rest centres was a 'clothing racket'; evacuees would tell 'long tragic stories of their experience and beg for clothing. . .which they then went out and pawned'.

Lisburn was regarded by the Ministry of Home Affairs as one of the most efficiently organised reception areas in the North. None the less, over two weeks passed before its four schools were cleared and billets found for those who had taken refuge in them. In the context of such rural saturation, on 27 April the Government had abandoned its own official evacuation scheme, which had been launched immediately after the Dockside raid. The decision aroused considerable confusion. The military authorities later complained that even the city's police were totally unaware of what official evacuation arrangements had been made.

It was not just the numbers of refugees which confounded government plans, it was also their social composition. Amidst the chaotic scenes at city rest centres and rural reception areas, the mainly middle-class volunteers readily appreciated that they were facing people not only traumatised by a terrifying ordeal but also, in many cases, suffering from a degree of poverty of which the volunteers had no previous conception. Almost with disbelief, Emma Duffin wrote of

> the incredible dirt of the people, of children crawling with lice, not even house trained, who destroyed mattresses and stuffed clothes down W.C.'s in order to get new ones, women turning up with naked children who were fully clothed and the same women and the same children turning up at another rest centre the following day, the children once more naked.

It was, she concluded, 'all a terrible indictment of our way of life.' In essence, a new social category was emerging that had not previously entered into the calculations of government ministers or their departments. Northern Ireland's official wartime historian, John Blake, referred to it as 'the submerged one-tenth of the population'. At the time Dawson Bates wrote: 'There is unfortunately a class that can only be described as unbilletable and which the Ministry would be very loathe to billet on any householder in Northern Ireland, such people are so inhuman in their habits.' In a joint memorandum with John MacDermott, he informed the cabinet that: 'Lice and vermin are being spread through the country, buses and trains are being infected, and clean and well kept households are having billeted upon them filthy and verminous persons.'

Moya Woodside could have confirmed this from her knowledge of and contact with the eleven evacuees staying with her mother. They were, she noted, 'all filthy, the smell of the room is terrible, they refuse all food except tea and bread, the children have made puddles all over the floor, etc. [Her mother] feels terribly sorry for them and is kindness itself but finds this revelation of how the other half lives somewhat overpowering.' Later it was discovered that several of the children had tuberculosis and two had a skin disease on their scalps. Similarly, Moya Woodside's sister, a member of the Women's Voluntary Service, who lived in a small country town thirty miles from Belfast, complained of

> the appalling influx from the slums the day after the raid. They were totally unprepared for such numbers and for the type of people arriving. The whole town is horrified by the filth of these evacuees and by their filthy habits and take-it-for-granted attitude. . . The smell is awful. . . They don't even use the lavatory, they just do it on the floor, grown-ups and children, our blankets in two nights have been absolutely ruined. She was ashamed to have to ask decent working people with clean houses to take in such guests.

From the experience of her family and of others, Moya Woodside observed that 'bed wetting and skin disease amongst children are the commonest complaints and vermin accepted as an inevitability'. She consoled herself with the thought that 'At least it may be good in one way if it makes people think about housing and the slums. Complacency and ignorance have been widely shattered these last few days.' Overall, she concluded that the crash evacuation in all its varied aspects presented a 'problem of the first priority for Stormont'. Of course such a mass elemental movement lay far beyond the powers of any government department to prevent. As John MacDermott himself observed: 'People just wandered into the country. . . no record could possibly be taken of them.' Ministers regarded their migration as unexpected and selfish, because those with undamaged houses appropriated billets earmarked for the genuinely homeless. But it was also thought to be understandable – few doubted that the Luftwaffe would return.

The Duke and Duchess of Gloucester, on a morale-boosting tour of the blitz areas of Belfast, are seen here at Percy Street, Shank Road, on 22 April 1941. (*Belfast Telegraph*)

For the Government to have accepted such a total dislocation of the normal life of the city and of Northern Ireland was tantamount to conceding complete morale victory to the enemy; an urgent response was necessary in order to restore order from the chaos and to prepare for a further attack. Immediately, consideration was given to the restoration of public morale. William D. Scott, permanent secretary at the Ministry of Commerce, suggested to Prime Minister John Andrews that he should make a personal appeal emphasising that 'our best reply. . . was redoubled effort'. He quoted, as a possible source of inspiration, lines from Abraham Lincoln's Gettysburg Address: 'It is for us the living, rather, to be dedicated here to the unfinished work.' Its sentiments, if not its eloquence, are discernable in Andrews's subsequent press statements. In them he referred to the 'gigantic task ahead' and declared: 'We will see this thing through to the end so that we may rejoice together in the day of victory.' Newspapers elaborated on the same theme. Much publicised official visits to the bombed areas were also hastily arranged, including one by the Duke and Duchess of Gloucester, and much prominence was given to a telegram received by the Stormont government from Herbert Morrison, the British Home Secretary. It congratulated both the 'leaders and their people on their grit and courage' and ended with a vague, though reassuring commitment: 'all help we can send is at your disposal'. Moya Woodside was not impressed. She wrote:

DUKE AND DUCHESS OF GLOUCESTER

Admiration For The Spirit of Belfast

TOUR OF DEVASTATED AREAS

THE DUKE and DUCHESS OF GLOUCESTER spent three hours yesterday inspecting Belfast's bombed areas. Everywhere they were received with cheers. They spoke words of comfort and encouragement to many humble folk.

People standing amid the ruins of their homes waved Union Jacks and sang the National Anthem. In one of the districts that had suffered severely women and children shouted " We're not beaten."

Belfast News-Letter, 22 April 1941

> There is not much point patting people on the back for their 'spirit' when there is nowhere for them to go, [when] Rest Centres overflowing are temporarily closed, when thousands are thrown out of work, when terrified refugees are spending nights under hedges in the countryside.

In the meantime, however, the Government was at least beginning to address these problems. It appealed to the public to stay in or return to their homes if possible, and soon afterwards indicated that empty and habitable houses would be requisitioned for the homeless and destitute. On 19 April 1941 the *Irish Times* considered that this threat helped staunch the flow of evacuees to Éire. Other observers, inside Northern Ireland, believed that they could already detect public opinion 'veering around to disapproval of those who bolted from undamaged homes'. At the same time the authorities stressed that it was the duty of householders to receive the homeless, threatened to apply compulsion if they refused, and prepared legislation to prevent rent profiteering. An urgent effort was made using requisitioned transport to clear the city's rest centres and move people from 'the more grossly overcrowded and unmanageable' areas of the country to others which soon became similarly overcrowded and unmanageable. In addition, while these measures were being taken, it was found necessary to drastically modify the Government's own emergency machinery. Under the Hiram Plan it had been the duty of the Ministry of Public Security to restore at least a semblance of normality to the city and then hand it back to the usual administrative departments. However, it was soon evident that John MacDermott's Ministry of Public Security had been grossly overloaded and, consequently, major areas of responsibility were transferred to the Ministry of Home Affairs and to the Ministry of Agriculture. Inevitably this caused criticism as both departments resented being asked to take over responsi-

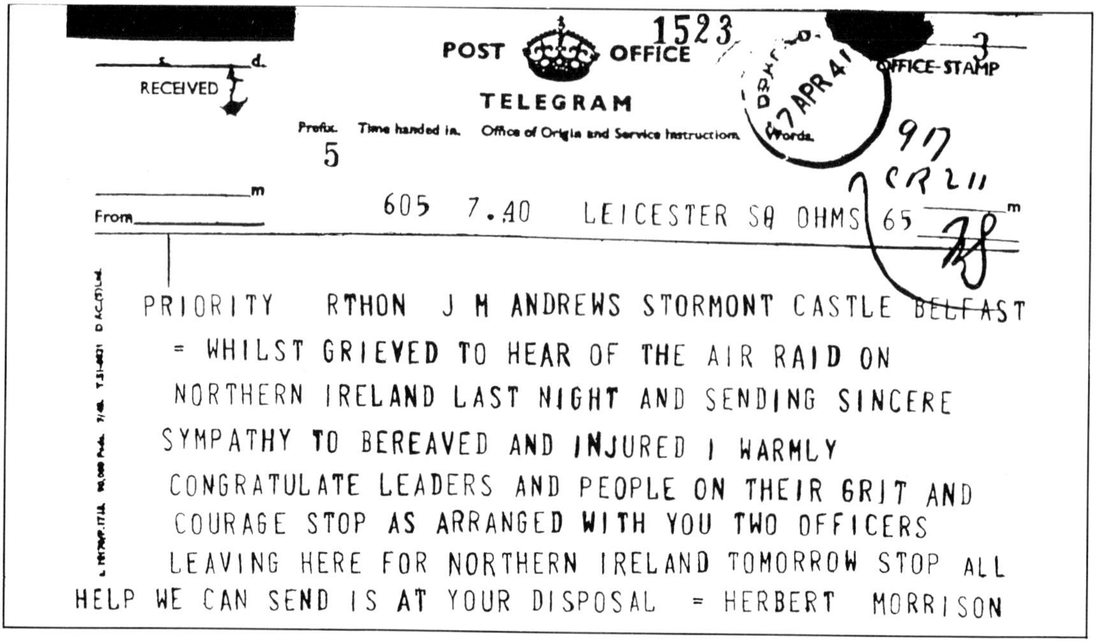

POST OFFICE TELEGRAM

RECEIVED

OFFICE STAMP

Prefix. Time handed in. Office of Origin and Service Instructions. Words.

5

From

605 7.40 LEICESTER SQ OHMS 65

PRIORITY RTHON J M ANDREWS STORMONT CASTLE BELFAST
= WHILST GRIEVED TO HEAR OF THE AIR RAID ON
NORTHERN IRELAND LAST NIGHT AND SENDING SINCERE
SYMPATHY TO BEREAVED AND INJURED I WARMLY
CONGRATULATE LEADERS AND PEOPLE ON THEIR GRIT AND
COURAGE STOP AS ARRANGED WITH YOU TWO OFFICERS
LEAVING HERE FOR NORTHERN IRELAND TOMORROW STOP ALL
HELP WE CAN SEND IS AT YOUR DISPOSAL = HERBERT MORRISON

Northern Ireland Prime Minister John Andrews received this telegram on 17 April, expressing Home Secretary Herbert Morrison's concern abo the 15–16 April raid. (Public Record Office of Northern Ireland)

bility for services which had fallen into such complete chaos. Meanwhile MacDermott was also strongly attacked at Stormont in some of the most bitter speeches made in the history of the Northern Ireland parliament. Jack Beattie, Independent Labour MP, whom MacDermott was convinced had 'Sinn Féin sympathies', said of MacDermott: 'The sooner he gets out of the post, the sooner will Belfast be safe and fit for the people. . . he has not got the human touch.'

Parliamentary debate and governmental concern concentrated almost exclusively on the impact of the blitz on Belfast. But there were a number of bombing incidents elsewhere in Northern Ireland, scattered along the Luftwaffe's flight path. In the most serious of these, at Londonderry, Newtownards and Bangor, the features of the attack that had characterised the experience of the capital were paralleled though on an infinitely smaller scale: most of the bombs were dropped on residential property; the public were unprotected and unprepared for the raid; active defences were weak or nonexistent; and blackout measures defective. Local press reports afterwards also reflected on the widespread preference for remaining in bed or for taking cover behind a ditch rather than in the few shelters available.

No provincial city or town in the North suffered more at the hands of the Luftwaffe than Londonderry. This was not unexpected. On 15 March 1941 the *Londonderry Sentinel* had warned its readers that they could not 'hope to escape the attention of the Nazi airmen throughout the war. Our immunity hitherto may well prove our greatest peril because of the false sense of security it has given.' MacDermott had already reached the conclusion that the city was as probable a target as Belfast. Its port was steadily emerging as an important base for the protection of the western approaches (at its peak, in 1943, it hosted 150 ships and 20,000 sailors). In addition, its significance as a ship-repair and ship-construction yard was also growing.

However, its active defences, comprised of thirty barrage balloons and sixteen anti-aircraft guns, had failed to keep pace with its developing strategic and economic role.

The alert came at just before midnight on Easter Tuesday evening. Charlie Gallagher, a local air raid precautions warden, recalls that there was no great sense of panic as he and his colleagues assembled at their post in Church House, Great James' Street. There had been, after all, 'dozens' of alarms before. However, the mood became more sombre when a telephone message was received indicating that 'Belfast was taking a hammering'. On hearing this news, Miss O'Neill, one of the first-aid personnel present, requested: 'Let us pray for those who may die tonight.' In respectful silence they bowed their heads in prayer. Soon afterwards, at a little after midnight, a post lookout reported that flares were being dropped over the city. This was followed almost immediately by two 'deafening explosions', and minutes later, an emergency call for ambulances to be dispatched. As Gallagher dashed towards one of the vehicles he heard a colleague mutter: 'I never thought that I would live to curse the night when bright moonlight shines.'

Two large parachute mines had been dropped, possibly by a single raider, near a small colony of ex-servicemen's homes in the Messines Park area, off the Buncrana Road. One fell harmlessly into a field, leaving an eighteen-foot crater and causing blast damage to houses and railway carriages. The other had devastated much of Messines Park. When Charlie Gallagher arrived, he was enveloped by a 'pall of dust' and his ambulance suddenly ground to a halt – 'It seemed like I was in the middle of a ploughed field.' Five houses had been totally demolished, 15 people had been killed, all of them members of ex-servicemen's families, and 150 made homeless. One of the bodies was not found until several weeks later. It had been blown into a sandpit and was eventually uncovered by some American construction workers, collecting building material for a new road development.

At the time officials concluded that the bombs had been dropped entirely at random. A civil defence report stated that the attack was 'indiscriminate and not directed against any naval, military or industrial concern'. This view was shared by the local naval authorities who claimed that the bombed houses lay in 'the worst blacked out area' of the city. However, some well-informed air raid precautions members, who had also witnessed the raid, concluded that the objective had been to disrupt the port by blocking the river, which was particularly narrow adjacent to where the mines had fallen.

Other areas nearer to Belfast also suffered during this raid. At about 1 a.m. the aerodrome at Newtownards, Co. Down, was struck by explosives and incendiaries; it was the only specifically military target to sustain damage outside the capital. Ten guards were killed and a number of civilians injured. Simultaneously, Bangor, also in Co. Down, was attacked for the second time. From a bedroom window in Bristow Park, south Belfast, Jean

Number 5 Hazeldene Gardens, Bangor, was struck by a bomb during t 15–16 April raid, killing c occupant, Margaret B. Watt. (Ian McQuiston)

Stewart 'could see the sky lighted by fires in the direction' of the town. At first flares were dropped lighting up the whole area and the surrounding countryside, and subsequently fourteen bombing incidents were reported. The most serious was at Ashley Gardens where six houses were damaged by high explosives. In all five civilians were killed and thirty-five injured. Although there appeared to be no obvious strategic target for the raid, on 19 April 1941 the *County Down Spectator* was firmly convinced the objective had been a 'large, white painted cinema'. On 3 May it returned to this conjecture, commenting that 'the white was beautiful, but now is more reminiscent of sunny Italy than our grey Northern skies. Today we are doubly fond of anything British and a sober quiet tone would be more pleasant.'

However, in Bangor, as in many more distant areas, the public's sense of the tragedy of the blitz focused on Belfast, its awareness and perception sharpened by the unending flood of refugees who had streamed into the borough. All of them were weary, confused and frightened. Many were ragged and pitifully poor; the sight aroused the consciences of this mainly middle-class town. On 26 April 1941 the *County Down Spectator* commented:

> The blitz has brought home to us the amount of absolute destitution in the poorer quarters of Belfast. The poverty that these enemy visitations has exposed is a disgrace to our much vaunted civilization. If the squalidness of many of the evacuees is indicative of the hovels that have been swept away in

> Belfast, Hitler has done these poor folk a service, so far at least as destroying their 'homes' is concerned. . . We are suffering so much in common that we have a feeling that the downtrodden amongst us are to have a better chance after the war.

In Belfast itself, Moya Woodside noted, even at the end of April, people 'still leaving. . . driving to a seaside town sixty miles away. We continuously passed lorries laden with bedding and furniture.' Days later, she returned to 'the blitzed area'. The experience made a profound emotional impact. It was, she recorded,

> bitterly cold and a wind swirled dust, plaster and ashes about the ruins so that one could hardly see. . . There was a sense of desolation; whole streets of windowless and roofless houses, with an occasional notice chalked on the door 'Gone to Ballymena' or some other country address. Not a soul about except demolition workers. Enormous gaps or mounds of bricks where once some familiar building had stood. More than a fortnight now since the raid, yet it still looks raw and obscene.

She concluded: 'People who survived that night of horror will surely never be the same again. Easy to understand why even still habitable houses are deserted.'

The devastation in High Street in the aftermath of th 4–5 May raid. (Public Record Office of Northern Ireland)

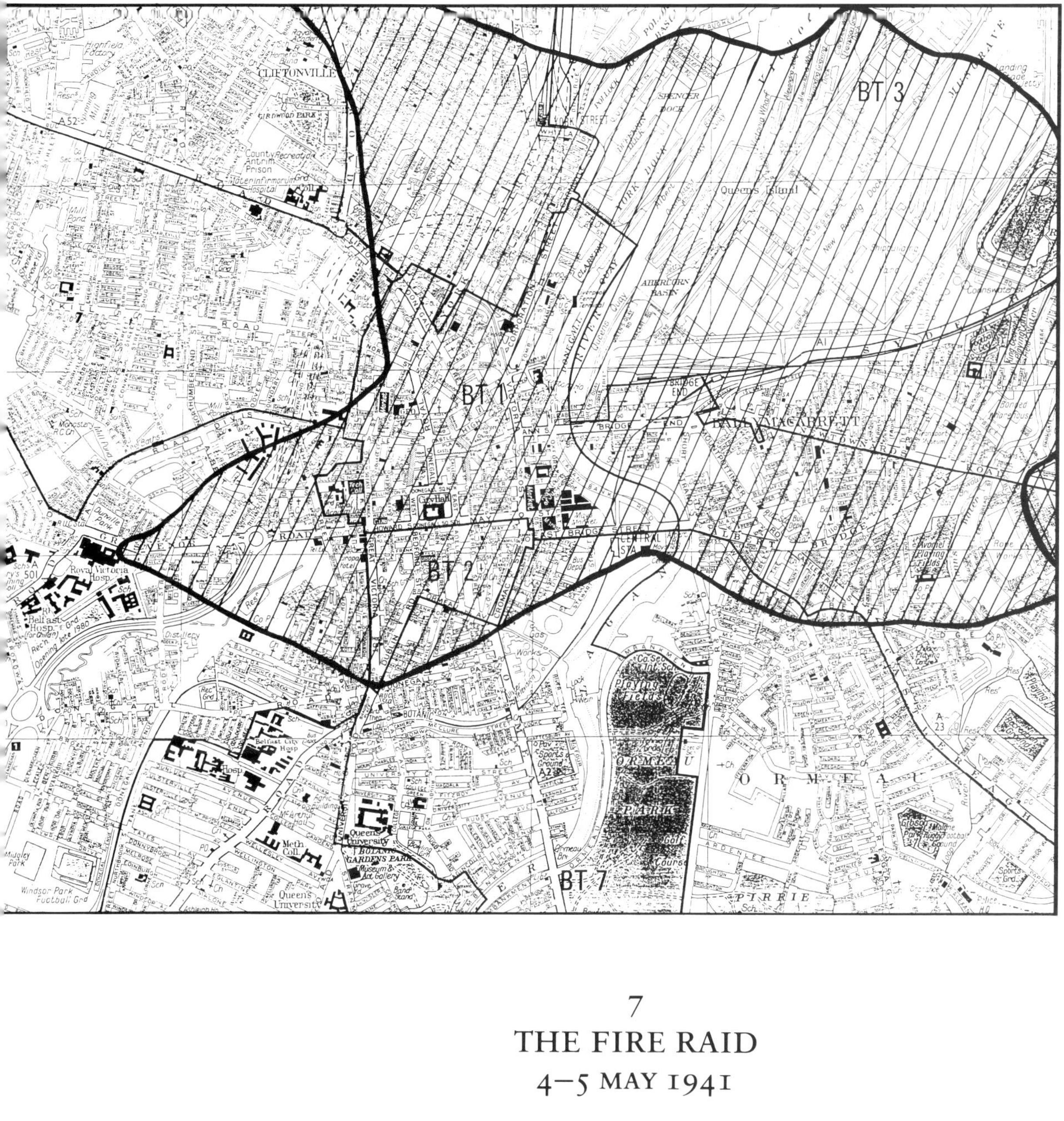

Based on official records, this map indicates the most severely stricken areas in Belfast during the 4–5 May raid.

7
THE FIRE RAID
4–5 MAY 1941

Almost every evening during the weeks following Easter Tuesday, 15 April 1941, the Luftwaffe returned in force to launch major attacks on Britain's cities and ports. London continued to bear the brunt of much of the assault. During the night of 19–20 April, enemy aircraft dropped over one thousand tons of high explosives on the capital – the biggest single bombing it sustained in the entire war. Urban areas on the south coast were struck repeatedly; lying just across the English Channel, they presented German bombers with soft targets. At least 775 tons of bombs and mines fell on Plymouth in the course of five raids between 21 and 30 April. From the vantage point of the Northern Ireland government, perhaps most ominous of all was the continuing onslaught against the western ports. Merseyside was attacked on three successive nights, from 1 to 4 May, and as a result nineteen hundred people died.

In this alarming context, efforts were made within Northern Ireland to heighten Belfast's preparedness for the Luftwaffe's anticipated return. During late April, its anti-aircraft barrage was strengthened: some anti-aircraft guns were transported from Britain, and others relocated from Londonderry and Larne. They were deployed with a view to improving the protective screen, particularly on the northern side of the city. The number of balloons was also increased and additional searchlight regiments were transferred from Britain. At the same time consideration was given to augmenting the city's passive defences. Boosted in part by official appeals, enrolment for the civil defence services was brisk in some districts after the Easter Tuesday raid. However, although this may have helped to restore their morale, both their total membership and supplies of vital equipment remained hopelessly inadequate. Any benefit derived from new recruitment was more than counteracted by the continuing loss of personnel caused by the crash evacuation and consequent expulsions from the service, and, to a lesser extent, the effect of military enlistment and the gradual movement of industry out of Belfast to less vulnerable locations beyond its boundaries. In addition to these measures, the Stormont government, following Westminster's example, assumed new powers to ensure that fire-watching orders were being fully complied with. It also earmarked a further £400,000 to provide more shelter accommodation in congested working-class districts.

Unfortunately, little that was tangible could be achieved during these vital weeks, due mainly to the acute shortage of supplies in Britain and the lack of time available. None the less, two measures of public protection were fully implemented. One was the decision to shoot those animals considered to be dangerous at Bellevue Zoo. At the time John MacDermott explained that this was necessary in the interests of public safety and morale; his ministry had been informed of widespread uneasiness in the neighbourhood of Bellevue. Accordingly, thirty-two animals were destroyed; the list includes lions, tigers, bears, wolves, vultures and a giant rat. The 'sentences' were carried out by a police constable and a sergeant in the Local Defence Volunteers. On 19 April 1941 the *Belfast Telegraph* described the head-keeper watching with 'tears streaming down his face, as the executioners proceeded from cage to cage'. The Government's compensation of £815 was clearly inadequate consolation. On the eastern side of the city, an attempt was made to camouflage the Stormont building. Ministers regarded it as both an obvious target in itself and a potential marker for the identification of others. Consequently, its walls were blackened and internal approach roads strewn with cinder making them almost impassable. To

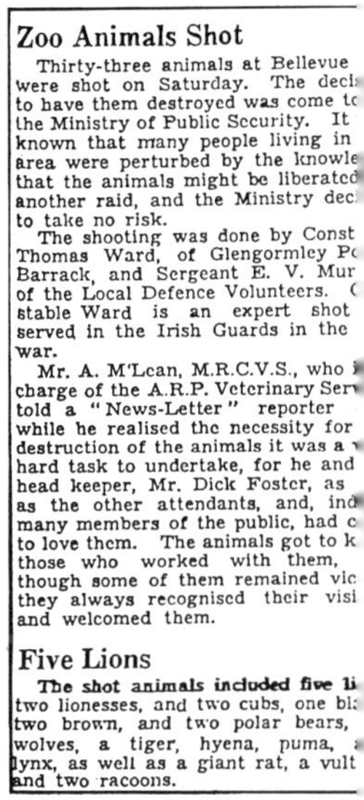
Zoo Animals Shot

Thirty-three animals at Bellevue were shot on Saturday. The deci to have them destroyed was come tc the Ministry of Public Security. It known that many people living in area were perturbed by the knowle that the animals might be liberated another raid, and the Ministry dec to take no risk.

The shooting was done by Const Thomas Ward, of Glengormley Pc Barrack, and Sergeant E. V. Mur of the Local Defence Volunteers. (stable Ward is an expert shot served in the Irish Guards in the war.

Mr. A. M'Lean, M.R.C.V.S., who charge of the A.R.P. Veterinary Ser told a "News-Letter" reporter while he realised the necessity for destruction of the animals it was a hard task to undertake, for he and head keeper, Mr. Dick Foster, as as the other attendants, and, ind many members of the public, had c to love them. The animals got to k those who worked with them, though some of them remained vic they always recognised their visi and welcomed them.

Five Lions

The shot animals included five li two lionesses, and two cubs, one bl two brown, and two polar bears, wolves, a tiger, hyena, puma, lynx, as well as a giant rat, a vult and two racoons.

Northern Whig, 21 April 1941

The unfamiliarly dark profile of Stormont (Northern Ireland's parliament building). Its white Portland stone has [b]een camouflaged beneath a [c]oating of pitch. (Ulster Folk and Transport Museum)

Belfast citizens both of these measures must have seemed potent evidence of the Government's presumption that another attack was imminent.

Throughout these weeks, rumours of further raids proliferated but though the sirens frequently wailed, no bombs actually fell. On the morning of Sunday, 4 May, Moya Woodside recorded with reviving confidence: 'Alert last night of about two hours' duration, but nothing happened. Stayed in bed. I am glad to discover that each time it sounds I feel less nervous. Eventually, I suppose, one can become accustomed to anything.' That Sunday was the first day of double summertime, a wartime innovation. The clocks went forward by one hour with the effect that sunset was 'delayed' until almost 9.30 p.m. Both the sudden lengthening of the evening and the mild, late spring weather were heartening. Lady Spender noted: 'We all had a late breakfast. It was a halcyon day, a light frost early and very hot later with a drenching dew and lovely tang in the air. We were in the garden all day.' After dusk, the night continued fine, almost cloudless, with a slight industrial haze, light south-south-westerly winds and a bright moon beaming down in its first quarter. Eileen Powderly remembers it vividly. She was on fire-watching duty at the office where she worked, off High Street, and because it was so clear and pleasant her employer suggested that she go home early, at about 10 p.m. Even before she had left her work place in the city centre, at about 9.45 p.m. the first Luftwaffe squadrons had already taken off from their bases in northern France, most of them 'bound for Belfast in Ireland'. As they travelled north over the Continent and crossed the English coast they reported occasional low cloud and rain and fog. But

Nur für den Dienstgebrauch

Zielstammkarte

Land: Grossbritannien
Nord-Irland

Ort: Belfast
(Nähere Lage):
O-Ufer des Victoria Kanals

Geogr. Werte: 54° 36' 45" N
5° 54' 30" W

Ziel-Nr. G.B. 83 5

Kartenbl.-Nr. Irl.5/1:100000
Irl.7/1:63360

E. B. Nr.

1. Bezeichnung des Zieles: Schiffswerft Harland & Wolff Ltd.

Vgl. mit Ziel-Nr G.B. 74 13: Short & Harland Aircraft Factory.

2. Bedeutung: Bedeutende Bau- und Reparaturwerft Englands für Kriegs- und Handelsschiffe jeder Grösse. Die viertgrösste Reparaturwerft Grossbritanniens

3. Beschreibung des Zieles:

a) Verkehrsanschlüsse: Wasser-, Bahn- und Strassenanschluss.

b) Ausdehnung insgesamt: NO-SW etwa 7 km
SO-NW etwa 3,5 km
etwa 1100000 qm

Bebaute Fläche: Etwa 275000 qm

c) Bauweise, Bauausführung, Luftempfindlichkeit, Brandgefahr:

Im SO-Teil der Anlage die eigentliche Bauwerft (s. Bildauswertung 1-5).
Im südlichen Mittelteil der Anlagen ausgedehnte Werkhallen zur Herstellung und Montage von Maschinen und Schiffsteilen (s. Bildauswertung 6-10).
Im Mittelteil der Anlage Schiffs- und Maschinen-Ausbesserungswerke (s. Bilauswertung 11-14).
Im nördlichen Mittelteil Lagerhallen und Materiallagerplätze (s. Bildauswertung 16-18).
Längs des ganzen NW-Teils der Anlagen am Victoria Kanal ausgedehnte Dock- und Werftanlagen (s. Bildauswertung 19-22).
Brand-, Explosions- und Einsturzgefahr.

g) Lebenswichtige Teile, Wasser- und Kraftversorgung, Sabotage:

Kraftstation im nordöstlichen Mittelteil (s. G.B. 50 49).
Die Trockendocks und Hellinge im N-Teil und S-Teil der Werft.
Die Hallen für Schiffsbau und -Ausbesserung.

h) Rohstoffversorgung:

i) Sonstiges:

Etwa 20 km im WNW Belfast Stadtmitte (City Hall) liegt der Flugplatz Aldergrove	(G.B. 10 6)
" 13½ km " OSO " der Flugplatz Newtownards	(G.B. 10 158)
Im O anschliessend " der Flugplatz Belfast	(G.B. 10 13)
Am NO-Ende der Halbinsel gebildet vom Victoria Channel und dem Musgrave Channel im Hafenberefch liegt das Hauptkraftwerk Nordirlands	(G.B. 50 49)
Im NW-Teil der Hafenanlagen am Pollock Dock liegt die Grossmühle Rank & Co.	(G.B. 56 77)
Im NO-Teil des Hafengebietes liegt das Flugzeugwerk Short & Harland	(G.B. 74 13)
" SO-Teil " " " " die Tankstelle Conns Water	(G.B. 21 26)
Etwa 2 km im SW liegt das Gaswerk der Stadt Belfast	(G.B. 52 49)
" 2 km " SW " die Kasernenanlagen Victoria Barracks	(G.B. 13 800)
" 3 km " NW " das Wasserwerk Belfast	(G.B. 53 75)

Part of Luftwaffe target fi
for Harland and Wolff an
Short and Harland, which
was drawn up in late 194
detailing their position,
military significance and
strength of local active
defences. (Imperial War
Museum)

when they reached Northern Ireland, they found, in the words of one German pilot, that 'visibility was wonderful. In the clear moonlight I could make out my targets perfectly.' Unlike Easter Tuesday, so it remained throughout the entire attack. The conditions were, in fact, as William Ward, the caretaker at St Ninian's parish church, later observed, 'ideal [for] bombing'.

Local assessments of the numbers of enemy bombers involved vary widely as once more radar communications between Aldergrove and Preston failed at an early stage in the raid. Also there were, in any case, such large numbers of aircraft arriving in a short space of time that radar plots were difficult to count. Anti-aircraft gunners complained that there were 'too many on the screen to effectively concentrate on one'. Rear Admiral Richard King, Flag Officer in Charge, suggested that there were perhaps fifty bombers over Belfast, but airforce personnel considered the figure to be substantially higher. Thus John Blake, in his official war history, estimated that about 150 were involved. Luftwaffe records indicate that 471 aircraft set out from their continental bases on the night of 4–5 May, and that of these 204 attacked Belfast, which was their chief objective and suffered a sustained and heavy attack. Secondary raids were also launched against industrial targets and docks in Liverpool and Barrow in Furness, and numerous minor assaults were experienced elsewhere.

At 12.10 a.m. a red alert echoed through the silent streets of Belfast. Three minutes later the anti-aircraft gunners stood by; from as early as 11.30 p.m. a smoke screen had shrouded the area of the port in anticipation of a possible attack. At 12.47 a.m. the first plots began to appear on local radar screens and soon afterwards the uneven hum of approaching Heinkel He111s and Junkers Ju88s could be heard over towns and villages neighbouring the city. David Davidson sat at his home in High Street, Bangor, Co. Down, listening to the bombers pass over in ominously large numbers. 'There was a constant drone,' he recalls. 'It was a petrifying noise.' By 1.02 a.m. the first waves of enemy aircraft were in the vicinity of Belfast, and simultaneously, the anti-aircraft guns erupted into action.

Eyewitnesses later recalled the 'pincer type' formation of the subsequent attack. Some of the bombers appeared from a north-easterly direction. They had come via the Copeland Islands, off the Co. Down coast, crossing from these to Carrickfergus in Co. Antrim, and then travelling along the northern shore of Belfast Lough towards the city. Others arrived from the south-west, having followed a northern course up the Irish coast, before passing over Carlingford Lough, Rostrevor, Hilltown and Dromara in Co. Down. The actual attack began at 1.07 a.m., with, in general, each aircraft participating singly rather than in group formation. A Luftwaffe pilot later reported that they first 'circled the docks', and then 'carefully, picking our targets, let loose our bombs'. The crews aimed their incendiaries, mines and high explosives 'entirely visually throughout', mainly from a height of seven to nine thousand feet, just above the level of the balloon barrage. But some swooped in as low as twenty-five hundred feet to attack anti-aircraft batteries and other specific objectives, while others remained at seventeen thousand feet or more. In the bright moonlight few flares were needed. None the less, local air raid precautions wardens reported seeing a number descend like 'gigantic ropes of luminous crystal', and anti-aircraft gunners recorded that some of their early fire was directed towards extinguishing them.

Within the first half-hour of the attack, reports had reached the civil defence control room that fires had broken out and explosives had been dropped along a broad sweep of the city, stretching from Greencastle to Sydenham. None the less, from Luftwaffe records, it is evident that their main objective or 'concentration point' throughout lay in the north-east where the strategically vital targets were clustered – the shipyards, the aircraft factory and the harbour. During its opening phase, the élite pathfinder squadron, Kampfgruppe 100, focused its destructive energies exclusively on this area. Its crews delivered no fewer than six thousand incendiary bombs as well as a substantial tonnage of high explosives. They subsequently reported that large explosions and fires had resulted at Harland and Wolff, the docks and the 'area East-South-East of the port facility'. By 1.55 a.m. Kampfgruppe 100's work was completed. Their final written assessments justifiably claimed that 'several fire bomb areas are linking up' in the target area. Unlike the Easter Tuesday raid, these were not extinguished quickly. They thus provided a vital aiming mark for the later waves of approaching aircraft crews for whom the 'red glow in the sky, started by earlier attackers, was clearly visible'. In little over an hour of this attack incendiaries had kindled fires in Belfast which were already on a scale far beyond the resources of the local brigades.

The extensive use of incendiaries at the outset set a pattern for the entire raid – in less than three and a half hours, 95,992 were dropped, along with 237 tons of high explosives. Incendiaries had for some time been regarded by MacDermott's Ministry of Public Security as the 'greatest menace with which the enemy's present tactics confronts us'. (In the course of the war they accounted for up to 75 per cent of the damage to British, German and Japanese cities and towns which suffered attack.)

On the evening of 3 May, William Strachan, the director in charge of air raid precautions at Harland and Wolff, had been awarding first-aid certificates. In the course of the proceedings he had advised the men: 'Tell yourself there is not going to be a raid.' In fact the harbour and particularly the shipyard were the most obvious and the most legitimate military targets in Northern Ireland. During preceding years, Harland and Wolff had headed the tonnage output of shipbuilding firms throughout the world on twenty-four separate occasions. By May 1941 it had a work force of over twenty-three thousand and was at that time completing contract work for five different Westminster government departments – the Admiralty, and the Ministries of War, Supply, Transport and Aircraft Production. Sir Wilfrid Spender and some Stormont back-bench MPs later suggested that indiscreet boasting by Unionist ministers that ships built in Belfast were 'knocking hell out of the Bosh' had helped attract the enemy's attention to the firm. In addition, Harland and Wolff presented, in the words of a subsequent Admiralty report, an 'almost ideal target'. It was easily identified from the air, being clearly defined by water. It was also extremely vulnerable and many of its buildings were of flimsy construction and made from materials which were an obvious fire hazard. It was especially unfortunate therefore that the firm's fire-fighting equipment was so grossly inadequate, and its air raid precautions organisation so gravely understaffed.

A later Admiralty report stated that the Luftwaffe attacked the shipyard in a distinct formation, with groups of five bombers participating in each assault. The raid began with incendiary bombs which 'fell like rain' in the centre of the works. These were accompanied later by bombs and parachute mines which ripped through sheds and offices, spread the flames, and

ort and Harland's aircraft factory after the 4–5 May raid. (Short Brothers)

pulverised water mains. The effect was devastating. At one point a large metal plate was blown clear of the shipyard and eventually impaled itself in the floor of one of the main buildings at Short and Harland aircraft factory virtually a mile away. Workers there at first mistook it for a new type of bomb which had failed to detonate. Elsewhere, high explosives struck baulk timber, transforming it into massive projectiles which totally demolished a shelter; fortunately, it was unoccupied. The noise level was deafening. So much so that when a crew member of a merchant vessel, contrary to standing orders, fired, single-handedly, all eighteen rounds of twelve-pounder ammunition stored in the gun's platform, neither his officers nor the gun-layer realised that their own gun was in action.

A total of seventy separate incidents resulted from the attack on the yard. They were concentrated particularly in the area between the Musgrave and Victoria Channels. Three corvettes nearing completion at the Musgrave Channel were incinerated and another was badly burned. At the Victoria Channel, sheds and timber were destroyed. The *Fairhead*, a transport ship loaded with military supplies, was sunk at its moorings by a parachute mine which broke its back (the wreckage blocked the Dufferin Dock for several months). Nearby, two other vessels were sunk and a further five damaged. At the Abercorn shipyard, three ships received direct hits, and the Queen's

Panoramic view of the electrical manufacturing shop, Queen's Works, Harland and Wolff, after t 4–5 May raid. (Harland and Wolff)

Works, Clarence Works, Alexandra Works and the Victoria shipyard each suffered crippling blows to production. Overall, almost two-thirds of Harland and Wolff's premises were devastated, including offices, sheds (some of them up to two hundred yards long), drawing offices, workshops, engine works, plant-repair shops, and stores. Even company records were destroyed. But perhaps the most serious set-back was the loss of the electrical manufacturing shop which took three months to repair. Fire was the major single cause of damage. Everything wooden was burned to the ground. Military personnel and the crews of ships in the port, including HMS *Furious*, helped the understrength fire services to tackle the flames. Their combined efforts, however, were frustrated by the acute shortage of basic fire-fighting equipment at the shipyard. This reached critical significance after high explosives had fractured underground water pipes, causing insufficient pressure in shore fire mains. Available hose lengths did not permit the drawing of alternative supplies of water from the deep docks, channels and

basins all around. Fires that had been subdued flared into life once more and much preventable damage resulted. At the Musgrave Channel, for example, a near miss caused an oil leak from a small ship, which was then ignited by incendiaries. It was as a direct consequence of this that the three corvettes under construction there caught fire and were totally destroyed. The Admiralty report concluded that they could have been saved had trailer pumps been available. Within an hour from the start of the raid, whole areas of the works were being consumed by flames, spouting hundreds of feet into the air. The fire at the pattern shop was among the worst. Fireman Reggie Briggs recalls that the blaze there 'spread as quickly as a man could walk', steel girders buckling with the intensity of the heat.

None of the Luftwaffe's strategic targets in the port area escaped the bombardment. As early as 1.45 a.m., fire-watchers at Short and Harland's aircraft factory reported that 'incendiary bombs have fallen' and that the 'situation is out of control'. When company firemen and members of the

BIG RAID ON BELFAST

MANY GREAT FIRES STARTED

HEAVY CAUSALTIES

Another savage air attack was made on Belfast last night.

The following joint communique was issued this morning by the Northern Ireland Ministry of Public Security and R.A.F. Headquarters:—

Last night enemy aircraft delivered a heavy attack on the Belfast area, during which considerable damage was done to industrial and residential property. A number of fires were started,

It is feared that casualties will be heavy. Further details will be announced later in the day.

Belfast News-Letter, 5 May 1941

Auxiliary Fire Service tackled the flames, they discovered that there was 'insufficient pressure in [nearby] hydrants'. Failure to get water from the mains forced reliance on the River Connswater. Unfortunately its level was 'very low' and was dropping still further as the tide receded. At 3.40 a.m. oil installations were struck, causing particularly heavy explosions and a pall of dense, thick smoke. This was observed and recorded by Luftwaffe crews. Two bombs crashed through and exploded on the floor of the flight hangar, destroying two planes; the others were salvageable. There was widespread damage to offices, stores, workshops and roofs, and unexploded bombs and large craters littered the airfield and internal roadways.

German war reporter Ernst von Kuhren flew with one of the Luftwaffe squadrons during the attack on Belfast. In triumphant tones he later described for German radio home stations his impressions of the city midway through the raid:

> When I saw [it] I can honestly say that I could not believe my eyes. When we approached the target at 2.30 we stared silently into a sea of flames such as no one had seen before. Then after a time, our squadron leader, who had already made over one hundred flights said: 'No one would believe it.' In Belfast there was not a large number of conflagrations, but one enormous conflagration

> which spread over the entire harbour and industrial area. . . Within the target area there is not one black spot. In the district of the docks and wharfs, factories and storehouses, an area of about one and a half square kilometres, everything was on fire. Here are the large shipbuilding yards. Here was the last hideout for unloading materials from the United States. Here the English had concentrated an important part of their war industries because they felt themselves safe, far up in the North, safe from the blows of the German airforce. This has come to an end.

German crew members were also reported as saying that it was a 'picture of destruction none of us will forget'.

It is evident that these descriptions and claims were not merely propagandist but, on the contrary, had considerable validity. Even Northern Ireland's official war history states that those witnessing the raid from neighbouring hillsides saw a 'great ring of fire as if the whole city was ablaze'. At the military hospital on the Stranmillis Road, Emma Duffin recorded:

> One of the orderlies asked if we would like to go and look out of the windows where the fire-watchers were. He led along a dark passage. I looked with something like despair at the town. The sky was red and above, the great clouds of smoke were eddying and billowing from the direction of the Lough. I thought of the people who had already endured the last blitz cowering in terror in the shelters in the already blitzed areas.

The German accounts were incomplete rather than inaccurate. By no means all of the high explosives and incendiaries dropped by the Luftwaffe had struck the obvious military targets concentrated in the harbour area. Just as during the Easter Tuesday raid, a heavy weight of bombs fell on commercial and residential property elsewhere in the city. Air raid precautions wardens later reported that there were the 'same crowds of panic-stricken people rushing' from the damaged terraces, often 'leaving relations, friends, or neighbours buried, wounded or dead in the debris, [and that] groups of benumbed citizens wandered about the burning streets'. From the outset the residential district that suffered most during this attack was east Belfast, stretching from Ballymacarrett to Sydenham.

M.I. McClure was a surgeon on duty at the Ulster Hospital on Templemore Avenue, which had already suffered damage three weeks earlier and was once more in the centre of the severely stricken area. Afterwards, he lucidly recalled his experience:

> The first bomb to fall near us fell at 1.05 a.m. We heard the crump quite readily and the first evidence of damage was that the gas fires began to flicker. At this point we turned off gas and electricity mains and sat waiting in the dim light of hurricane lamps. Bombs then fell in quick succession. . . uncomfortably close. Within a few minutes they seemed to be falling all the time. . . one had not the time to remove one's steel helmet to adjust the chin strap before another fell. The building at this stage was beginning to shake and tremble with each explosion. . . it soon became evident that we were going to

be hit sooner or later. . . incendiary bombs began to fall thickly around the building.

The shell of Templemore Avenue library stands in midst of this stricken are[a] after the 4–5 May raid. (Ulster Museum)

When the hospital was itself hit, he continues, 'We tried to use our internal hoses but the water mains must have been struck and no water came through. [Soon afterwards] a series of bombs or one fairly large bomb fell on and through the roof, immediately the area burst into flames'; the building had to be evacuated. An ambulance which had arrived on the scene at the moment of impact was caught by the blast and blown into the air, further injuring the patients inside.

Eyewitnesses stated later that the Newtownards Road and adjoining streets in the neighbourhood of St Patrick's Church of Ireland church were transformed into unrecognisable ruins in the course of the raid. The district was struck by successive bombs and by incendiaries which fell in such large numbers that the resulting fires could not be contained. Charlie Gallagher was among those who volunteered to bring ambulances and other equipment down from Londonderry midway through the raid in response to a request for assistance from Belfast. He was sent to east Belfast and recalls that the area was 'a sea of flames which were flaring up' and that local people were 'very despondent' in the midst of so much destruction and death. He himself 'felt superfluous' given the scale of their tragedy and was 'deeply dispirited' during the journey back home later that afternoon.

The list of streets in this area where extensive damage was reported to

Ravenscroft Avenue sustained substantial damage in the 4–6 May raids. (Ulster Museum)

have occurred included Chater Street, Avondale Street, Witham Street, Tower Street, Westcott Street, Hornby Street, Ravenscroft Avenue, Skipper Street, Tamar Street, Bryson Street, Mersey Street, Westbourne Street and Donegore Street. In most of these at least half of the houses were destroyed; in Chater Street none was left standing. The worst single incident was at Avondale Street where a parachute mine fell within ten yards of a public shelter, blasting it twelve inches along the pavement and killing twenty-five of its occupants. At Witham Street thirty-five houses were demolished as a result of the raid and after the all-clear, a delayed-action bomb exploded causing the deaths of nine people. When Robert Watson, a joiner in the shipyard, arrived at his home in Westcott Street that morning, having evacuated to beyond Lisburn two weeks earlier, he found that 'half of it had gone and rescue workers were digging bodies out of the rubble'. Mary Wallace who lived nearby recalls that during the attack, when she and her mother opened their front door to go to a neighbouring shelter, the blast from a bomb blew them back through the living room and into the working kitchen. They decided to take cover under the kitchen table. Civil defence officials later recorded that there was 'much confusion and panic' throughout this district. Meanwhile bodies that had been recovered from the debris were already being laid out on the cratered streets and pavements prior to being taken to the morgue.

The explosions and the fires also spilled over into the more suburban parts of east Belfast. From a very early stage in the attack high explosives and incendiary bombs were dropped along the Holywood Road. The

A near miss from an unexploded parachute mi[ne] in the 4–5 May raid cause[d] heated debate about the safety of the Carson statu[e] at Stormont. (Public Reco[rd] Office of Northern Irelan[d])

ambulance depot located there sustained a direct hit. Denise Chambers, one of the nurses on duty, recalled: 'It is the awful smell of burning and dust everywhere that I will always remember about that night.' Belmont Road, where Lady Spender lived, was blocked by debris and she noted that on this occasion there was 'lots of damage in [the] neighbourhood'. Both Prime Minister John Andrews, and Minister of Public Security John MacDermott were satisfied that an attempt had been made to bomb Stormont. Shortly after the raid was over, an unexploded parachute mine was discovered by police near the base of Carson's statue in the estate grounds and the entire area had to be evacuated. Andrews immediately telephoned Sir Wilfrid Spender to discuss his acute worries about the protection of the statue and set up a cabinet committee to investigate the vexed question. He consulted Carson's widow and was eventually reassured when informed that the

Salvage and rescue work in progress at Westbourne Street, on the Newtownards Road in east Belfast, after the 4–5 May raid. (Public Record Office of Northern Ireland)

sculptor had retained a cast of its head. It was then decided that it should remain where it was, surrounded with sandbags. Spender, who had a most profound admiration for Carson, regarding him as the greatest statesman of his generation, noted: 'I feel sure that Carson himself would not have wished this matter to be regarded as of major importance in the circumstances.'

In addition to the widespread destruction of residential property in east Belfast, inevitably some strategically significant objectives also suffered from the bombing. Roads in Ballymacarrett were so extensively blocked and cratered that a two-mile ambulance journey from Mersey Street to the Royal Victoria Hospital on the Grosvenor Road took at least two hours. The railway service between Bangor and Belfast was disrupted by a crater on the line adjacent to Tamar Street and an unexploded bomb at Connswater. The Bangor and County Down Railway Station itself sustained extensive damage to offices and stores. High explosives and incendiaries caused a serious fire at the ropeworks, which was still burning brightly twenty-four hours after the all-clear. Here, as elsewhere throughout the Newtownards Road–Bloomfield Road area, the extensive rupturing of water mains and the turning of the tide, which reduced the River Connswater to a muddy trickle, enabled the flames to spread unchecked. As a result, factories, shops and churches, as well as houses, were gutted and fire-fighters forced to stand aside, frustrated and impotent.

Identical problems arose in the other part of Belfast to be extensively damaged in the course of this attack – the city centre. Within little over an hour, the air raid precautions control room was virtually overwhelmed by reports of fires mushrooming up throughout this area. Among the locations that had already been struck by high explosives and incendiaries were

The gutted International B (corner of Lower Donegal Street and York Street) shortly after the 4–5 May raid. (Ulster Museum)

Shaftesbury Square, the city hall, Bedford Street, Chichester Street, Donegall Place, Castle Place and Castle Lane. On 6 May in the *Irish Times* one fire-watcher commented that the 'first incendiary bombs were quickly dealt with', but when succeeding waves of aircraft continued to drop them by the thousands, 'we didn't have the slightest chance'. Some of Belfast's oldest and finest thoroughfares were reduced to smouldering debris. Rosemary Street, High Street, Waring Street and North Street were extensively damaged; Bridge Street was effectively destroyed. It was so devastated that after the attack, groundless rumours proliferated claiming that a German bomber had been shot down and had crashed into and pulverised the surrounding buildings. Nora Carse remembers that early next morning as she walked from the nurses' hostel into the Royal Victoria Hospital, the ground was littered with billheads from Arnott's drapers and outfitters shop on Bridge Street – almost a mile away; some were burned, others were more or less intact. They had been borne upwards in the swirling air currents generated by the intense fires which were rampant throughout this area.

Bridge Street after the 4–5 May raid, seen here from High Street. (Public Record Office of Northern Ireland)

Blitzed buildings in Lower Donegall Street, still smouldering after the 4–5 May raid: St Anne's Cathedral was fortunate to survive intact. (Public Record Office of Northern Ireland)

When Ernie Logan cycled into work at his accountancy firm on High Street, he noted that the 'whole left-hand side [of the street] looking towards the Albert Memorial Clock was ablaze; practically every building being gutted' The whole area skirting the cathedral also became an inferno which stretched along Donegall Street, engulfed the International Bar and cascaded into the lower end of York Street. In the process, the casualty post on Academy Street was almost encircled by flame. During the raid, post personnel had been compelled to stand at rear entrances, armed with stirrup pumps and buckets of water in a forlorn effort to keep the rapacious flames at bay. When eventually they were forced to evacuate, many of the casualties were 'afraid to pass through the doorway owing to the flames'. At Tomb Street air raid precautions post close by, auxiliary lights were switched on when the electricity supply failed at 2.45 a.m. However, the wardens discovered soon afterwards that it was considerably brighter inside with the lights off and the window shutters open, 'so fiercely were the fires burning all around the building'.

Fortunately, the city centre was virtually deserted at the time of the attack

Repairs underway on the severely damaged roof of Belfast City Hall, 3 June 1941. (Ulster Museum)

– the early hours of Sunday morning. None the less, there were fatalities among those who lived and worked there. At Glenravel Street police station seven young policemen were killed when the building was demolished after receiving a direct hit. They had been transferred from the training depot weeks before in order to augment the strength of the force in Belfast. High explosives also struck the corner of Chichester Street police barracks and deflected into the street. Police Constable Donald Fleck, who was working as a telephone operator there that night, believes that he and his colleagues were 'saved by the angle of the bomb'. Nearby, decaying working-class terraces also suffered at Gloucester Street, where twelve residents were killed when a parachute mine devastated twelve houses.

In the course of the raid a number of Belfast's most attractive inner-city buildings were destroyed or severely damaged; among them were Rosemary Street Presbyterian Church, the banqueting chamber at the city hall, and the Belfast Water Commissioner's Office. The printing presses at three of Belfast's four daily newspapers were unable to function on 5 May. Many of its leading business premises were obliterated or, at least, partially demolished. Apart from Arnott's, these included, Gallaher's, Dunville's

Stores, the Bank Buildings, Robb's Garage, the Co-operative Timber Stores, Mackenzie and McMullan's, the Ulster Arcade, Jackson's, the Athletic Stores and Thornton's. Such extensive destruction inevitably provided

Rescue and salvage work in High Street. (William Cono sketch, private collection)

ample opportunity for looting. Billy McNeill, then a police constable, recalls that it was 'widespread' in the city centre, especially 'where windows had gone and there were no police patrols on duty'. This view is confirmed by the experience of a publican who arrived at his premises in Callender Street several hours after the all-clear to find that his entire stock had all but disappeared; even fixtures screwed to the counter had been removed.

From the outset the city centre was extremely vulnerable to the Luftwaffe's tactical use of incendiaries and high explosives. Its water mains were old and friable and also much too narrow to provide adequate pressure in fire hoses. This dropped catastrophically after bombs had ruptured piping and when larger numbers of firemen attempted to draw water at the same time in response to the growing number of fires. A temporary respite was gained when access was made to the Farset river below High Street. For a time the river provided a welcome volume of water. However, the tide turned and, as in east Belfast, the water level fell to a depth which the suction pipes could no longer reach and the flow from hoses contracted once more to a minute trickle. It was a grave misfortune that the quantities of fire-

Bridge Street, looking towards High Street, on 5 [M]ay 1941. (Ulster Museum)

fighting equipment available were not adequate to enable sufficient alternative supplies to be drawn from the River Lagan. An official report later concluded that if this had been possible, many valuable premises could have been saved. Instead firemen were once again powerless to prevent the flames from spreading, and as a consequence, many confined themselves to rescue work, identifying the dead, tending the injured, and comforting the panic-stricken. At 2.20 a.m., little over an hour from the beginning of the attack, help was requested from Éire. In response, thirteen crews were hastily dispatched from Dublin and Dundalk. They helped combat fires in the city centre and harbour area and were again cheered by crowds north of the border. After 2.30 a.m., the various districts within Northern Ireland were also asked to send whatever assistance they could provide, including fire pumps, ambulances and rescue parties. Six squads later arrived from Londonderry, the others remaining in case the northern city would itself be the target of an attack. Worse was to come: according to J.B. Meehan, at about 3.15 a.m., a 'particularly heavy blitz fell on the centre of the city and the York Street area. . . in a holocaust of destruction. Fresh fires added their blaze to the general conflagration. It now seemed that only the coming of

Belfast city centre: soldi
demolish the unstable s
of a burnt out building.
(Major H. John F. Potte

daylight could save the city.' At approximately 3.40 a.m. a telegrammed appeal for fifty pumps was transmitted to the Home Security War Room. As before, the Westminster government knew little regarding the actual scale of the attack on Belfast at the time, believing that just fifty bombers had participated out of an estimated total of three hundred over Britain. None the less, it was aware that there were 'large fires throughout the city' and forty-two pumps with crews were promptly assembled and consigned. Not surprisingly in the circumstances, Northern Ireland ministers later proved very reluctant to part with these additional reserves of men and equipment.

Although none of the other areas of Belfast suffered such extensive damage in the course of this raid as the city centre, the harbour area and east Belfast, few escaped entirely, and in some areas incidents occurred which bore an uncanny similarity to those experienced during the Easter Tuesday attack. In north Belfast, Sarah Nelson, who lived opposite the waterworks, spent the entire night under the dining-room table. She recalls feeling on this occasion, a 'greater sense of terror, knowing what had happened before' and noted that the sound of bombs was 'more continuous' than previously,

Soldiers try to make safe blitzed premises in Belfast after the 4–5 May raid. (Major H. John F. Potter)

The devastation at York Street mill, seen here on 7 May 1941. (Imperial War Museum)

but that 'there was nothing so near'. Similarly, local air raid precautions wardens concluded that though damage was 'more widespread' than during earlier raids, the 'district suffered less overall' and there were 'periods when no messages were received'.

By about 2.30 a.m. reports arriving at air raid precautions control centre indicated that high explosives and incendiaries had fallen on more than half a dozen locations to the north of the city, including Lismoyle Park, Alworthy Avenue, Ballysillan Park, Sunningdale Park, Cooldarragh Park and Whitewell Road. The most serious incident had occurred at Greencastle. After the alert, a number of people in the neighbourhood gathered in the boiler house of St Ninian's parish church. It had been placed at the disposal of women, children and the elderly – Catholic as well as Protestant – by the Reverend W.J. Finlay Maguire. He had done so in response to the 'extensive damage and grave loss of life' experienced locally during the Easter Tuesday raid and also because of the 'entire lack of air-raid shelters of any description' in the area. William Ward, the caretaker, later recorded: 'At first the hum of enemy aircraft overhead did not worry us overmuch as we had had small alerts previously, but as the sound increased we knew we were going to have a heavy raid. . . more people arrived so fast we could not get all the names recorded.' Finally, about eighty or so were packed tightly into the little room, less than fifteen feet square, and lit by a single candle. They sang 'hymns most of the time' and felt 'of course fear but no panic'.

Sadly, soon afterwards, the events of three weeks earlier virtually repeated themselves, with equally tragic consequences. Once more, early in the attack at 1.20 a.m., two parachute mines descended almost simultaneously on the Greencastle district. They landed in the Barbour Street–Whitewell Road area with devastating effect. Police Constable James Hawthorne, standing about four hundred yards away, had seen the bombs 'drifting slowly down' and braced himself for the 'tremendous blast'. All around him windows shattered and slates were ripped off. Within moments, 'dazed occupants staggered into the street covered in grime and soot'. He immediately 'attended to the dead bodies strewn around' and sought to comfort the many injured. A district nurse, Susan Storey, was one of the thirty people who had been killed. She lived on the Whitewell Road, beside the Orange Hall. It had been suggested to her, shortly after the alert, that she should go to a 'safer place'. She had refused to do so, however, explaining that she was 'expecting a call to a birth' and had to remain at her home so

7 May 1941: Royal Welsh siliers help clear up bomb image opposite the Belfast -operative Stores in York Street. (Imperial War Museum)

that she could be contacted. Her daughter, who had stayed with her, died as well; their house and the Orange Hall were both demolished.

York Street mill was also struck once again by incendiary bombs and high explosives. At 3 a.m. it was already enveloped by flames and was possibly the largest conflagration of the entire raid. To Jimmy Doherty it seemed like an 'island of fire'. Bryce Millar had been one of three thousand employees there before joining the shipyard and he knew the building well. 'The truly astonishing thing,' he recalls, 'was that flames were coming from every window, the spinning-room, twisting-rooms and roving-rooms. Every floor was engulfed by flames, from North Queen Street to York Street.' On this occasion the entire works was destroyed, the machinery was buckled and twisted, the company's records were burned, and the debris blocked adjacent roads. Only the mill horses escaped, having been led to safety by local youths. The heat was intense. It could be felt by people standing over one hundred yards away; nearer, it rose up from the pavement and caused pain through the soles of leather shoes. Women in adjoining streets splashed water around the windows of their homes to prevent the glass from

The charred iron skeleton of rolling stock burnt out the track near the London Midland and Scottish Railway Station, York Street, after the 4–5 May raid. (Ulster Museum)

cracking. William Topping, a mill worker, recorded: 'It was pathetic [next morning] to see the employees around the ruins, many of whom had spent their entire working life in the firm and wondering what would happen to their livelihood.' For months the stench of burning pervaded the air throughout the district, deepening the sense of desolation and loss.

Other business premises nearby sustained damage. High explosives blasted a taxi through the roof of O.D. Cars on Alexandra Park Avenue; it finally collapsed on top of a pile of rubble on the street outside. Bombs and incendiaries struck the London, Midland and Scottish Railway Station which was forced to close for three days after the attack. Fire had swept through offices, sheds and stores, and coaches and engines were burned out on the platform. Craters and an unexploded bomb, discovered beside Greencastle bridge, disrupted services so that trains using this line could at first approach the city only as far as Whiteabbey or Whitehouse. The Midland Hotel was also gutted, and the railway's engineering works did not recover pre-raid production levels until mid-June.

West and south Belfast escaped the worst of the devastation. Casualty posts on the Shankill Road reported that the 'work was not so heavy' as on the night of 15–16 April. Mackies' foundry, the one major strategic target on the Springfield Road, was little affected by the raid and had regained normal weekly output by mid-May. But the Falls Road area generally suffered more during this attack than it had done previously. In his parish diary Father Hendley described it as a 'terrible night'. James McConville, then a boy, remembers clearly the period after the alert: 'all fifteen of us' in the house 'with neighbours from four or five houses away crowded together for reassurance. . . We spent the night in prayer. No one could possibly remember how many decades of the rosary were recited.' The distribution of the bombing outside appeared to him to be 'scattered and much more haphazard'. Certainly, Belfast air raid precautions control centre received reports of incidents which were widely dispersed throughout the area from Albert Street to Ballymurphy. In one case a bomb exploded at the top of Beechmount Crescent and Beechmount Street, destroying eight houses and wiping out three families. Eyewitnesses later recalled seeing the 'headless trunk of the man of the house still standing at the kitchen sink'. Elsewhere, a land mine plunged into soft earth at a local brickworks and failed to explode, and a number of delayed-action bombs were discovered. On Tuesday, 6 May, two days after the raid, at 5.30 a.m., James McConville remembers local residents being 'rudely awakened'. The buried land mine 'was to be exploded at 6 a.m. . . . We were allowed back into our house on Thursday afternoon and eleven days later, at 4.15 in the afternoon, the bomb eventually was exploded without one word of warning to any of us and without a ha'pworth of damage.'

Many local people sought safety at Clonard Chapel. Rita McKittrick remembers that among them were Protestant women and children from the North Howard Street–Cupar Street area of the Shankill, who joined with

Catholics from nearby streets. The two communities were thus united, however briefly, by a common bond of fear. That they should have met together in such an unlikely setting became one of the most enduring images and memories of the Belfast blitz. An entry in the monastic 'Domestic Chronicles', written shortly after this raid, states simply that

> the crypt under the sanctuary, also the cellar under the working sacristy has been fitted out and is opened to the people, women and children only, as an air-raid shelter. This act of ours is very much appeciated by all, Protestants included. Prayers are said and hymns sung by the occupants during the bombing. The Fathers and Brothers go to the kitchen cellar.

On the night of 4–5 May a group of between two to three hundred mothers and children congregated together in the crypt. Eileen Powderly remembers that at the height of the attack a bomb fell, narrowly missing the chapel. There was a deafening explosion and the force of the blast blew open the doors of the vault which gave access to the building from the street. The atmosphere of terror and doom was heightened by the sound of horses that had escaped from neighbouring business premises and in panic were pounding up and down the stone pavement outside. With death apparently imminent, one of the priests, Father Tom Murphy, wearing a tin helmet for protection, stepped forward and gave all present a general absolution. Early next morning, a girl returned to her home in Beechmount Parade and was warned by her father: 'Don't use the bathroom; there's a horse in it.' After further enquiry, she discovered that the horse was dead; it had been blown into the house by a bomb which had detonated in the road nearby.

As in previous raids, south Belfast was the area of the city which suffered least in this attack. 'Again this part of town has been lucky,' noted Moya Woodside. From her home in Elmwood Avenue, she considered that the 'bombs and barrage were louder and nearer than on the 15th [April], but perhaps seemed worse in the imagination'. She 'stayed in bed until the noise became too shattering and then put on slacks and dressing gown and came down to join the maid in the kitchen. We got under the table, with pillows, rugs and eiderdown and stayed uncomfortable, bored and scared till about 4.30 am.' She concluded despondently: 'How boring it is, utterly boring, thus to spend one's night.' At the military hospital on the Stranmillis Road, Emma Duffin 'soon realized that it was an even worse blitz than the last. The thud of bombs continued at very short intervals and the great hall door shuddered and shook in the blast but stood fast. . . Having seen the pathetic streets smashed to dust and those distorted bodies, the horror was brought home to me more.' She added with some relief: 'I am glad to say, though I felt horrified, I did not feel fear. . . [but] I sensed a slight shudder as bomb after bomb dropped.'

Patrick Shea was at his lodgings in number 50 Elmwood Avenue. In *Voices and the Sound of Drums* he describes the scene:

> When the alert sounded the more active [lodgers] saw to it that the shutters

direct hit at Gallaher's roll factory; photograph c. 12 May 1941. (Gallaher Limited)

were securely bolted, the bath, handbasins and sinks filled with water in case of fire, candles brought out lest the electricity should fail, fires extinguished. The assembly point for the whole household was the large ground-floor living room. Miss Mack, an elderly, socially superior person who kept herself to herself in her first-floor bedsitter, would make one of her rare appearances amongst us. She would come downstairs, draped in her fur coat and carrying her jewel case. Tenderly she would be manoeuvred into a recumbent position on a mattress under the large dining-room table; for the period of the alert she would lie there, her furs wrapped around her, her jewels clasped to her bosom. . . Those who were not lying down or on a fire-watching tour of inspection of the top floor, sat or stood around the empty fireplace. . . That was how our household was disposed on Whit Sunday night as we listened to the frightening drone of the raiding aircraft, the sounds of the city centre being torn apart, the detonations of the exploding bombs and the return fire of the anti-aircraft guns. On that night fear was in every heart in Belfast.

Towards the end of the raid, it was the sheer number and size of the fires which continued to make the most profound impression on those who witnessed the stricken city. Christoph v.d. Ropp, a war reporter for the

Aus Belfast zurück

Brände an allen Ecken und Enden

PK. . . ., 6. Mai.

Wir sind vor einer halben Stunde vom Feindflug zurückgekehrt. Die Spiegeleier und der Kakao haben uns gut gemundet, einer nach dem anderen ist dann zu Bett gegangen. Man ist müde und hat ein Recht, es zu sein, denn der Flug hat viele Stunden gedauert. Der Morgen blickt in die Fenster hinein, und die ersten Vogelstimmen hallen durch die stille Welt.

Viele Stunden waren wir unterwegs. Wir sahen England und das [illegible] im Mondschein liegen, sahen das Licht des Mondes sich an den Küsten und in den Buchten spiegeln. Über dem Land und über dem Wasser lag Dunst, aber die Sicht war doch gut.

Das nächtliche England war im Aufruhr. Überall standen die Scheinwerfer im dunstigen Nachthimmel. Brände leuchteten zu uns herauf, zum Teil noch von früheren Angriffen; nächtelang lohen sie schon zum Himmel, es scheint den Engländern tatsächlich gar nicht möglich zu sein, sie zu löschen. Dann ließen wir große Industriestädte seitlich liegen, auf die heute nacht deutsche Kampfflugzeuge ihre Bombenlast abwarfen. Das heftige Abwehrfeuer blitzte von weitem herüber zu uns, die wir unsere Bahn weiterzogen, unserem Ziele zu.

Dann kam Belfast in Sicht, ein Strahlenkranz von Lichtern in verschiedenen Farben, weißliche, gelbe, rötliche; Qualmwolken über der großen Stadt. Es waren Hunderte von kleineren und mehrere große Brände, die wir ausmachen konnten. Unter einem schwarzen Rauchpilz brannte im Hafen ein Ölbehälter aus. Kein Zweifel: die große nordirische Stadt, jener wichtige Industrie- und Hafenort und bedeutende Umschlagplatz für Güter nach England, war ganz entscheidend getroffen!

Wir umflogen die Stadt in einem weiten Bogen, während uns die Flakartillerie des Feindes umbellte. Dann verschwand die Vision Nordirlands, unwahrscheinlich schon wegen ihrer weiten Entfernung, im Dunst der Mondnacht.

Wir spähten nach Nachtjägern aus. Ein Flugzeug unserer Staffel ist heute nacht lange Zeit von solch einem unheimlichen Gesellen begleitet worden, den man im ungewissen Licht mehr ahnen als sehen konnte. Der Weg war noch lang, und die Nacht neigte sich schon dem Morgen zu. Zu einer Zeit, wo andere im tiefsten Schlafe liegen, fliegen deutsche Kampfflieger gegen England, mit gespannten Sinnen, jede Müdigkeit mit eiserner Willenskraft niederkämpfend! Wir kehrten alle unversehrt heim. Das braucht kaum betont zu werden, denn wir sind es gewohnt, daß die Engländer unserer Nachtfliegerei nichts anhaben können. England selbst aber brennt an allen Ecken und Enden, wie wir das heute noch mit eigenen Augen sehen konnten.

Kriegsberichter Christoph v. d. Ropp

Schwere Besorgnis über die deutschen Angriffe auf Nordirland

Sonderdienst des „VB."

Bern, 6. Mai.

Die unablässigen harten Schläge der deutschen Luftwaffe auf die großen britischen Umschlaghäfen rufen in England eine zunehmende Besorgnis hervor. In einem Leitartikel erklärt die „Times", Deutschland verstärke mit diesen Angriffen auf die britischen Westhäfen wie auf Belfast seinen Feldzug zur See. Die Aufgaben der britischen Flotte würden dadurch aufs äußerste erschwert. „Eine einschneidende Behinderung besteht ohnehin darin, daß unsere Flotte im Mittelmeer und im Fernen Osten wie im Atlantik für eine Aufgabe beansprucht wird, in die sich 1914 die Flotten der Alliierten teilten, die selbst große Seemächte waren."

In Meldungen aus London zu den letzten schweren Luftangriffen auf die Kriegsindustrieanlagen und Hafeneinrichtungen von Belfast heißt es, man könne auch heute noch nicht den angerichteten Schaden voll überblicken. Bei dem vorletzten Großangriff fanden, wie der britische Minister für öffentliche Sicherheit, MacDermott, vor dem nordirischen Unterhaus bekanntgab, 500 Personen den Tod, 420 sind schwer- und 1142 leichter verletzt worden.

Der neue Angriff auf Belfast

Beträchtliche Wirkung

Amsterdam, 6. Mai.

Wie der Londoner Nachrichtendienst meldet, wurden auch in den frühen Morgenstunden des Dienstag Belfast, sowie einige andere Gebiete Nordirlands, wieder von der deutschen Luftwaffe angegriffen und mit Bomben belegt. Wieder habe der Angriff eine beträchtliche Zahl von Opfern gefordert. Auch auf Westschottland sowie das Gebiet des Merseyflusses seien Angriffe erfolgt, die, wie der Nachrichtendienst mitteilt, „ziemlich beträchtlichen Charakter" angenommen hätten.

An account of the 4–5 M
raid on Belfast, written b
war reporter, Christoph
Ropp, appeared in the N
Party newspaper,
Völkischer Beobachter, c
May 1941. (British Libr

Völkischer Beobachter, flew with the final wave of German bombers and wrote an account of his experience, shortly after the pilots had returned to base and retired to bed, 'having enjoyed their fried eggs and cocoa'. When they were leaving Belfast, he observed:

> Clouds of dense smoke covered the city. There were hundreds of smaller and several big fires which we could make out. Under a black mushroom of smoke an oil storage tank was burning in the harbour. . . There is no doubt the big Irish city. . . was quite decisively hit. Then this vision of Northern Ireland already incredible because of its great distance away disappeared into the mist of the moonlight night.

In confidential reports, completed after their final assault, the Luftwaffe crews also observed 'numerous simultaneous fires, new fires, powerful jets of flame'. The vibration from their bomb explosions could, they claimed, be felt up to a height of '3,500 metres'. On their journey home, the smoke clouds above Belfast, which had by then risen to over '4,000 metres', were clearly visible from as far distant as Liverpool.

Depictions and impressions from inside Northern Ireland fully confirm these awesome descriptions from the air. At her home in east Belfast, Lady Spender was appalled by the 'red and angry glare' radiating upwards from the harbour area. The official history states that by 4 a.m. those watching from surrounding hillsides were witnessing 'such an inferno as they will long remember; below them a great ring of fire as if the whole city was ablaze. And every now and then the sudden glow in the sky as oil bomb or parachute mine suddenly erupted.' In Bangor, Co. Down, David Davidson could not only see the 'huge glow in the sky' but he could also hear the sound of the explosions faintly in the distance. At Aghalee, beyond Lisburn, Robert Watson, an evacuee from east Belfast, was awakened by the noise of the raid. To Charlie Gallagher, standing at the top of the Glenshane Pass (about forty-five miles from Belfast), the fires were clearly visible and appeared to 'pulsate up and down'. He was driving his ambulance south from Londonderry in such haste that it had overheated and he had paused there to allow the engine to cool down. As he proceeded he was aware of the

Ann Street suffered extensively during the 4–5 May raid. (Ulster Museum)

distinctive uneven drone of enemy aircraft overhead. After reaching Antrim he found that the air was so thick with ash and soot that he was forced to stop once more to clean his windscreen and restore his vision of the road.

At peak there were over two hundred fires burning in Belfast. They were officially classified as 2 conflagrations, spreading and out of control; 22 major fires, each requiring the attention of 30 or more pumps; 58 serious fires, each requiring 11 to 30 pumps; and 125 smaller fires. Outbreaks on such a scale lay far beyond the resources of the local full-time and part-time brigades, with their combined strength of just 1,830 men and 254 pumps. Later assessments of their performance varied. John MacDermott considered that they were better organised than in April, but it was the opinion of Lord Abercorn, the Governor of Northern Ireland, that the whole service urgently needed to be 'tightened up'. Certainly it was ludicrously small, relatively untrained, and its supplies of equipment were lamentably inadequate; some of the hose and other materials damaged in the Easter Tuesday raid had not yet been repaired.

During the height of the attack, an emergency system of government was established, under a modified version of the Hiram Plan. Soon afterwards, at 4.25 a.m., two hours before sunrise, the raid at last came to an end, and at 5.13 a.m. the all-clear sounded. Due to bomb damage at the harbour power station, the sirens had been silenced. Instead, citizens were informed that the raiders had gone by wardens moving through the streets, ringing handbells.

On hearing the welcome news in the packed boiler house at St Ninian's parish church, the Reverend Finlay Maguire 'offered a prayer of grateful thanks to Almighty God for his deliverance after such a night's ordeal'.

On 6 May 1941 the *Irish Times* commented that on the morning after the raid, 'outside the city the sun was shining on a sylvan scene. Inside it was hell.' Moya Woodside wrote in similar vein: 'One can't believe to look at green trees and white blossoms and birds singing that these nights of horror have not been some evil dream.' Without trams or trolley buses, people walked wearily to work, crowding the footpaths. The familiar roadways along which they passed had become suddenly unfamiliar, fringed now by the smoking ruins and charred skeletons of barely recognisable buildings. The condition of Belfast was such, newspaper reports claimed, that some who had lived there for all of their lives lost their way. Emma Duffin 'peered along the street but could see only smouldering rubble. Parties of soldiers aided civilians to clean up. Large gaps have appeared where flourishing shops had stood'; most of those still standing were closed. Masonry was collapsing into pavements, water cascading down from upper storeys and the rumble of exploding bombs continued to be heard from areas cordoned-off by police and troops. Eyewitnesses record that many wept when they first saw the extent of the devastation, appalled that so much had gone. In shelters, local clergy sought to bring comfort and minister to those despairing and distressed.

Many fires were still blazing fiercely. Jimmy Mackey, a regular fireman, had worked to contain them with little success throughout the night and carried on next day, before eventually falling asleep, exhausted, in Donegall Street, his head resting against a lamppost. He recalls:

> It was not normal fire-fighting. You had to fight the fires from the street. They were burning so intensely that it was impossible to get access to buildings. At the larger fires, there were firestorms. As the flames took hold, there was a great in-rush of air; they sucked it in creating a shortage of oxygen and making breathing difficult.

A number were not finally extinguished until Wednesday, 7 May, forty-eight hours after the all-clear. Some civil defence personnel later considered that it was the bright glow, which they continued to cast over parts of the city, that was responsible for attracting the attentions of the Luftwaffe yet again. On the night of 5–6 May, at 12.45 a.m., a small force of possibly three enemy aircraft dropped incendiary bombs and high explosives on east Belfast. The worst single incident occurred at 2 a.m., when a parachute mine demolished two public shelters and a number of houses in Ravenscroft Avenue. Fourteen people died, forty were seriously injured and three hundred made homeless. Air raid precautions warden Harold Allen remembers seeing Queen's University medical students next morning, loading bodies and parts of bodies into waiting ambulances. At 3 a.m. enemy bombers returned, showering the same district with incendiaries. In most

The stark façade of the International Bar at the corner of York Street and Lower Donegall Street as it awaits the demolition squads tidying up after the raid of 4–5 May. (Public Record Office of Northern Ireland)

cases these were quickly extinguished and by 3.35 a.m. the raiders had passed.

It is almost certain that the attack was carried out by 'strays' from the major raid on Clydeside by over one hundred aircraft between 12.30 a.m. and 3.40 a.m. on the early morning of 6 May. Possibly Belfast was mistaken for a GB city despite the fact that Luftwaffe crews considered visibility over Britain to be good. However, a number of local wardens were convinced that the German aircraft involved had been conducting a routine reconnaissance flight until they observed fires still showing light at the rope-works. The wardens' report suggests that the bombers then closed in and launched their mines and incendiaries against this target, missing it by the narrowest of margins. Their account also claimed that the port had been in grave danger of further bombardment, stating: 'At McGinn's public house, on the corner of Tomb Street and Gamble Street, a fire smouldering all day burst out again at 11.30 pm and lit up the harbour area. But fortunately the fire service was able to kill the glare before the planes arrived, thus in all probability saving the harbour from further attack.'

On the night of 6–7 May there was a further alert and there were some early indications that the port had been struck. Moya Woodside heard the aircraft overhead, noting: 'Back they came last night with intermittent bangs and gunfire. Although I had gone to bed at 9.30, I was not able to sleep until the all-clear, but at least got a rest.' Initial reports, at 2.30 a.m., stated that enemy aircraft had dropped incendiaries over the docks, causing fires, but that the raid was not developing. It later emerged that in fact no bombs had fallen on Belfast. The confusion was probably caused by fresh combustion continuing to erupt from below the debris of fires thought to have cooled down.

During that night and early next day, at last, those fires still smouldering finally expired. Throughout the city, suburban gardens had been coated with the scorched and shrivelled evidence of their destructive power. On the morning of 5 May, Moya Woodside had found her flowerbeds and yard 'littered' with singed fragments, ashes, and 'lots of shrapnel'. And on the Stranmillis Road Emma Duffin walked out on to the hospital lawn. She recorded:

> The smell of burning was in the air. The grass was strewn with blackened and charred papers. There was a sheet from a child's essay book. On the top of the page, I read, 'The End of the World'. It seemed appropriate. It was the end of the world as we knew it.

8
CRISIS OF MORALE
5 MAY–31 DECEMBER 1941

The conflagration at Arnott's (corner of High Street and Bridge Street) after the 4–5 May raid. (Ulster Museum)

On Wednesday, 7 May 1941, Major H. John F. Potter, then a young boy, was travelling through Belfast on his way back to school in England, his return journey having been delayed for two days because the boats were not running. He later recorded in his diary:

> We caught the 2.35 train from Portstewart, and had a good journey into Belfast. We had to go right into Whitehouse and the train there changed ends;

this was because a goods-train had been hit, and was blocking the line. There were a good many bomb craters all along the line from here, but though some were very close, as far as we could see, they had all missed; several had fallen [in] the mud of the Lough. The first damage we saw was to some houses on the Lower Antrim Road, below Cavehill; there was a rescue party at work, the only one we saw. On coming in to York Street station, the damage was appalling; we passed between two rows of burnt out carriages, and tangled wreckage of goods trains; the houses and ware-houses on the right of the line had mostly been burnt out, and in many cases, only the walls were left; York Street station was for the most part burnt out; the roof was gone, and many of the offices, including the Gentlemens, had been hit. All the flagstones on the platform were chipped and broken, and the Midland Hotel had been burnt out; soldiers were busy with a crane clearing part of the line; our porter told us that ours was the first train to get into the station since the 'blitz'. I had to sit and wait outside the station for some time. . . Just up the road, a row of houses had been hit and wrecked; soldiers in lorries, nearly all with Union Jacks, were going to and fro, clearing away the debris; another soldier was directing the traffic, whilst others were giving people lifts; a big lorry stopped, and people jumped on it from every direction. Then the porter came with a taxi, and we went down to the docks. A good many of the little houses off Corporation Street had been hit, and at one place, a police car told us to go slow as demolition work was in progress; a pub had been wrecked, and soldiers were pulling down one of the walls; later on, we heard it go. On coming to the docks, we saw that the Liverpool wharf had been completely burnt out, and there was nothing left but a twisted mass of girders; there was no Liverpool boat. After dumping our luggage, we went off to see some of the damage. The Albert Clock seemed to have sunk in the ground, for it was leaning over like a tower of Pisa; all the top part of the High Street was closed, and traffic was being directed down the street past Woolworths; many of the shops on the left of the High Street, Arnotts and others, were just piles of rubble; they were most of them still smoking, and AFS men were busy playing hoses on them. Other big shops destroyed were the Bank Buildings, Thorntons, Davies and Greys, Stewarts, the Castle Toy Shop, and many others. The Cathedral had had a very lucky escape, for houses on both sides of it were in ruins, and still burning. Up by the Cathedral, we saw a notice warning people not to pick up pens and pencils they saw, as they might contain high-explosives, dropped by the Germans. I wonder who put that notice up; I don't believe it. It was now time we went on board ship. . . On going down the Lagan, we saw an awful amount of damage. Several of the wharves were wrecked and still burning, and we saw at least one crane that had collapsed. The planning offices of Harland & Wolff's had completely disappeared. It looked as if Short & Harland's had been hit, and the hangars had been hit. I don't remember seeing any work going on in the docks; we saw at least one ship partially under water. I'm afraid the damage to Belfast docks is [very] serious. As we sailed down the Lagan, it was dusk. The AA guns were pointing to the skies, their crews were waiting. We passed a sloop, its decks cleared for action, and its guns ready elevated. [Everyone] was watching,

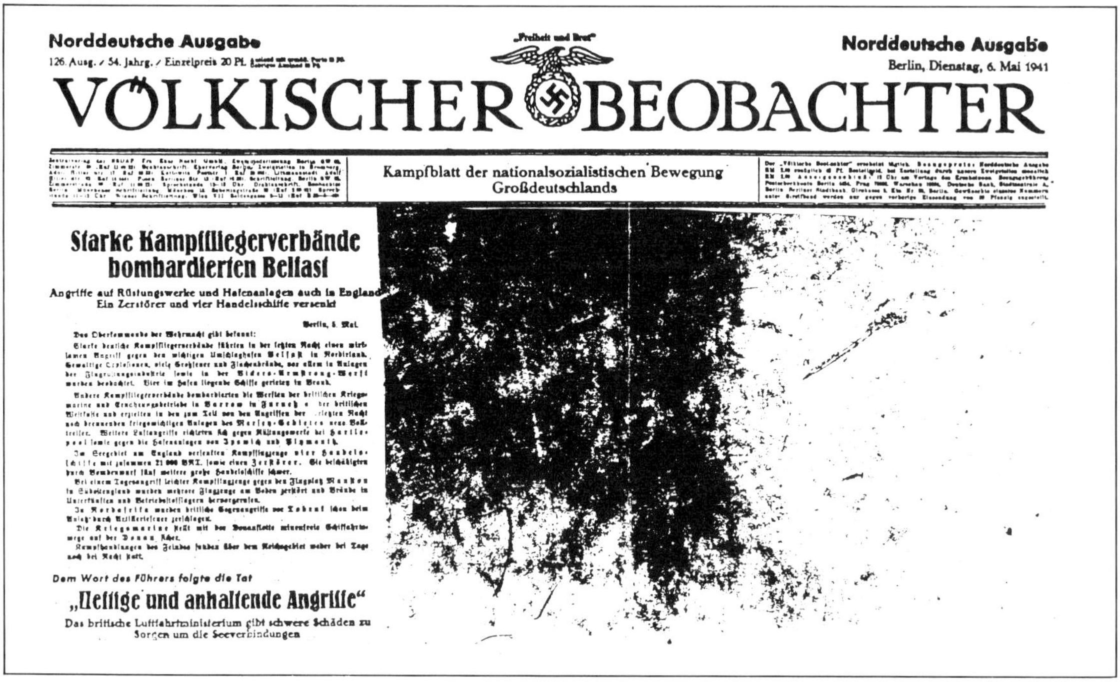

Norddeutsche Ausgabe

126. Ausg. / 54. Jahrg. / Einzelpreis 20 Pf.

„Freiheit und Brot"

Norddeutsche Ausgabe

Berlin, Dienstag, 6. Mai 1941

VÖLKISCHER BEOBACHTER

Kampfblatt der nationalsozialistischen Bewegung Großdeutschlands

Starke Kampffliegerverbände bombardierten Belfast

Angriffe auf Rüstungswerke und Hafenanlagen auch in England
Ein Zerstörer und vier Handelsschiffe versenkt

Berlin, 5. Mai.

Das Oberkommando der Wehrmacht gibt bekannt:

Starke deutsche Kampffliegerverbände führten in der letzten Nacht einen wirksamen Angriff gegen den wichtigen Umschlaghafen Belfast in Nordirland. Gewaltige Explosionen, viele Großfeuer und Flächenbrände, vor allem in Anlagen der Flugrüstungsindustrie sowie in der Vickers-Armstrong-Werft wurden beobachtet. Vier im Hafen liegende Schiffe gerieten in Brand.

Andere Kampffliegerverbände bombardierten die Werften der britischen Kriegsmarine und Ernährungsbetriebe in Barrow in Furneß an der britischen Westküste und erzielten in den zum Teil von den Angriffen der letzten Nacht noch brennenden kriegswichtigen Anlagen des Mersey-Gebietes neue Volltreffer. Weitere Luftangriffe richteten sich gegen Rüstungswerke bei Hartlepool sowie gegen die Hafenanlagen von Ipswich und Plymouth.

Im Seegebiet um England versenkten Kampfflugzeuge vier Handelsschiffe mit zusammen 21 000 BRT. sowie einen Zerstörer. Sie beschädigten durch Bombenwurf fünf weitere große Handelsschiffe schwer.

Bei einem Tagesangriff leichter Kampfflugzeuge gegen den Flugplatz Manston in Südostengland wurden mehrere Flugzeuge am Boden zerstört und Brände in Unterkünften und Betriebsstofflagern hervorgerufen.

In Nordafrika wurden britische Gegenangriffe vor Tobruk schon beim Ansatz durch Artilleriefeuer zerschlagen.

Die Kriegsmarine stellt mit der Donauflotte minenfreie Schiffahrtswege auf der Donau sicher.

Kampfhandlungen des Feindes fanden über dem Reichsgebiet weder bei Tage noch bei Nacht statt.

Dem Wort des Führers folgte die Tat

„Heftige und anhaltende Angriffe"

Das britische Luftfahrtministerium gibt schwere Schäden zu Sorgen um die Seeverbindungen

he 4–5 May raid on Belfast made headline news in the Nazi Party newspaper, *Völkischer Beobachter*, on 6 May 1941. (British Library)

waiting in case they should come back, to rain bombs on Belfast, to destroy houses and docks, shops and churches. But they did not come. . . Part of our cargo were some of the victims of the 'blitz', soldiers being taken back to England. There were about a dozen coffins. Grim fellow passengers.

Not surprisingly, the Luftwaffe bomber crews were supremely confident of the success of their raid on Belfast during the night of 4–5 May. Their reports make repeated and enthusiastic references to 'enormous' fires at the shipyard and the aircraft factory, 'heavy explosions' at the nearby oil installations and numerous ships being engulfed by flame at the port. In their overall 'evaluation of the effect' of the attack they concluded, with obvious satisfaction, that 'since there was good visibility and there were fierce connected fires in the ordered target area, we can be sure of a very good effect'. Subsequent enemy reconnaissance flights, operating both by day and night and beginning within hours of the all-clear, further evaluated the raid's impact. Early on Monday morning, 5 May, William Kennedy, a Southern fireman, was damping down the fire at the ropeworks when he noticed a German aircraft flying high above. Emma Duffin was at the Belfast Union Infirmary when she heard the alert and hastily reached for her steel helmet and gas mask.

When processed, the photographic evidence seemed fully to justify the optimistic assessments of the German bomber crews. As a result, for the first and only time in the entire war, Belfast made headline news in the German press. *Der Adler* published two aerial views of the city, and devoted a full page to post-raid evaluation, itemising the extent of the destruction: 'Around 100,000 square metres destroyed in the Belfast harbour area; the big Harland and Wolff shipyard completely destroyed; in the slipway three ships have undoubtedly suffered devastation and damage', and the aircraft factory 'severely affected'. Reports in *Völkischer Beobachter* were briefer but written in similar vein under bold headlines which read 'Strong Air Fighter Units Bomb Belfast' and 'Back from Belfast: Fires Everywhere'. On German radio, listeners were also assured that 'Belfast shipyard and industry have been completely destroyed', and both in broadcasts as well as in the press the significance of their achievement was underlined. The city was not only projected as a vital industrial base, with its naval construction, aircraft factory and grain mills, but also as a trading centre of supreme importance. It was stressed that 'since the crippling of the London docks and ports on the east coast, Liverpool, Belfast and Glasgow have been the main channels through which foodstuffs and war materials have entered Britain'.

In Belfast itself many would have accepted these doom-laden descriptions and analyses of the impact of the attack on the city's economic life. On the morning of Monday, 5 May, observers described shipyard employees arriving for work and gazing helplessly at the ruins of the 'Island', tears streaming down their faces. One was heard to remark, 'Well, we'll never

Harland and Wolff electrical shop after the attack on 4–5 May. (Harland and Wolff)

build ships here again', and another, 'There is virtually nothing left. The Yard is destroyed.' Moya Woodside had no doubt as to the gravity of its consequences. On 6 May she wrote:

> The tale of Sunday night's havoc is not yet told. We now have an unemployment problem of staggering proportions. *Thousands* and *thousands* are walking the streets with only the faintest hope of being employed again until *after* the war. What is going to become of all these people, many of them homeless and bereaved (or they will be), as well as without work. At present this side of things has scarcely been realized but material repair and reconstruction is of small importance beside the human problem.

In fact the prospects for industrial reconstruction and recovery, even in the harbour area, were much less gloomy than was widely assumed. Although it had borne the full fury of the attack and had been partially demolished, it had not been obliterated as German reports supposed and claimed. At Harland and Wolff a number of important structures survived intact – including the power station, building slips, pumping station and

me of the damage at Short nd Harland after the 4–5 1ay raid. (Short Brothers)

Admiralty offices. However, no other British shipyard sustained such damage to plant and machinery in the course of the war or suffered so much devastation during a single raid. Ultimately Harland and Wolff's claim for bomb damage to its property, both in Belfast and in Great Britain, totalled almost £3 million; it was the biggest single amount demanded from the Westminster government during the entire conflict. Admiralty officials, who later analysed the impact of the attack, concluded that it was a 'very interesting example owing to the concentration of the raid and the size of the yard' and that it was a 'matter of reconstitution and reorganization for the whole works'. The process of clearance and reconstruction was initially delayed by the presence of numerous unexploded bombs in the harbour area, including ten parachute mines. Production was halted completely until 8 May and during the week following the attack, it fell to 10 per cent anticipated levels. In the longer term a major cause of diminished output was the disruption of night-shift work. This had been carried out spasmodically before the raids when urgent work was required to ships and engines. However, employees had become more aware of their vulnerability when working at the yard during the hours of darkness, especially as the very limited protective cover provided by wooden roofs had been demol-

Work begins on a damage
Stirling bomber wing at
Short and Harland after th
4–5 May raid.
(Short Brothers)

ished. Consequently, they now refused to operate shifts between 10 p.m. and 6 a.m. Employment at the yard, which fell by 3,200 between March and May, had returned to pre-raid levels of 23,000 by late August 1941. Production also gradually revived. By 21 May 1941, it had reached approximately 40 per cent of normal levels, 65 per cent by late June, and full output had been restored by November 1941.

The Luftwaffe's other strategic targets in the port area escaped relatively lightly. At Short and Harland a post-raid inquiry concluded that damage was actually 'not extensive'. There, the 'serious delay in production' (by an estimated three months) was caused almost exclusively by the devastation of the aircraft shop at Harland and Wolff's Alexandra Works. It was the only local source of supply for Stirling fuselages and had already sustained severe damage during the Dockside raid. No aircraft parts were made there between 4 May and 12 June. At Short and Harland's own works one week's output was totally lost because of the raid. It was eventually restarted using converted bicycle sheds to accommodate plant and machinery. In the short-term, production was disrupted by the loss of electricity supplies due mainly to high explosive and incendiary bomb damage at the nearby harbour power station. From 2.45 a.m. the city was without lights or power for twenty-four hours. In common with the shipyard, the recovery of aircraft

irling bombers stand amid :he rubble at the Short and Harland aircraft factory after the 4–5 May raid. (Short Brothers)

output was also hampered by the subsequent reluctance of the industry's employees to work night-shifts. These did not restart at the machine shop until November 1942.

Assessing the damage to Stirling bombers at Short and Harland after the 4– May raid. (Short Brothers

Although there had been considerable bomb damage at the harbour power station, the vital generating plant had not been affected. Elsewhere, at major industrial sites outside the harbour, the recovery of output was, in some instances, surprisingly brisk. At the ropeworks, where the post-raid fires had been particularly intense, normal output had resumed by mid-September 1941. Overall, in the seven months between December 1940 and June 1941, unemployment fell locally by thirty thousand, and by August 1941, just 5 per cent of the adult male labour force was without work. In October, Sir Basil Brooke, the Minister of Commerce, described the situation as 'very satisfactory'. That same month Moya Woodside observed: 'Unemployment at any rate amongst men has dropped tremendously over here and one result is that our Welfare office has many fewer applicants.' Her pessimistic comments after the May raids were a symptom of the all-enveloping mood of despair and anguish which was then gripping the people of Belfast. They were tense, emotionally drained and fearful of more and worse to come. They were overwhelmed by the scale of physical destruction, the growing number of the dead and the extent of the dis-

"BUSINESS AS USUAL"

AFTER its second successive scourge of Nazi savagery, Belfast once more took for its slogan the words "Business as usual", and behind boarded windows where glass had been shattered the wheels of commerce and industry began turning once more.

Belfast News-Letter, 7 May 1941

location and hardship. There is ample evidence of war weariness, of disintegrating morale, even of defeatism among a population which was at no point psychologically prepared for the suffering and sacrifices of modern warfare.

Local newspapers at the time described the devastation in the anonymous and optimistic phrases imposed by censorship. They implied that public morale was unshaken and that the pattern of normal life had survived more or less intact. There were descriptions of 'business as usual notices' appearing defiantly in blitzed areas, of 'women brushing up the broken glass', their spirit unshaken, and even of 'typists on their way to work [on 5 May, finding] time to pause and admire the new spring fashions'. 'People,' Moya Woodside stated tersely, 'distrust newspapers.' She herself fumed:

> Press reports of the raid are nauseating. Of course they are hampered by not being allowed to mention any street or building by name. But, even so, it should not be necessary to turn out all the usual journalistic clichés and clap-trap about 'stricken mothers', 'citizen's courage', 'stoicism', 'traders carried on with a smile', etc., etc. The truth is that people are dazed, worn out, many despairing, nerves and irritability everywhere.

Both physical and psychological factors contributed to deep and widespread demoralisation. In the short-term at least, life for many people had suddenly and violently been transformed into a bleak and grim struggle to survive. On Monday, 5 May, Moya Woodside noted: 'I don't think I have ever been so tired in my life. This lack of sleep plus nervous strain is so exhausting.' Later that evening when the siren sounded, she noted despondently: 'I didn't get up. [I] felt so tired that I didn't care what happened.' In any case, she found that sleep was 'impossible', writing: 'In spite of all my efforts of reason and self-control I do feel frightened when I hear the drone' of aircraft engines overhead. Her experience was obviously not unique; clearly, the sense of fear must have been infinitely greater for those living in areas that had been blitzed. A few days later, after alerts 'five nights in succession', she commented, 'everyone looks about ten years older'. Among those remaining in the city, she observed:

> Inability to sleep seems very common. People lie awake listening for the sirens or the planes. Others go to bed with all their clothes on. I heard yesterday of

two old ladies who had not undressed for three weeks. Some sit up every night till 2.30 am or so when the danger has presumably passed. No wonder so many look wrecks. [Her friends spent] all their leisure time in bed [and] as for making plans or inviting [them] for a meal, one just feels too tired and irritable even to contemplate it.

Blitz Square (corner of Bridge Street and High Street) being cleared after the 4–5 May raid. In the foreground a static water tank is under construction (Ulster Museum)

In fact it was evident that the 4–5 May raid, remembered locally as the

'Fire raid', had extensively and profoundly disrupted the entire life of the city; its very heart seemed almost to stop. In early May Jimmy Doherty vividly remembers that 'there was nothing in Belfast. No food in the shops, no security, no fire protection, water mains gone, sewerage in the streets, water carts in use for fear of contamination, people afraid because it was out of their control.' Shortages of essential foodstuffs became more acute as a

result of the attack. On Monday, 5 May, many grocery shops and restaurants were closed, and hot food was almost impossible to buy. During the following weeks, Moya Woodside constantly complained of inadequate supplies, particularly of meat, and queues at bread shops on a scale that she 'had never seen before in [her] life'. She estimated that her weekly purchases took 'twice as long' as formerly, despite the 'compulsion to patronize one or two places', and she shared the 'depressing' presumption that conditions would deteriorate further in the immediate future. This seemed to be confirmed by the introduction of clothes rationing in late May, which 'killed this kind of trade'; as a consequence, large city-centre stores were 'dead'. Tobacco was also frequently difficult to obtain as so many thousands of people sat up and smoked night after night. Shop owners had of course their own problems of damaged and, in some cases, looted premises, lost records which made debts difficult or impossible to trace, and lost customers owing to the crash evacuation. Some faced additional complications: one large and long-established city-centre hairdressing business, which was unfortunately named Hoffmanns, felt obliged in mid-May to advertise that it employed 'All British staff'.

The city's essential services, with the exception of the telephone system, suffered greater interruption in early May than they had done after the Easter Tuesday raid. Lady Spender complained that for several days 'all our cooking had to be done on the tiny open grate in the maid's sitting room'. Numerous gas pipes had been smashed, particularly in east Belfast and the city centre. Ballymacarrett had no supply for a full week, and repairs were still being carried out in late June. The whole city was without electricity for twenty-four hours and only gradually over the period up to 11 May was normal voltage output restored. Due to the initial power failure, the main sewage pumping station was unable to function. Trams and trolley buses were also temporarily immobilised; thus normal timetables were not fully operational until 23 May, and for a time the Castle Junction terminus could not be used because of the extensive devastation of this whole area. An additional cause of transport chaos was the closure of thirteen major roads after the raid which were blocked by fires, debris and craters. They included Bridge Street, High Street, North Street, Rosemary Street, Victoria Street, Donegall Street, Castlereagh Road, Newtownards Road and Holywood Road. Railway services from the London, Midland and Scottish, and Bangor and County Down railway stations were also suspended for several days because of damage to buildings and track. There were emergency plans at the Great Northern Railway Station to sell tickets in booklets from a nearby grocery shop.

The large number of unexploded bombs were a further major cause of dislocation throughout the city: almost 150 were reported to the authorities. One found in Donegall Square South temporarily debarred the civil authorities from the use of the city hall. Another was discovered off Dundela Avenue in east Belfast on 10 May, six days after the raid. It was a

Debris and rubble scattered in front of the impressive façade of the London, Midland and Scottish Railway Station, York Street, after the 4–5 May raid. (Public Record Office of Northern Ireland)

'G', also known as a 'Monica', mine, weighing one thousand kilograms, with a distinctive glass window which housed a photo-electric cell detonating device. According to Northern Ireland's Prime Minister, John Andrews, it was of a 'type that has only just come to light'. Experts were eventually brought over from Britain to examine and dismantle it, and three thousand people, living in surrounding houses in the Strandtown area, were forced to evacuate. From Hillsborough, the Governor, Lord Abercorn, urged Andrews to ensure that all of these bombs were defused as an absolute priority. He considered that the disruption which they caused was having a most 'grievous effect on morale'.

The virtual failure of the local water supply, however, was a much more acute cause of concern to the Stormont government. The system suffered much more extensive damage in the 4–5 May raid than it had done previously. In addition to the sixty-seven mains which were fractured, the Woodburn conduit was crushed by high explosives; it carried one-third of the total volume consumed in Belfast. As a consequence, 'three-quarters of the city was [still] without water for fire-fighting purposes' five days after the raid; additional hose lengths would have been required to relay it from rivers and dock basins. Also thousands of citizens had an intermittent supply of water for up to ten days after the attack and a small number had no supply whatever over the same period.

Such cumulative deprivation and disruption was inevitably corrosive of public morale and likely to induce feelings of weariness. In mid-May Moya Woodside recorded her sense of shock and outrage at the remarks of a nurse, 'a sensible, secondary-school educated woman', whom she had been talking to. The nurse had been for a week 'without gas, light, water or phone', had no charwoman, and travelled 'one and a half hours to her evacuation place daily'. Having gone through her litany of discomforts, she declared: 'How I wish it was over! I don't care how it ends, if only it was over. I don't believe it will make much difference for ordinary people even if Hitler wins.'

However, the most vital reason for the widespread depression and despair was public awareness of the unprecedented scale of human and physical loss that Belfast had by then suffered at the hands of the Luftwaffe. During the May raids, it was the narrow working-class terraces of Ballymacarrett and the commercial heart of the city which had suffered most severely. Once again newspapers reflected on how pathetic it was to see women and children searching in the rubble for anything they could retrieve. The effect of these most recent attacks on popular morale was heightened by the context in which they had occurred. In less than a month enemy aircraft had launched four assaults of contrasting strength on the city. Their cumulative impact had been traumatic. Although the precise number of those who had been killed was at the time uncertain, it was widely assumed that the final death toll would be measured in thousands. The destruction of property was such that, later in 1941, the Government admitted liability for war claims totalling £20 million. Over 130 industrial premises, almost 1,400 businesses and offices, 70 churches, including gospel halls, and 197 public buildings, including schools, had sustained varying degrees of damage. In the stricken residential areas German bombs had demolished 3,200 houses and almost 4,000 had been reduced to a state of acute disrepair. A total of 56,600 dwellings had suffered in some measure from the attacks. The figure represented over half (53.3 per cent) of the city's housing stock, a proportion higher than the national average for blitz damage in urban areas in Britain. As a consequence of all raids, one hundred thousand Belfast people had been left temporarily homeless while repairs were being carried out, and fifteen thousand had no homes. At the time it seemed certain that these horrifying statistics would rise still higher, whenever the Luftwaffe chose to demonstrate its awesome destructive power yet again.

William McCready found these devastated surroundings profoundly distressing and the atmosphere deeply oppressive. Soon after the Easter Tuesday raid he had moved from his home in Keadyville Avenue to Whiteabbey. He had spent the night of 4–5 May closeted in the coal hole of his

ower North Street – tidied up but still showing extensive physical scars in late 1941. (Major H. John F. Potter)

new home, only next day hearing of the extensive damage to property and loss of human life. He wrote despondently:

> I was very fatigued and depressed at this time. I was reporting each day for duty at the head post office, and on my journey in by bike the scenes of destruction were deeply impressed on my mind. [During the evenings] I tried to read but I could not concentrate. . . from time to time an involuntary shudder passed over me and I would see again the demolished houses, with I suppose the bodies of the occupants, and hear the whistling, tearing sound of bombs, followed by the heavy dull thud. I found myself thinking at times that perhaps after all the people who had been killed outright were possibly not the most unfortunate ones. . . It all seemed like a terrible nightmare.

Amidst the debris and rubble, rescue workers resumed the unenviable work of recovering the dead and injured. As in April, they were hopelessly overwhelmed by the scale of the task. They were too few in number, having roughly one-quarter of the personnel necessary to conform to British establishment levels. In addition, their supplies of the requisite tools and materials were grossly inadequate. The chief district officer for east Belfast, Major G. Thompson, later recalled that 'volunteers were not wanting. . . women as well as men in several cases tore at the debris with their bare hands in an attempt to rescue the buried'. However, he concluded: 'Without doubt

Westbourne Street: salvaging what is left from the devastation of the German air raids. (Public Record Office of Northern Ireland)

more lives could have been saved had the necessary equipment been to hand.' Invaluable assistance was received not just from the public, but also from the Royal Ulster Constabulary, from other civil defence districts within Northern Ireland and, above all, from the large military contingent based locally. The heavy dependence of the civil authorities on the army's resources of manpower and supplies had been deeply resented by its commanding officers after the Easter Tuesday raid. They now reiterated strongly their earlier complaints. They criticised, in particular, the considerable 'number of able-bodied men loafing around in the vicinity of work when soldiers were putting so much effort, at great inconvenience, into the work of clearance'. John MacDermott was well aware of these stirrings of resentment and he himself observed that the rank and file no longer had the same 'zest in their work'. The Governor, Lord Abercorn, raised the matter with Prime Minister John Andrews, stating that he had 'heard [of] a feeling in military circles against some of the civilian population. . . who came to stare at the damage and do not lend a hand'. He suggested that police constables should be 'keeping people on the move' and should prevent them from being 'parked in prohibited areas'.

While rescue work continued, the death toll climbed steadily. On 5 May, at 1.30 p.m., the number of bodies recovered stood at 55 and 75 people were known to have been seriously injured. By 6 p.m. that evening these figures had increased to 69 and 126 respectively and both rose further as a result of the minor attack on the Ravenscroft Avenue area a few hours later. By 2.30 p.m. on 7 May the air raid precautions control centre was informed that almost all of the bodies had been dug out at the blitzed sites in the city centre and in north and west Belfast. A notable exception was Glenravel Street police station where three young police officers remained buried. In east Belfast rescue work was still in full progress. Due mainly to the lack of men and equipment, it was frequently a painstaking task, even where the location and number of those trapped beneath the debris was known. In the Newtownards Road area, air raid precautions warden John Devenport had arranged after the alert for the accommodation of local people in various shelters and had hurriedly composed a list of those in each. He had just left Donegore Street shelter when it was demolished, along with much of the street, by a large high-explosive bomb. From his register he knew that eight people had been buried beneath the rubble and he immediately attempted to rescue them. A later wardens' report stated that the first person Devenport found he recognised to be Mrs McClenaghan, to whom he had spoken moments earlier. She was dead as was her son who was brought out minutes later. Two other men were then brought out 'in a dying condition'. Devenport continued to dig for bodies, working alone, with bombs still falling and fresh fires burning. After the debris had been removed to a depth of five to six feet, 'he felt that there was no hope of anyone being found alive and he made his way to other stricken districts'. He later returned 'when he could snatch an hour or so from his duties', helped occasionally by students, corporation workmen, soldiers, and relatives of those buried. Eventually 'on the following Sunday [11 May], a week later, he uncovered a hand and sent for the police. The four bodies were then recovered.' Elsewhere, within this area, rescue operations were on occasion much more protracted. At Westbourne Street sixty-five houses were destroyed or damaged by a parachute mine. Members of a military squad began rescue work at the site on 5 May, shortly after the all-clear, but were halted prematurely when a large unexploded bomb was discovered close by. They eventually resumed their efforts on 15 May and had not finished extricating the dead until ten days later. The soldiers were themselves uncertain how many they had finally succeeded in digging out, owing to the state of mutilation.

The total number of bodies recovered after the May raids was much less than those recovered after the Easter Tuesday attack. Then, public scandal in the handling of the corpses had been narrowly avoided through last-minute improvisation by Ministry of Public Security officials. On this occasion mortuary services were able to cope more easily and benefited from the experience of three weeks earlier. In east Belfast Major G. Thompson's only cause for concern and criticism was that during the attack, 'the morgue was closed and bodies were left on the street to the detriment of morale'. Those unidentified were again brought to St George's Market – a building even less suited to this purpose than formerly as its glass roof had sustained extensive blast damage on the night of 4–5 May. The dead were made available for public inspection from Tuesday, 6 May, and the funeral of those unclaimed was conducted next day. Newspapers reported that, in a solemn atmosphere, Mass was celebrated, followed by a united Protestant service. The bodies, thirty-one in all, were then placed in camouflaged military lorries, and the two funeral processions progressed slowly towards the city cemetery and Milltown cemetery, past the dense crowds that lined the pavement. Military and civilian rescue squads paused and bowed their heads in silence; their arduous task of recovering the dead had not yet been completed. By 14 May, the official death toll for both May raids had reached 119. According to Northern Ireland government figures, it finally rose to 191, of which 81 were men, 86 women, 18 children, 3 unclassified and 3 missing; in addition, 189 people had been seriously injured.

After the Fire raid, Emma Duffin observed: 'This time tremendous damage had been done [but] though it looked worse, not so many lives were lost.' Many factors account for the much lower mortality level: important among them was the distribution and timing of the Luftwaffe attack. Moya Woodside noted, with obvious justification, that 'Less people were killed as this one was directed mainly at the city centre and shipyards.' When the assault began late that Sunday night, after midnight, both were largely deserted. As a result, during the next three hours, casualty posts, even in these heavily bombed areas, were generally much less busy than during the previous raid. At the first-aid post in Academy Street twenty-three injured people were treated, compared to over one hundred three weeks earlier. At the old town hall in Victoria Street local first-aid personnel had been 'heavily reinforced from areas outside the city' but most of this additional staff was 'not called upon and obliged to stand-by'. Similarly, in east Belfast, Major G. Thompson reported that the posts had 'less to do than expected'.

Amazingly, there were no fatalities among the work force of either Harland and Wolff or Short and Harland. None the less, deaths did occur in the harbour area, including four seamen – one on board ship and three ashore, and at least forty people were injured, mainly fire-watchers, firemen, soldiers and naval personnel. Most of the casualties were fortunate enough to escape with burns, cuts and shock; one of them 'dropped to his knees in the ambulance and gave thanks to Almighty God for his survival'.

'he offices of the *Northern Whig*, gutted but still anding – the only building in Bridge Street to survive the blitz. (Major H. John F. Potter)

The death rate would undoubtedly have been substantially higher had normal weekday shifts been in operation. At the aircraft factory alone fourteen hundred men regularly worked through the hours of darkness prior to this raid. They would have been gravely exposed to the fury of the bombing as there was no adequate protection for employees in the harbour area. The shelters provided at the shipyard were later criticised by Admiralty officials who strongly recommended that their walls should be strengthened. Two of them had been demolished during the course of the assault.

It is often assumed that the nature of the attack itself also contributed to the smaller number of deaths in May. It was in the words of a later air raid precautions wardens' report 'predominantly a fire-raid' and Luftwaffe records indicate that 95,992 incendiary bombs were dropped, more than three times the figure for the night of 15–16 April. However, German sources reveal that the weight of high explosives delivered was also greater on 4–5 May: 237 tons compared to 203 tons three weeks earlier. Although a substantial proportion of this larger volume fell on industrial and commercial property, residential areas were also very severely stricken, particularly in east Belfast. The death toll would certainly have been higher had so many people not left the city. As the *Northern Whig* stated on 6 May:

Annadale Street, off the Antrim Road, after the blit virtually all the houses we destroyed or damaged beyond repair. (Ulster Museum)

'Working class areas again suffered. . . fortunately many had evacuated.' On Saturday, 3 May, Sir Wilfrid Spender estimated that one hundred thousand citizens, roughly one-quarter of Belfast's population, had taken refuge in the country. In addition, thousands of ditchers were continuing to trek out of the city every evening. On the night of the raid their numbers swelled during the long delay between the alert at 12.10 a.m. and the arrival of the Luftwaffe over fifty minutes later. In west Belfast Father Hendley observed that 'there were no further deaths as the people had all cleared out of the houses to the fields'. A government official also noted that

> since Easter, 1,000's of citizens made a [nightly] pilgrimage from the city to sleep in the country. The last of these voluntary evacuees had scarcely left the boundary when the sirens sounded. Those in bed rose hastily and gathering a few belongings, sought refuge in cellars, beneath stairways, in shelters or camped in fields or public parks. . . in eerie silence they listened.

Despite this massive voluntary evacuation, well over half of those who died in the raid were women and children.

Within the city itself other factors may help to account for the lower level of mortality. Certainly the local active defences put up greater resistance in May than they had done three weeks earlier, but they were still only marginally more effective and were powerless to prevent the very extensive damage that occurred. Although the smoke screen was abandoned as futile at 2 a.m., the recently reinforced anti-aircraft gun barrage resisted strongly throughout. It discharged a total of three thousand rounds – twice the number fired during the much longer Easter Tuesday attack. Also, once again the HMS *Furious* was co-operating with the anti-aircraft gun control system and joined in with the shore batteries when enemy aircraft were on a safe bearing. The ship was extremely fortunate when a mine narrowly missed it and then failed to explode, its clock stopping three seconds from zero hour. A later Admiralty report confirmed the popularly held view that the carrier's massive guns had 'put up a very effective barrage which undoubtedly reduced the effect of the attack'. On this occasion the German bomber crews were more impressed by Belfast's anti-aircraft defences than they had been before. They now described the flak over the city as 'moderate to strong' and in some areas 'well positioned'. None the less, their reports indicate that they attacked from approximately seven thousand feet – the same height as in previous raids. Their altitude varied widely but generally bombs were delivered from just above the level of the balloon barrage. The anti-aircraft gunners fired into the crimson sky without success, though at least two enemy bombers had already perished over Great Britain on the outward journey to Northern Ireland. On the following night, 5–6 May, the local active defences had a rare success. A Junkers Ju88 was intercepted and brought down near Ardglass, Co. Down, by the squadron leader at Aldergrove, J.W.C. Simpson DFC, who had earlier registered one 'hit' during the Dockside raid. On this occasion the debris of the aircraft was recovered, and later drawn through Belfast with, it was hoped, beneficial effects on public morale.

Possibly a more plausible explanation for the lower death rate may be that Belfast citizens were now more shelter conscious. Shelters, however, continued to be too few in number, unevenly distributed, underequipped and, above all, unpopular with the public. As in previous raids, the shelters' performance was uneven. In some instances they were spectacularly effective. At Hornby Street, off the Newtownards Road, a parachute mine fell within five feet of one, demolishing part of it, yet its seventeen occupants survived unhurt. Similarly, in Chater Street a large high-explosive bomb caused a thirty-eight-foot-wide crater, twelve yards from a packed public shelter, and once again there were no casualties. But on other occasions they provided inadequate protection. A total of forty-seven people died in shelters at Avondale Street, Donegore Street and Ravenscroft Avenue. In these and other cases, they either suffered direct hits or were exposed to blast forces more intense than they were designed to withstand, their floors 'surged and rocked' several inches, and the walls and roof collapsed. After reviewing their performance, John MacDermott concluded that public shelters had 'proved' themselves and he reaffirmed his commitment to accelerating their rate of construction whenever labour, transport and materials became available. None the less, he was aware that they aroused considerable 'social distrust' and doubted whether, in future attacks, people

ANOTHER SHARP RAID ON BELFAST

MANY WORKERS' HOMES DEMOLISHED

Bravery of Men and Women in Fighting Fires

GALLANT RESCUE SQUADS

ON Monday night — the second night in succession — Belfast received the attention of Nazi raiders. The attack was short and sharp. Among the property hit was a working class residential area.

In this district some people were killed outright in a shelter which received a direct hit. A large crater was driven in the centre of the roadway and houses on either side had miraculous escapes from complete destruction.

Throughout the day rescue and demolition squads worked untiringly with the military to clear up the debris from demolished buildings. Fires which had been started in Sunday night's raid had all been brought under control.

Belfast News-Letter, 7 May 1941

would be willing to remain in the city and utilise them.

Reflecting on the May raids, MacDermott was more satisfied than he had been previously with the performance of the civil defence services. In his view their personnel had shown less sense of shock and had been better organised than before, while continuing to demonstrate a heartening dedication to their task. He was also relieved that the Government's own preparations had not fallen into the same degree of disarray as it had done during the mid-April raid, though they clearly required considerable modification in response to the strong military criticism. His advance emergency headquarters, set up under the Hiram Plan, was withdrawn on Tuesday, 6 May. On this occasion, there was much less pressure on the city's welfare services. No more than ten thousand people had stayed in Belfast's rest centres on the night of 5 May, one-quarter of the 16 April figure, and just twenty thousand meals were served in them on the day following the raid, compared with seventy thousand after the Easter Tuesday attack.

On 6 May the *Irish Times* noted that 'The wild-eyed people of 3 weeks ago are no longer noticeable. . . there are no tears and no evidence of the terrible fear that a raid on such a scale is calculated to create.' However, MacDermott himself would have utterly rejected this optimistic assessment. He had become increasingly alarmed by the low level of civilian morale, informing the cabinet in mid-May that it had 'not shown itself as good over the two, recent, heavy raids'. He continued: 'I bore recent testimony to the morale of the people most affected but it is impossible to resist the conclusion that the morale of the city is not first class. . . in some ways, definitely disappointing.' He noted that there were 'many rumours of an alarming character' in circulation and that there was 'much fear'. Privately to Sir Wilfrid Spender he 'painted a very gloomy picture of the discontent' in Belfast, even anticipating that 'opposition demonstrations would take on organized forms and that he expected an attack on Stormont buildings by our population'. As Minister of Public Security, he was particularly exposed to and aware of the widespread symptoms of despair, resentment and demoralisation. He had become increasingly frustrated at the difficulty of recruiting adequate numbers of volunteers to the civil defence services, even to act as fire-watchers. Belfast dockers had refused to comply with the terms of the fire-watchers' order, which obliged workers in industry and business to participate in fire-watching duties in their work place during the hours of darkness. He was disturbed by the sizeable groups of able-bodied men who stood by watching military rescue squads in action without offering to assist them. He was concerned at the widespread unwillingness of employees to work night-shifts, particularly in the port area, and also at their propensity to strike. Most of all, he was depressed by the scale of the crash evacuation from the city and the reluctance of rural householders to accommodate the evacuees. The evacuation convinced him that there was 'more panic amongst the people of Belfast than in cities in Great Britain which had been subjected to worse bombardment'.

Inevitably, the 4–6 May raids accelerated the mass exodus which had begun after the Easter Tuesday attack. The number of homeless people had dramatically increased. Also, earlier public anxieties and fears had been heightened and confirmed. James McConville recalls that 'two nights of severe attack had brought home to us how vulnerable we were'. There was a widespread presumption that the Luftwaffe would return. As Moya Woodside recorded dolefully on 7 May, 'the Nazis have evidently decided to wipe out the harbour and all surrounding it'. This appeared all the more likely as the active defences in Britain rapidly became more effective. In February 1941, 12 enemy aircraft were shot down over Britain; by May the number had soared to 127. Local ministers and civil servants feared that, as a consequence, Belfast might be regarded as a soft target, particularly as the coast of neutral Éire could provide bombers with easy access to and from Northern Ireland. As one official observed, the crash evacuation represented a 'sound instinct'. In the view of air raid precautions warden Jimmy Doherty it was 'natural to run. Those who stayed were mad.'

From the early morning of 5 May, the Great Northern Railway Station and bus terminus were once again besieged by thousands of panic-stricken people determined to leave the city; their outward surge was facilitated as transport services gradually recovered. As before, a number crossed the border, though fewer than in April. On 7 May the *Irish Times* reported that a few arrived in Dublin on stretchers; others carried all their worldly goods in a single shopping bag. Many of them had spent the greater part of the

night in the fields and under hedges. Emma Duffin recounted the tale of 'little Mrs Sloan', a nurse who had been to Dublin on leave and had travelled on a train packed with evacuees. In one of the coaches she noticed a woman who 'had a dead baby in her arms and was asking for a bottle for it from everyone she met'.

When Charlie Gallagher from Londonderry arrived in Belfast with his ambulance, he was immediately sent to the Short Strand area and spent the day transporting families to suburban church halls. He was struck by the mood of despair and the degree of poverty. He was conscious of the 'smell of unwashed bodies'; some of his passengers indicated that they had not taken their clothes off since Easter Tuesday. 'They brought nothing with them,' he recalls. 'They had nothing to bring. They kept asking me, a Derry man, where so and so was. No one knew where anyone was.' Later that afternoon, when returning home, he saw streams of people, 'walking along the roadside, with cases in their hands, getting out'. The whole experience had been a revelation for him. Due to distance, press censorship and the fact that few, if any, Belfast refugees had gone to Londonderry, he had previously known little either of the scale of the devastation in the capital, or of its deep psychological impact.

The renewed flood of refugees from the city increased to bursting point the level of congestion in surrounding reception areas, aggravating their already grave problems of housing, public health and food supply. As before, householders whose homes were undamaged occupied houses and rooms suitable for women and children and, as a Ministry of Home Affairs official remarked, 'chaos was the result'. The pressure on accommodation

September 1941: A group Inst (Royal Belfast Academical Institution) pupils standing on the platform at the Great Northern Railway Statior Great Victoria Street, befc being evacuated to Royal School Dungannon. (Bill McCourt)

throughout Northern Ireland had gradually been increasing. At the end of 1940 there were seventy thousand British troops based in Northern Ireland, many of them in rural districts, and the Secretary of State for War, Sir Anthony Eden, had expressed his conviction that no more could possibly be accommodated except under canvas. To this was added one hundred thousand panic-stricken refugees from Belfast after the Easter Tuesday raid, and it was then being suggested that the countryside could not physically absorb more than twenty-five thousand additional people. However, according to one official estimate, during late May and early June 1941, the number of evacuees, both voluntary and government-organised, peaked at over 220,000. By its nature, the precise figure is difficult to quantify, but certainly at least one-third of the population of the city was, at that time, sleeping beyond its boundaries.

The process of providing billets for such large numbers was even slower in May than after Easter Tuesday, despite more active Ministry of Home Affairs intervention. At Lisburn it took three weeks to clear the emergency rest centres after the May raids; it had taken a fortnight in late April. Moya Woodside had some direct experience of the overcrowding which resulted. On a 'shopping expedition' to a village six miles from Belfast, she found 'almost less for sale than in town' because the local population had been 'swollen by military wives, blitz evacuees, ordinary evacuees, a school evacuated and a Teacher Training College'. Two months later she described the tribulations of a family friend whose car had broken down in a tiny seaside village. Despite walking around the neighbourhood for several miles, he

> could not find anyone to mend the car or anywhere to stay the night and had to sleep in the sand hills. . . He was unable to get anything to eat nor would anyone give him a meal, even of tea and bread. Village shops were completely sold out and householders around about told him that they could hardly get enough for themselves let alone their evacuees.

None the less, the desire to escape from the oppressive atmosphere of the city affected all districts and all classes. Emma Duffin recorded how she 'longed for peaceful time in the country', away from 'blitzes' and 'worries'. William McCready stated with conviction: 'I wanted more than anything to get out into the country where I could hear no sound except. . . the birds.' He experienced what he himself described as a state of 'mental debility', adding, 'I have never wanted so much to go off and live in the country away from it all. Mentally I feel at a very low ebb.' For a long period many working-class areas, in particular, remained bleak and depressing, with adequate housing at a premium. Moya Woodside described being 'out in a slum district', six weeks after the May raids. She wrote: 'The place is still a terrible mess, with whole sides of the street lying in disorderly ruins. Not much chance of forgetting things if you lived here I thought.' When she returned almost four weeks later, she noted: 'The extent of the destruction again appalls me. . . still everywhere one looks are streets of roofless houses and great piles of bricks and mortar.' She traced a blitzed-out family to a nearby street and was appalled to find that the full rent of 5s.4d. (27p) was being paid 'for a house in which two upper rooms were quite uninhabitable, downstairs windows were covered in felt, gas supply cut off, all cooking in semi-darkness over an open fire'. It was 'iniquitous', she concluded, that landlords should charge so much for 'little more than a shelter. . . Yet, there is competition even to get this.'

Those who joined the exodus to rural areas had contrasting experiences. David Davidson recalls that a number of the refugees who moved to Bangor liked it and settled there permanently. Similarly, Charlie Gallagher could name at least a 'score of families, who went from Londonderry to Donegal and never came back'. Mary Wallace was just eleven years old when she was evacuated from Bloomfield with her mother, and she also relished her new and unfamiliar environment. They went first to Portstewart, Co. Londonderry, and from there to a large house seven miles from Enniskillen, Co. Fermanagh, where they stayed for nine months. She remembers how she

All that remained of Annadale Street, off the Antrim Road, after the German air raids. (Public Record Office of Northern Ireland)

'loved it. [It was] heaven, no school as it was too far away, no worries', and even a supply of chocolate, courtesy of the American troops bivouacked at nearby Ely Lodge. However, other children were less fortunate. A welfare officer from Cookstown, Co. Tyrone, later recalled how 'deeply ashamed' she felt at the extent to which orphans from Dr Barnardo's and other homes were exploited as cheap labour on farms in Armagh and around Ballycastle and Ballymena in Co. Antrim.

For most evacuees, living in the country involved considerable inconvenience, sometimes in ways that were not anticipated. As newlyweds, Nellie Bell and her husband Bob ended up sharing a cottage with a family at Donacloney, near Lurgan in Co. Armagh. She recalled that they had the 'room to ourselves but the girl of the house had a baby and to get to her room she had to go through ours, as the man says: "God be the judge of that". The baby needed a lot of attention.' She also found that rural life had other more predictable disadvantages:

> Bob was working shifts 6.00 to 2.00 and 2.00 till 10.00. Well, to get to work on early shifts, Bob and me both had to get up about 3.00 or 3.30 am. Though this is 1941, the cottage had no gas or electric. I had to light a fire with bellows to make him a cup of tea or boil an egg or something. He walked the 4 or 5 miles to Lurgan to get a train to leave him into Belfast. After a couple of weeks he got a bicycle which helped a bit but after a puncture or two, it didn't work very well either. For the 2.00 till 10.00 pm it was just as bad. He had to leave Donacloney about 11.00 in the morning.

For middle-class families the experience both of the blitz and of evacuation was generally much less traumatic or disruptive. The leafy suburbs escaped the worst of the attacks. Also, if there were no shelters within easy access, an option was to have one constructed for private use. A not untypical advertisement in a local newspaper read: 'Maid required, two in family, wages £40.00. Good air raid shelter.' Even if it was decided to remain in the city, holidays elsewhere were affordable and could provide a welcome relief. Moya Woodside described the frenetic atmosphere of a Co. Donegal hotel during the summer of 1941. It was, she wrote,

> almost the last place in Europe where the lights are still alight. . . Last year it was only half-full and those wearing evening dress were in a minority. This year it is crowded out mainly with Belfast's wealthier citizens and about 75 per cent are in evening wear. In fact the display of jewellery and furs is terrific. I am amused to note that a man's economic status is indicated by the number and size of the precious stones which adorn his wife's person and by the comparative length of her silver fur and mink shoulder cape.

She also noted that, unlike twelve months previously, news of the war was received with 'apathy'; the wireless was ignored. Such families could also readily afford, if they chose, the cost of temporary evacuation out of the city. The considerable numbers who did so were a cause of concern to the Governor, Lord Abercorn. He wrote to Prime Minister John Andrews:

'From my own knowledge I have seen people of means leaving Belfast nightly in their cars to spend the night in a safer area', and he suggested that they were, thereby, 'adding extra burdens to the wardens'. Enclosed with his letter was a short piece of doggerel, written by a member of the Governor's staff and sent to the secretary of the Stormont cabinet. The object of the derision was the flood of middle-class evacuees pouring out of the city after the Fire raid.

THE YELLOW CONVOY

They sing the songs of Ulster with all their lusty might,
  But do they think of Ulster's 'grit' when bunking off at night?
They leave before the black-out and in cars which travel fast,
  To make quite sure of sweet repose before the 'raiders passed'.

Their keys they hand to neighbours and wish them all 'Good Luck',
  Until to-morrow morning when back returns their pluck.
They waste the country's petrol to gain their safe retreat,
  But where they get their coupons from is up another street.

They may hear 'planes pass over them' but they can go to bed,
  And find out in the morning if many souls are dead.
They come back after breakfast all smiles and in the 'pink',
  Not thinking of the volunteers who haven't had a wink.

Then they go off to business to do their little bit,
  By urging all to 'work like Hell' while they prepare to flit.
They need sing songs of Ulster these lily-livered lads,
  For men like these will always please Old Hitler and his Cad.

Moya Woodside was critical of her neighbours in south Belfast: 'I think of people I know with cars and friends and homes in the country, who have comfortably evacuated themselves and now complain of inconvenience or slow trains or a few broken windows.' She had frequent contact with working-class families partly for the purpose of allocating a distress relief fund. Reflecting on the contrast between their experience and her own, she commented: 'I feel almost ashamed when interviewing people who have lost homes, belongings, jobs, sometimes relatives, all kinds of worry and trouble. . . Some people have suffered such a terrible upheaval and for the most part they are uncomplaining and philosophical.'

The May raids and subsequent alerts also encouraged the now well-established response of trekking each evening into the suburbs and beyond. 'Going up the road' was a predominantly working-class phenomenon and quite widespread throughout Northern Ireland. In Londonderry, Charlie Gallagher witnessed hundreds ditching in the area of the present-day

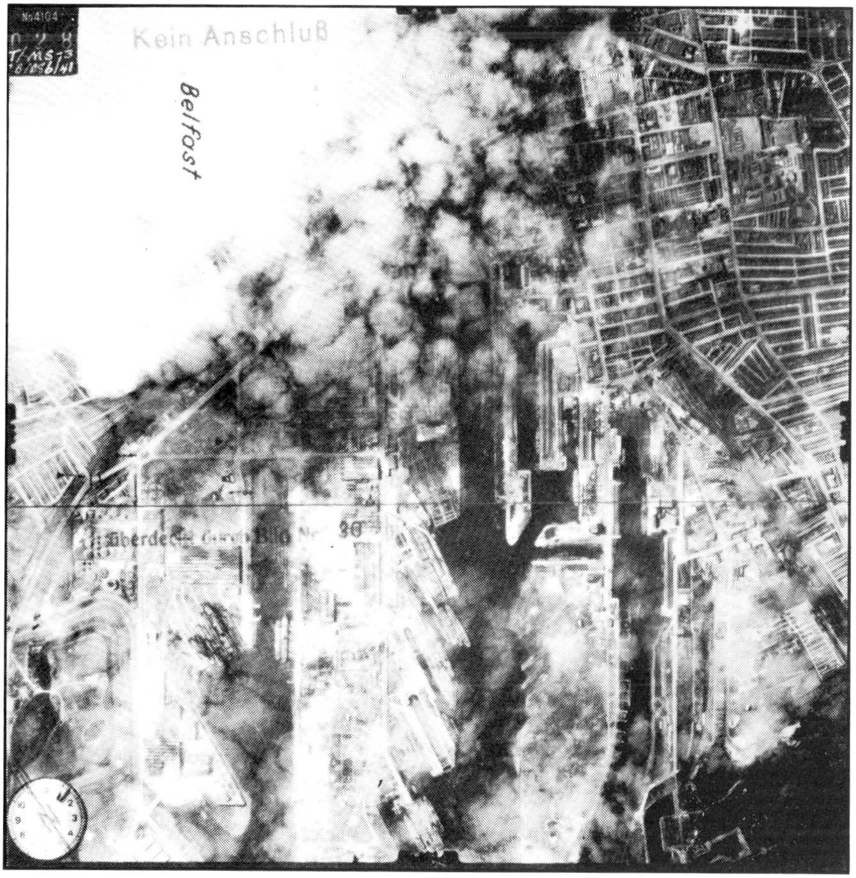

Luftwaffe reconnaissance aircraft took this photograph of the dock area, still in flames, hours after the 4–5 May raid. (British Library)

Creggan estate, then open fields, and on the 'old hill' in Waterside. In Belfast, John MacDermott could hear the sound of their footsteps passing up the lane outside his home near the Stormont estate. He informed the cabinet: 'Many are still leaving the town nightly to stay in the fields or walk on the roads till the danger of a raid is thought to be passed.' On 6 May, Moya Woodside described her 'maid's brother [arriving] from the country on bicycle; he had spent the night under a haystack'. She added: 'It seems that the entire population of working class districts or what is left of them trek out every night with food and bedding. It is the only thing for them to do when there are no shelters.' One week later, she called at a house 'close to railway lines and a possible military objective'. She continued:

> The woman told us that everyone left there went out to the suburbs at night and sat in the fields till about 2.30 before returning. She looked a wreck, naturally enough; her little boy of seven has hysterics every night. . . What is to be done about all these people? There is absolutely no accommodation for them where they go and they are under hedges and under trees all around the city.

Police officers and government officials inquired into ditching in west Belfast on the night of 20 May 1941, and concluded that it was already 'less bad than immediately after the blitz' but that 'appalling conditions' still existed. Three farms were visited on the Falls Road and about five hundred people were found sleeping there in barns and byres and under open

Staff of Mackies pose with pilots in front of a completed Stirling bomber (James Mackie and Sons)

haystacks; most of them had a covering of some description. The officials considered that 'they could not stay in a decent state of health under such conditions of hardship'. There were no sanitary arrangements. A significant proportion were pensioners who had not remained in their homes overnight since Easter Tuesday. The others were mainly women and children, some of them very young. The mothers stated emphatically that they had no intention of sleeping in Belfast again, preferring instead to walk two to three miles beyond the city boundary each evening and return shortly before dawn, at about 5 a.m. Many of them lived in houses close to Mackies' foundry on the Springfield Road, which was widely regarded as a Luftwaffe target.

A further inquiry, conducted two weeks later on the night of 6 June, indicated that parallel nightly movements were taking place along the Springfield, Glen, and Whiterock Roads. There also, people were found sleeping mostly in barns, with the farmers' consent, but with some still seeking shelter under hedgerows. But, in addition, the report confirmed that there was a substantial nocturnal migration on virtually all of the major roads leading out of Belfast. People walked 'a considerable distance into the mountain' at Ballygomartin, and in 'particularly dense numbers' along the Braniel Road as far as Ballygowan. 'A great many' trekked up the Craigantlet Road into the hills or up the Newtownards Road towards Dundonald village. The Ligoniel and Castlereagh Roads were especially popular, with much 'true ditching' continuing in both districts. 'A very great number' continued to go out along the Glengormley, Antrim and Shore Roads, some on foot, others in cars – 'not necessarily posh cars'. Some main routes, however, did not attract ditchers for a variety of reasons. The Holywood Road remained unpopular owing to its proximity to Sydenham airport and because bombs had fallen there in early May. Similarly, the presence of two demolished houses on the Comber Road served as a deterrent. In other areas, such as Newtownbreda, the city boundary was too far distant from the tram terminus to make it a convenient location for nightly evacuees. Having reached their destinations, the behaviour of ditchers varied. The report stated:

> Very substantial numbers remain out until they think the likelihood of a raid is passed and then come back into their houses. Some stay out all night. There is an interesting difference between the appearance of those who come back early and those who stay out late. They say that you can almost notice the difference in the sound of their footsteps. The former proceed back slowly and in a hesitating manner and the latter more confidently.

The numbers of those who trekked into the suburbs nightly peaked during the period of panic after the May raids. Thereafter, their volume was determined by many factors, including weather conditions, the phase of the moon, or the circulation of a Lord Haw Haw rumour. Officials also considered that the Government's threat to requisition habitable houses encouraged nocturnal evacuation as some, who would otherwise have fled to the country more permanently, felt constrained to remain in Belfast. However, easily the most important single determinant of the level of ditching was the incidence of an alert. While some people walked out to the boundary every night, many sat up and waited until they heard the sirens. On 20 June, Moya Woodside visited a 'house in a slum area'. She continued: 'Two boys of school age were sitting about half dead. On asking why they weren't at school, I was told: "Oh they often sleep in now. We always stay up till about 2.30. Everybody does the same, so we have plenty of company."' The 6 June report stated that when an 'alert goes now roads out of Belfast become completely blocked by refugees, essential traffic is immobilized and the people present an obvious target to enemy machine-gunning from the air'. Having reached the outskirts of the city, 'they do not settle but wander around until raiders passed' and then return back home.

By its nature it is difficult to assess with any precision how many people took part in ditching during its most popular phase. On 18 May 1941, German radio claimed that over '20,000 women and children escaped every evening from Belfast to the outskirts of the city'. John Blake, the official war historian, calculated the figure around ten thousand. However, the two reports, produced shortly after the raids, would suggest that both these figures may be an underestimation. In early June, on nights when there were

20,000 SLEEPING IN THE FIELDS

NIGHTLY ORDEAL OF BELFAST FAMILIES

THE nightly evacuation of Belfast by women and children, who sought shelter in the fields and hillsides, was raised in the Northern House of Commons yesterday, following an announcement by the Premier (Mr. J. M. Andrews) to the effect that the Government had decided not to hold a secret session of Parliament.

It was stated during the debate that in one district 20,000 people were sleeping out at night, and the fear was expressed that if 40,000 family huts were not provided around the city before the winter there might be an unspeakable calamity.

Irish Times, 14 May 1941

no sirens, police stated that approximately 500 ditchers walked out the Falls, Glen, Whiterock and Springfield Roads; 600 trekked along the Castlereagh Road; 300 went towards Ligoniel; and a further 150 along the Glengormley and Antrim Roads. They established that this was about one-tenth the level of four weeks earlier and that, even at the time when they were making their inquiries, these figures could be multiplied at least tenfold in the event of an alert. In either circumstance, the number of nocturnal evacuees using these roads alone could well have reached fifteen to sixteen thousand.

Events on the night of 23–24 July 1941 provide an insight into how many people might still flee from the city when the sirens sounded. The alert was heard that evening at 1.52 a.m. and radar plots were received of several enemy aircraft flying north-east from Ardglass. Almost simultaneously, large numbers of ditchers filed towards the city boundaries, in particular, along the Castlereagh, Ormeau, Malone, Lisburn, Falls, Springfield, Ballygomartin and Antrim Roads. They were 'hurrying but not panicky', and there was also a 'considerable exodus by car'. Ministry of Public Security officials estimated that they totalled at least thirty thousand, even though no bombing incidents were actually reported in Belfast. So large a figure was no doubt partly related to the return of some former evacuees who had briefly settled in the country. However, it is also an indication of the high level of public fear that continued to exist. Moya Woodside recorded the experience of her brother who lived 'near the end of the tram lines on one of the roads out of town'. He told her that when the sirens sounded, he 'walked down to the road and was astonished to see the rush out that was still going on. "First, there were the cars," he said, "and then after a bit, streams and streams of people, mostly running. It was like the crowds at a football match." This, nearly three months after the blitz and before even a gun had gone off or a plane been heard.' Ironically, several weeks before the first raid on Belfast, the fact that very few people left their houses when the sirens sounded was cause for comment among local civil servants; in contrast, mass ditching had already become a characteristic way of life in bombed cities in Britain.

The Government was broadly sympathetic in its response to the nocturnal evacuees. Prime Minister John Andrews wrote to Minister of Home Affairs Dawson Bates: 'I would agree with MacDermott that we should not actively encourage people to leave the city but. . . we should not tolerate a condition of affairs under which people are compelled to sleep in fields or wander through country lanes during night-times especially in winter.' The Government could also defend the practice. After all, many of the ditchers were women, some with husbands on night-shifts, or were themselves female linen workers. A significant proportion of the remainder were children, or the aged and infirm. Most lived in small houses near large factories. Officials estimated that 150,000 Belfast citizens still lived in target areas, without access to shelters. Also, trekking into the countryside did not clutter up further the overcrowded, rural reception areas, though it did congest roads and cause water and sanitation problems. Fortunately, the weather remained generally mild and as John Blake writes in his official wartime history, 'By the grace of God, disease and pestilence were avoided.'

One government response was to appropriate buildings, such as schools and halls, where they were available close to the city boundary, and use them as emergency rest centres. In some districts vans, equipped with loudspeakers, were then dispatched at night in an effort to enduce 'hedge-sleepers' to avail themselves of these facilities. Alternatively, in other areas, it was decided to offer basic accommodation in suburban hutments erected for this purpose. The provision of tents was considered but rejected as they were thought likely to foster 'immorality'. Initially, Dawson Bates ordered three thousand huts from Westminster, sufficient to meet the needs of thirty to forty thousand ditchers. The Westminster government was, however, extremely hostile in its response to this request. It was regarded as not being British practice to encourage night evacuation, which was considered to be corrosive of morale and likely to exacerbate the problems of fire-fighting in the event of another raid. The Stormont proposal was criticised severely in the *Evening Standard.* Eventually, the Ministry of Home Affairs received permission to construct 150 huts, and one-third of these was available for use by September 1941.

Sir Basil Brooke, the Minister of Commerce, also regarded hutments as a partial solution to the problems raised by the crash evacuation from Belfast. Specifically, he urged that a number should be erected in suburban areas to serve as living quarters for key workers employed on munitions contracts. In his opinion this would accelerate the return of those who had evacuated and so stimulate production by reducing the time-loss caused by travel to and from the countryside, and by making night-shift duties less inconvenient. At the same time, it would ease the pressure of overcrowding in reception areas. In addition, he argued that women would refuse to evacuate with their children unless they considered that their husbands were safe. He was convinced that if this type of accommodation was not provided and further air raids took place, there would be 'no labour. . . left to carry on'. Such fears were probably well founded. In 1941, 80 per cent of the work force at Harland and Wolff lived within two miles of the shipyard, which was the most obvious strategic target in Northern Ireland. Eventually two hundred huts were constructed to house two thousand men 'selected from the point of view of their importance to war production'.

The Government's main response to the crash evacuation was to encourage all unofficial evacuees to return to the city. Meanwhile the official evacuation scheme was relaunched on 21 May; it had been suspended on the morning after the Easter Tuesday raid. Its aim was to ensure that women, children, the aged, blind and infirm moved to the safety of the country, so 'diminishing the feeling of fear'. In early July 1941, it was estimated that there were still 150,000 mothers and children living in Belfast. In the short-term, urgent steps were taken to clear the rest centres. Consideration was also given to preventing rack-renting. Dawson Bates explained to cabinet that earlier legislation had not been fully effective as

Damage at the furniture a naval store, Alexandra Dock, Harland and Wolf (Harland and Wolff)

families feared dispossession if inflated rents were reported to the authorities. Moreover, barns and sheds had not been included in any of the earlier rent restrictions legislation. In a desperate attempt to find additional accommodation in the countryside, Bates requisitioned large stately houses and other buildings for use by 'respectable' families. On 15 May he even suggested that the Governor's residence at Hillsborough be 'turned over to refugees' as everywhere else 'had been swamped'. In addition, he urged that camps for 'absolutely unbilletable persons' should be instituted 'under suitable supervision', and advised Andrews that additional huts should be ordered and constructed outside the city to accommodate up to one hundred thousand people. At the time as many as thirty evacuees were being billeted in each of the small rural houses.

The Government was deeply concerned at the predictable reluctance of some country households to receive billetees from Belfast, especially in cases where children were accompanied by adults. Despite the threat of prosecution, various subterfuges, apart from downright refusal, were employed in order to avoid accepting them. These included houses 'suddenly filling up with visitors', absence from home, and deliberate efforts to make rooms appear as unattractive as possible by removing all furniture, even to the extent of lifting linoleum from the floor. The Ministry of Home Affairs considered that the occasional prosecution had a 'useful propaganda effect' in discouraging this sort of negative response. It also sought support from church leaders in encouraging rural householders to react more sympathetically. Although John MacDermott at the Ministry of Public Security generally applauded these measures, he considered them to be insufficiently far-reaching. To him the crash evacuation and the indifference of some country residents towards refugees from the city were symptoms of a fundamental defect – the collapse of morale.

By early June 1941 the flow of official evacuees to rural areas had reached its highest total – approximately seventy thousand. However, by September, this had dropped to sixty thousand and by Christmas of that year, to less than thirty thousand. The level of unofficial evacuation also fell dramatically during these months. A Ministry of Home Affairs inquiry stated that the drift back to Belfast had rapidly 'reached alarming proportions'. It concluded that the 'greatest reason' for it was the 'boredom' and 'inconvenience' of life in the countryside. Generally, city people had no friends or interests there, and few felt really at home in the unfamiliar environment. Rural houses on the whole were less well provided with basic amenities, such as water supply or electric light. There was less choice in village shops and they were more remote; there were no cinemas or chip shops round the corner and it was no longer possible to talk to neighbours over the half-door. Children became homesick and distressed at having to walk, perhaps two miles or more, to school. Adults, like Bob Bell, who had to work in the city, found the time and cost of travel an unacceptable additional burden. Nevertheless for many people, their happiest memories of the blitz, at least in retrospect, are associated with evacuation, and perhaps even more with ditching in the early summer of 1941. As the evenings lengthened and the risk of attack diminished, there was greater opportunity to indulge in some friendly banter and to enjoy the 'crack'. Tommy Mack, a local comedian, recounted with relish the dubious tale of his 'going up the road' to Falls Park by car one evening. Soon people were passing him so rapidly on all sides that he became convinced that the vehicle had stopped, jumped out and promptly fell on his behind.

Within four weeks of the raids, Moya Woodside found working-class women generally 'anxious to return to their houses, even in vulnerable areas'. The most frequent remarks of those who had already come back were: 'We couldn't stick it' or 'We couldn't afford the fares [and] the time and expense involved in coming up for the rations.' When it was suggested that they might register with a country shop, the usual response was: 'We would rather stay with Co-op or so and so cash stores or some chain grocery.' There was also often a lack of sympathy between evacuees and the householders and residents of rural areas. Moya Woodside concluded: 'The sort of billeting where inhabitants of one street have been billeted with the next or nearby and when habits and standard of living are similar is obviously much more successful than the transfer to the suburbs.'

Ditching continued on a gradually diminishing scale for many more months. In mid-September Prime Minister John Andrews wrote to Dawson Bates, the Minister of Home Affairs, expressing his concern that people 'were still sleeping out' in rural districts around the city. Journalist James Kelly claims that nine months after the last raid on Belfast he discovered an old man and his wife sitting beneath a country hedge at three in the morning. But increasingly, officials observed that those who had 'formerly left the danger areas are now staying in their own homes, but are not going to bed until about 2.00 in the morning when they think the danger of an air raid is passed'. The decline of the trekking habit was mainly due to fewer alerts, lighter evenings, and the obvious discomfort that it involved. But the crucial reason for the return of evacuees and the decline in ditching was that the fear, which had inspired both, receded. This was due in part to the infrequency of air raids on the west and south-west of England from mid-May 1941. It was related to events on mainland Europe as well – specifically, the German invasion of Russia. When German troops crossed the Russian border on 26 June 1941, in Northern Ireland, as elsewhere, a dramatic readjustment in political attitudes occurred. Moya Woodside noted that Russians ceased to be 'the anti-christ or the Communist menace but our gallant allies'. Unionist newspapers began to contain advertisements for Communist Party meetings to be addressed by Betty Sinclair and W.H. McCullough on such themes as 'What the Red Army is fighting for'. (Ironically, the two speakers had been sentenced to a total of five years' imprisonment during 1940 for publishing 'sedition'; the sentence had been reduced to five months when eminent counsel was engaged on their behalf

Devastation at Gallaher's covered yards; photograph c. 12 May 1941. (Gallaher Limited)

by public subscription.)

The opening of the Eastern Front also stimulated sentiments of hope. From late June, Moya Woodside detected 'a feeling of cheerfulness abroad. People express the view that so long as Hitler is embroiled with Russia he won't have time to come over and bomb us. One woman said: "Well, everybody can go ahead with their holiday now."' Several weeks later she again noted:

> There is a widespread feeling of optimism. On all sides one hears remarks: 'The Russians are doing well, aren't they?' Almost equally common is the expression: 'Maybe it will be over before the winter or sooner than we think.' There almost seems to be an assumption that the US and the Russians will finish off the Germans without much effort or loss of life on the British side.

Eyewitnesses observed unmistakeable indications that panic had receded and normality was returning. By late June, gas-mask carrying, which was at its peak after the Easter Tuesday raid, had fallen off again: 'One sees the occasional woman with a mask but no men.' During the next few weeks Churchillian 'v' signs appeared, 'daubed all over the place'. Moreover, there is evidence of social opprobrium and disapproval for those who had fled from the city. Two pieces of graffiti could be seen on Broadway picture house, on the Falls Road. One read: 'Be a woman and not a hen, come back from the country and feed your men.' The other was politically less neutral in tone; it commented: 'Men of Ulster, loyal and true, fled to the hills when the sirens blew.' Elsewhere in Belfast similar statements were painted on walls. A particularly common one was: 'Be a man and not a mouse. Come down from the hills and sleep in your house.'

Vacant ground in Doneg
Place in July 1941, wher
previously Brands
Emporium had stood.
(Public Record Office of
Northern Ireland)

6 BLACKOUT POINTS

THIS WINTER may bring renewed enemy activity over our Province, and it is the duty of everyone to make sure that not one chink of light gleams from their windows to help the raiders.

Blackout Carelessness may bring disaster to yourself or to your neighbour; a glint of light may guide a bomber to vital targets. Leave nothing to chance. Blackout your windows thoroughly — and remember these six simple points:—

1. Make your blackout before turning on the light.
2. After you have made your blackout, look at your windows from outside.
3. Switch off your hall light before opening the door.
4. Don't carry lights past unscreened windows. Remember this particularly during an alert or in a raid.
5. Be conscientious, and blackout your back windows and skylights. The warden or police may not see them; the enemy raider will.
6. Don't forget that blackout is as important in the dark of early morning as at night.

Don't wait for the Warden's Warning or a Police Prosecution . . .

BLACKOUT YOUR WINDOWS NOW!

Issued by Ministry of Public Security, Stormont.

None the less, fear of a further raid still lingered. On 24 July, Moya Woodside recorded meeting a woman, who, like so many in the city, did not retire to bed before 2. a.m. Moya Woodside suggested to her that 'Hitler was pretty busy in Russia and that we might hope for further respite until the Autumn', and received the reply: 'You never know you can't trust that man. Look how he broke his promise to Mr Chamberlain.' However, Moya Woodside herself noted one week later:

> Everyone is dreading the prospect of another winter. Black-out was bad enough, but now with food shortage, expected fuel shortage, and the experience of the blitz, probably to be repeated and maybe with gas, even the most sanguine cannot suppress a feeling of anxiety.

Officials predicted, with good reason, that 'if a bomb were again to fall on Belfast, there would be as great an exodus as before'.

The presumption that the Luftwaffe would return was shared fully by Stormont ministers. Consequently, with a greater sense of urgency, the Government sought to improve Northern Ireland's active and passive defences. It met with greater success than previously. By July 1941, Belfast was protected by seventy-four anti-aircraft guns and eighty barrage balloons, and Churchill could justifiably claim that, in its military equipment, it 'approached the approved scale more nearly than in other parts of the world'. Ballyhalbert airport was opened on 28 June 1941, as Aldergrove was considered to be poorly sited for the purpose of intercepting enemy aircraft. Northern Ireland's importance in the war strategy of the Allies was steadily increasing and this was reflected in the arrival of a night-fighter squadron of Defiants and more day-fighters to reinforce the existing fighter squadron. In October 1941 John Andrews acknowledged the extent of the improvement in the North's defensive screen and confidently predicted that, as a consequence, 'future raids would not be as long or as severe'. Local passive defences were also strengthened: by the end of 1941 the city had 3,000 firemen, a 50 per cent increase from May, and six months later, sufficient shelter accommodation to provide protection for 430,000 people.

These improvements in both active and passive defences were never to be tested. After the night of 5–6 May, no more raids on Belfast occurred. However, the blitz on Ireland was not yet over. Ironically, Dublin, capital of neutral Éire, had the unenviable distinction of being the last Irish city to suffer significant damage at the hands of the Luftwaffe. Early on Saturday morning, 31 May, at just after midnight, aerial activity was reported overhead and a number of the forty-five hundred local air raid precautions wardens made their way to their posts. When the drone of approaching aircraft was first heard, flares were sent up to inform the German pilots that they were flying over neutral territory. The wardens can have felt no great sense of apprehension: no warning was given to the public, though a system of sirens had been in operation since the autumn of 1940. Large numbers of foreign aircraft flying in local skies was by no means unusual – during the

Enemy aircraft were reported over Northern Ireland yesterday afternoon.

So far no reports of bombs having been dropped have been received.

Belfast News-Letter, 7 May 1941

month of May alone, twenty-seven hundred were seen or heard over or near Irish territory. However, on this occasion a succession of explosions shattered the silence of Dublin's streets. Southern government records indicate that at 1.30 a.m. a 250-pound bomb was dropped on North Circular Road, demolishing a house. (A popluar explanation for the attack suggested that this area was targeted because of its significant Jewish population; similar interpretations had been put forward to account for the bombs dropped on the Antrim Road area of Belfast.) Almost simultaneously, two identical bombs fell; one on Summerhill Parade, destroying two dwellings and killing one person, and the other in Phoenix Park where no loss of life and little damage to property was reported. The final and by far the most serious incident occurred at 2.05 a.m. when five hundred pounds of high explosives detonated in North Strand, within half a mile of Amiens Street Railway Station, prompting some to speculate that it had been the intended target. Twenty-five houses were demolished, 345 were later declared unfit for use and a further 1,000 sustained minor damage. The resulting fires were extinguished within one hour. However, rescue work was slow, hampered by the large groups of curious sightseers who gathered moments after the blast. By 10 p.m. on Saturday evening the death toll had reached 17, one week later it stood at 23, with 145 suffering from injuries of varying severity. Twelve of the dead were given a public funeral on 5 June. During the weeks which followed, eleven more bodies were recovered from the debris, bringing the final total to thirty-four; over half were women and children. Among them were the sister, brother-in-law, and two nieces of Patrick Finlay, one of the Dublin firemen who had helped fight the flames in Belfast on 16 April.

The attack caused a profound sense of shock and outrage in Dublin. Carnage on such a scale had not been witnessed there since the first weeks of the Irish civil war in 1922. In *In Time of War* Robert Fisk describes surviving newsreel film showing air raid precautions wardens standing to attention and saluting as each corpse was removed from the bomb site at North Strand, with Taoiseach Eamon de Valera and Frank Aiken, the Minister for the Co-ordination of Defensive Measures, staring dumbfounded at the crater. Immediately, the Irish representative in Berlin, William Warnock, registered an official protest. As de Valera spoke in the Dáil denouncing the atrocity and expressing sympathy with the bereaved, the members stood silently in their places. The incident heightened popular awareness that the Irish capital was extremely vulnerable. It had virtually no active defences and had shelter accommodation for fewer than 30,000 people, though 370,000 had respirators. No one had been evacuated from the city and it had many densely populated, decaying tenements near its centre.

Eduard Hempel, the German minister to Éire, seemed fully to share the pervading incomprehension as to how the attack could have occurred. When he was informed of it, he records feeling 'staggered', adding, 'my first, immediate reaction was one of suspicion and I wondered if the bombing had been done by the British with captured German planes. . . to upset Irish neutrality and get Ireland into the war'. Three weeks earlier there had been a peculiar transmission on the German radio English language service, which seemed to forewarn listeners of the possibility of such an event. It stated: 'It is conceivable that to gain their ends the British intend to bomb Eire and then declare that the crime was committed by Germany.' In a broadcast after the Easter Tuesday raid on Belfast, one of the Luftwaffe crew members spoke of their strict instructions that they should take great care not to bomb neutral Éire. (Possibly it was to reduce the risks of this occurring that pilots approaching Belfast from the south-east and failing to identify the Isle of Man first to guarantee that they were on course for Northern Ireland were ordered to abort and attack a target in Great Britain.) However, when the minute fragments at the sites of the explosions in Dublin were examined, it was proved conclusively that the bombs were of German origin. It was clear that the Luftwaffe had been responsible; in the words of one Irish cabinet member, 'Of course, we knew it was the Germans.' The German leadership itself admitted responsibility and offered to pay compensation. In 1944 the Southern Ministry of Finance estimated that this would amount to £460,000. Eventually, fourteen years later, £327,000 was paid over by the German federal government as a final settlement.

At the time the incident was given widespread publicity in news broadcasts transmitted in Axis-controlled European countries (that is, countries controlled by the alliance of Nazi Germany and Fascist Italy). On each occasion Germany's 'moral innocence' was strongly asserted. On 5 June 1941 Budapest radio announced that in the

> Wilhelmstrasse. . . the Irish minister to Berlin today protested against the recent Dublin bombing. As far as is known in Berlin political circles, the Irish minister was told that it was impossible that the Germans bombed Dublin intentionally. Investigations are in progress, as it must be established whether at the time of the bombing, German planes were active around Dublin.

Yet it does seem difficult to explain how such an attack could have taken place accidentally. During the debate in the Dáil, one member stated bluntly: 'Is it not true that a one-eyed imbecile could see the difference between our cities and the belligerent's cities if he wanted to see it but we know that he damn well did not.'

Such circumstances might suggest that the attack had in fact been deliberate. This had been the general feeling among better-informed Dubliners, when on 1–3 January 1941, the Luftwaffe had dropped bombs on various parts of the city and the south of it killing three people. Several weeks later, Count Jan Balinsky had visited Éire on behalf of the Polish Research Centre in London and he commented on the widely held view that they had been

> dropped to intimidate the Irish and show them what would happen to them should they make concessions to the English such as the grant of naval bases. It is commonly said: 'We have no anti aircraft defences, no shelters, no balloon barrage, no aeroplanes. Dublin could be smashed by German bombardment with great loss of life. Britain is wealthy enough to rebuild London and other cities but Ireland is poor and would not be helped by Britain when the time came to rebuild the country'. . . In my opinion, for what it is worth, if the Germans intended to intimidate the Irish by the bombing, they have achieved their purpose.

After all, despite Éire's declared policy of neutrality, Ireland had not acted in a totally non-partisan manner in the course of the conflict. Most recently it had on two occasions sent brigades north to help extinguish the fires in Belfast and had opened its arms to Northern Ireland's refugees. There are other indications of a measure of bias in Irish administration. For example, during the war the authorities there recorded that over 160 Allied and German aircraft crashed or force-landed in Éire. At least 223 fatalities resulted; however, some of the surviving airmen were interned at the Curragh. Among these, there were constantly many more Germans held than British or American, even though far fewer German aircraft had for one reason or another actually put down in the twenty-six-county area. (In 1943, 260 Germans were held and just 46 Allied crew members.) Also, intriguingly, on 29 May 1941, a little more than twenty-four hours before the Dublin attack, British fighter planes engaged an enemy bomber over the city between 9.50 p.m. and 10 p.m. It was last seen limping towards the south at a very low altitude, with black smoke pouring from its fuselage.

An altogether different explanation for the raid on the Irish capital was eventually favoured by Eduard Hempel, the German minister. He claimed that it was an accident caused by 'interference with our planes. . . They thought they were attacking British towns.' This interpretation is corroborated from an improbable source – Winston Churchill. Writing of the incident after the war, Churchill suggested that the attack on Dublin was an unforeseen result of British interference with the radio beams used by Luftwaffe pilots to locate their targets in Britain. For many months the Germans had been transmitting radio navigation signals on intersecting lines to guide their planes to cities in the United Kingdom. The British countered by jamming the German radios and distorting their signals. This could be extremely effective. On the night of the 4–5 May raid on Belfast, one Luftwaffe crew member recorded despondently that there was 'total interference with the radio navigation system', adding that 'since last December the precision of the target finding has suffered extremely from British radio jamming'. He also noted that the transmitter was 'suddenly giving a signal which was 100° out over England. Is Tommy deflecting it or am I myself reading it wrongly? It makes you sick.' As a consequence, in order to establish his true position, he was forced, against orders, to fly at very low altitude in an attempt to identify the shape of the coastline and then compare it with his map. It has been suggested that such interference from Britain may help account for a number of near misses that Dublin experienced before the 30–31 May raid. For example, on the night of 28–29 May, about fifty unidentified planes crossed over the south-east coast of Éire at just after midnight, flying northwards. A raid on the city seems to have been aborted at the last minute, perhaps when the airmen realised belatedly that they were over Ireland and not Britain.

Some experts, however, do not accept the 'bending of the beams' interpretation of the attack. They would argue that British radio countermeasures were not as effective as is generally believed; both German military records and surviving Luftwaffe crew members suggest that their radio aids were usable for most of the night-blitz period. In any case, it is unlikely that the VHF signals used by enemy aircraft could have been received as far away as Dublin. Also, it is almost certain that neither of the German pathfinder squadrons – Kampfgruppe 100 or Kampfgruppe 26 – which exclusively used the radio-beam system, were operating on the night of 30–31 May 1941. Critics of the radio-jamming theory would suggest an alternative explanation of the incident. From Fighter Command Intelligence reports of operations on that Friday evening, it is clear that German activity was widespread, though not heavy, over west and south-west England. At first, visibility was good and their high explosives and incendiaries would have been delivered visually. However, the easterly winds were significantly stronger than had been forecast. Bombing and minelaying incidents were recorded at Merseyside, Cardiff, Bristol and Newport, as well as at Dublin, which was attacked by 'raiders returning southward'. Probably the bombs were dropped on the city by a crew or crews which had failed to find Liverpool, either because they had been blown well west of their desired track outbound or as a result of the low cloud which spread westward during the course of the night. They would have homed onto one of the powerful radio beacons on the coast of Brittany, but would have been anxious not to land back at base with their bombs still on board. As they travelled southwards the lights of Dublin would have come into view and probably they decided to direct their bombs at this target of opportunity. From a good height, with perhaps a thin layer of cloud or even well-broken cloud, the night-time glow over Dublin may not have seemed to be particularly significant or striking. There were, after all, a considerable number of lights still showing over England from fires burning here and there – railway and tram systems, steel works, docks and industrial sites. In addition, many were deliberately displayed from decoy towns or airports and night-fighter patrol line turning points. With a strong easterly wind, the lights of Dublin might well have been diffused by mist off the Irish Sea or salt-laden air, caused by the strong onshore wind. At the time of the attack the lights would have been mainly from street lamps and these had been cowled precisely in order to prevent sky glare. The German government's comment, made several weeks after the raid, that it 'may have been due to high wind', lends additional strength to this interpretation.

Whether the Dublin attack had been intentional or otherwise, certainly the German blitz on British cities and ports had come to an end. During the fortnight following the May raids on Belfast, first Glasgow, then Liverpool, London and finally Birmingham bore severe attacks. However, after the night of 16–17 May, the sustained and heavy bombing was over. The German leadership had become preoccupied with their preparation for the Russian invasion and the opening of the Eastern Front. From 23 May, British intelligence was aware that an 'attack on Russia was likely'. 'Enigma' decoded messages indicated that the German air fleet was being transferred to the east. By late June 1941, only 299 of the Luftwaffe's bombers re-

Corner of Lower Donegall Street and York Street in la 1941. (Public Record Offi of Northern Ireland)

mained at their western bases; of these one-half were not serviceable. For Hitler, the 'be all and end all of National socialism' was not, after all, the destruction of Belfast, or even the invasion of Britain, but rather the 'acquisition of living space in Eastern Europe'.

9
FROM WAR TO PEACE
JANUARY 1942–MAY 1945

With the passage of years, it has become easier to evaluate the overall impact of the blitz on Northern Ireland. At the time it traumatised the city of Belfast and its citizens. It had come on such a scale and with such suddenness and ferocity, striking a population which was psychologically and physically so woefully unprepared. Of course some sort of normality did gradually begin to return, and the raids themselves, however horrific, could not entirely suppress the dry, cynical, earthy humour of the local people – public morale was profoundly shaken, not destroyed.

The anguish and suffering that the Luftwaffe had caused is grimly reflected in post-blitz statistics. During the two mass attacks on Belfast, German records indicate that some four hundred metric tonnes of high explosives were dropped. As a consequence of all the raids on Belfast at least 1,100 of its citizens were killed, and 650 severely injured. In the United Kingdom as a whole, 60,500 people died and 86,000 sustained serious injury because of bomber attacks and the various forms of long-range bombardment; 80,000 of the casualties occurred in the London civil defence region. In the list of all British cities struck by enemy action between 7 September 1940 and 16 May 1941, Belfast ranks twelfth by weight of bombing, a little behind Manchester, and some way ahead of Cardiff, Nottingham, Sheffield and Newcastle upon Tyne. Plymouth, the urban area, which before the war defence experts had classified as at comparable strategic risk, came fifth; it suffered eight mass attacks, during which over twelve hundred metric tonnes fell.

Something of the enormity of the human tragedy behind these statistics was brought home to Moya Woodside in mid-June 1941.

> [I] visited a woman in the Poor Law Infirmary, who had been there since the 15 April blitz suffering from burns and a broken leg. All her four children had been killed but she was still in total ignorance of this and believed them to have been evacuated. . . The sister told me that her husband had not plucked up enough courage to tell her yet and that he was supposed to have returned to work in England that Saturday. Mrs— described her experience to me saying that the last thing she could remember was being pinned under a mass of bricks and hearing the children screaming that they were being burnt. Curiously enough she scarcely made any enquiry about them.

Amidst the mayhem of death and destruction, streets as well as people died.

One of the survivors: the elfast Co-operative Stores York Street came through the blitz relatively ınscathed, although there as massive destruction on : opposite side of the road. Photograph September 1948. (Ulster Folk and Transport Museum)

'Hogarth Street never got over it,' Arthur Jackson recalls. 'The loss of neighbours, of chums you had grown up with, gone to Hillman Street school with or to Newington Presbyterian Church – the community was gone, shattered. The people who had lived there never returned after the raids. It brought back too many memories, though they might settle somewhere in the neighbourhood and their sons or their daughters might go back to the street itself.' A number moved out of the city completely or even left Northern Ireland altogether as soon as the war was over.

For many survivors, the experience had a lasting effect in other ways. There were those, especially among the elderly, who never fully recovered from the trauma and the anxiety of the blitz: it shortened their lives. Some found that their attitudes and values had been permanently altered. For Bryce Millar, the raids shook his religious faith and ended his active church involvement. York Street Presbyterian Church, which he had attended, was destroyed; its activities and organisations amalgamated with a neighbouring congregation. The Boys' Brigade Company, to which he had been dedicated, also merged in the new arrangement. But he found that after the raids, he had 'lost interest. It all seemed false, unimportant. For a time I felt a deep resentment towards all that life was.'

Alternatively, the religious commitment of others remained intact and was even strengthened. In Billy Boyd's opinion, to regard the pain and sorrow caused by the Luftwaffe as 'God's will is simply blasphemy. The innocent suffer for no logical reason; individuals exercise their own free will and inflict suffering on others.' Harold Allen still remembers clearly his thoughts as he lay in the gutter on Knock Road, blown there by the blast from high explosives, with bombs continuing to fall all around. It occurred to him then, with total clarity, that 'human life, the family, personal relationships are in the end the only thing that really matter. They are irreplaceable.' Whether his house would still be standing when he returned home seemed, by comparison, a matter of the most total insignificance. It is a perspective on life which never left him during his subsequent years of service as a minister in the Presbyterian Church.

In fact little was left unchanged by the blitz. The devotional life of the community suffered from the extensive destruction of church premises throughout much of the city. During the fifteen years after the war, more new churches were built in Belfast than in any other period of comparable length in its history. The reconstructed buildings differed from the old: they were usually much smaller in size and few had galleries. These developments reflected the steady movement of population away from the most densely populated districts; a process which the blitz had undoubtedly helped to accelerate. The raids also contributed to an acute shortage of housing. In 1944 the Government's first comprehensive survey estimated that over 23,500 new houses were required in the city. At that time Belfast had an average density of 28.7 persons per acre. Over 37 per cent of its citizens inhabited 'overcrowded or unfit dwellings'; in Smithfield ward the figure was 76.1 per cent, in Court ward 65.8 per cent and in Falls ward 62.1 per cent. Sixty per cent of its total population lived in poorer areas such as these, with at least sixty houses per acre. The housing problem became acute in wartime, owing to bomb damage, the lack of new building and inadequate maintenance. There was also substantial rural migration into some districts; for example, the numbers living in west Belfast, specifically in the Smithfield–Falls area, rose from 78,000 in 1938 to 111,000 in 1945. At successive post-war Unionist Party conferences, resolutions were passed criticising ministerial delay in constructing an adequate number of houses in 'good working class' areas.

Inevitably, Belfast's educational services were severely dislocated by extensive physical damage to schools, the disruptive impact of the crash evacuation and the deleterious effect of the air raids on the receptivity of pupils. A total of thirty-nine public elementary schools were either destroyed or seriously damaged during the blitz – some were never to reopen. In mid-September 1941, after the summer holidays, A.J. Tulip, a school inspector in Belfast, reported that attendance was less than half pre-blitz levels and was lowest in the areas which had been most severely

A Stirling bomber (left) and a Halifax bomber (right) stand in Blitz Square, High Street, during Wings for Victory week, April 1943. (Ernie Cromie, Ulster Aviation Society)

bombed. Substantial numbers of teachers had also evacuated and there were instances of up to ninety children of all ages being taught by a single teacher, such as at Hillman Street school. It was noted that those pupils attending class were 'jumpy', had considerable difficulty in concentrating and had experienced 'an appreciable gap' in their school lives. Many of the absentees could be seen playing in surrounding streets during school hours. Chief casualty officer Professor T.T. Flynn drew attention to a less obvious educational lapse by predicting that when 'normal pre-war traffic returns, the accident rate, especially amongst children, will be appalling. They have lost their road sense due to the wartime absence of traffic.'

Industrial and commercial property had also sustained very considerable damage, particularly during the 4–5 May raid. In some cases this represented a tragic and irreparable loss to the cultural heritage of the city. For example, the Cambridge Bar in Sugar House Entry, which ran between High Street and Waring Street, with its historic links back to the United Irishmen, was gone. Throughout the bombed districts there were yawning gaps where business premises had once stood. 'Blitz Square', the waste area left after the obliteration of Arnott's on High Street, became for many years a favourite location for circuses and fairs and the tents of travelling evangelical preachers. It typified the use made of other similar bombed sites elsewhere in Belfast.

Given the widespread devastation of factory plant and machinery, it is surprising that unemployment should have fallen substantially even during 1941. By August of that year, just 5 per cent of the adult male labour force was without work. This was partly due to voluntary enlistment in the forces; there were roughly twenty thousand recruits from Northern Ireland during the first two years of war. In the same period twenty-eight thousand transferred to work in Britain, though an unknown number returned, particularly, as one Home Office official wryly observed on 6 May 1941, 'if bombs fell in their vicinity whilst over here'. Meanwhile the flow of war contracts to local industry markedly increased as the productive capacity of GB firms became more fully utilised. Also, the local linen industry continued to employ considerable numbers until early 1942, while the building and contracting industry expanded rapidly. Aerodromes and bases were being constructed for American and British troops, as well as large numbers of public shelters for the belated protection of Belfast citizens.

None the less, though male unemployment continued to fall with only slight interruption, the blitz aggravated the problems of Belfast industry. This was not just because of the extensive physical destruction and the disruption of night-shift work which it caused. It also helped raise issues which contributed to a further deterioration in labour relations. In autumn 1941, workers in the port area held protest meetings criticising the alleged apathy of management towards air raid precautions and forcefully demanding that greater provision be made for their protection. After the attacks, the dispersal of production to less vulnerable sites outside the city generated potentially derisive questions related to wage levels, work schedules, transport costs, allowance for time spent travelling, and accommodation. At the same time it exposed the dearth, even in the largest firms, of managerial talent needed to plan and co-ordinate efficiently the output of the scattered factory units. Overall, agreement that was urgently needed on vital though sensitive matters, such as dilution (that is, the replacement of skilled by semi-skilled and unskilled workers), became much more difficult. Cumulatively, the scale of war production in Northern Ireland was considerable. Between 1939 and 1945, Belfast's shipbuilding industry produced 170 ships, including 34 corvettes used in escort convoys to protect British shipping from German submarine attack. In addition, 54 merchant ships were launched, 3,000 vessels were repaired or converted (up to 100 at any one time), and numerous ships were accommodated at expanded berths in the harbour area. Londonderry was also an important centre of ship construction and repair.

Local industry contributed to the needs of the forces in other ways. Harland and Wolff, for example, produced 505 tanks, numerous gun mountings and ordnance pieces, and over 13 million aircraft parts. At Short and Harland, 1,200 Stirling bombers and 125 Sunderland flying boats were built, its work force expanding to 23,000, employed not only at Sydenham but at 11 dispersal factories in such locations as Newtownards in Co. Down

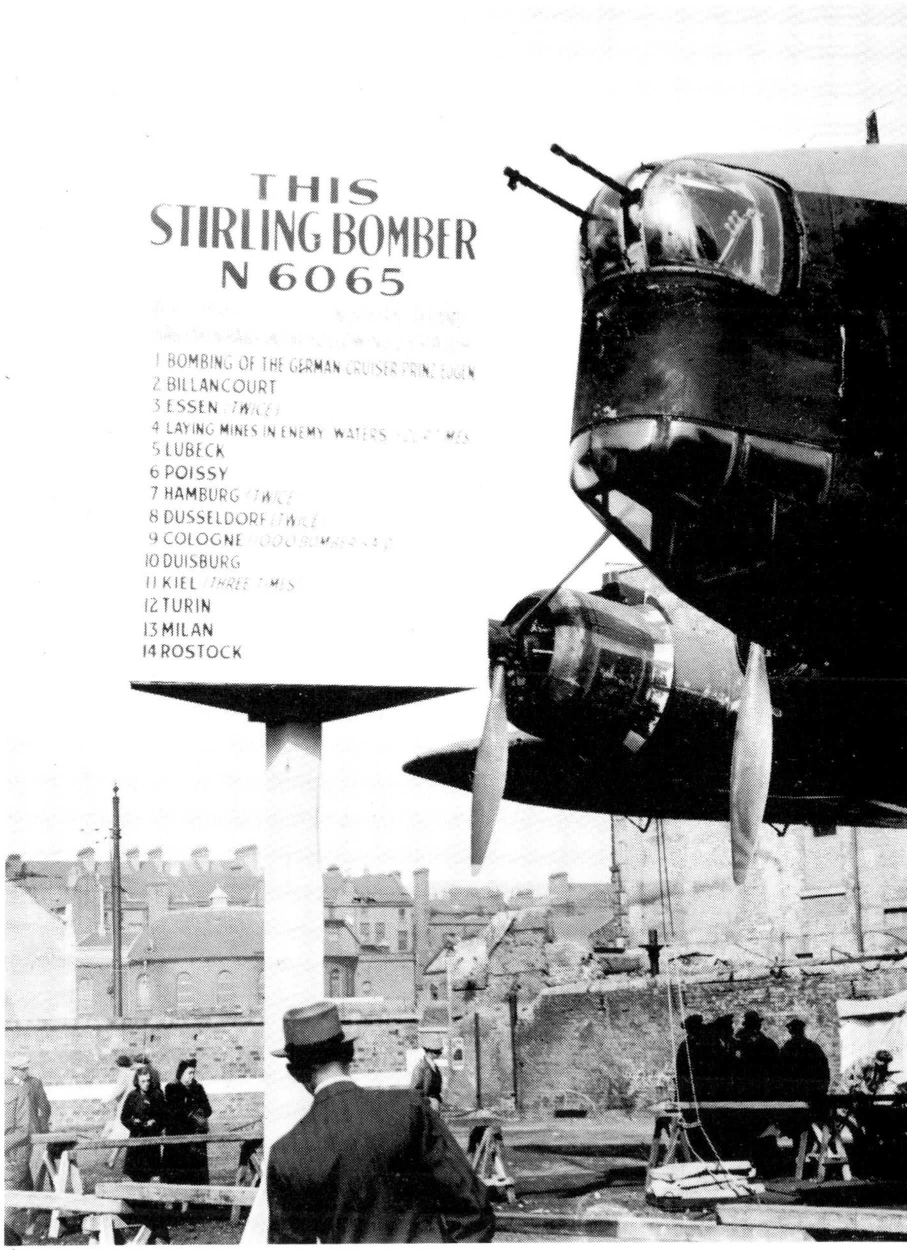

A veteran Stirling bomber returns to Belfast, where it was built. Wings for victory week, April 1943. (Ernie Cromie, Ulster Aviation Society)

and Lambeg, Long Kesh and Aldergrove in Co. Antrim. One-third of the ropes required by the War Office were made at Belfast Ropeworks. The textile and clothing industry had greater difficulty in adjusting to war conditions. Its output was restricted both by raw material shortages, and the disruption of exports, which forced some firms to close or to operate only on a part-time basis. None the less, hundreds of thousands of uniforms were made in the North for the growing number of British servicemen, and 90 per cent of the shirts required by the forces were produced locally, particularly in Londonderry. Linen firms diversified their production – making parachute webbing and harnesses (two million flax fabric parachutes were manufactured in Northern Ireland during the war years,

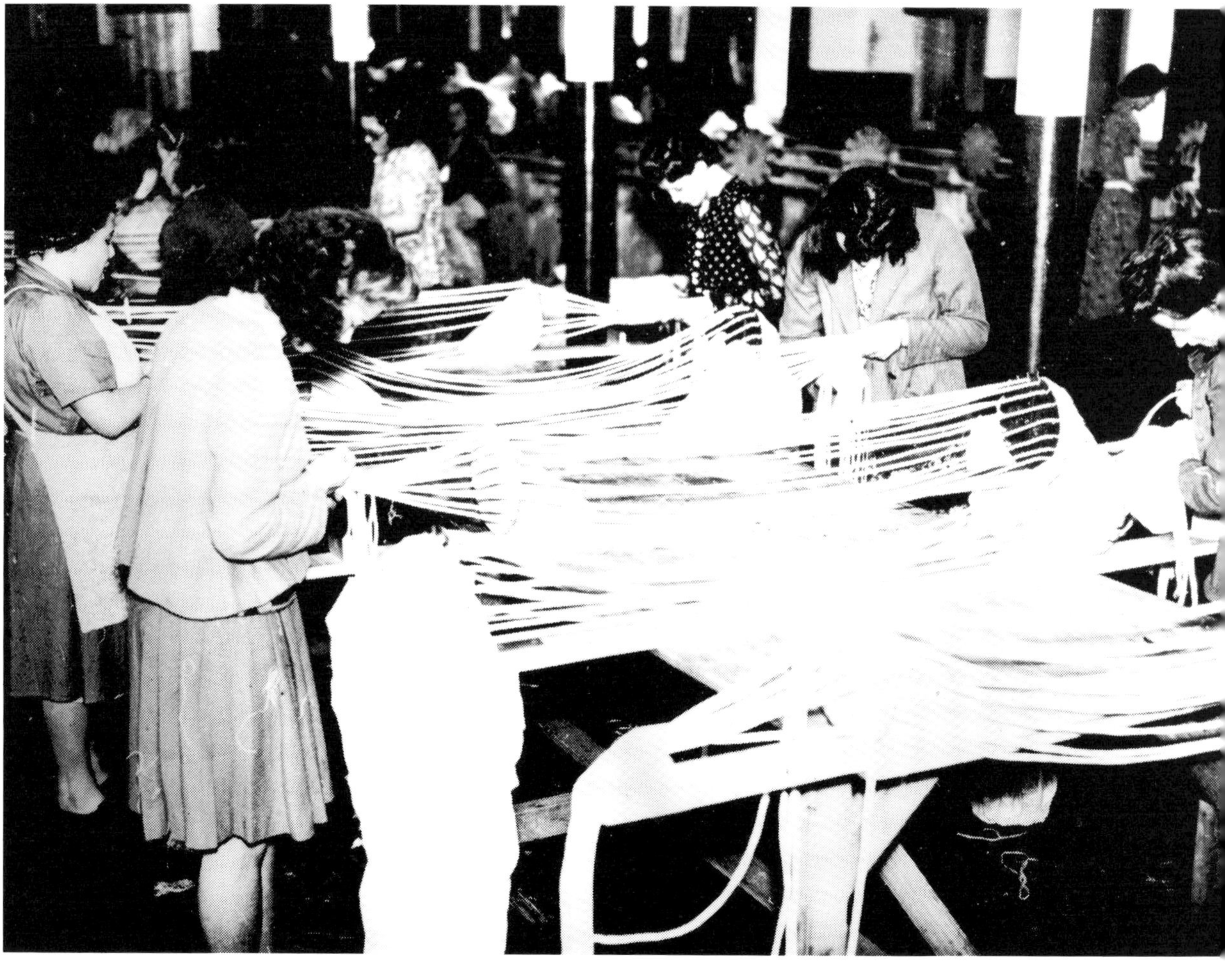

September 1943. Wome[n] workers contribute to th[e] war effort: parachute-making at Littlewood's, Carrickfergus, a major centre for parachute production. (Ulster Folk [&] Transport Museum)

particularly in Carrickfergus, Co. Antrim), machine-gun belts, canvas and wagon covers.

In some cases linen firms stored their textile machinery and converted to munitions production. These, with other small engineering firms, generally subcontracted work from the main munitions factories. James Mackie and Sons, whose foundry was established in 1840, was exceptionally dynamic and successful. In the war years its production included seventy-five million shells and sixty-five million components for bombs. After the blitz, the firm took over factory space in a number of spinning and weaving firms – including Herdman's of Sion Mills, Dickson's of Dungannon, both in Co. Tyrone, and John Allen's of Lurgan, in Co. Armagh – and used it for war production. A feature of Mackies' expansion was its increased use of female labour. In 1938 it had employed an exclusively male labour force of approximately 2,000 at its Springfield Road works. By 1943 its work force there was comprised of 3,800 men and 3,700 women. After Dunkirk, women munitions workers were functioning on a three-shift system, each eight hours long, seven days per week. Their introduction on such a scale into this male domain raised problems such as the need for separate cloakroom facilities, and more especially, the considerable opposition from skilled male engineering workers. Eric W. Scales, secretary at the Ministry

Camouflage nets being produced at Littlewood's, Carrickfergus, September 1943. (Ulster Folk and Transport Museum)

of Public Security, described the Amalgamated Engineering Union in Northern Ireland as 'the last remaining stronghold of unyielding trade unionism'. John T. Gailey, a director at Mackies recalled: 'If a strike occurred, the firm ignored the strike. . . and brought in more unskilled labour to take the place of the skilled. . . The [female employees] were very heterogeneous, ranging from doctors' wives downwards, a considerable proportion. . . were married.'

Although in Northern Ireland the expansion of female employment in industry was a feature of the war, it was perhaps less dramatic than in other parts of the United Kingdom. In 1935, 46.5 per cent of the industrial labour force in the North was female, compared to 26.4 per cent in Great Britain. The total number of female insured workers in the six counties increased from 111,900 in 1939 to a wartime peak of 118,600 in 1943. However, the character of their work in local industry changed significantly. Traditionally, women had been employed almost exclusively in local linen and clothing firms. In the war period, not only did the nature of output in this sector change, but also, increasing numbers found work in other industries and 7,500 transferred to find work in Great Britain. The scale of female employment in the aircraft industry increased and in rope and twine making, and most spectacularly, in the engineering industry as a whole.

panic from Belfast, served to illuminate dramatically the extent of poverty in the city and to blast away popular complacency. The newly appointed moderator of the Presbyterian Church, the Reverend W.A. Watson, made an awesome prediction in the course of his installation speech on 2 June 1941:

> After the big blitz of a few weeks ago, I was inexpressibly shocked at the wrecked houses and shops but I was more inexpressibly shocked at the sight of the people I saw walking the streets. I have been working nineteen years in Belfast and I never saw the like of them before – wretched people, very undersized and underfed, down-and-out-looking men and women. They had been bombed out of their homes and were wandering the street. Is it creditable to us that there should be such people in a Christian country?. . . If something is not done now to remedy this rank inequality, there will be a revolution after the war.

In John Oliver's phrase, the mass evacuation 'lifted the lid off' the scale of social deprivation and need; it was as much a revelation to the officials and the political leadership, both at Stormont and at Westminster, as it was to those members of the public who were not directly affected. For twenty years Northern Ireland people had been treated in large part as second-class citizens, paying the same level of taxation as in Britain but being provided with unequal services, whether in health, housing, education or Poor Relief. In response, junior ministers urged upon the Prime Minister the necessity of producing detailed plans for the post-war period to 'arouse enthusiasm and capture the imagination of the great majority of the people'. They regarded it as 'essential for the future of the province as well as the party'.

Andrews responded by appointing a profusion of committees and making a single speech in the Commons on 30 July 1942 committing himself to such laudable goals as improved housing and expansion in education. He concluded that if 'foresight, energy and courage' could solve post-war problems, 'they will be solved'. However, his words had a hollow and unconvincing ring. Doubts as to his competence not only to mobilise the country for war but also to prepare it for peace contributed to his fall. Meanwhile, by September 1942 Belfast Corporation's reputation for corruption and incompetence was such that he was forced reluctantly to take action. He and his colleagues took the controversial decision to appoint city commissioners, who would relieve councillors of a number of their functions. This legislation served to alienate some influential elements within the Unionist Party, who opposed the bill, while failing to satisfy those who believed that firmer action was justified. From the spring of that year, Andrews himself became convinced that if a general election was called his government would be defeated. Twelve months later, on 28 April 1943, amongst growing criticism of his administration from within the ranks of the Unionist Party and even his own government, he was forced to resign. One of the first acts of his successor, Sir Basil Brooke, was to formulate

The task of demolishing tz-damaged houses went on for several years; this Belfast terrace is being cleared in January 1948. (Ulster Folk and Transport Museum)

plans for all the major social services during the post-war years. Officials involved with civil defence played a crucial role in this process; their experience during the blitz had heightened both their awareness of poverty and their zeal to eradicate it. In the financial negotiations which followed, British ministers were broadly sympathetic. They also had become more conscious of Northern Ireland's relative backwardness in areas such as health and housing.

It is sometimes suggested that the air raids, at least in the short-term, helped to ease sectarian tension and divisions. Police Constable Billy McNeill, based at Mountpottinger station, recalled: 'The Catholic community felt and lived the situation just like the Protestant people.' There are numerous dramatic illustrations of the validity of this observation. Women and children from the Shankill as well as the Falls sought sanctuary in the vaults of Clonard Monastery. In north Belfast members of both communities sang hymns together in shelters on the community interface at Isabella Street, close to the area where six years earlier the worst sectarian riots had occurred since the troubles of the early 1920s. In bombed areas of the city air raid precautions members and others had worked to free those trapped by debris, had fought fires and had cared for the injured. The matter of religious identity, normally so vital, became irrelevant. On two occasions, despairing citizens from all parts of Belfast had sought to identify their dead at St George's Market, though the unclaimed were given religious rites appropriate to their presumed faith and were interred in separate burial grounds.

Post-war improvement in housing conditions: new houses on the Shore Road, April 1946. (Ulster Folk and Transport Museum)

Both Protestants and Catholics had fled in panic and fear into the countryside to seek refuge in rest centres and billets, or in suburban ditches. For a time it seemed to some that they might make common cause and turn their combined anger on the people and the institutions which they saw as responsible for their suffering. Tommy Henderson, the Shankill Road Independent Unionist MP, who had comforted John MacDermott after the Easter Tuesday raid, referred to this danger in an impassioned speech at Stormont in mid-May. 'I broke down,' he told the Stormont parliament, 'when I saw lying dead men I had been reared beside. When I saw the whole district where I had roamed in my bare feet razed to the ground and the people murdered by the Nazis, I certainly broke down. It was no shame to break down'. Then attacking the Prime Minister, John Andrews, he asked:

> Will he come to the hills and to the Divis Mountain? Will he go to the barns and the sheughs throughout Northern Ireland to see the people of Belfast, some of them lying on damp ground?. . . Will he come to Hannahstown and the Falls Road? The Catholics and the Protestants are going up there mixed and they are talking to one another. They are sleeping in the same sheughs, below the same trees and in the same barns. They all say the same thing, that the Government is no good.

Citizens from both traditions also co-operated closely in the civil defence organisation. In his autobiography, *Working at Stormont*, John Oliver observed: 'Religion in fact played little part in the wartime administration story. All were at risk and all played their part in the processes of survival.' He concluded that sectarian strife did not seriously affect the administration of services: 'For a contentious people, we were remarkably unified in face of the dangers of war.' On the Shankill, Rita McKittrick joined the air raid precautions service after the blitz and remembers spending as much time at Divis Street post (Lower Falls) as at her own home base in Beverley Street. She explains: 'War brought us together. It's only now that you ask were there undercurrents even then?' Similarly, Charlie Gallagher recalls that in Londonderry 'community tensions were at an all-time low during the war. It became a boom town and this helped transform attitudes. Catholics were encouraged to join the civil defence services by the local bishop, Bishop Neil Farren, and the atmosphere was one of friendly co-operation.'

However, the extent to which the two communities came together in Belfast might easily be overstated. Such short-term unity as emerged was rooted not in common love and mutual tolerance but in shared fear, grief and panic. The police inquiry into ditching near Falls Road bus terminus on the night of 20 May 1941 noted with surprise that large numbers went there from areas as far distant as Carlisle Circus, the Antrim Road, and even from the east of the city. Clearly they did so partly because they felt safe there, but the report considered that this was not the only explanation. It was also because 'the people, being mostly Roman Catholic, wish to get into an area where there is a large proportion of their own persuasion'. They therefore preferred to join nocturnal evacuees in west Belfast rather than go to other, in some cases, more accessible suburban districts. However, in Belfast, as in Londonderry, this sectarian division of the population was mostly facilitated by 'the geography of the town'. Likewise, volunteers at the schools and halls, which served as rest centres, observed that the refugees tended to divide on religious lines soon after their arrival. Moreover, in towns such as Lisburn, the Catholic Church operated its own centres, administered by its own personnel, and inevitably these attracted almost exclusively its own communicants.

There is evidence that sectarian suspicion remained strong throughout the war, including the period of the blitz. This was partially related to competition for employment. In May 1941 Ernest Bevin, British Minister of Labour and National Service, commented on the ubiquitous fear in Northern Ireland that the region would 'experience substantial unemployment after the war'. He continued: 'Men are not willing to give up their jobs to go into the armed forces unless they are assured that the obligation is general and that their jobs will not be taken permanently by others, possibly of a different religion.' Andrews discussed this fraught issue with Herbert Morrison during his brief visit to Northern Ireland two months later.

Also, particularly in Belfast, there was a tendency amongst unionists to regard the nationalist community as a sort of fifth column, pro-German and anti-British by instinct, and ever willing to aid and abet the enemy by passing on sensitive information mainly via German agents across the border. Joseph McCann recalls building shelters in the Antrim Road–Artillery Street area soon after the Easter Tuesday raid. He quickly became aware of the widespread local Protestant presumption that people had 'filed up and down the Falls Road' during the attack, with lights in their hands, in order to indicate to the Luftwaffe that it was a Catholic–Nationalist area with pro-German sympathies. The rumour was of course groundless – though Hugh Crossan does remember one individual, who was somewhat 'simple-minded', lighting matches for this purpose in his back yard, to much local amusement.

Moreover, there were rumours of mysterious lights appearing in the night sky, after the sirens had gone, to serve as navigational guides for enemy pilots; inevitably it was assumed that the more extreme republican elements were responsible. The existence of these signals would seem to have been given some credibility even by the authorities. Donald Fleck was on switchboard duty at the police station in Chichester Street during the 4–5 May raid, when a sinister report was filed by military personnel. It stated that an inexplicable bright light had been observed shining to the north of Belfast and another to the south. The police inquiry into ditching, two weeks later, would appear to provide at least partial confirmation of this sighting. It noted that exceptionally large numbers of nocturnal evacuees went up the Ligoniel, Hightown and Crumlin Roads, and continued:

> It is suggested not only by the evacuees but by the police themselves that one reason for the safe nature of this area has been attributed to the fact that during 'alert periods', lights are seen in the vicinity of Wolf Hill. These lights are presumed to have been signalling to enemy aircraft and as a consequence no bombs have been dropped in this locality.

The basis for much of the speculation about nationalist subversion and possible German respect for Irish neutrality lay in the distribution of death and devastation sustained by the city during the raids. Many unionists were convinced that Protestant areas bore more than their share of the destruction – a viewpoint summed up in the emotive jibe that the 'pope was in the first airplane'. There is some evidence to suggest that they did suffer disproportionately. B District, which was made up of Falls, Smithfield and parts of St Anne's and Woodvale wards, had a population of roughly one hundred thousand and was over 90 per cent nationalist. The Easter Tuesday raid resulted in just 50 deaths throughout this area; in addition, 60 houses were demolished and 350 damaged. The Catholic community did of course endure loss and distress in other parts of Belfast, notably in the area of York Street mill. However, of the ninety-two bodies claimed and removed from St George's Market after the attack, seventy-five were Protestant. On the other hand, at the public funeral after the 4–5 May raid, eleven of the thirty-one bodies were believed to have been Catholic – a figure which reflects accurately the respective religious proportions of the city.

In addition, almost all of the churches that sustained serious damage as a consequence of the air raids were Protestant (nineteen Presbyterian, twelve Church of Ireland, eight Methodist and two Catholic). It was with little exaggeration that the Clonard Monastery's 'Domestic Chronicles' recorded

S.P.1.

ÉIRE—IRELAND

SCRÚDÓIREACHT PHUIST

Postal Censorship

Ní hí an Scrúdóireacht Éireannach fé ndeár an leitir seo do chiorrbhadh.

The Irish Censorship is not responsible for the mutilation of this letter.

after the May attacks that 'in no raid so far has any Roman Catholic Church been hit. Deo Gratias et Mariae.' The Catholic Church's schools, however, suffered more than proportionately. Of the ten public elementary schools destroyed by fire or bomb blast in the county borough of Belfast, six were under Catholic management and so also were twelve of the twenty-nine that required major repairs. It would be difficult as well as pointless now to quantify accurately the precise extent of the loss borne by each community. If Protestant districts did suffer more, the only plausible explanation would be that they contained a substantial majority of the city's population and that most of the Luftwaffe's major targets were located in predominantly Protestant areas.

Protestant suspicion of the minority population was fully shared by the Stormont government. For example, when establishing a home guard – the Local Defence Volunteers – Craigavon had been determined that the B Specials, the predominantly Protestant auxiliary police force, should form its nucleus and that it should be placed under the control of the Royal Ulster Constabulary. In cabinet he referred to the 'grave objections', of which his colleagues were 'fully cognizant', to such a body being raised in Northern Ireland on the same basis as in Great Britain. The Opposition condemned the procedures adopted, claiming they were 'creating a sectarian and political force' by making 'political loyalty' a precondition of membership. Similarly, in 1940 a military recruitment campaign had been conducted using a Unionist Party official as co-ordinator, on the grounds that he knew 'everybody in the country'. Critics stressed that this type of approach 'did not happen in Britain'. Craigavon and his colleagues had also been concerned that nationalist sympathisers were fostering dissatisfaction and fomenting strike action in local industry, and also leaking sensitive information to Germany via Dublin. Westminster shared at least some of this anxiety. The British authorities, therefore, decided not to establish a system of decoy lighting in the North shortly after the Dockside raid; it was feared by Air Commodore Carr that details of the scheme would be 'conveyed elsewhere by subversive elements in Northern Ireland'.

Inevitably local ministers were especially anxious about the activities of the Irish Republican Army. Comparing Belfast with cities in Britain, informed observers considered that the security forces were extremely vigilant, 'due to factors not connected with the war but traditional alertness against IRA sabotage'. In early September 1939, unlike any other part of the United Kingdom, regular troops in Northern Ireland had been 'located with a view to the maintenance of internal security'. The cabinet immediately urged the British government to open an internment camp at Ballykinler, 'not only for the acceptance of enemy aliens but also those who may be required to be interned in the interests of the defence of the realm'. Next day, on 3 September, the B Specials were placed on patrol category and, later that evening, forty-five IRA suspects, 'the king's enemies', were interned for the duration of hostilities. By July 1940 the number of internees had risen to 155. They were eventually held on board a prison ship, anchored in Strangford Lough. However, Home Affairs officials regarded the extreme republican activists as anti-British rather than pro-German and did not believe that they were either armed or subsidised by Germany.

By late 1940 the IRA had become quiescent, due mainly to the security measures taken by both the Northern and Southern Irish governments. However, its activities revived early in 1942, and were directed as much towards sabotaging war industry as attacking specifically military objectives. The most serious incident to occur was the murder of Police Constable Patrick Murphy, on 5 April 1942, during a gun battle in Cawnpore Street, off the Lower Falls Road. Six men were subsequently convicted and sentenced to death. In contrast to Éire, no republican had previously been executed in Northern Ireland and an effective protest campaign against these sentences was organised, involving the Northern Ireland Labour Party, the Communist Party of Northern Ireland and some trade unions. Appeals for clemency also came from Eamon de Valera and the United States. Eventually, all but one of the prisoners was reprieved. Tom Williams, however, was hung at Crumlin Road jail on 2 September. As a token of sympathy, black flags were flown in parts of west Belfast and women knelt outside the prison at the time of his execution. Across the street, Protestant women and girls sang the British national anthem and 'There'll always be an England'.

The incident highlighted contrasting sectional opinions and responses. This contrast was observable in other ways. John Oliver noted that the civil defence services had a greater appeal to Protestants 'for they are by nature and tradition, organizers and devotees of order and efficiency'. Anything in the nature of an appeal for national service evoked a readier response from them as they 'identified themselves more fully with the British state'. According to Oliver, the Catholic contribution lay more in 'neighbourliness and spontaneous help'. Some Catholics were air raid precautions members but 'less prominently and with some inhibitions'. Royal visits were an 'embarrassment' for them; they 'kept their heads down'. The obligatory oath of allegiance uncovered 'a divided loyalty in the hearts of many Catholics' and was a potent factor in deterring nationalist recruitment. (At least partly for this reason, the Belfast Fire Service was by tradition an almost exclusively Protestant force.) There was clearly considerable

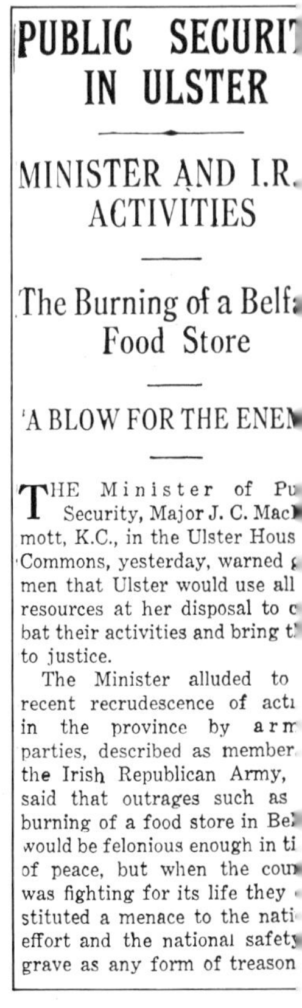
PUBLIC SECURIT
IN ULSTER

MINISTER AND I.R.
ACTIVITIES

The Burning of a Belf
Food Store

'A BLOW FOR THE ENE

THE Minister of Pu
Security, Major J. C. Mac
mott, K.C., in the Ulster Hous
Commons, yesterday, warned
men that Ulster would use all
resources at her disposal to c
bat their activities and bring t
to justice.

The Minister alluded to
recent recrudescence of acti
in the province by arm
parties, described as member
the Irish Republican Army,
said that outrages such as
burning of a food store in Be
would be felonious enough in ti
of peace, but when the cou
was fighting for its life they
stituted a menace to the nati
effort and the national safety
grave as any form of treason

Belfast News-Letter, 25 July 1940

A republican reminder of a longer conflict: 'Honour Ireland's dead, attend Milltown' (Belfast's Catholic cemetery) is the slogan on this wall in Corporation Street, June 1941. (Ulster Museum)

hostility felt towards air raid precautions in west Belfast, even though as a general rule Catholic personnel served in Catholic areas. Joseph Goss, a World War I veteran, was the chief district officer in B District. In organising civil defence there he faced a greater level of active antagonism and passive resistance than found elsewhere. This included, according to government reports, the burning of gas masks by the IRA, the receipt of threatening anonymous letters, physical attacks on Goss's friends and 'armed hold-ups'. In addition, there was a notable shortage of volunteers from the Falls Road, which was partially compensated for by a larger proportion joining from the Glen Road. Mr Davies, inspector general of the Royal Ulster Constabulary, even suspected that some air raid precautions men of 'not particularly proven loyalty' were involved in burning an inadequately guarded butter store close by their post. Even in Londonderry, Charlie Gallagher also commented on the tendency among extreme republicans there to 'see the Union Jack in everything'.

In July 1940 William McCready attempted to analyse the perceptions of the young Catholic employees with whom he worked at the central post office in Belfast:

> Generally speaking, [they] appear to take a very light-hearted view of the war. Physically they were here in Ulster but mentally they are members of the Eire community. In other words they are united Ireland men. I believe that they have such a strong dislike or at least distrust of Britain that they would as

Belfast Telegraph,
27 January 1942

ENEMY PLANES OVER ULSTER FIRED ON AS AMERICAN ARMY VANGUARD ARRIVES

SPLENDIDLY EQUIPPED DIVISION

Led by Youngest Officer of His Rank

WHEN AMERICAN TROOPS WERE DISEMBARKING AT A NORTHERN IRELAND PORT ON MONDAY THEY HAD NOT LONG TO WAIT FOR CONFIRMATION OF SIR ARCHIBALD SINCLAIR'S WARNING—GIVEN JUST BEFORE THEY STEPPED ASHORE—THAT THEY WERE NOW IN THE COMBAT ZONE.

Over the Province prowling enemy planes received a hot reception from ground defences, and for a time the thudding of distant heavy gunfire synchronised with the tramp of marching Yanks as they clattered down the gangways and on to the square-setts of the landing stage.

The American troops—part of a United States Army Division—were under the command of one of America's "live-wire" commanders, Major-General Hartle, reputed the youngest officer of that rank in the Army.

The contingent was fully equipped with all the latest infantry weapons and included engineers, artillery, signals and even their own nursing sisters.

The steel-helmeted troops were all fighting fit. They included many Irish - Americans, men of Scandinavian descent, one full-blooded Sioux Indian and one smiling Chinese.

The contingent received a hearty Ulster welcome at the various camps to which they were assigned. They submitted freely to be interviewed by the hundreds of newspapermen present at the disembarkation.

PLEASANTLY SURPRISED.

Many of the Americans had thought that at the beginning in camp they would have to live "rough," and they were pleasantly surprised when they found not only a better camp than they had expected, but also that the British Army staff had prepared their beds, cooked a special dinner and made all arrangements for their comfort.

The inevitable dog mascot has made its appearance, an American soldier somehow managing to bring along a mongrel known as "Jitterbug."

U.S. TROOPS CATCHING THEIR FIRST GLIMPSE OF NORTHERN IRELAND

"The Star-Spangled Banner"

By FRANCIS SCOTT KEY.

Oh, say, can you see by the dawn's early light
What so proudly we hailed at the twilight's last gleaming
Whose broad stripes and bright

Oh, thus be it ever, when freemen shall stand
Between their loved homes and the war's desolation!
Blest with victory and peace.

NORTHERN HOUSE AND U.S. TROOPS.

HISTORIC OCCASION.

GOD SPEED VICTORY.

Prior to the prorogation of the Northern Ireland Parliament to-day the Prime Minister told the House of Commons:

"Twenty-four years ago the Union Jack and the Stars and Stripes flew side by side at a Northern Ireland port when a military contingent from the United States landed on our shores.

"An event so historic and so significant is worthy of a permanent record in the annals of this House.

"Those who witnessed as I did the arrival of the troops felt a thrill of emotion when the Governor representing his Majesty the King greeted the officer in command and the Secretary of State for Air spoke eloquent and stirring words of welcome it was my pleasure to join in the greeting in the name of the Government and people of Northern Ireland.

"I deemed it fitting to express through the Press the satisfaction we all feel at the presence of the American troops in our midst and I take the earliest opportunity in this House of assuring the General Officer Commanding the American Troops in the United Kingdom and all the officers and men serving under him that Northern Ireland bids them a heartfelt welcome.

"SPLENDID BODY."

"President Roosevelt, whose statesmanship, vision, and courage have won the admiration of us all told the world a few months ago that American forces would be sent across the ocean to take their place in the fighting line. He has kept that promise.

"The troops now in Northern Ireland are a splendid body of men, young, alert, well disciplined and equipped.

"Between the United States and Ulster there are many bonds that can never be broken, bonds created by kinship and language, identity of outlook and a common faith in democracy.

"Many men and women of Ulster birth have gone to the United States and are playing their part in the life of that great Republic. I am confident that the officers and men of the American Army now in

soon trust the Germans and that means Nazi Germany. . . They look upon the war as being none of their business. . . they have such a strong dislike of England and have such a strong desire to have a united Ireland that it blinds them to the possibility of German invasion.

He recorded an impression that the Falls Road was 'delighted by every success on the part of Hitler'. Others living there then recall little anti-German feeling. Hugh Crossan remembers Celtic supporters taunting their Linfield rivals by giving them a Nazi-style salute.

There is some evidence that local attitudes towards the stationing of American troops in Northern Ireland also diverged on religious lines. From as early as January 1941, highly confidential discussions began, relating to the establishment of the V (US) Army Corps bases in Northern Ireland and Scotland. Twelve months later, on 26 January 1942, the first divisions disembarked at Dufferin Quay in Belfast. It was a milestone in the course of World War II and in the history of Anglo-American relations. They were welcomed as they strode ashore by the strains of the 'Star-Spangled Banner',

Late January 1942: the first units of American troops arrive in Belfast. (Public Record Office of Northern Ireland)

played by the band of the Royal Ulster Rifles. Despite attempts at secrecy, their imminent arrival had for some time been a common topic of conversation both in Northern Ireland and Éire. By May 1942 their total number had built up to a peak of over thirty-seven thousand. Four months later, the first arrivals were dispatched to North Africa. More arrived during the autumn of 1943, so that immediately before the Normandy landings, United States Army strength in the North had reached one hundred and twenty thousand.

Numerous airfields, military camps and barracks were constructed to accommodate them. Among the most impressive was a virtual new town, erected by August 1942, at Langford Lodge, on the shores of Lough Neagh. It served as a depot for the Lockheed Overseas Corporation (the American firm nominated by the United States government to operate the base), and was used for the repair and maintenance of aircraft. In Londonderry, 75 million dollars was spent on facilities mainly in the vicinity of the port. This base was used by United States forces until August 1944 and massive facilities for the repair, maintenance and fuelling of escort vessels were established there. At peak 149 ships were based there to help protect the Western Approaches, along with the 20,000 sailors to crew them. Most were British, American and Canadian, but other nationalities, including Free French, Dutch, Polish and Russian, were represented. The American forces' area headquarters was at Talbot House, near Magee College, which contained a heavily fortified, underground bunker. This would have be-

Canadian seamen rent ro
skates at a rink in
Londonderry, January
1945. (Charlie
Gallagher/National
Archives of Canada)

'You could not help but like them.' Jokes involving them abounded. In Ballymena, Co. Antrim, so the story ran, the first exchange between an American soldier and an attractive passer-by foundered on a misunderstanding. 'Say honey, what do you do about sex over here?' he asked hopefully. 'Oh,' she replied, 'we be havin' our tea about that time.' A woman living in a Co. Down seaside village, which was quiet even by local standards and a favourite spot for retirement, remembers a typical GI wisecrack: 'Gee, Rostrevor's a swell little place but why the hell don't they bury their dead?' Among the troops there was a surprising lack of knowledge of recent wartime events. When the 'walls of Belfast were plastered with the slogan "Remember Dunkirk"', one man, then working as a tea-boy at an American camp, was amazed to hear a United States sergeant remark 'that [Dunkirk] must have been one hell of a guy'; though this may be a better example of GI leg-pulling than of genuine ignorance.

Star-Spangled Manner

Friction could and did of course arise. In his 'History of American Forces in Northern Ireland', Lieutenant-Colonel Leonard Webster comments that in mid-August 1942, the soldiers were instructed 'not to go out alone after dark, not to carry weapons and to be discreet'. They were better educated and more sophisticated than the native population and on occasion gave the impression of 'knowing it all', which could infuriate local people. They were also well paid and generous – so much so that they were ordered to 'refrain from encouraging begging'. Inevitably, much of their high income was spent on alcoholic drink. Alternative forms of entertainment were frequently lacking – hotels overcrowded, newspapers and radio programmes incomprehensible, films dated, and sports facilities unsuitable or nonexistent. Their drinking could leave local supplies short or lead to aggressive or insensitive behaviour. The Mass Observation reporter described their off-duty life style as essentially one of 'pubs and pickups'. Arguments might well develop over local girls, most of whom liked the American troops with their easy manner and their affluence. Train loads of prostitutes from Belfast descended on American bases in rural towns, and imitating American fashion, large numbers of peroxide blondes appeared at local dance halls, such as the Plaza in Belfast. An additional and related cause of tension was the fact that a number of the US soldiers were black. Graham Smith, in *When Jim Crow met John Bull*, even suggests that for a time 'racial violence temporarily replaced sectarian violence' in Northern Ireland. As a result of a street brawl in Antrim, involving local men and American soldiers, during October 1942, one black GI died. Weeks earlier, a white American quartermaster, based locally, had commented: 'The girls really go for them in preference to white boys, a fact that irks the [white] boys no end.' He predicted 'No doubt there will be some bloodshed in the near future.' Local reaction, from both Protestant and Catholic communities, to women fraternising with American troops was largely the same. On the Protestant Shankill, Rita McKittrick recalls that such women were regarded as 'brash and had a fast reputation. You were sort of blacklisted if you went out with them.' Her mother warned her to have 'nothing to do with them' or she would 'get killed'. In dance halls, the management was always eager for their custom and 'required you to dance with them. You couldn't refuse.' But, overall, most of those living in the district were 'friendly to them'. In another Protestant area, Jimmy Penton claims that they were 'warned off' Dee Street and 'never came near it'. On the Catholic Falls, in Joseph McCann's view, the general reaction to them was one of 'hostility and suspicion. Girls who had gone out with them were likely to get their hair cut off. It was a common occurrence. Fights were sometimes sparked off by troops asking for girls.'

'I wanna get me a street car.'

However, in other ways, the religious identity of local people does seem to have influenced their perception of the American troops. A Mass Observation reporter, who studied public attitudes in Northern Ireland towards the American soldiers during June 1942, concluded that they were generally well liked, but that this generalisation had to be 'qualified' on a 'religious basis'. The Protestant population was genuinely 'favourable often enthusiastic' about them, and 'biased towards approval'. It welcomed them for themselves, as well as for their contribution to the war effort and 'almost sub-consciously, as a strengthening of the forces of order against the constant fear of Catholic [nationalist] trouble'. In contrast, the Catholic com-

conscription should be extended to Northern Ireland. Ernest Bevin, the Minister of Labour and National Service, anticipated that, given the danger of Éire being invaded, most Irishmen would welcome the opportunity of coming together to 'defend their soil'. At the same time compulsory recruitment would 'help resolve unemployment in Northern Ireland' and raise, it was hoped, forty thousand additional men, then sorely needed by the British Army. When asked for an 'expression of views' on the matter, the Stormont cabinet replied that it was 'emphatically of the opinion that conscription should be applied' to Northern Ireland. In late May 1941, however, the British government decided against its introduction. In the background, opposition to the proposal had steadily mounted. Strongly worded protests were received from the United States and Canada, and most especially from Southern Ireland. As the British representative in Dublin warned: 'Even if the case for [conscription in Northern Ireland was] unanswerable', its effect would be to 'strengthen de Valera and weaken the Opposition'. He added: 'We shall not get any move forward here until we have a clash with de Valera; when that comes we shall need the Opposition. . . Facilities on the west coast are vastly more important than Ulster's present needs.' In other words, it was his opinion that the acquisition of naval bases in the South was more vital than the raising of additional troops in the North.

However, crucial in determining the negative decision taken at Westminster was the accumulating evidence that there would be powerful opposition from within Northern Ireland itself. The Inspector General of the Royal Ulster Constabulary Lieutenant-Colonel Sir Charles Wickham, warned that there would be massive resistance from the local nationalist minority, encouraged by the Catholic hierarchy. As evidence he cited the statement, issued by Cardinal MacRory from the archbishop's palace in Armagh on 22 May, which declared:

> The people of all creeds and classes in Belfast recently suffered at the hands of the Germans. However regrettable that may be, it does not touch the essence of the question which is that an ancient land, made one by God, has been partitioned by a foreign power, against the vehement protests of its people. Conscription would now seek to compel those who writhe under this grievous wrong to fight on the side of its perpetrators.

In Wickham's opinion, it could be 'safely assumed' that the whole Catholic community would 'follow the cardinal's lead'. He therefore anticipated that there would be a wholesale refusal to register for military service in nationalist areas, with many of its opponents escaping across the border. He feared that this resistance would lead to arrests by the police, which would provoke hunger strikes and the probable use of firearms in street violence. Such incidents, he suggested, would provide 'the press gang up the Falls Road' with its 'full share of publicity', giving 'new life to the IRA', a force then estimated by the Home Office to have two thousand members, and that its 'new strength and prestige [might last] for a long while after the war is over'. He and others expressed concern that a significant proportion of those called up would be from the Catholic community and fervently anti-British, as so many Protestants were working in reserved occupations, such as the police or the special constabulary.

From his enquiries, Herbert Morrison, the Home Secretary, became convinced that compulsory military service would lead to a 'renewal of the strife between Protestant and Roman Catholic workmen, with disorder at the shipyards and other places'. If the policy was proceeded with, he advised that 'the Government must be prepared to deal with large scale resistance', even to the extent of setting up 'concentration camps for thousands of resistors'. He pointed out that 'Prison accommodation in Northern Ireland is nearly full.' Meanwhile, the scale of nationalist opposition had also impressed Andrews. Their protest activity culminated in a rally held in Belfast on Sunday, 25 May, and attended by up to ten thousand people. Next morning Andrews telephoned Morrison to say that the level of local resistance was greater than he had anticipated and that though his government still favoured conscription, 'the real test' must be 'whether it would be for the good of the empire'. This is likely to have influenced the attitude of the British cabinet, when on Tuesday, 27 May, it agreed a statement, later cheered at Westminster, indicating that it would be 'more trouble than it was worth'. In Belfast Moya Woodside had watched with deepening disapproval the changing mood of public opinion in Northern Ireland. She noted:

> Anti-conscription feeling seems to be growing. Nationalists and Catholic clergy condemn it absolutely, using arguments based on Irish history and not on present-day facts. What a pity these people must always live in the past and at the same time be deliberately kept in ignorance of what Nazi rule means. The fate of Catholics in Poland and in the Reich means nothing to these revenge-on-England-at-all-cost fanatics.

However, she acknowledged: 'It is a pity that the Stormont government by their handling made a party issue out of this and other matters such as the Ulster Home Guard and its control by the police, etc.' Later, she observed that the 'feeling seems to be that Stormont is clutching at this as a way out of the unemployment problem, to be solved at England's expense'.

Overall, the whole episode would suggest that many Northern Catholics felt, at best, indifference towards the war effort. Certainly, few if any felt enthusiastic about fighting to defend a government whose existence they had consistently opposed and which they considered had brought them nothing but discrimination and humiliation over the previous twenty years. Even those who supported the war would have opposed conscription on the grounds that Westminster did not have the moral right to demand military service from a people who clearly had never wished to live under its rule. They would have agreed with Cardinal MacRory that this was 'the essence

Some answered the call t
fight for king and countr
The Central Recruiting
Office, Belfast 1941.
(Imperial War Museum)

of the question'. Anti-British feeling also remained a potent and deep-rooted emotion and was to some extent reinforced by the policy of neutrality adopted by de Valera's government in Éire.

The war undoubtedly exposed profound and far-reaching differences in perception between the nationalist and unionist populations in Northern Ireland. Yet the contrast could be overstated. For example, it is far from clear that the Protestant community would have genuinely welcomed the introduction of conscription either. Growing uncertainty that unionists would respond favourably, may help account for Andrews's increasing uneasiness and hesitancy on the issue; in the course of the negotiations he had consulted both the party and his cabinet colleagues. Jack Beattie, Independent Labour MP, taunted ministers by stating that 'if they want to go ahead with this, [they] should test the feeling of the electorate. Everyone knows here what the outcome would be.' Similarly, Wickham, in his confidential assessment, stated: 'It is extremely doubtful if conscription has the whole-hearted support of either section of the population.' Moya Woodside also noted at the time that the 'no-conscription decision is welcomed by most, except ardent Unionists'.

Doubts as to the extent of Protestant backing for its imposition are reinforced by the consistently poor level of voluntary enlistment from the Northern Ireland area by the local population. After an initial surge during the early months of the conflict, nothing seemed to revive it. The War Office regarded the money spent on a special recruiting campaign in the summer of 1940 as having been largely wasted. The volume of recruits remained small during and after the blitz, despite the undoubted stimulus it gave to anti-German feeling. The numbers coming forward for each of the four months, April–July 1941 inclusive, were among the lowest from the outbreak of war; only February and December 1940 produced fewer. It was precisely because the voluntary system was regarded as a failure that Ernest Bevin had urged the application of conscription to Northern Ireland. This and the inadequate flow of volunteers to the civil defence services had also prompted John MacDermott to favour strongly its introduction.

The final decision not to introduce compulsory military service can readily be justified. It was estimated during the autumn of 1941 that forty thousand men from Northern Ireland would have been raised had it been enforced then. Of these (according to Northern Ireland government statistics), only 11,500 actually came forward voluntarily between September 1941 and August 1945. However, in this same period the number of recruits from Éire formally approved in the Northern Ireland recruiting area was 18,600. Clearly few, if any, of these would have offered themselves had conscription been introduced north of the border. Thus little, if any, advantage would have accrued from its imposition and the conclusion that it would have been 'more trouble than it was worth' appears to be totally vindicated. (Over the whole course of the war the total number of volunteers recruited in Northern Ireland was 30,664 from the six counties and 28,774 from Éire.) None the less, the decision irritated some British ministers, notably Ernest Bevin, who complained that Northern Ireland was 'asking for a privileged position, because we had not had conscription'. He suggested that this was the 'fault' of the Stormont government, as it had 'got cold feet'; and in Andrews's phrase, Bevin 'used this argument to prevent work coming' to the North.

No doubt partly because of the lack of conscription, visitors from Britain continued to find that the mood and the attitudes of Northern Irish people contrasted starkly with those across the water. This impression was based on detailed studies of both the Protestant and Catholic communities. In 1944 Tom Harrisson, from Mass Observation, noted how local people, presumably unionist, 'shock our soldiers by saying of the war: "I hope England will win."' Two years earlier, another Mass Observation reporter concluded that: 'Even the blitz in Belfast has not really awakened the people. It is regarded in some ways as almost an insult and a grievance that Ulster should have been attacked in this way. There are of course many enthusiastic and patriotic citizens, especially among the middle- and upper-class Protestants. None the less, the slackness in the atmosphere is unmistakeable to any experienced student.' In 1943, even Churchill commented critically on the 'young fellows of the locality [who] loaf about with their hands in their pockets'. Indeed there is much evidence of a lack of real commitment to the war effort within Northern Ireland. There was, for instance, according to Sir Basil Brooke, a 'body of opinion at Stormont' which was 'outraged' at the idea that the North, a food-exporting region, should be obliged to introduce rationing. This response prompted Brooke, then Minister of Agriculture, to protest that the North's 'loyalty is only skin deep'. But nowhere was the laxity of local attitudes more explicit than in the persistently poor performance of Belfast's strategic industries. Throughout these years, Westminster ministries were acutely concerned at the inadequate output, poor record of contract completion, lack of dilution, and strained labour relations both in the aircraft factory and at the shipyard.

At Short and Harland the strike record was by far the worst of any major military services' supplier in Northern Ireland. Representatives of the work force reported structural defects in aircraft parts, including claims that wings and fuselages were dangerously out of line. Low worker morale was reflected in poor discipline, the misuse of tools, destruction of materials and extremely high absenteeism levels. In *In Time of War* Robert Fisk quotes an American employee of the Lockheed Overseas Corporation, on loan to Short and Harland, who wrote home to his parents after the Easter Tuesday raid: 'You have heard about how tough the Irish are – well, all I can say is that the tough Irish must come from Southern Ireland because the boys up in Northern Ireland are a bunch of chicken-shit yellow bastards. Ninety per cent of them left everything and ran like hell.' In 1943, Mr Smiles of the Ministry of Aircraft Production estimated that the firm was not working at more than 65 per cent efficiency and that 'any amount of people are drawing pay for loafing about'. Other contemporary reports estimated that production at Short and Harland was three times slower than at comparable British firms.

Similarly, according to G.H. Hall, financial secretary to the Admiralty, absenteeism at Harland and Wolff shipyard remained at a level two times higher than at the worst yards in Great Britain; Churchill himself noted that it was 'less active' than those on the mainland. Bevin claimed that if the firm 'were properly organized, production. . . could be raised to an extent equivalent to the additional production which would result from adding 7–8,000 men to the labour force employed in Admiralty shipyards in England'. There was much criticism of Sir Frederick Rebbeck, the firm's manager, who, it was alleged, concentrated too much on reconstruction after the blitz at the expense of war production and consideration was even given to reopening Workman Clark's old yard. In exasperation, Bevin declared, during the spring of 1943, that 'due to small production per worker, orders cannot be placed in Ulster. In my opinion, [it] will become a derelict province after the war. . . due as much to bad management as workmen slacking.' At Westminster he stated bluntly that the firm's output had been 'nothing like' the level he had hoped for.

Lower Ann Street: workers homeward bound from the shipyard, still busy in 1946. (Ulster Folk and Transport Museum)

Some British journalists, reporting on Northern Ireland, used more unrestrained and emotive language to describe how life there differed from Britain. One such criticism appeared in the *Sunday Pictorial* on 4 April 1943, under the headline 'Look at this, Mr Bevin': '"What is this all about?" you say to yourself surveying this wondrous scene of inactivity and petty squabbling. "Is ours a private war or can't Northern Ireland join in?" Because (believe it or not) there are 25,000 men and women loitering on Ulster's street corners, 25,000 who haven't a thing to do other than line up for the dole.' The report ridiculed local carters and dockers who had recently gone on strike and had felt 'justified in letting the ships look after themselves and letting the war go to hell'. It claimed that over the previous nine months, three million working days had been lost in Northern Ireland owing to strike action. Its conclusion was that the 'young, fit men and women twiddling their thumbs or playing pitch-and-toss on the pavement are obviously a disgrace to Britain and the Empire'. As a possible solution, it suggested that they should 'go to England'. In fact the flow of surplus labour crossing from Northern Ireland to take up employment in Britain had shown a marked and permanent decline after the first fifteen months of war.

Overall, there was much for the British government to criticise in Northern Ireland's wartime performance. The evidence would suggest that there was, in John MacDermott's phrase, a lack of 'equality of sacrifice', not only within Northern Ireland but within the United Kingdom as a whole. Conscription was not applied to the North and voluntary enlistment there persisted at a low level. Its industrial production record was unimpressive, even unsatisfactory. Its government and many of its people displayed a unique absence of commitment to the war effort. In addition, when in mid-1940 the nation faced military defeat – Churchill's 'abyss of a new dark age' – Craigavon's greatest priority remained the preservation of the Union, rather than the survival of Britain and of the empire. He refused to make any concessions regarding Irish unity at a time when Westminster ministers were hoping to lure Eamon de Valera away from neutrality through an offer of constitutional change.

Yet the relationship between Great Britain and Northern Ireland undoubtedly became closer during the course of the conflict. This was due to their shared experience of war and of Luftwaffe attack. Their closer friendship was not, however, primarily related to any outstanding commitment shown or sacrifices made by the Northern Ireland people, though its generals did serve the British Army well. Rather, it was due to external, even accidental, factors. German control of much of western Europe, combined with Éire's neutrality, dramatically enhanced the significance of the North's geographical position. As a direct consequence, its role in Allied victory became a vital one. Northern Ireland had greatness thrust upon it: it became a base for convoys, escorts, maritime reconnaissance, coastal command, and anti-submarine aircraft, as well as a launching pad for American forces prior to their landing in North Africa and on the beaches of Normandy. As Prime Minister, Sir Basil Brooke came close to understanding the true nature of the association between Northern Ireland and Great Britain in the course of a speech given to an audience in London. He stated that while the North had never doubted that Britain was necessary for its survival, 'we hope that you now realize that we are necessary to you'. His 'hope' would appear to have been fully vindicated. In July 1943, Home Secretary Herbert Morrison said of Northern Ireland: 'Her strategic position alone ensures that her contribution is a crucial one. The unprotected gap in mid-Atlantic, the stretch of ocean that could not be covered by shore-based aircraft from either side, would have been far wider if it had not been for the coastal command bases in Northern Ireland.'

Two months earlier, Churchill also stressed primarily Northern Ireland's strategic role in a letter of appreciation to John Andrews, who had just resigned as Prime Minister:

> That was a dark and dangerous hour. We were alone and had to face

'Mae West' life jacket
oduction at Ewart's mill –
ı example of the Northern
Ireland war effort, 1941.
Ulster Folk and Transport
Museum)

> single-handed the full fury of the German attacks raining down death and destruction on our cities and, still more deadly, seeking to strangle our life by cutting off the entry to our ports of the ships which brought us our food and the weapons we sorely needed. Only one great channel of entry remained open. That channel remained open because loyal Ulster gave us the full use of the North Irish ports and waters and thus ensured the free working of the Clyde and the Mersey. But for the loyalty of Northern Ireland and its devotion to what has now become the cause of thirty governments or nations we should have been confronted with slavery and death and the light which now shines so brightly throughout the world would have been quenched.

In conclusion, he declared emphatically: 'During your premiership the bonds of affection between Great Britain and the people of Northern Ireland have been tempered by fire and are now, I believe, unbreakable.'

Meanwhile one might reasonably have expected that the war, and especially the blitz, would also have led to an improvement in the relationship between Northern Ireland and Éire. Without doubt, the readiness of the Southern government to dispatch its fire brigades to the devastated areas of Belfast and to provide support for its panic-stricken refugees made a profoundly favourable impression on Northern Irish people at the time. One of John MacDermott's leading officials, Eric W. Scales, observed appreciatively:

> Perhaps the most spectacular feature of each of the raids was the immediate dispatch on each occasion of these voluntary firemen from a neutral state, racing through the night, with their peacetime headlamps blazing, to fires that none of them could ever previously have imagined. Such transcends the ordinary business of regional reinforcement.

After the Easter Tuesday raid, Moya Woodside considered that the arrival of crews from across the border was the 'one encouraging piece of news'; they had come 'in spite of animosity between North and South and the almost total lack of petrol in Eire'. She suggested that 'an action like this does more for Irish unity than the words of politicians'. (However, she also commented that 'the arrival of a large detachment of AFS from Glasgow, complete with equipment, make us conscious of a comforting solidarity with Britain'.) Likewise, Emma Duffin mused when she heard of the spontaneous and generous response from Dublin: 'Perhaps, this will draw North and South closer together. I wonder.'

Hope of reconciliation must have been reinforced by the sincere expressions of support made by Southern political leaders. Eamon de Valera stated publicly that 'their sorrows in the present instance are also our sorrows; and I want to say that any help we can give them in the present time we will give to them wholeheartedly'. The Fine Gael leader, William T. Cosgrave, wrote to Andrews: 'Our hearts go out in respectful, sorrowful sympathy with the Government and people of Northern Ireland. We pray God to comfort and console them and ward off any further destruction and damage.' Both politicians and newspapers in the South certainly hoped that their 'act of friendship' would lead to a 'new understanding' between the people of Ireland. On 17 April 1941 an *Irish Times* editorial, under the headline 'A Terrible Beauty', stated:

> Humanity knows no borders, no politics, no difference of religious belief. Yesterday for once the people of Ireland were united under the shadow of a national blow. The constitution of Eire claims all Ireland's thirty-two counties as the national territory and yesterday's events proved the basic justice of that claim. . . The bombs that were hurled on Belfast made no question of political or religious difference. Orangemen and 'Fenians' alike fell victims to the destruction that was rained on Northern Ireland. . . The men, women and children of Belfast whether they live in the Falls or the Shankill are as Irish as those of Dublin. . . When all is said and done the people of the six counties are our own folk and blood is stronger than the highest explosive.

Two days later, de Valera spoke in similar vein: 'In the past, and probably in the present too, a number of them did not see eye to eye with us politically, but they are all our people – we are one and the same people.'

Occasionally in the midst of the carnage and chaos caused by the blitz, increased understanding could and did occur, however briefly. Edward Lennon, the crew member up with the Dun Laoghaire fire brigade, recalls a break during the fire-fighting near the ropeworks after the Easter Tuesday raid. He was sitting on a low wall next to a Belfast fireman, an 'Orangeman'. As they surveyed the devastation the Northerner commented, in a quiet voice, 'We should be all one.' Lennon considered that 'he was very fair in what he said'. Not all were embued with the ecumenical spirit, however; some of the Southern firemen were asked on their return why they had risked their lives for Northern Ireland citizens. In the council chamber in Dundalk one member, a Mr Brannigan, stated that he 'would like to know where the orders came from that the brigades should go outside Eire'. One month earlier, James Larkin, a councillor, had raised this and other related issues during a meeting of the Dublin Corporation. At the same time strong allegations were made that the Stormont government had failed to acknowledge sufficiently the help which the North had received from the South. Jack Beattie, Independent Labour MP, claimed that 'the Prime Minister had not the decency to thank the bogeyman for what he had done'. Earlier, the Nationalist Party leader, Thomas J. Campbell, had given notice of a private member's question in the Commons. He intended 'to ask the Prime Minister to express his gratitude' to Dublin, Dundalk, Dun Laoghaire and Drogheda for dispatching their brigades and for the 'generous hospitality' shown by Éire towards the 'destitute refugees'.

If Northern ministers were reticent about openly declaring their feelings of indebtedness, there may be an honourable explanation for it. After private discussions, Andrews succeeded in persuading Campbell to withdraw his question by arguing that too public or formal a statement might embarrass Éire by raising the 'neutrality issue' and sensitive 'questions of international relations'. On 17 April, MacDermott wrote personally to the Southern Minister of Local Government and Public Health, expressing his deep appreciation for the assistance received. In parliament five days later, he stated: 'The help offered by our neighbour Eire was not related to any bond of war or any political consideration and was above and beyond politics. It was based on a common humanity; we gratefully accept and acknowledge it as such.' Subsequently, Andrews offered to pay for the cost of the aid provided but this was declined by the Irish Minister of Finance in March 1942. The only 'payment' made by the Stormont government was in the form of tea and cocoa which it supplied to the Irish Red Cross – the organisation which had accommodated more than one thousand of the Northern refugees who had fled to Dublin. In late May 1941, when the Southern capital was itself bombed, the Belfast Fire Service indicated its willingness to assist; in the event, its services were not required.

The response of the Stormont government to Southern aid was more complex than their restrained statements of gratitude and counter-offers of help and payment might suggest. By no means everyone in the North would have agreed with MacDermott's comment that the 'help offered by our neighbour Eire' had been 'above and beyond' politics. On the contrary, some would have shared Sir Wilfrid Spender's opinion that the Éire government was 'utilizing the occasion to indulge in further propaganda for a united Ireland. In my view this entirely discounts the value of its not very heavy expenditure on charitable lines.' There had always been discreet and informal collaboration between the two governments over a wide range of practical issues. However, close and open association with the South during the blitz was a policy which was forced by tragic circumstances upon hesitant Northern ministers. When, in the early hours of 16 April 1941, Sir Basil Brooke sanctioned MacDermott's proposal that fire engines should be requested from Dublin, he described it as a 'matter of expediency'. Later, when the cabinet was discussing the refugee problem in mid-May, it concluded with obvious reluctance that 'co-operation' with Éire was the 'only course available'. After all, the surge of evacuees into the South could not be stopped and it was helping to ease the problem of overcrowded reception areas in the North. Also, it was obvious that if further raids occurred, as was anticipated, many more would flood across the border and not just from Belfast. Officials estimated that as many as fifteen thousand might evacuate from Londonderry city into Co. Donegal.

Although their expressions of gratitude were no doubt sincere, there was, none the less, a strong feeling among Northern ministers that Éire, in a number of ways, positively contributed to their security difficulties. Dublin was still 'ablaze with lights' and it was widely assumed that these were being used as a navigational guide by the Luftwaffe. Moreover, Andrews considered that Northern Ireland was not being 'sufficiently protected owing to [its] proximity to Eire'. He alleged that, at Westminster, 'the susceptibilities of Eire are being too much considered', and claimed that its leaders 'simply look upon this policy of appeasement as weakness'. At the same time Southern Ireland was regarded as a source of leaked information for the Axis powers. John Oliver writes: 'German envoys had free run of Dublin and their outrunners were doubtless taking the train from Amiens Street [in Dublin] to Great Victoria Street [in Belfast] any day they chose. This all contributed to make our job very hard indeed.' Consequently, the Stormont cabinet sought to monitor more closely the movement of people across the border through such measures as the introduction of travel permits and the operation of special constabulary patrols. By July 1941 the control of telephone calls was said to be 'pretty well complete'. As the popularity of the Andrews government declined, so it became more sensitive to criticisms of the 'infiltration' of workers from Éire into Northern Ireland. At the end of the war, however, Home Affairs officials did not believe that espionage in Northern Ireland had been either widespread or effective. Despite having an embassy in Dublin, Germany received no advance warning of either the North African expedition in 1942 or the Allied invasion of Europe two years later. In both instances many of the American troops involved were based in the North. A few days before the Normandy landings, a US battle fleet was moored off Bangor bay; local citizens were astonished at the speed and secrecy of the moves.

In addition, during the early stages of the war, the Northern government was concerned at the danger of a German invasion of the South. At the time the Prime Minister, John Andrews, described this in a letter to Churchill as the 'matter which gives me most anxiety', adding that he had 'no great faith in Eire's power or intention to defend herself'. As early as May 1940, Sir Basil Brooke had advised Craigavon that the Government should 'watch this possibility'. Such a step, he believed, would enable Hitler to 'threaten the Western Approaches to Britain' and he regarded Éire as 'the easiest place, in view of IRA activity' and because an invading force could take advantage of local 'hostility to England in the Eire population'. John Oliver also observed: 'where better than Donegal or Sligo' for German troops to land? 'What handier fifth column inside the United Kingdom than the IRA in Derry or Fermanagh?'

In the view of Stormont ministers, Éire not only compromised Northern Ireland's security but also constantly meddled in its internal affairs. For example, it had encouraged resistance to conscription and, it was alleged, discouraged the North's unemployed from crossing over to Britain to find work. Even the custody of IRA internees in the North was complicated by the border: a local military leader, Major-General Sir James Cooke-Collis, opposed holding them in Londonderry, owing to the danger that an attempt might be made to free them, and suggested instead that they be transferred to the Isle of Man. The Northern Ireland government, however, rejected this proposal as it feared that if they were handed over to the Home Office, Éire might succeed in negotiating their release.

However, by far the greatest cause of anxiety for the Stormont cabinet during the early stages of the war was the prospect of Eamon de Valera reaching an agreement with the British government whereby he traded his neutrality for the ending of partition. Lord Londonderry, whose perspective was regarded as 'somewhat broader than his colleagues', wrote to Churchill when this danger was at its height in June 1940:

> I have heard of proposals that Craig should make a gesture but I am quite convinced that there is no gesture that he can make which would have any effect on Southern Ireland, and moreover that that gesture, if he made it, would lose the support he can count on in the North of Ireland, because the people up there are under no illusions as to the attitude of the south.

Such mutual suspicion and primal hatreds, both within Northern Ireland and throughout the island as a whole, ran too deep to be obliterated by the trauma of the blitz. They survived the war undiminished; there was in Yeats's phrase, 'More substance in our enmities than in our love.'

The external danger, which had imposed co-operation between North and South and, however incompletely, fused the North's sectarian factions together in fear, soon passed. In the end Belfast sustained just two major attacks by the Luftwaffe, despite widespread expectations at the time that the force would return in strength. John Oliver recalls that the period which followed, from early May 1941, was one of 'starting all over again' for the Ministry of Public Security, and of 'making much more far-reaching civil defence preparations for further air raids that never came'. Most of this effort was of course entirely wasted; none the less, some of the measures taken were of permanent value. Officials at the Ministry of Public Security regarded the formation of a National Fire Service in 1942 as 'one of the most significant things' which they ever achieved. Professor T.T. Flynn claimed that as a result of the reforms which they introduced then, Belfast had the 'best and cheapest ambulance service in Great Britain outside the city of Westminster. It takes a war to awaken people to the need.'

Progressively the fear of further attacks receded, though there were occasional alerts until the final months of the conflict and as a result, the problems and pressures faced by William Grant, who had succeeded John MacDermott as Minister of Public Security on 11 November 1941, steadily eased. (On leaving the ministry, MacDermott became Attorney General.) In late 1942 United States troops landed in North Africa, British forces won their first victory over the German army at El Alamein, and at Stalingrad the German divisions were facing surrender. Earlier that year, Bomber Command launched its first thousand-bomber raid on the German city of Lubeck, a campaign which culminated in attacks on Berlin, and finally, three assaults on Dresden, lasting 70 minutes in total and causing fatalities estimated at between 27,000 and 135,000. The outcome of the war would soon be inevitable; as a consequence, from late spring 1943, Belfast's defensive screen began to be dismantled. By September of that year it was common knowledge that both the city's anti-aircraft guns and its balloon barrage had been withdrawn. Simultaneously, the British Air Ministry removed Northern Ireland's allocation of night-fighters. It seemed somehow predictable that it should have done so without bothering to consult or forewarn the Northern Ireland cabinet; to the end, the level of the North's active defences was a source of friction between the regional and Westminster governments. At the same time, as if to reassure the public, the protective brickwork around parliament buildings at Stormont was removed, and paintings that had been put into storage at the beginning of the war were returned to the city hall. By then, on 21 June 1943, the *Belfast News-Letter* was complaining that the static water tanks in the city centre had become 'almost useless', owing to the accumulation of litter casually dropped in them by passers-by.

(J. Mercer)

Indications that normality was returning came thick and fast. During the spring of 1945, construction work began on houses that had been devastated at Greencastle in north Belfast during the blitz. They had been among the first to suffer damage in both major raids on the city, now locals proudly boasted that they were the first to be rebuilt. On the night of 16 February 1945 the gaslights in neighbouring streets had been turned on for the first

Opposite
The Albert Memorial Clc casts a reflection on the static water tank at the bottom of High Street, March 1944. There was some concern that the stagnant water in these tanks was a public health risk. (Ulster Folk and Transport Museum)

time since being blacked-out at the beginning of the war. Ten weeks later, on 5 May, air raid precautions members in Belfast received a brief impersonal note from Civil Defence Authority headquarters on the Lisburn Road, stating that they were being stood down forthwith. For several years their posts had served as little more than social centres. None the less, such cursory treatment caused deep resentment among personnel. Finally, on VE Day, Tuesday, 8 May 1945, fire-watching regulations were revoked by order in council.

Preparations to celebrate the Allies' long-anticipated victory in Europe had been gathering pace in Belfast over the previous week; a government announcement, specifying which day had been chosen for the festivities, was eagerly awaited. Steadily, expectations rose, finally erupting in spontaneous expressions of relief and jubilation during the evening of Monday, 7 May. Belfast became, in the words of one newspaper reporter, 'a city without strangers'. On 8 May the *Belfast News-Letter* stated that:

> People from all parts gathered in festive mood. Along Donegall Place and Royal Avenue, long lines of revellers joined in snake-like formation, dancing in and out among rows of tramcars immobilized by the crowds. Songs were in

An unexpected but welc visitor to the static water tank in front of Michael Reynold's public house, North Queen Street. (Artillery Unemploymen Group)

Black-out Ends September 17

Curtains and Blinds Sufficient

RELIEF FOR FIRE WATCHERS

THE complete black-out, perhaps the most depressing of all wartime restrictions, will end with Double Summer Time on September 17.

Belfast News-Letter, 7 September 1944

> the air everywhere. They ranged from 'Tipperary' and the favourites of 1918 to a completely new 'number' composed for the occasion which began: 'Hitler thought he had us with a Ya, Ya, Ya.'

For the first time in six years the sky above the crowded streets glowed with the light from bonfires. Bunting festooned thoroughfares, shelters were painted in party colours, drums were beaten and bin lids clattered. In fact, the report claimed, 'all the spirit of the twelfth was there doubled and redoubled', adding that it was an opportunity not only for 'rejoicing but to stage demonstrations of loyalty to crown and constitution'. Mary Wallace, who lived off Bloomfield Avenue, was among those who converged on the city centre. She had gone to bed and was asleep when she and her sisters were wakened by their mother. Outside, 'everyone was on the street', shouting and yelling, many of them still in their pyjamas. She pulled a coat over her night clothes, put on her shoes and joined them, following the delirious human tide along the Newtownards Road and over the Albert Bridge. It was 'as bright as day' by the time she returned home, 'freezing but so happy'. Momentously, at one minute after midnight, hostilities in Europe had officially ended.

The carnival atmosphere of VE Day itself has left a vivid and lasting impression on the minds of many people then living in the city. At 3 p.m. Winston Churchill announced the absorbing details of German capitulation. His statement was greeted by the ringing of church bells, and the celebratory wail of ships' sirens and factory hooters. Workers were given two days' paid holiday. At Stormont, the House was adjourned without transacting any business and the Prime Minister, Sir Basil Brooke, made the decision to hold an immediate general election. At the city hall the biggest crowd seen there since Covenant Day in 1912 had gathered to hear Churchill's speech broadcast live. At 10.40 that evening the building was bathed in floodlight for the first time since the conflict began. It was, by then, engulfed by thousands of dancing, drinking, cheering citizens, total strangers kissed each other and soldiers were embraced by all and sundry. Bands were improvised, using a motley collection of instruments – bugles, accordions, drums and once again bin lids. Bryce Millar made his way there after returning home to Michael Street from his work at the shipyard. He recalls:

> Outside everyone was going in the same direction. You wanted to be part of the atmosphere. It was as though you had been carrying a huge burden that had been suddenly taken off. You felt as light as a feather. The relief that it was over. War had seemed endless, dreary, with its rationing and restrictions; now it was back to normal.

Meanwhile Joseph McCann had ended up at a house on the Shankill Road, where he was invited to sing republican songs. Despite the general euphoria, he thought it wiser to decline. Rita McKittrick had walked down to the Albert Memorial Clock, also floodlit, where the large and excited crowd was exuberantly re-enacting a traditional old-year's-night ritual in Belfast, smashing empty bottles against its cut-stone base and iron railings. She 'didn't get home until after one in the morning, but nothing was said'. At a public house in Callender Street, the owner had procured an Ulster flag; it was flown as a symbol of celebration and of unity.

Elsewhere, away from the centre of the town, street parties were held. Effigies of Hitler were burned from lamp standards. On 9 May the *Belfast News-Letter* described, on the Shore Road, a 'bugle band leading a procession of youngsters in the midst of whom was carried the figure of Hitler wearing his swastika but hanging from gallows'. Thanksgiving services were organised in churches throughout the city. The congregation at St Ninian's was addressed that evening by the Reverend Finlay Maguire. William Ward, the caretaker, recorded that 'the pews filled with people, many of whom used the boiler house as a place of refuge. The King's speech [at 9 p.m.] was heard on the wireless at the close.' On a smaller scale, similar scenes of celebration and worship were reported in other parts of Northern Ireland. In Bangor David Davidson remembers an 'explosion of joy', free beer in the public houses, and large numbers gathering joyfully around the McKee Clock at the seafront.

In Londonderry, as well, there were popular expressions of delight but Charlie Gallagher recalls that the celebrations there were somewhat muted. There was a mood of apprehension, concern that the end of the war might also bring an abrupt end to the city's unfamiliar affluence. Many people throughout Northern Ireland must also have been haunted by the spectre of economic recession returning, and with it, unemployment and poverty. Moya Woodside recorded the comments of her maid, whose father was working at Harland and Wolff: 'She said, "Father is earning good money now. But he's saving like mad to have something left when the war is over and he'll be out of work again."' For all the suffering that had occurred, the conflict had also brought a level of prosperity not known since World War I. The declaration of peace on 8 May 1945 should have brought an uncomplicated sense of relief; instead it revived for many in Northern Ireland disturbing memories of the Depression.

Opposite
Donegall Place, 8 May 1945: the people of Belfa jubilantly gather for the V Day celebrations. (*Belfas Telegraph*)

APPENDIX I

CASUALTY LISTS OF THE 15–16 APRIL 1941 AIR RAIDS

There appears to be no complete list of the casualties of the blitz. No list, in any case, could be fully comprehensive given the considerable number of bodies that were never identified. Included are facsimiles of the lists of the killed and injured drawn up by Belfast's Civil Defence Authority between 7 p.m. on Thursday, 17 April, and 1 p.m. on Monday, 21 April 1941. This is followed by the names of all the dead who were identified at St George's Market, Belfast, between Friday, 18 April, and Sunday, 20 April 1941. The names of those who died during the 15–16 April 1941 attacks on Londonderry and Bangor are also included. The Londonderry list is incomplete as two further bodies were recovered after it had been drawn up. There is no casualty list available for the 15–16 April attack on the aerodrome at Newtownards.

(These lists appear by permission of the Public Record Office of Northern Ireland.)

The gravestone erected at Milltown cemetery, Belfa in memory of the unidentified victims of th 15–16 April raid in 1941 (Ulster Museum)

BELFAST CIVIL DEFENCE AUTHORITY

CENTRAL ENQUIRY OFFICE

CITY HALL BELFAST

Fourth List (19.00 hrs.) 17th April, 1941

List of killed and injured

DEAD

Name	Address	Mortuary
Anderson, ? Elizabeth	26 Sylvan Street	Mater
Barr, Mrs.	74 York Road	Mater
Bell, Rev. Thos., B.A.	138 Antrim Road	Mater
Bennet, R.	21 Serpentine Road	Falls Baths
Benton, Wm.	224 Upper Meadow St.	Falls Baths
Briggs, Jack (Body No.35)	47 Veryan Gardens	Falls Baths
Castle, H.	80 Malone Ave.	Falls Baths
Clarke, James Finlay	Glenrosa House, Glenrosa Street	Melville & Co.
Clarke, Mabel Alexandra	Glenrosa House, Glenrosa Street.	Melville & Co.
Denby, Dorothy	20 Evelyn Gardens	Mater
Duff, John M., (Identity Card No. UABL/299/4)		Mater
Duffy, John	-	Falls Baths
Ferguson, Charles	18 Ohio Street	Union
Flood, Thomas	45 Pilot Street	Mater
Fullerton, C. (Male)	77 Sussex St.	Falls Baths
Gardner, Amelia	18 Ohio Street	Union
Gilmore, Daniel, (Identity Card No. UADF/201/6)		Mater
Graham or Grahm Francis	25 Sheridan Street	Mater
Greer, June	57 Estoril Park	Falls Baths
Long, Norman	175 Cliftonpark Ave.	Union
Long, Ralph A.	175 Cliftonpark Ave.	Union
Long, Ivers	175 Cliftonpark Ave.	Union
McCaffery, Catherine	85 Gracehill Street	Mater
McCarey, Josias, Junr.	17 Kilronan Street	Melville & Co.
McCullough, Eileen Lousine	19 Hogarth Street	Melville & Co.
McCullough, Brian	19 Hogarth Street	Melville & Co.
McCullough, Eileen	19 Hogarth Street	Melville & Co.
McGradden or McGladden John	59 Summers Street	Falls Baths
McKenna, ?, (Male) age 18)	66 Ferris Street	Falls Baths
McKenna, Francis	66 Vere Street	Mater
McKenna, John	64 Regent Street	Melville & Co.
McWhinney, James	24 Unity Street	Melville & Co.
McWhinney, Eileen	24 Unity Street	Melville & Co.
McWhinney, Mary	24 Unity Street	Melville & Co.
Meeklen, Constable James	York Rd.R.U.C. Barracks	Mater
Millar, John Forsythe	69 Lockesley Park	Melville & Co.
Moore, William,	185 Duncairn Gardens	Melville & Co.
Moore, Hugh Hanna,	Glenrosa Ho. Glenrosa St.	Melville & Co.
Mulholland, Sarah Freeburn	95 Lilliput Street	Melville & Co.
Power, Patrick	20 Veryan Gardens	Falls Baths
Renton, William,	140 Duncairn Gardens	Melville & Co.
Scott, Albert	202 Cliftonville Road	Falls Baths
Stevenson, James	26 Ohio Street	Melville & Co.
Valence, Agnes (Body No133)	-	Falls Baths
Weldon, S. (Male)	71 Ballycorry Street	Falls Baths

DEAD

Unidentified

	Mortuary
Female child	Falls Baths
Female	Falls Baths
Female	Falls Baths
Female	Falls Baths
Male	Falls Baths
Male	Falls Baths
Male	Falls Baths
Male, 20, Evelyn Gardens, Body No.36. Mrs Harriett Denby	Falls Baths
Male, 20, Evelyn Gardens, Body No.37. Isable Denby	Falls Baths
Male, age about 45 years, 33 Avoca Street.	Falls Baths
Female age about 45 years, found 33 Avoca Street. Alice or Ellen Nesbitt	Falls Baths
Male, age about 6 years, 140 Manor Street.	Falls Baths
Female, age about 45 years, 140 Manor Street	Falls Baths

INJURED

Name	Address	Injury	Hospital
Anderson, William	29, Westbourne St.	Light	Royal Vict.
Bell, Mary	19, Thomas Street.	Light	Union
Boyle, Rose	25, Southport Street	Serious	Mater
Brett, Maria	142, Argyle Street	Light	Union
Brown, Peter	3, Etna Drive.	Light	Belfast Hosp. for Sick Children
Charley, Maud	14, Nth. Thomas St.	Serious	Mater
Cravaghan, Henry	63, Gracehill St.	Serious	Union
Doherty, Agnes	47, Walton Street.	Light	Union
Doherty, James	60 Stanhope Street	Serious	Mater
Finlay, Jane	6, Sultan Street	Light	Royal Vict. sent home
Gates, Margaret.	11 or 19 Ballyclare St.	Serious	Mater
Hairwood, Sarah	12 Michon Street	Light	Royal Vict.
Heenan, Elizabeth	6 Nth. Thomas Street	Serious	Union
Heanney, Susan	14 Percy Street	Serious	Belfast Hosp. for Sick Children
Holland, Rachel	18 Heathfield Parade	Serious	Mater
Housten, Vera	10 Chichester Park	Serious	Mater
Howe, Stanley	9 Indiana Ave.	Serious	Mater
Johnstone, Robert	15 Ballynure Street	Serious	Mater
Liddy, Thomas	60, Wall Street or 29 Carlisle Street	Serious	Mater
Lowens, Thomas	9 Ballynure Street	Serious	Mater
McAdams, E.	15 Fairview Street	Serious	Mater
McCann, Irene	21 Glasgow Street	Light	Royal Vict.
McCatney, Joseph	87, Chatham Street	Light	Royal Vict.
McIlvenny, John	3, Jackson Street	Serious	Mater
Maguire, Patrick	28 Alexandra St. West	Light	Royal Vict. sent home
Mason Thomas	103 Dawson Street	Serious	Mater
Millar, David	Dock Lane	Serious	Mater
Muckian, Brigid	58, Unity Street	Serious	Mater
Murray Ernest	5 Percy Street	Light	Belfast Hosp. for sick Children
Murray Violet	41, Lepper Street	Serious	Union
Park, James	62, Vere Street	Serious	Mater
Pritchard, Catherine	164, Blythe Street	Light	Royal Vict. sent home
Ray, Ernest	No particulars	Serious	Mater

List of killed and injured contd.

INJURED

Name	Address	Injury	Hospital
Reilly, Patrick	69, Holmdene Gardens	Serious	Mater
Rodgers, Fred	57 Harcourt Drive	Serious	Mater
Scott, Albert	202 Cliftonville Road	Serious	Mater
Skelton, Samuel	69 Ballycarry Street	Serious	Mater
Spence, Catherine	30 Brookfield Street	Light	Royal V.
Taylor, Sarah	156 Sylvia Street	Light	Royal V.
Thompson, Jeannie	9 Warwoxthy Street	Light	sent home Royal V.
Tumelty, John	26 Regent Street	Light sent home	Belfast Hosp. for Sick Children
Turbin, James	251 Antrim Road	Serious	Mater
Vallance, Agnes	24 Mt. Collyer Road	Serious	Mater
Walsh, Emily	20 Walton Street	Serious	Mater

FURTHER LIST WILL BE ISSUED

TO-MORROW, 18th April, 1941.

Sheets 125/155

~~5th List (15,00 hours)~~

18th April, 1941.

List of Killed [redacted]

DEAD

Name	Address
Black, ?	Southport St.
Black, Mary	1, Southport St.
Boyd, Hugh	8, Percy St.
Boyd, Elias J.	do.
Brady, Mary	24, Unity St.
Campbell, Arthur	89, Lilliput St.
do Margaret	do
do Roberta	do
do Lillian	do
Cinnamond Art. M.	11, Madigan Park.
Cooke, Ernest V. (Jnr.)	184, Blythe St.
Crothers, Alexr. (Jnr.)	23, Louisa St.
Convery, Jane	24, Unity St.
Campbell, Robt.	89, Lilliput St.
Fletcher, Martha	62, Heather St.
Harbinson, Robt. J.	31, Heather St.
Harper, Ann Jane	12, Ebor Pde.
Hillis, David	55, Hallidays Road.
Irvine, Hamilton	14, Thorndyke St.
Kingham, George Stuart	144, Duncairn Gdns.
Millar, Henry	91, Blythe St.
Millar, Rebecca	91, Blythe St.
Morton, Thomas	174, Manor St.
McAuley, Joseph	27, Unity St.
McCann,	Glasgow St.
McCann, Anna	do.
McClements, Hamilton (Jnr.)	13, Thorndyke St.
McCormick, Sarah	31, Heather St.
McGrodey, John	59, Summer St.

McKinty, John 52, Duncairn Gdns.
Nesbitt, Jean 33, Avoca St.
Nesbitt, Saml. do.
O'Boyle, James 74, Artillery St.
O'Hare, Josephine 29, Unity St.
Quinn, John R. 46, California St.
Quinn, Roderick 46, California St.
Roberts, Mrs. 140, Manor St.
Roberts, Thos. do.
Skelton, Samuel 69, Ballycarry St.
Skelton, Audrey do.
Slavin, Henry 50, Joseph St.
Smith, W. J. 63, Malvern St.
Stevenson, Ellen 26, Ohio St.
Stevenson, Richard do.
Stevenson, Samuel do.
Swan, John 61, Brussels St.
Swan, Margt. 32, Westmoreland St.
Swan, William do.
Totten, Jeffrey 53, Eastland St.
Tate, Bessie Jeffrey 174, Manor St.
Tate Evelyn do.
Welsh, Phores Hill 28, Paxton St.

LIST OF DEAD

Name	Address	Hospital or Mortuary
1st list		
McClements, Hamilton	13 Thorndyke Street	Templemore Ave.
Baird, Murdock	26 Eastland Street	R.V.H.
Barr, James Alec.	74 York Road	Belfast Union
Boyd, Mrs.	Bromley Street	R.V.H.
Gardner, Amelia	18 Ohio Street	Belfast Union
McAuley, Mrs.	Bromley Street	R.V.H.
McDonald, Neta	26 Enfield Street	R.V.H.
McDonald, Meta	26 Enfield Street	R.V.H.
McGarvey or McGlady, Samuel		R.V.H.
O'Neill, Hugh	26 Marcus Street	R.V.H.
Swann, Martha	32 Westmoreland Street	R.V.H.
Totton, Mrs.	53 Eastland Street	R.V.H.
Totton, Thos.	53 Eastland Street	R.V.H.
Wallace, James	89 Heather Street	Belfast Union
Wilson, Alexander	55 Eastland Street	R.V.H.
Bothwell - (Female Child)	(?) 13 Rock Street	R.V.H.

McCann, Mrs.	Found back of L.M.S.	R.V.H.
McCann, Anna	do.	R.V.H.
McCann - (Female)	Found Glasgow Street	R.V.H.
McCann, Sarah	Glasgow Street	R.V.H.

Sixth List
(20.00 hours)

18th April, 1941.

List of Killed and Injured

DEAD

Name		Address
Bradshaw,	David	57, Eastland Street
Briggs	John - see list 2	47, Veryan Gardens
Burton	Sarah	45, Columbia Street
Cochrane	Gertrude	43, Columbia Street
Craig	Robert	93, Blythe Street
Douglas	Emily	8, Ballynure Street
Douglas	Margaret	do
Douglas	Sarah	do
Harper	Ann J.	12, Ebor Parade
Higgiston	Mary M.	13, Main St. Greencastle
McCartney	Matthew	23, Whitewell Crescent
McDermott	Kathleen	45, Veryan Gardens, G/Castle
McDermott	Maureen	do do
McDermott	Patrick	do do
McPolin	Norah	12, McDowell's Rows G/Castle
Spence	George	65, Tates Avenue
Wallace	John	57, Eastland Street

UNIDENTIFIED

Female Age 65
Pale complexion. Bad congenital deformity
(Belfast Union)

INJURIED

Name	Address	Injury	Hospital
Abbott Eileen	195 Clifton Pk.Ave	Light	Royal Victoria
Aiken Alexander	107, Mervue St.	Serious	Belfast Infirmary
Bultitude Margt.	3, Hatrick's Court	Serious	dc Union
do Richard	do	Light	do
Bunting William	8 Lebanan Street	Serious	Royal Victoria
Carlisle, W.	80, Leopold St.	Light	do treated & sent home
Coard John	31, Ivan Street	Serious	B/fast Union Infrm.
Coulon ?	Hillview Street Greencastle	Critical	Belfast Hospital for Sick Children
Corr, Annie	155, Sydney St.W.	Serious	Belfast Infirmary
Craig, John	93, Blythe Street	Serious	Belfast Union
Curran Robt	?	Light	Royal Victoria treated & sent home
Donnelly, Mary	30, Vulcan Street	Serious	Royal Victoria Ward No. 7
Dougan, William	52, Enfield Street	Serious	Royal Victoria Ward No. 2
Fairfield Agnes	4, Ohic Street	Serious	Belfast Infirmary
Ferson William	90, Bellevue Street	Light	Royal Victoria treated & sent home

List of killed and Injured, Contd.

Name	Address	Injury	Hospital
Gardiner, Andrew	25 Paris Street	Serious	Royal Victoria
Gorman, Bridget	23 Garnoyle St.	Light	Royal Victoria
Henderson, Bridget	35 Holmdene Gdns.	Serious	Belfast Union
Houston, Jane	33 Greenmount St.	Serious	Belfast Union
Hughes, Sarah	12 Thorndyke St.	Serious	Royal Victoria
Ireland, John (?)	-----	Light	Royal Victoria treated and sent home
Kelly, Elizabeth	47 Eureka St.	Serious	Belfast Union
Kielty, John	46 Hopeton St.	Light	Royal Victoria treated and sent home
McKane, Mary	90 Havana St.	Serious	Belfast Union
McKeown, Agnes	227 Oldpark Rd.	Serious	Belfast Union
McMullan, Gertie	8 North Queen St.	Slight	Children's Hospital treated and sent home
McNeill, Catherine	3 Short Street	Serious	Belfast Union
Montgomery, (?)	8 Enniskillen St.	Serious	Belfast Union
Montgomery, William	109 Jamaica St.	Serious	Belfast Union
Mulholland, Patrick	7 Seaford St.	Serious	Royal Victoria
Mulholland, Susan	11 Ardilea St.	Serious	Belfast Union
O'Hare, Mary	82 Hanover St.	Serious	Belfast Union
Polley, James	33 Oberon St.	Serious	Royal Victoria
Rutledge, Margaret	15 Carl St.	Serious	Belfast Union
Thompson, John	7 Trinity St.	Serious	Royal Victoria
Topping, Allen	145 Mayo St.	Light	Royal Victoria treated and sent home
Tumilnson, Jane	9 Thorndyke St.	Serious	Royal Victoria
Tumilnson, Annie	39 Thorndyke St	Serious	Royal Victoria
Ward, Elizabeth	3 Ballynure St.	Serious	Belfast Union
Watson, Wm.	Cooldaragh Pk.	Light	Royal Victoria Trtd & senthome
Wilkinson, Margt.	2 Riersdal Cott. Andersonstown	Light	Royal Victoria trtd & sent home
Winterhalder, Ed.	99 Antrim Rd.	Light	Royal Victoria trtd & sent home

FURTHER LISTS WILL BE ISSUED TOMMORROW 19th APRIL.

Sheets 179/192

7th List (18.00 hours) 19th April, 1941.

List of Killed and Injured.

DEAD

Name	Body No.	Address	
Anderson, Elizabeth		26 Sylvan Street	Mater
Ball, Samuel		47 Harcourt Drive	Mater
Barr, Jennie		74 York Road	
Beggs, Phyllis Irene		45 Upr. Meadow Street	
Bell, John		21 Ballymena Street	
Belshaw, Robert		56 Shankill Road	
Bennett, Robert		21 Serpentine Road	Mater
Boyd, Edith		14 Bromley Street	
Boyd, Jessie		38 Upper Meadow Street	
Bradley, Miss		27 Glencoe Park	
Bradley, Mrs.		27 Glencoe Park	
Bradley, Sydney		27 Glencoe Park	
Brown, Annie English		22 Christopher Street	
Burdett, - Dorothy Kathleen	(63)	20 Evelyn Gardens	Mater
Conlon, James		68 Vere Street	
Convery Miss		26 Unity Street	
Cooke, Mary Ann		34 Unity Street	
Cooke, Thomas		34 Unity Street	
Corr, Frederick		76 Vere Street	
Corr, Mary Anne		76 Vere Street	
Corry, Elizabeth		53 Joseph Street	
Corry, Martha		53 Joseph Street	
Corry, Samuel		53 Joseph Street	
Crothers, Sandy		23 Louisa Street	
Denby, William		20 Evelyn Gardens	Mater
Duff, Kathleen		90 Hanover Street	
Duffy, James		11 Lincoln Avenue	
Duffy, Josephine		11 Lincoln Avenue	
Duffy, Kathleen		11 Lincoln Avenue	
Duffy, Seamus		11 Lincoln Avenue	
Farrelly, Maurice		3 Kinnaird Street	
Fullerton, -		Sussex Street	Mater
Fullerton, Denis		77 Sussex Street	
Fullerton, Elizth.		77 Sussex Street	
~~Gay~~, Henry William		22 Percy Street	
~~Gay~~, Doreen Mary		22 Percy Street	
~~Gay~~, Mary		22 Percy Street	
~~Gay~~, Reginald		22 Percy Street	
~~Gay~~, Sydney		22 Percy Street	
Gilmore, Daniel		42 Eskdale Street	Mater
Gribbin, Nancy S.		25 Percy Street	
Grimes, Christopher		70 Vere Street	
Hawthorne, David H.		3 Tyne Street	
Heaney, A.J.		14 Percy Street	
Heaney, Mrs. Edith		14 Percy Street	
Heaney, George		14 Percy Street	
Heaney, Vera		14 Percy Street	
Hendron, Thomas		Colin, Dunmurry	
Holmes, Mary Jane		177 Upper Meadow Street	
Howe, William Maurice		9 Indiana Avenue	
Hutchison, Lily		261 York Street	
Hutchison, Mary		261 York Street	

List of killed and injured (continued)

Hutchison, Martin,	261 York Street.	
Hutchison, Rita,	261 York Street.	
Hutchison, Sadie,	261 York Street.	
Hutchison, Sarah, White	261 York Street.	
Hutchison, William	261 York Street.	
Irvine, Agnes	16 Percy Street.	
Jackson, Georgina	11 Ballymena Street.	
Jackson, Thomas	11 Ballymena Street.	
Jackson, Thomas (Junior)	11 Ballymena Street.	
Kearney, Elizabeth	34 Unity Street.	
King, Joseph	7 Tyne Street.	Royal Victoria Hospl.
Magill, Margaret. (see 8th list)	23 Heather Street	Mater Hospital.
Mahaffey, William J., ~~99~~	99 Sussex Street.	
Mells, Jane Mary	68 Crosby Street.	
Millar, David,	4 Dock Lane.	Mater Hospital.
Montgomery, Andrew,	66 Heather Street.	Mater Hospital.
Morris, William T.A.	124 Disraeli Street.	
Murray, William	13 Cherryville Street.	
McAnally, Agnes,	93 Sussex Street.	
McAnally, Elizabeth	93 Sussex Street.	
McAnally, Hugh	93 Sussex Street.	
McAnally, Mary	93 Sussex Street.	
McAuley, George	12 Bromley Street.	
McAuley, Margaret	12 Bromley Street.	
McCartney, Ethel	???? Percy Street.	
McClements, Agnes	13 Thorndyke Street.	
McCluskey, Dr. Gerald.		Mater Hospital.
McDolphin, Vera or Nora	12 McDowell's Row, Greencastle.	
McDonald, Martha	70 Disraeli Street.	
McDowell, William	20 Ballyclare Street.	
McFall, Joseph (Senior)	33 Louisa Street.	
McFall, Joseph (Junior)	33 Louisa Street.	
McFall, Sarah	33 Louisa Street.	
McHugh, Margaret	57 Halliday's Road.	
McHugh, Mary	57 Halliday's Road.	
McIlhern, Catherine	93 Sussex Street.	
McIntyre, William	140 Duncairn Gardens.	
McKay, Marcus,	13 Louisa Street.	
McSorley, Sarah	74 Vere Street.	Mater Hospital.
McWhinney, Joseph (Senior)	22 Unity Street.	
McWhinney, Joseph (Junior)	22 Unity Street.	
Power, Bridget,	38 Veryan Gardens.	
Power, Gerald,	38 Veryan Gardens.	
Power, Patrick	38 Veryan Gardens.	Mater Hospital.
Robinson, James Henry	21 Donaldson Crescent.	
Russell, Sophia,	34 Unity Street.	
Scullion, Bridget	76 Harcourt Drive.	
Skelton, Audrey	20 Ballycarry Street.	Mater Hospital.
Skelton, Samuel	69 Ballycarry Street.	Mater Hospital.
Tate, Ellen O.	174 Manor Street.	
Totton, Agnes	53 Eastland Street.	
Unsworth, Thomas	20 Ohio Street.	
Venn, Mrs. Trethena A.	144 Duncairn Gardens.	
Vigors, Forbes	70 Disraeli Street.	
Walsh, Angela,	71 Stratheden Street.	Mater Hospital.
Walsh, Mrs. Annie	71 Stratheden Street.	Mater Hospital.
Wilson, Ellen	55 Eastland Street.	
Wilson, Euphimia	55 Eastland Street.	
Wilson, Mrs. Jane (Pension Book No.WA.3194)		Mater Hospital.
Wilson, Sarah,	55 Eastland Street.	
Wilson, William,	55 Eastland Street.	
Wylie, Annie,	24 Sylvan Street.	Mater Hospital

List of Dead - Unidentified

9 Bodies - Female:	Belfast Public Mortuary, Lagan Bank.
1 Body - Male:	Belfast Public Mortuary, Lagan Bank.-Removed from Greencastle.
1 Body - Female:	Belfast Public Mortuary, Lagan Bank. - Removed from Earl St.
1 Body - Male:	Belfast Public Mortuary, Lagan Bank. - Removed from Vere St.
17 Bodies - Male:	Belfast Public Mortuary, Lagan Bank. - Removed from Percy St.
1 Body - Female:	Johnson Mortuary - Found at Regent St., understood to have lived with Jane Brady, 24 Unity St.
1 Body - Female:	Johnson Mortuary - From Mountcollyer Rest Centre.
1 Body - Male:	Johnson Mortuary.
15 Bodies:	D. Ireland, Lisburn Road.
14 Bodies:	
23 Bodies:	Lagan Bank Mortuary.

List of Injured.

Name	Address	Injury	Hospital	Sent
Armstrong, Edward	Hunts Pk., Donaghadee.	Light.	Royal Vict.	Home.
Baker, John	13 Trillick St.	Light.	Royal Vict.	"
Barker, John	"	Light.	Ulster.	"
Barr, Andrew	53 Hatton Dr.	Light.	Ulster.	"
Blair, Joseph	111 Riga St.	Light.	Royal Vict.	"
Boal, James	24 Roxburgh St.	Light.	Ulster.	"
Bowen, Clara	5 Lowry St.	Light.	Ulster.	"
Browne, Edward	43 Etna St.	Light.	Ulster.	"
Burch, Joseph	86 Sydney St. West.	Light.	Royal Vict.	"
Burns, Jean	11 Thorndyke St.	Light.	Ulster.	"
Burns, Kathleen	11 Thorndyke St.	Light.	Ulster.	"
Campbell, Wm.	2 Galway St.	Light.	Royal Vict.	"
Curley, Jane	68 Stanhope St., now at Ravarra, Ballygowan.	Light.	Royal Vict.	"
Davison, Jeremiah	Glengormley R. U. C.	Light.	Royal Vict.	"
Doran, John	72 Clyde St.	Light.	Ulster.	"
Haywood, Sarah	12 Meekon St.	? Serious	Ulster.	"
Irvine, Robert	14 Thorndyke St.	Light.	Ulster.	"
Johnston, Mrs.	181 Madrid St.	Light.	Ulster.	"
Kelly, Bridget	18 Holmdene Gdns.	Light.	Ulster.	"
Kelly, James	78 Holmdene Gdns.	Light.	Ulster.	"
Lynch, Charles	45 Whiterock Dr.	Light.	Royal Vict.	"
Mercer, Elizabeth	60 Dunedin Pk., Ardoyne	Light.	Royal Vict.	"
Monaghan, Edward.	46 Hanover St.	Light.	Royal Vict.	"
Morrison, Robert	54 Strathedin St, now at 41 Dhu-Varren Pde.	Light.	Royal Vict.	"
Murray, Rose	65 Holmdene Gdns.	Light.	Ulster.	"
McClernon, Michael	2 Nanson St.	Light.	Royal Vict.	"
McCluskey, Mary	20 Mossvale St., now at The Mount, Carrickfergus	Light.	Royal Vict.	"
		Light.	Royal Vict.	"
McCullough, George	Central Fire Station.	Light.	Royal Vict.	"
McGeery, Margaret	65 Holmdene Gdns.	Light.	Ulster.	"
McGuinness, Allen	20 Crumlin St.		Belfast Hosp. for Sick Children.	
McGurk, James	82 Henry St.	Light.	Royal Vict.	"
Russel, Louisa	28 Ardilann St.	Light.	Ulster.	"

Previously returned as unidentified.

Stewart, Leonard — Belfast Hosp. for Sick Children.

Sheets 156/178.

FURTHER LIST WILL BE ISSUED LATER

8th List. (15.00 hours) 20th April, 1941

List of Killed and Injured

INJURED

Name	Address	Injury	Hospital
Dancell, Charles	50 Mervue Street	Serious	Mater
Darragh, Margt.	26 Sylvan Street	Serious	Mater
Fisher, John	128 Whitewell Road, Greencastle	Serious	Royal Victoria Hospital.
Johnstone, David	13 Taylor Street	Light	Royal Victoria
Kelly, Annie	97 Sussex Street	Light	Royal Victoria
McAlea, Annabella	25 Wall Street	Serious	Mater
McConville, James	19 Fleetwood St.	Serious	Mater
McPolin, Ellen	12 McDowell's Row	Serious	Mater
Marshall, Patrick	117 McTier Street	Serious	Mater
Mills, Joseph	Ballynure Street	Serious	Mater
Page, Jim	218 Matilda Street	Slight	Belfast Hospital for Sick Children
Swan, Mary	2a Aberdeen Street	Serious	Royal Victoria
McVicker, Ann	34 Annadale Street, Antrim Road	Slight	Belfast Hospital for Sick Children
Wylie, Hugh	37 Unity Street	Serious	Mater

Sheets 193 - 210

DEAD

Name	Address
Anderson, William John	3 Annadale Street
Balmer, James	172 Manor Street
Ballantine, Wm. Vincent	126 Whitewell Road
Bleakley, Thos. Wm.,	8 Thorndyke Street
Bothwell, Lily	13 Dock Street
Brothers, Margaret	6 Annadale Street
Brown, Annie English	22 Walton Street
Brown, Florence E.	28 Ohio Street
Brown, Henry	18 Burke Street
Brown, Mary Jane	18 Burke Street
Brown, William Thomas	22 Walton Street
Briggs, Rowland	47 Veryan Gardens
Carter, Joseph (Junr.)	13 Dock Street
Carter, Kathleen	13 Dock Street
Cash, Mary Ann	77 Sussex Street
Connelly, Annie	64 Heather Street
Connolly, Charlotte	64 Heather Street
Connelly, James	64 Heather Street
Connolly John	9 Annadale Street
Corr, Mary Ann	76 Vere Street
Crossen David	20 Ohio Street
Curran, Patrick	72 Vere Street
Curran, William	72 Vere Street
Deering, Martha	28 Ohio Street
Deering, Mary	28 Ohio Street
Denby, Isabel (or Isable)	20 Evelyn Gardens
Denby, Mrs. Harriett	20 Evelyn Gardens
Douglas, William	8 Ballynure Road

8th List (Contd.) (15.00 hours) 20th April, 1941.

DEAD

Name.	Address
Drummond, Martha	61 Disraeli Street
Duff, John	1 Thorndale Avenue
Dunwoody, Edith	13 Lincoln Avenue
Dunwoody, Henry	13 Lincoln Avenue
Dunwoody, Isabella	13 Lincoln Avenue
Dunwoody, William	13 Lincoln Avenue
Ferguson, Agnes	24 Ohio Street
Ferguson, Andrew	24 Ohio Street
Ferguson, Eliz. Shaw	24 Ohio Street
Ferguson, Richard	24 Ohio Street
Graham Francis	1st door (?25) Sheridan St.
Graham, Jane	1st door (?25) Sheridan St.
Gray, Sarah	18 Ballyclare St.
Guiness, William	3 Annadale Street
Halliday, Harold C.	27 Hogarth Street
Hamilton, Catherine	18 Walton Street
Hanna, Eliza	25 Heather Street
Hanna, Thomas	28 Ohio Street
Harron, May (Mrs.)	126 Whitewell Road
Harvey, William	56 Heather Street
Hawthorne, David	3 Tyne Street — See 9th list —
Hillock, Sarah Ann	24 Sylvan Street
Hood, Robert D.	15 Hartley Street
Hood, William	15 Hartley Street
Hunter, Joseph M.	1 Annadale Street
Jamison, Margaret	25 Heather Street
Kennedy, Benjamin	33 Earl Street
Lennon, John	32 Louisa Street
McAteer, Adam	14 Ballynure Street
McAteer, Martha	14 Ballynure Street
McDonald, Thomas	70 Disraeli Street
McDonald, Thomas M.	78 Harcourt Drive
McErlean, John J.	40 Glenview Street
NcFall, Meta	33 Louisa Street
McFall, Violet	33 Louisa Street
McGennity, Rita	74 or 75 Holmdene Gardens
McPolin, Bernadette	12 McDowell's Row, Greencastle
McPolin, Bridget	12 McDowell's Row, Greencastle
McSorley, Mary	74 Vere Street
McVeigh, Francis	2 Vere Street
Magill, Annie (Mrs)	23 Heather Street
Magill, Hugh	23 Heather Street
Magill, Margaret (See 9th list)	23 Heather Street
Mateer, D.	28 Sylvan Street
Mateer, F.	28 Sylvan Street
Millan, Daniel	4 Dock Lane
Moore, Mary R.	263 York Street
Morris, Wm.	124 Disraeli Street
Murry, Margaret	Gracehill Street, Oldpark
Murry, Miss R. E.	Gracehill Street, Oldpark

8th List (contd.) (15.00 hours) 20th April, 1941

DEAD

Name	Address
Nesbitt, Alice	33 Avoca Street
Nesbitt, Ellen	33 Avoca Street
O'Neill, Margaret Jane	85 Jamaica Street
Patterson, Emma	15 Ohio Street
Patterson, William	15 Ohio Street
Power, Thomas	38 Veryan Gardens
Reid, Martha	33 Louisa Street
? Reilly, Mary See [illegible] lists of 19th & 17th.	101 Sussex Street
Riecken, William	6 Annadale Street
Skelly, Samuel	71 Strathcden Street
Smiley, Thomas	59 Vere Street
Smyth, Elizabeth	24 Ohio Street
Smyth, Hugh	5 Cambridge Street.
Stewart, Alice	73 Holmdene Gardens
Stewart, Raymond,	73 Holmdene Gardens
Stewart, Stella	73 Holmdene Gardens
Torley, Frances	9 Annadale Street
Unsworth, Sarah	20 Ohio Street
Walsh, Catherine	20 Walton Street
Ward, Sarah	9 Annadale Street.

Sheets 211-216

A further list will be issued

9th List. (13.00 hours) 21st April, 1941.

LIST OF KILLED.

Name.	Address.
Andrews, David Harold	62, Whitewell Crescent.
Andrews, Mary	62, Whitewell Crescent
Bell, Hannah	61, Disraeli Street
Beech, Margaret Eileen W.	170 Manor Street
Beeth (or Beech) Margaret Slane Williamson	170 Manor Street
Brown, Mrs. Rachel	11, Hogarth Street
Caldwell, Francis E.	17, Glasgow Street.
Christie, James	17, Hogarth Street
Christie, Margaret Stewart	17, Hogarth Street
Christie, Sylvia	17, Hogarth Street.
Cook, Mrs. Mary	34, Unity Street.
Curry, Wm. John	57, Belgrave Street
Doherty, Mary	30, Veryan Gardens.
Donnelly, Annie	23, Hogarth Street
Donnelly, Arthur	2 3, Hogarth Street
Donnelly, Maggie	23, Hogarth Street

Donnelly, Robt. Moorehead	23, Hogarth Street
Donnelly, Susan	23, Hogarth Street
Donnelly, Susannah H.	23, Hogarth Street
Dornan, Cissy	70, Nickerfield St. Glasgow. (Place of death, Hogarth St.)
Duffy, Sarah Annie	59, Hogarth Street
Faux, C. Y.	213 Antrim Road.
Ferguson, Andrew (Jnr.)	24, Ohio Street
Ferris, Daniel	32 Carlow Street
Finlay, Robert	20, Rowan Street.
Fisher, Rose	128 Whitewell Road.
Forbes, James	255 York Street
Garrett, John	58 Heather Street
Geddis, Agnes	48 Heather Street
Geddis, James	48 Heather Street
Gilmore, John	43 Eskdale Gardens.
Gray, John	18 Ballyclare Street
Irwin, Albert J.	72 Hogarth Street
Irwin, James	72 Hogarth Street
Hillock, Sarah	24 Sylvan Street
Kenney, Sarah	Castle St, Antrim. (visiting 41 Ponsonby Avenue)
Larkin, William	Carrick House, Regent St.
Larkin, William	3 Abbey Gardens, Whiteabbey.
Lilley, Albert	72 Hogarth St.
Lilley, Frances E. T.	72 Hogarth St.
Lynas, Richard	35 Ruth Street
McCallum, Cecil	56 Hogarth Street
McDonald, Thomas	70 Disraeli Street
McGinty, William	75 Holmdene Gardens.
McKnight, Maggie	23 Hogarth Street
McLellan, James (Jnr.)	25 Hogarth Street
McLellan, James (Sr.)	25 Hogarth Street
McLellan, Sarah	25 Hogarth Street
McCartney, Ethel	49 Pernau Street
McErlean, John	40 Glenview Street.

9th List (continued) (13.00 hours) 21st April, 1941.

Name.	Address.
McNeill, Hugh	65 Hogarth Street
Magee, Jane	12 Percy Street
Magee, Thomas	12 Percy Street
Magee, Thomasina	12 Percy Street
Magee, Mary (Jnr.)	12 Percy Street
Magee, Mary	12 Percy Street
Malone, Kathleen	31 Sussex Street
Mason, Anthony	9 Burke Street
Mason, Mary	9 Burke Street
Mason, Richard	9 Burke Street
Mason, Rose	9 Burke Street
O'Hare, Mary	29 Unity Street
Orr, Raymond	213 Antrim Road.

Renton, Elizabeth	140 Duncairn Gardens.
Simon, Florence	7 Sunningdale Park.
Simon, Henry	7 Sunningdale Park.
Venton, Wm. Anson	140 Duncairn Gardens. (home address Killalshard, Newtownbutler)
Wallace, Wm. John	57 Eastland Street
Wherry, May	16 Thorndyke Street
Wherry, John	16 Thorndyke Street

Sheets 218 - 223.

BELFAST CIVIL DEFENCE AUTHORITY.

List of dead identified at St. George's Market.

18th April, 1941.

NAME	No. of body	ADDRESS
+Anderson, William John		3, Armadale Road.
+Brown, Henry		18, Burke Street.
+Brown, Mary Jane		18, Burke Street.
Briggs, Rowland	35	47, Veryan Gardens (see list 2)
Bothwell, David		13, Dock Street.
+Burdett, Dorothy Kathleen	63	20, Evelyn Gardens.
Carter, Joseph (Junr)		13, Dock Street.
Carter, Kathleen		13, Dock Street.
Castles, H.		80, Malone Avenue.
Connolly, John		9, Annadale Street.
Connolly, Charlotte		64, Heather Street.
Curran, William		72, Vere Street.
Curran, Patrick		72, Vere Street.
+Denby, Wm. Henry (Senr).	76	20, Evelyn Gardens.
+Denby, Isabel	37	20, Evelyn Gardens.
+Denby, Mrs. Harriett	36	20, Evelyn Gardens.
Douglas, William		8, Ballynure Road.
Fullerton, Elizabeth		77, Sussex Street.
Gray, Sarah		18, Ballyclare Street.
Grimes, Christopher		70, Vere Street.
Greer, June		57, Estoril Park
Guiness, William		3, Annadale Street.
+Hutchinson, William		261, York Street.
+Hutchinson, Sarah White		261, York Street.
+Hutchinson, Mary		261, York Street.
+Hutchinson, Lily		261, York Street.
+Hutchinson, Rita		261, York Street.
+Hutchinson, Sadie		261, York Street.
+Hutchinson, Martin		261, York Street.
Hood, William		15, Hartley Street.
+Hawthorne, David		3, Tyne Street.
+Meekin, Const. James	16	R.U.C. Barracks, York Road.
Magill, Margaret		23, Heather Street.
Moore, Mary R.		263, York Street.
Millan, Daniel		4, Dock Lane.
+Murry, Miss R.E.	54	Gracehill Street, Oldpark Rd.
+Murry, Margaret	42	Gracehill Street, Oldpark Rd.
Mateer, D.		28, Sylvan St. (off Manor St.)
Mateer, F.		do.
McGennity, Rita		74 or 75 Holmdene Gardens.
Morris, William		124, Disraeli Street.
+McSorley, Mary		74, Vere Street.
+O'Hare, Josephine		29, Unity Street.
+O'Neill, Margaret J.	72	85, Jamaica Street, Oldpark Rd.
+Philips, Sgt.-Major		Military funeral
Riley, Mary, (nee Burns)		Sussex Street.
Smyth, Hugh		5, Cambridge Street.
Smyth, Hugh		5, Cambridge Street.
+Stewart, Raymond		73, Holmdene Gardens.
+Smiley, Thomas		59, Vere Street.

Scott, Albert	202, Cliftonville Road.
Torley, Francis	9, Annadale Street.
+Totton, Geoffrey	53, Eastland Street.
Tate, Ellen Ogle	174, Manor Street.
Venn, Tryphene	144, Duncairn Gardens.
Vigors, Forbes	70, Disraeli Street.
+Walsh, Angela	71, Stratheden Street.
+Walsh, Annie (Mrs.)	71, Stratheden Street.
Ward, Sarah	9, Annadale Street.

+ Removed from St. George's Market for Private Burial.

2.

BELFAST CIVIL DEFENCE AUTHORITY

List of dead identified at St. George's Market.

19th April, 1941.

	Name.	No.	Address.
+	Anderson, Elizabeth		26, Sylvan Street.
+	Ballantine, Wm. Vincent		126, Whitewell Road.
+	Balmer, James		172, Manor Street.
	Bell, Hanna		61, Disraeli Street.
	Bothwell, Lily		13, Dock Street.
	Bradley, Mrs.		25, Glencoe Park.
	Bradley, Miss		25, Glencoe Park.
+	Brady, Mary	4	24, Unity Street.
+	Brown, Mrs. Rachel		11, Hogarth Street.
+	Cash, Mrs. Mary Ann	19	77, Sussex Street.
+	Connolly, Annie		64, Heather Street.
+	Connolly, James		64, Heather Street.
	Convery, Jane	11	24, Unity Street.
+	Cook, Mrs. Mary Ann		34, Unity Street.
+	Donnelly, Annie		23, Hogarth Street.
	Drummond, Martha		61, Disraeli Street.
+	Dunwoody, Edith		13, Lincoln Avenue.
+	Dunwoody, Henry		13, Lincoln Avenue.
+	Dunwoody, Isabella		13, Lincoln Avenue.
+	Dunwoody William		13, Lincoln Avenue.
+	Ferguson, Andrew		24, Ohio Street.
+	Ferguson, Agnes		24, Ohio Street.
+	Ferguson, Richard		24, Ohio Street.
+	Ferguson, Elizabeth Shaw		24, Ohio Street.
	Graham, Francis		Sheridan Street.
	Graham, Jane	15	Sheridan Street.
+	Gribben, Nancy Simms		25, Percy Street.

+ Hamilton, Catherine		18, Walton Street.
+ Hanna, Elizabeth	65	25, Heather Street.
+ Harron, Mrs. May		126, Whitewell Road.
+ Harvey, William		56, Heather Street.
+ Hillock, Sarah Ann		24, Sylvan Street.
+ Holmes, Mary Jane		177, Upper Meadow Street.
+ Jamison, Margaret	59	25, Heather Street.
+ Kearney, Elizabeth		34, Unity Street.
+ Kinghan, George Stewart		144, Duncairn Gardens.

NAME	No.	ADDRESS
+Larkin. William		3, Abbey Gardens. Whiteabbey.
+M'Ateer, Adam		14, Ballynure Street.
+M'Ateer, Martha		14, Ballynure Street.
+M'Cartney, Ethel	45	49, Pernau Street.
+M'Donald, Thomas		70, Disraeli Street.
+McErlean, John	38	40, Glenview Street.
+McGinty, William	19	75, Holmdene Gardens.
+McHugh, Margaret		57, Halliday's Road.
+McHugh, Mary		57, Halliday's Road.
+Magill, Mrs. Annie		23, Heather Street.
+Magill, Hugh		23, Heather Street.
+Mason, Richard		9, Burke Street.
+Mehaffy, William John		99, Sussex Street.
+Nesbitt, Alice		33, Avoca Street.
+Nesbitt, Ellen		33, Avoca Street.
+Orr, Raymond		213, Antrim Road.
+Patterson, William		15, Ohio Street.
+Patterson, Emma		15, Ohio Street.
+Power, Bridgett		38, Veryan Gardens.
+Power, Gerald		38, Veryan Gardens.
+Power, Patrick	32	38, Veryan Gardens.
Pinning, Alfred J. No. 40. L.C. 1879347 R.E –		
+Reilly, Mrs. Mary		101, Sussex Street.
+Renton, Elizabeth		140, Duncairn Gardens.
+Robinson, James Henry	69	21, Donaldson Crescent.
+Russell, Sophia		34, Unity Street.
+Simon, Henry		7, Sunningdale Park.
+Simon, Florence (Mrs.		7, Sunningdale Park.
+Smyth, Elizabeth		24, Ohio Street.
+Stewart, Alice		73, Holmdene Gardens.
+Stewart, Stella		73, Holmdene Gardens.
+Venton, William Anson		140, Duncairn Gardens (lodgings) Home address: Killalahard,
+Wallace, James	38	29, Heather Street.
+Walsh, Mrs. Catherine		20, Walton Street.

+ Being removed for private burial.

BELFAST CIVIL DEFENCE AUTHORITY.

List of Dead Identified at St. George's Market on 20th April, 1941.

No. on Coffin	Name	Address
501	Bradley (Man)	25 Glencoe Park
505	Bradley (Female)	" " "
	~~Cume~~ Currie, William J.	57 Belgrave Street
503	Clarke (Boy)	Found 4 Ballynure Street
489	Conroy (Mrs.)	
	Doherty, Mary	30 Veryan Gardens
	+ Donnelly, Maggie	23 Hogarth Street
504	Elliott	31 Percy Street
	Ferguson, Andrew (Junr.)	20 Ohio Street
491	Forbes, James	255 York Street
	Gilmore, John	43 Eskdale Street
	Gilmore, Daniel	43 Eskdale Street
488	Gordon, Wm.	29 Hogarth Street
496	? Graham	Sheridan Street
507	Greer, Jane (1 yr + 10 months)	57 Estoril Park (Protestant)
490	Hamilton, Kathleen	10 Springmount Street
512	Hunter, Joseph	1 Annadale Street
494	Lemon, John	32 Louisa Street
	Lynas, Richard	23 Ruth Street
	Lynas, Richard	35 Ruth Street
	O'Hare, Mary	29 Unity Street
514	Taylor, Jack	87 Sussex Street

NORTHERN IRELAND

COUNTY LONDONDERRY

RURAL DISTRICT OF LONDONDERRY

COLLINS, Ellen, age 21. Daughter of James and Elizabeth Collins, of 55 Messines Park. 16th April 1941, at 55 Messines Park. Glendermott New Cemetery.

COLLINS, James, age 60. Husband of Elizabeth Collins, of 55 Messines Park. 16th April 1941, at 55 Messines Park. Glendermott New Cemetery.

McFARLAND, William Alexander, age 44; Home Guard, of 57 Messines Park. Son of Alexander and Annie McFarland, of 16 Hawkin Street; husband of Elizabeth McFarland, removed to 16 Hawkin Street. 16th April 1941, at 57 Messines Park, Londonderry City Cemetery.

MURRAY, Ita, age 13. Daughter of William S. and Mollie Murray, of 59 Messines Park. 16th April, 1941, at Messines Park.

MURRAY, Kathleen, (see County Borough of Londonderry List).

MURRAY, Mollie, age 39. Wife of William S. Murray of 59 Messines Park. 16th April 1941, at Messines Park.

MURRAY, Philomena, age 10. Daughter of William S. and Mollie Murray, of 59 Messines Park. 16th April, 1941, at Messines Park.

MURRAY, Sheila, age 10 months. Daughter of William S. and Mollie Murray of 59 Messines Park. 16th April 1941, at Messines Park.

MURRAY, William S, age 50. Husband of Mollie Murray, of 59 Messines Park. 16th April 1941, at Messines Park.

RICHMOND, Bridie, age 14 months. Daughter of John and Winifred Richmond, of 61 Messines Park. 16th April 1941, at 61 Messines Park. Londonderry City Cemetery.

RICHMOND, John, age 53. Son of John and Margaret Richmond (nee Caulfield), of 23 Long Tower Street, Londonderry; husband of Winifred Richmond of 61 Messines Park. 16th April 1941, at 61 Messines Park, Londonderry City Cemetery.

RICHMOND, Owen, age 18. Son of John and Winifred Richmond, of 61 Messines Park. 16th April, 1941, at 61 Messines Park. Londonderry City Cemetery.

RICHMOND, Winifred, age 45. Daughter of Dorby and Rose Coyle, of Carrigart, Co. Donegal; wife of John Richmond, of 61 Messines Park. 16th April 1941, at 61 Messines Park. Londonderry City Cemetery.

NORTHERN IRELAND

COUNTY DOWN

BOROUGH OF BANGOR

GRATTAN, Angeline, age 18, of 40 Ashley Gardens. Daughter of Mataldia Grattan and of Andrew F. Grattan, removed to Bullagh, Newcastle, Co. Down. 16th April 1941, at 40 Ashley Gardens. Bangor New Cemetery.

GRATTAN, Mataldia, age 54, of 40 Ashley Gardens. Wife of Andrew F. Grattan, removed to Bullagh, Newcastle, Co. Down. 16th April 1941, at 40 Ashley Gardens. Bangor New Cemetery.

GRATTAN, Shelagh, age 20, of 40 Ashley Gardens. Daughter of Mataldia Grattan and of Andrew F. Grattan, removed to Bullagh, Newcastle, Co. Down. 16th April, 1941, at 40 Ashley Gardens. Bangor New Cemetery.

WATT, Margaret Byers, age 60, of 5 Hazeldene Gardens. 16th April, 1941, at 5 Hazeldene Gardens. Buried at Balmoral, Co. Antrim.

WRIGHT, Robert E., age 41, of 32 Avenue Baylands. 17th April 1941, at Bangor Hospital.

APPENDIX 2

PEOPLE INTERVIEWED

NOTE: An asterisk indicates the use of a fictitious name for a person who wished to remain anonymous.

Harold Allen
William Allen
Father Hugh Arthurs
George Batchelor
Billy Boyd
John Boyles
Reggie Briggs
Nora Carse
Joseph Crilly
Hugh Crossan
David Davidson
Josephine Downey
Patrick Finlay
Donald Fleck
Charlie Gallagher
Fred Heatley
Elizabeth Henry
Elizabeth Hurst
Arthur Jackson
Jim Jenkins
Sean Kelly
Tom Kenny
Edward Lennon
Ernie Logan
Joseph McCann
John MacDermott
Jimmy Mackey
Rita McKittrick
Billy McNeill
Agnes Mary Mercer
Bryce Millar
Sarah Nelson*
Nan Nicholl
Father Paddy O'Donnell
John Oliver
Jimmy Penton
Eileen Powderly
Frank Skillen
Mary Taggart*
Robert Watson

The following people provided written memoirs or archive material relating to the blitz:

Harold Allen
Nellie Bell
Jim Jenkins
Ernie Logan
Jim McConville
H. John F. Potter
Joan Urquhart

In addition, information was gained at Jimmy Doherty's public lecture on the blitz, held in Belfast on 28 May 1987.

BIBLIOGRAPHY

MANUSCRIPT SOURCES

NOTE: All files marked with an asterisk were of particular value.

Northern Ireland

PUBLIC RECORD OFFICE OF NORTHERN IRELAND, BELFAST

CAB 3A The Official War History of Northern Ireland: Official Papers and Copies of Official Papers

CAB 3/A/3
CAB 3/A/4
CAB 3/A/5
CAB 3/A/15
CAB 3/A/47
CAB 3/A/57
CAB 3/A/58*
CAB 3/A/60*
CAB 3/A/61
CAB 3/A/62*
CAB 3/A/64
CAB 3/A/65*
CAB 3/A/68*
CAB 3/A/69
CAB 3/A/71*
CAB 3/A/87
CAB 3/A/89

CAB 3D War Diaries and Campaign Accounts

CAB 3/D/2
CAB 3/D/7
CAB 3/D/8

CAB 4 Cabinet Conclusion files

CAB 4/333–568* (16 January 1935–23 December 1943)

CAB 9CD Cabinet Secretariat Civil Defence files

CAB 9CD/33*
CAB 9CD/35
CAB 9CD/36/2
CAB 9CD/42/2
CAB 9CD/91
CAB 9CD/117
CAB 9CD/136
CAB 9CD/176*
CAB 9CD/178
CAB 9CD/180
CAB 9CD/186/7
CAB 9CD/207*
CAB 9CD/209*
CAB 9CD/216
CAB 9CD/217*

COM 61 Ministry of Commerce, National Emergency files

COM 61/459
COM 61/532
COM 61/533
COM 61/541
COM 61/905
COM 61/915
COM 61/939

DEV 9 Ministry of Development, Main Registry files

DEV 9/1/54*
DEV 9/1/56*

ED 13 Ministry of Education, 'G' General and Policy files

ED 13/1/2019*

FIN 17 Ministry of Finance, Public Record Office files

FIN 17/2/4C*
FIN 17/2/4D
FIN 17/2/19*

FIN 18 Ministry of Finance, Treasury Division, 'A' Registry files

FIN 18/20/19
FIN 18/21/64
FIN 18/21/228

HA 6 Ministry of Home Affairs and Public Security Civil Defence files

HA 6/2/1*
HA 6/2/4
HA 6/2/9
HA 6/2/16*
HA 6/3/4
HA 6/3/8
HA 6/3/11*
HA 6/3/70
HA 6/3/75
HA 6/3/78
HA 6/3/91
HA 6/3/98
HA 6/3/99*
HA 6/3/100
HA 6/3/101

HA 6/3/117
HA 6/3/153
HA 6/3/156A
HA 6/3/205*
HA 6/3/206
HA 6/3/241
HA 6/3/249*
HA 6/3/255
HA 6/3/259
HA 6/3/271
HA 6/3/294
HA 6/6/7*

HA 18 Ministry of Public Security files

HA 18/3/1
HA 18/3/2*
HA 18/3/3*
HA 18/3/5*
HA 18/3/6
HA 18/3/7

INF 7 Information Service Photographs

UTA 12 Ulster Transport Authority, Northern Counties Committee files

UTA 12/CG/4

PRIVATE PAPERS:

D 715/6–24*	Sir Wilfrid Spender Financial Diary (December 1934–June 1944)
D 770/1/1–4	McElborough Papers
D 1415/D/14	Lord Craigavon Papers
D 1633/2/40	Lady Spender Diary (1941–3)
D 1896/1,2	Luftwaffe aerial photographs
D 2109/13*	Emma Duffin Diary (pages 86–111)
D 2742/1*	St Ninian's Church of Ireland Church; notes of air raids by the caretaker, William Ward
D 3004/D/31,32	Sir Basil Brooke Diaries (September 1939–December 1941)
D 3041/3,4	Whelan Papers
D 3134	Topping Papers
D 3304/1–3	Templemore Avenue First Aid Post (30 January 1941–20 January 1944)

CLONARD MONASTERY, BELFAST

'Domestic Chronicles', April–May 1941

LINEN HALL LIBRARY, BELFAST

Diary of William McCready

QUEEN'S UNIVERSITY BELFAST

R.M. Henry Collection

TEACHERS' CENTRE, BELFAST

'Ulster and the World Wars', teachers' project (booklets and tapes)

ULSTER FOLK AND TRANSPORT MUSEUM, CULTRA

ORAL HISTORY ARCHIVE

R88/20
R88/21
R88/22
R88/23

Republic of Ireland

STATE PAPER OFFICE, DUBLIN

CABINET MINUTES (SEPTEMBER 1940–DECEMBER 1941)

G 3/5
G 3/6

CABINET FILES OF DÁIL ÉIREANN

S 1221
S 8658
S 11582
S 12125
S 12164
S 12242
S 12405
S 12432
S 12728A
S 12939
S 13504

Great Britain

BRITISH BROADCASTING CORPORATION, LONDON

German radio extracts from the 'Survey of World Broadcasting' (8 April–15 May 1941)

THE BRITISH LIBRARY (REFERENCE DIVISION)

Newspaper Library

IMPERIAL WAR MUSEUM, LONDON

Luftwaffe Target files

KG SS 77452*
GB 835*
GB 5049*
GB 5377*
GB 5677*
GB 10915*
GB 10916*

GB 10918*
GB 10919*
GB 10923*

PUBLIC RECORD OFFICE, LONDON

CAB 2, 12, 13 Papers of Committee of Imperial Defence and of the Home Defence Committee

CAB 2/9*
CAB 12/3*
CAB 12/4*
CAB 13/8*
CAB 13/9*

CAB 21, 66, 123 Cabinet Conclusions, Memoranda, and Committees

CAB 21/648*
CAB 21/649
CAB 21/650
CAB 66/16*
CAB 123/92*

HO 45 Home Office Registered Correspondence

HO 45/18532
HO 45/18913
HO 45/19161
HO 45/19896
HO 45/20279
HO 45/20280
HO 45/20733
HO 45/23212
HO 45/24212
HO 45/25049
HO 45/25050
HO 45/25051*

HO 186–205 Ministry of Home Security, Air Raid Precautions files

HO 186/157
HO 186/446
HO 186/574
HO 192/1325*
HO 192/1661
HO 203/7
HO 205/174*

PREM 3,4 Prime Minister's Office

PREM 3/327/1A
PREM 3/327/2*
PREM 4/53/2*

TOM HARRISSON MASS OBSERVATION ARCHIVE, UNIVERSITY OF SUSSEX, BRIGHTON

Files and diaries relating to Northern Ireland

MO 1306
MO 1309
MO 2101
MO 5462* (Diary of Moya Woodside)

Federal Republic of Germany (West Germany)

BUNDESARCHIV-MILITÄRARCHIV, FREIBURG

Luftflotte 3 Operations Reports, and Air Force High Command, Intelligence Sector, Daily Situation Reports for Luftflotte 2 and 5

RL 7/95*
RL 7/98*
RL 7/99*

German Democratic Republic (East Germany)

NATIONALE VOLKSARMEE, MILITÄRARCHIV, POTSDAM

Luftwaffe Reports

PARLIAMENTARY PAPERS

United Kingdom

Official Report, 3rd and 5th series, Parliamentary Debates, House of Commons

Northern Ireland

Northern Ireland House of Commons Papers, 1931–42

Parliamentary Debates, Official Report, House of Commons

Parliamentary Debates, Official Report, Senate

Planning Advisory Committee Report on the general housing problem with particular reference to the clearance of slums, the provision of new housing in the post-war period, 1944. (Cmd 224, Government of Northern Ireland)

GOVERNMENT PUBLICATIONS

Belfast Gazette, Belfast, HMSO (1940–41)
Blake, John W. *Northern Ireland in the Second World War*, Belfast, HMSO, 1956
Isles, K.S. and Norman Cuthbert. *An Economic Survey of Northern Ireland*, Belfast, HMSO, 1957
Shearman, Hugh. *Northern Ireland 1921–1971*, Belfast, HMSO, 1971
Ulster Year Book, Belfast, HMSO (1926–56)

NEWSPAPERS AND PERIODICALS

Aeroplane
Aerospace Historian
Aviation News
Belfast News-Letter

Belfast Telegraph
County Down Spectator
Der Adler
Dundalk Democrat
Evening Standard
Flypast
Irish News
Irish Press
Irish Sword
Irish Times
Londonderry Sentinel
Northern Whig
Stars and Stripes
Sunday News
Sunday Pictorial
The Times
Völkischer Beobachter

THESES

Barton, B.E. 'Sir Basil Brooke: the making of a prime minister', Ph.D. thesis, Queen's University Belfast, 1986

Davidson, Robson. 'The German air-raids on Belfast of April and May 1941 and their consequences', unpublished Ph.D. thesis, Queen's University Belfast, 1976

Harbinson, John F. 'A history of the Northern Ireland Labour Party, 1891–1948', unpublished M.Sc. thesis, Queen's University Belfast, 1972

BOOKS, ARTICLES AND PAMPHLETS

Avon, Lord. *The Eden Memoirs: Facing the Dictators*, London, Cassell, 1962

The Eden Memoirs: The Reckoning, London, Cassell, 1965

Bardon, Jonathan. *Belfast: An Illustrated History*, Belfast, Blackstaff Press, 1982

Barton, Brian. *Brookeborough: The Making of a Prime Minister*, Belfast, Institute of Irish Studies, 1988

Beacham, A. 'Report of a Survey of Living Conditions made in a Representative Working Class Area in Belfast, November 1938–February 1939', Belfast, Presbyterian Church in Ireland Social Services Committee, 1939

Beckett, J.C., *et al. Belfast: The Making of the City, 1800–1914*, Belfast, Appletree Press, 1983

Beckett, J.C., and R.E. Glasscock. *Belfast, Origin and Growth of an Industrial City*, London, BBC Books, 1967

Bekker, Cajus. *The Luftwaffe War Diaries*, London, Macdonald, 1964

Belfast and Northern Ireland Directory, Belfast, *Belfast News-Letter*, (1921–48)

'Belfast District Synod, Temperance and Social Welfare Committee, Report of a Survey, 1938', Methodist Church in Ireland (1938)

Briggs, Asa. *The Birth of Broadcasting*, Oxford, Oxford University Press, 1961

Brodie, Malcolm. *One Hundred Years of Irish Football*, Belfast, Blackstaff Press, 1980

Linfield, 100 Years, Belfast, Linfield Football Club, 1985

Buckland, Patrick. *Irish Unionism: Ulster Unionism and the Origins of Northern Ireland, 1886–1922*, vol. II, Dublin, Gill and Macmillan, 1973

The Factory of Grievances: Devolved Government in Northern Ireland, 1921–39, Dublin, Gill and Macmillan, 1979

A History of Northern Ireland, Dublin, Gill and Macmillan, 1981

Budge, I., and C. O'Leary. *Belfast: Approach to Crisis: A Study of Belfast Politics 1603–1970*, London, Macmillan, 1973

Calder, Angus. *The People's War: Britain 1939–1945*, London, Panther, 1971

Calvocoressi, Peter, and Peter Wint. *Total War: Causes and Courses of the Second World War*, Harmondsworth, Penguin, 1972

Campbell, Winifred. 'Down the Shankill', *Ulster Folklife*, no. 22 (1976)

Carnwath, Dr Thomas. 'Report to the Special Committee of the Belfast Corporation on the Municipal Health Services of the City', typescript at Queen's University Belfast, dated 24 December 1941

Carroll, Joseph T. *Ireland in the War Years, 1939–1945*, Newton Abbot, David and Charles, 1975

Churchill, Winston S. *The Gathering Storm*, London, Macmillan, 1948

Curran, Father Danny. *The Story of St Paul's, Falls Road, Belfast, 1887–1987*, Belfast, Howard Publications, 1987

Devlin, Paddy. *Yes We Have No Bananas: Outdoor Relief in Belfast 1920–39*, Belfast, Blackstaff Press, 1981

Donne, Michael. *Pioneers of the Skies: A History of Short Brothers P.L.C.*, Belfast, Nicholson and Bass, 1987

Ervine, St John. *Craigavon: Ulsterman*, London, Allen and Unwin, 1949

Fisk, Robert. *In Time of War: Ireland, Ulster and the Price of Neutrality, 1939–1945*, London, André Deutsch, 1983

Fitz Gibbon, Constantine. *The Blitz*, London, Wingate, 1957

Glasscock, R.E. *see* Beckett, J.C., and R.E. Glasscock

Gray, John. *William McCready of Whiteabbey, 1909–1982. Diarist and Book Collector,* Belfast, Linen Hall Library, 1983

Harbinson, John. *The Ulster Unionist Party, 1882–1973,* Belfast, Blackstaff Press, 1973

Harkness, David. *Northern Ireland Since 1920,* Dublin, Helicon Press, 1983

Harrisson, Tom. *Living Through the Blitz,* Harmondsworth, Penguin, 1978

Hume, John, and Michael Moss. *Shipbuilders to the World: 125 Years of Harland and Wolff,* Belfast, Blackstaff Press, 1986

Irving, David. *Hitler's War,* London, Hodder and Stoughton, 1977

The War Path: Hitler's Germany 1933–1939, London, Michael Joseph, 1978

Johnson, David. 'The economic history of Ireland between the wars', *Irish Economic and Social History,* vol. I (1974)

Jones, Thomas. *Whitehall Diary: Ireland 1918–1925,* vol. III, ed. Keith Middlemass, Oxford, Oxford University Press, 1971

Kennedy, Liam, and Philip Ollerenshaw. *An Economic History of Ulster, 1830–1939,* Manchester, Manchester University Press, 1985

Krieger, Leonard, and Fritz Stern. *The Responsibility of Power,* London, Macmillan, 1968

Lawrence, R.J. *The Government of Northern Ireland: Public Finance and Public Services 1921–1964,* Oxford, Oxford University Press, 1965

Longmate, Norman. *The G.I.'s: The Americans in Britain 1942–1945,* London, Hutchinson, 1975

Air Raid: The Bombing of Coventry, London, Hutchinson, 1976

How We Lived Then: A History of Everyday Life in the Second World War, London, Hutchinson, 1976

McGimpsey, Christopher. *A Camera Record: Bombs on Belfast, The Blitz 1941,* Belfast, Pretani Press, 1984

Maltby, A. *The Government of Northern Ireland 1922–1972: A Catalogue and Breviate of Parliamentary Papers,* Dublin, Irish University Press, 1974

Messenger, Betty. *Picking up the Linen Threads: Life in Ulster's Mills,* Belfast, Blackstaff Press, 1988

Moore, Brian. *The Emperor of Ice Cream,* London, Mayflower, 1967

Moss, Michael *see* Hume, John, and Michael Moss

Munck, Ronnie, and Bill Rolston. *Belfast in the Thirties: An Oral History,* Belfast, Blackstaff Press, 1987

Nowlan, Kevin, and T. Desmond Williams. *Ireland in the War Years and After, 1939–1951,* Dublin, Gill and Macmillan, 1969

O'Leary, C. *see* Budge, I., and C. O'Leary

Oliver, John. *Working at Stormont,* Dublin, Institute of Public Administration, 1978

Ollerenshaw, Philip *see* Kennedy, Liam, and Philip Ollerenshaw

Open, Michael. *Fading Lights, Silver Screen: A History of Belfast Cinema,* Antrim, Greystone Press, 1983

Ramsey, Winston G. (ed.) *The Blitz Then and Now,* vols. I and II, London, Battle of Britain Prints International, 1987, 1988

Rolston, Bill *see* Munck, Ronnie, and Bill Rolston

Shea, Patrick. *Voices and the Sound of Drums: An Irish Autobiography,* Belfast, Blackstaff Press, 1981

Smith, David J. *Action Stations: Military Airfields of Scotland, the North-East, and Northern Ireland* Wellingborough, Patrick Stevens, 1985

Smith, Graham. *When Jim Crow met John Bull: Black American Soldiers in World War II Britain,* London, I.B. Taurus, 1987

Stern, Fritz *see* Krieger, Leonard, and Fritz Stern

Twyford, H.P. *It Came to Our Door,* Plymouth, Underhill, 1946

Ulster Unionist Council. 'Annual Reports', 1939–45

Wakefield, Kenneth. *The First Pathfinders: The Operational History of Kampfgruppe 100, 1939–1941,* London, William Kimber, 1981

Wint, Peter *see* Calvocoressi, Peter, and Peter Wint

INDEX

Brian Barton was born in Dunkineely, Co. Donegal, in 1944 and educated at Methodist College Belfast. He graduated from Queen's University Belfast in 1967 with a BA in Modern History; he was awarded an MA by the New University of Ulster in 1979 and a Ph.D. by Queen's in 1986. He taught at Glastry Secondary School in Ballyhalbert from 1969 to 1971, and since then has been a lecturer in the Department of Academic Studies at the College of Business Studies in Belfast. His most recent publication is *Brookeborough: The Making of a Prime Minister*, Institute of Irish Studies, 1988.